The
Also-Ran
but a
Champion

The Travels of a Kayak:
From Carriacou to Oahu

Alfred Fitzgerald Brathwaite

Copyright © 2025 Alfred Fitzgerald Brathwaite.

All rights reserved. No part of this book may be reproduced, stored, or transmitted by any means—whether auditory, graphic, mechanical, or electronic—without written permission of the author, except in the case of brief excerpts used in critical articles and reviews. Unauthorized reproduction of any part of this work is illegal and is punishable by law.

ISBN: 979-8-89419-569-8 (sc)
ISBN: 979-8-89419-570-4 (hc)
ISBN: 979-8-89419-571-1 (e)

Because of the dynamic nature of the Internet, any web addresses or links contained in this book may have changed since publication and may no longer be valid. The views expressed in this work are solely those of the author and do not necessarily reflect the views of the publisher, and the publisher hereby disclaims any responsibility for them.

One Galleria Blvd., Suite 1900, Metairie, LA 70001
(504) 702-6708

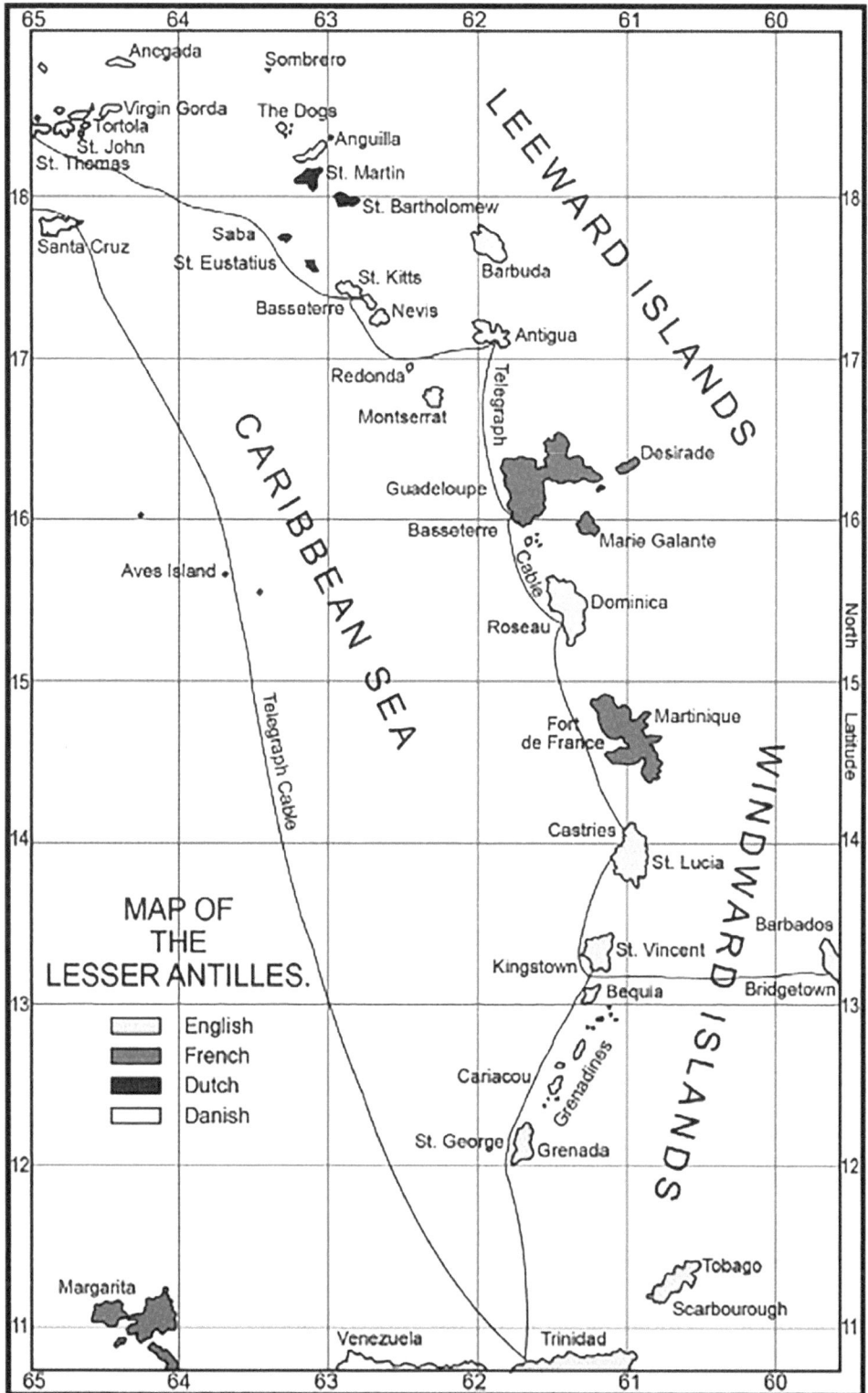

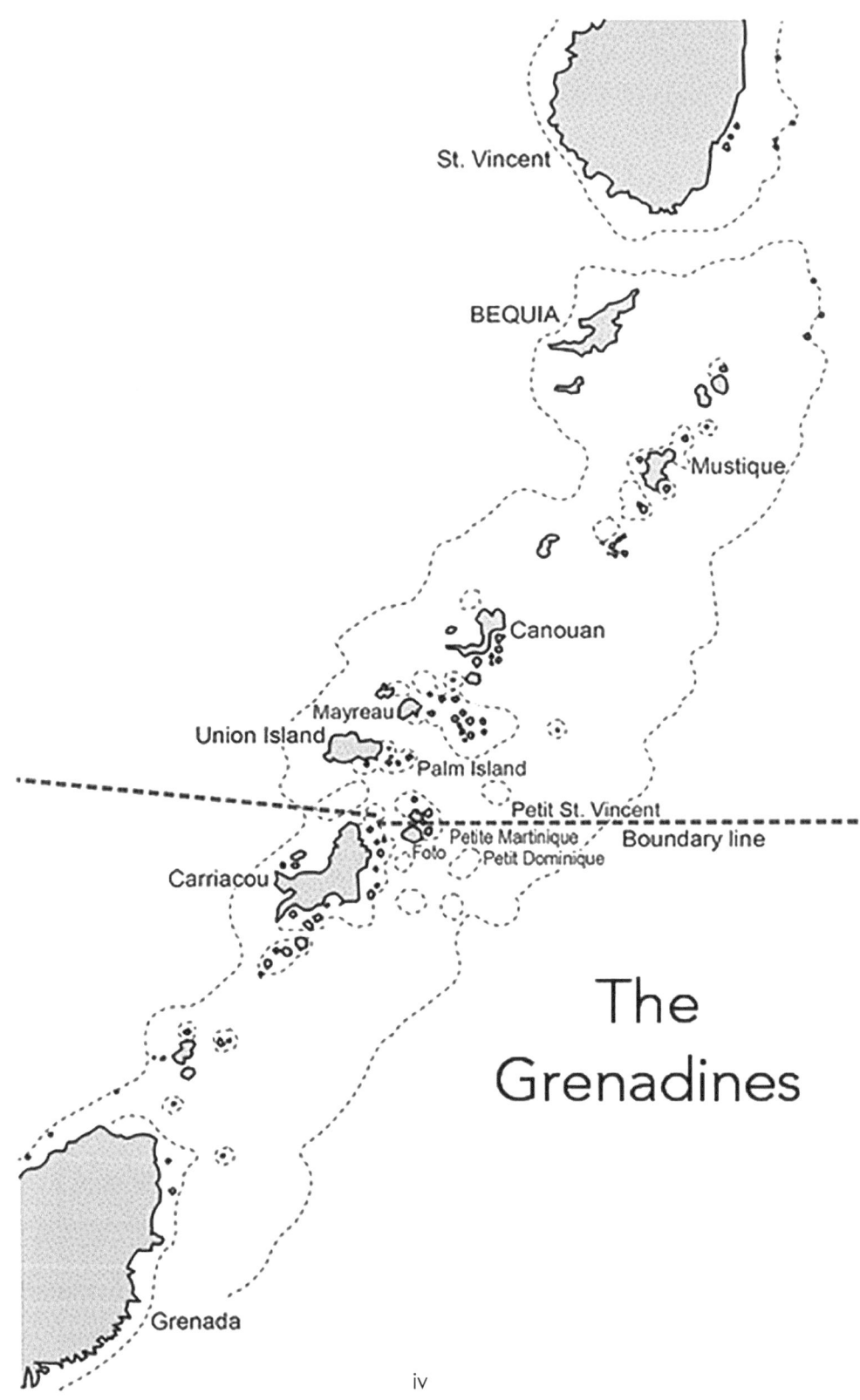

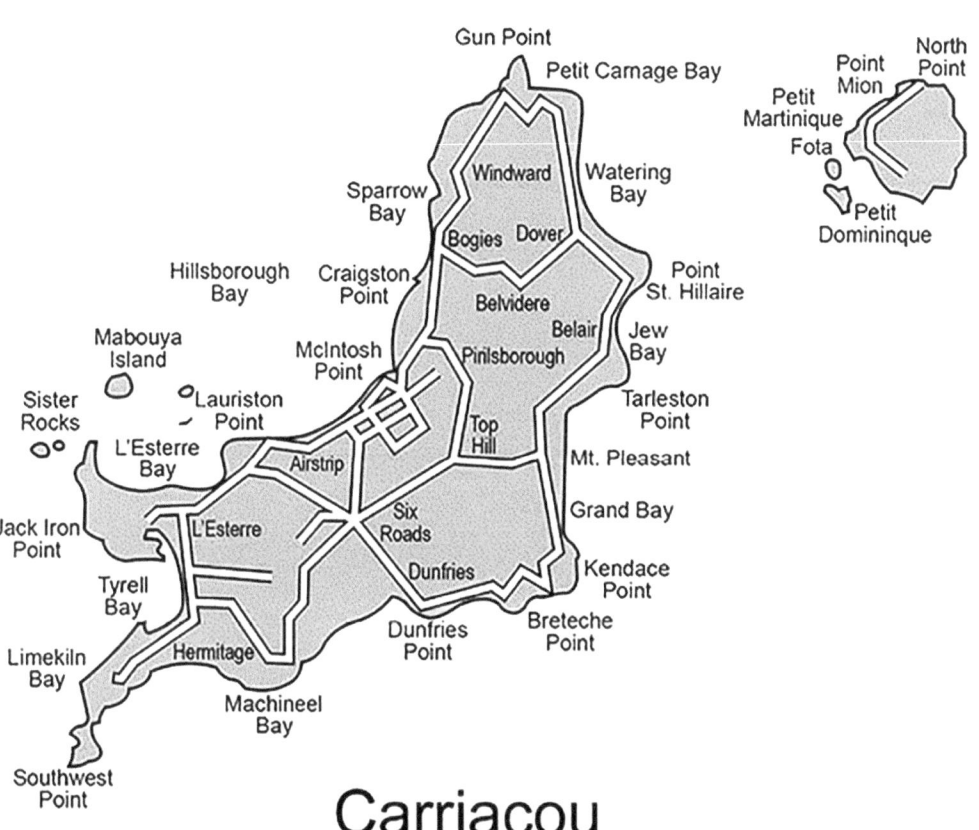

*To my world, which is in perpetual metamorphosis,
and to the memory of one who stood tall in it: a mother.*

CONTENTS

Map of the Lesser Antilles iii
The Grenadines iv
Carriacou v
Preface xiii

Part 1:
The Early Days of Old in the Present

1. Whence Cometh Thou? 3
   A Topographical Outline 15
   Home Sweet Home 18
   Beyond the house 28
2. Growing Up: The Family and the Neighbourhood 40
   The Liberty Shop—Thank u, from little comes much 47
   The Alpha: My Eldest Brother 57
   The Grand Bay Land 72
   The Days of Labour: Gritillia Commands 77
   Maternal Relatives 106
3. And Then There Were Men: Village Characters 115
4. Thy Daily Bread: Let Us Eat 131
5. Specific Events and Occasions: Bonhomie 146
   Carnival 146
   Regatta 152
   Christmas 153
   Island Tours 156
   Intravillage Relationships 158
   Events Related to Death 166
   Charles Gilbert 170
   Cassava Milling 175

    Emancipation Day 175
    A Wedding... 176
    As Children 179

6. Mt. Pleasant Elementary School: To Learn or Not to Learn..188
7. Other Personal Incidents in My Youth: Mischievous? 202
    Brawn or Brain 202
    Lysander 214
8. The Grenada Boys Secondary School: Another Small Step ..219
    Adeline 224
    The Kainash/Trafalgar Boys 246
9. UWI, Mona, Jamaica, (October 1961—November 1967)....253
    David "Jack" Radix.. 269
    George, My Immediate Older Brother 277
    Another Great Thinker, One with a Knighthood.......... 281
    Other Friends and Episodes 284

Part 2:
Extended Medical Training—With A Salary

10. Princess Margaret Hospital, Nassau, Bahamas.................... 305
11. Residency Programmes 309
    At First, an Educational Interlude 309
    The Second Act..312
    The Gods Dwell here 318
    Ottawa, Canada.. 322

Part 3:
An Independent Working Man

12. Grenada: What? No Fatted Calf? 331
13. One of the Original Three Guianas...................................... 343
14. Nassau, Bahamas, 1978–1981 357

15. Sporting a Laissez-Passer	363
16. One More Time	374
17. The Yachting Capital	387

Part 4:
The Revolving Door: A Time To Go

18. Whither Goest Thou?: Back Home	397
A Jumbled Miscellany of Thoughts—Nondoctrinal	401
Poems	411
Animating Pollination	413
Bridled Happiness	414
Acceptance	415
Golden Nature	416
Tensions	417
Projections	418
The Love Call	419
It Never Ends	420
Eating Ice Cream: The Wings of Love	421
The Triangle of Changing Emotions	422
Side One	422
Side Two	422
Side Three	423
Within the Triangle	423
Hotchpotching	425
Summer Blues	428
To Dream	429
To Pass Over	430
Epilogue	431
Appendix	437
Additional Photos	463

PREFACE

To reminisce is not unusual, whether doing so is purposely initiated or not. For no obvious or apparent reason, a past situation may spontaneously pop into one's mind but only evanescently—a fleeting image. However, when a memory is intentionally recalled, it may be allowed to linger awhile, to be dwelt on or even more deeply analysed.

Whether transitory or sustained, a look back may occur when one is idly relaxed or meditating, when one is prompted by one's present circumstance, or even when one is coerced so to do by another individual.

Reflections may either repose solely within the inner self as one becomes lost in a nostalgic reverie or be communicated to others, verbally or otherwise. But whichever form it takes, most people would admit or plead guilty to indulging in this mental exercise, and without doubt, some episodes may occur repeatedly.

To live is to reminisce.

Regardless, when such takes place, although one may smilingly relive a gladdening event or consider it in a different light, there is the possibility that the memory will invoke questions, doubts, what-ifs, and even regrets. This is because such reflections, when considered all together, may represent the many different aspects and issues encountered in one's journey through life.

Indeed, reminiscing may at times be likened to acting as a post-event armchair general or a Monday-morning quarterback who, after a weekend game or even many games, manages and dissects situations in which he or she may have been the major player, a participant, or, less likely, a mere bystander.

As I have purposely reflected on my own journey over time—a journey which at times I did not understand—occasions have arisen when, caught in a spell of hindsight, I have imagined what other outcomes there may have been had I acted differently. Admittedly, a few of these events engendered remorse at the time or shortly after. However, what has happened cannot be changed. As yet, none of these occasions has left me with any lasting regrets, and I hold no grudges. But any regret I have felt has not so much been about what I have done but more so about what more I could have done. Still, as I turn back the hands of time, I relive but cannot reshape, nor do I wish so to do.

It has been said that one can learn from history, and I agree. But for me at this point, although I am now intentionally allowing history to surface, it is with the knowledge that it cannot be altered or controlled. My objective in so doing is not to guide, predict, or create the future, despite the opinion of Peter Drucker.

Nevertheless, under normal circumstances, when past events resurface, they ought not be allowed to dwell for too long, lest in so doing they lessen one's enjoyment of the now times. As it is often expressed, carpe diem!

And yet, perhaps one's present time is unpleasant, and the future seems bleak. In such a case, one would tend to revert for longer periods of time. And yet, over 90 per cent of knowledge is based on the past and the rest on the present.

Hence, I acknowledge that, if allowed by the mythological Janus and in combination with other factors, historical events may contribute to the generation of ideas that may be put to good use in planning and laying a foundation for the times to come without repeating past mistakes.

Other than through innate inspiration, one's life is primarily shaped, in the general sense, by people or events. In my case, both have positively influenced my earthly journey, though as one might expect, some have done so less than others and some seem to have had no meaningful consequence. Hopefully, these experiences generated ideas that have borne fruit.

Despite some disappointments and what may even be considered outright failures, I believe that I have so far experienced a reasonably satisfying journey through this life, but whether it has been profoundly meaningful or not is open to conjecture and has no bearing on the primary reason I have written this memoir. As my years now seem to elapse more rapidly and my memories, like my old photographs, fade and wane in significance, I wish to relate how circumstances and persons in my life may have had, knowingly or not, some influence on me, although I know full well that it is virtually impossible to weigh what I consider to be immeasurable values.

This presentation is based on remembrances, which at times appear to be fully intact, at times are less so, even blurred, and at times are but only of fleeting images, and I have written it without the benefit of any in-depth research. For this reason, it should come as no surprise that other persons of my time may think, remember, or know otherwise. The situation is such that I have had cause to return to my address books to remember names only to find that many a name has no corresponding entry in my memory bank.

This therefore makes it likely that readers may hold different opinions, find discrepancies, and even strongly disagree with what I have written. So, if you, dear reader, know differently from my accounts of these past events, I beseech you to kindly bear with me, for my brain is becoming less and less responsive, as if a cloud or fog that was once absent from it has appeared and is becoming denser and increasingly infiltrative. I therefore welcome any expressed differences, because any thought of mine remains but only for one "brief shining moment" in my mind. Perhaps I seek that such thoughts ought not be forgot just as the challenge King Author gave to the lad in Camelot.

The title of this narrative has been strongly influenced by others, particularly by those I consider to be my friends, but the choice has remained mine, even though it undoubtedly has its roots in not just the words but also the essence of my high school song, which contains the lyrics 'The also-ran and the champion, each one can but do his best.' I have merely changed two words, one a conjunction.

It is also my belief that the word *also-ran*, though carrying a competitive connotation, can be applied more broadly to the majority of people throughout the course of their lives, although many of them have in the past behaved in a way that exemplifies a champion, even if only once.

Here I purposely expand the meaning of *champion*, using it to mean not simply *winner* (or in military terms, *general*) but more broadly, *warrior* (*soldier*). For the majority of us are, in a general sense, jacks of all trades, doing the ordinary but perhaps becoming masters just once, even performing heroic deeds.

Some persons may do many ordinary things but excel in only one.

Or, individuals may be incapable of doing great things but can do small things in a great way. Or, as otherwise stated, majoring in a minor key.

Bear in mind that those considered champions may, after time has passed, become also-rans. Do consider that despite their great achievements, some quarterbacks have never reached what is considered the mountain top—a super bowl winner. And still, Dan is the man in the van.

This discourse will not be a mere continuum of descriptions but will, in large measure, hopefully demonstrate how events and personalities interweave over time, despite that more recent events and some isolated events will, to a great extent, be completely unrelated to others.

Therefore, this exercise will hopefully not merely be a temporal portrayal of the past but rather a demonstration of the criss-crossings and linkages of the encounters and adventures of my life. To maintain one's perspective, it may be necessary to be repetitious.

Although this exposé may, at times, reflect my thoughts, I have certainly made no deliberate attempt to offer philosophical expressions.

The grammar is decisively that of British English, but it may drift into the colloquialism of the local lingo or dialect and, rarely, into other versions of the language. This is because at school or on formal occasions, one was expected to use the standard language—English, in my case. However, there was a casual reversion to the more usual and 'common' form of oral communication among friends and family—broken English. This meant that it was therefore necessary to hesitantly think before expressing oneself in formal speech or writing. I can only hope that any blending herein is appreciated.

The island of Carriacou features prominently in this story, for it was where I first knew myself, where my foundation was laid, and where I received an upstanding upbringing. It is a place in which I initially lived full time and then part time and which, since leaving, I have continued to visit.

I proffer no excuses for this, as it was here that my character received its frame. Then, it was imposed upon me and was perhaps confining, but over time, it has become self-modifiable but nevertheless inherently protective. Not unlike the exoskeleton of a crab, it can be adjusted, expanded, and remodelled to accommodate the growth that's taking place within.

Its influence has remained somewhere within me, a closed umbrella that awaits the often-untimely downpours that are expected throughout one's life.

I therefore do admit that there is more than just me in this autobiographical exercise. Some aspects of life which ought not to be lost are detailed here as accurately as possible, although, of course, from my perspective. I narrate events as I saw or experienced them, flavoured with my impressions.

Anaïs Nin once said, "We write to taste life twice, in the moment and in retrospect." I considered relating my story for many years, but these words prompted me to agonize no longer and to now disclose my experiences as I remember them, with no intention of replacing the existing circumstances. The aim is neither to enhance nor belittle myself.

PART 1

THE EARLY DAYS OF OLD IN THE PRESENT

1

WHENCE COMETH THOU?

Having so been told, I have accepted that I was born in 1941 on the island of Carriacou. In my youth, and for many years onward, my thoughts of this island were invariably dominated by a phrase commonly uttered by natives: "Oh me Lard, the sun goin' kill me today" (or sometimes, "Oh my goodness, the sun hot for so").

The island, like others in the region, was divided into villages or districts, and the place where I was born and spent my early years was a part of the eastern front. Here, the day broke all too early, as if very proud to herald a repeat of the same picture as yesterday, soon to be followed by the glow of a rising sun. The sun would first peep over the Atlantic horizon and then appear as an unclouded, huge, glisteningly yellow globe hovering over a purely white reef and the sea of varied blues. All too slowly but without hindrance, the blazing sun would traverse the sky for near ten hours before disappearing over and beyond the hills to the western villages.

By its placement in the sky, we were able to tell the time of day until sundown. That image has remained with me even after having left this land at age 11, returning only on school vacations until age 20 and, six years after that, on more conveniently planned but only temporary visits. It mattered nothing to us children, and perhaps to most adults, what the temperature was, as we were then ignorant of Fahrenheit and degrees.

Although seemingly a daily constant, the heat, for most people, understandably appeared to manifest more so on Saturdays and some holidays, when outdoor chores tended to be more numerous. Consider also that on weekdays, the youth and many adults would spend some five hours or more out of the direct sun either in a school building constructed to provide ample ventilation or in a suitable indoor work environment. And because Sundays were accepted and respected by most families as the Sabbath, outdoor work was limited then. Consequently, the heat seemed not as intense.

And yet, despite the stiflingly oppressive heat, it was not unusual—and indeed, it was generally possible—for one to find a shaded area when appropriate to feel some degree of delightful comfort by enjoying the gentle breezes of the trade winds, which occasionally emanated from the seashore and whiffed inward and upward over the land. Nevertheless, a lasting impression of a land as unceasingly and swelteringly hot as ever remained within me until well into the 1980s, after which, with my changing circumstances, the heat was no longer of any significant consequence to me.

Later in life, I understood that when the elder villagers described the weather as being "close", it was in reference to not just the heat but also the high humidity. Nonetheless, back then, I was uncertain whether that word was used as an uncomfortable synonym for oppressive nearness or a stifling antonym to joyful openness—or whether both meanings were simultaneously representative of how they felt about the atmospheric conditions. Although we, the younger ones, were at intervals uncomfortably warm and muggy on some days, when twilight faded into evenings and evenings into nights, the heat of the sun abated. And with the increasing glow of the starry sky, especially when it was enhanced by the growing fullness of the moon from a crescentic quarter, there arose in us an appreciation of our surroundings, of our atmosphere, especially when we experienced the sky from atop the hills.

In that mood, we no longer pensively roamed but were ready to start playing together and singing, "Twinkle, twinkle little star, how we wonder what you are, like a diamond in the sky!" Although we looked at the stars, the only constellations known to us were the Big Dipper, because we used it to locate the North Star, and the Seven Sisters, because it appeared before Christmas. Somehow, each of us children could count no more than six of the sisters, and with constant staring, the sixth disappeared.

As for the moon, our farmers and most villagers who depended primarily on their agricultural outputs tended to know how its different phases affected farming. Therefore, they planned and planted accordingly. They thought well of the children, who also knew those kinds of things. My mother always kept a copy of the current annual McDonald's Almanac in her shop to this end, but it was available to all, including to me, for it made for good reading.

I grew up knowing the island was (and remains) a dependency parish of the larger and main island, Grenada, which is geographically situated within the chain of islands still referred to as the Caribbean or West Indian islands. At the time, the majority were still colonies of Great Britain and thus were considered the British West Indies.

Historically, there may have been the odd change, but at that time, I understood further geographic subdivisions, referred to as the Greater and Lesser Antilles, with the latter separated into a northern leeward group and a southern windward group, not to be confused with the Windward Islands of the Netherland Antilles. The British Windward Islands, from north to south, were Dominica, St Lucia, St Vincent, and Grenada.

I never knew where the southernmost islands of the Antilles—Trinidad and its sister island, Tobago, which are located near South America—fitted in these geo-administrative divisions. Likewise, Barbados, the easternmost island, was seemingly out of the chain, closer to the Windwards but not in the Caribbean Sea. Apparently, primarily for the benefit of foreign travellers, both are just considered to be either parts of the Lesser Antilles or parts of the Southern or Eastern Caribbean.

It ought to be appreciated that, though the term is loosely applied, these West Indian islands were not and still are not all British colonies, and some, even though British, do not fit into the above descriptions. In this regard, one makes reference to Bermuda, the Bahamas, Turks and Caicos, and the Cayman Islands (within the Greater Antilles). Its being British notwithstanding, British Guiana is a country within the northern rim of the South American continent.

Let me add that the above referenced anglophone colonies, together with the British Virgin Islands within the Lesser Antilles and British Honduras in Central America, were never members of the West Indies Federation (1958–1962).

The majority of these West Indian territories are English-speaking islands, and most have chequered pasts of domination or colonization by European powers. Some others are of French, Dutch, and Spanish influences and languages and either are affiliated with non-British colonial powers or are independent. Interestingly, the three Guianas—French, Dutch (Surinam), and British (later, Guyana)—were all intracontinental, in the same general locale, in a row along the northern edge of South America. As a reflection of their histories of changed dominations, there is a retention of many recognisable non-English names and some aspects of culture of varied prominence within most of the English territories. Two in particular, Dominica and St Lucia, still have, in addition to English, a well-defined French Creole tongue, explainable perhaps by their proximity to French islands. Perhaps they remained in French hands longer than other islands. History records intermittent battles, primarily between the French and English powers, which occurred prior to the eventual British colonial rule.

Rule, Britannia! Britannia rule the waves! Always bent on making others slaves.

There is now a new twist to enslavement within some of the islands. Natives are lofted into elevated positions within organisations mainly so they can be controlled by the masters. Often, these self-satisfying, planned promotions certify the exactitude of the Peter principle. By default, many countries are ruled by politicians who already exemplified that principle long before being catapulted into power—not so much the power of the office but of that they take upon themselves. Some were never in the position of having achieved anything of consequence.

In many of the islands, retained names are found not only in those of locations, as noted in this presentation, but within other aspects of life—machete, pomerac, zaboca, shadon bene—as well as in people's names, such as de Gannes, Antoine, Cayenne, and Baptiste.

Also, within most countries of the region, there is a local lingo, dialect, or twang. Seemingly strange now but explainable then, the well-to-do once discouraged their children from speaking any form of Creole, particularly the French-derived sort. Now Creole is an asset to the many who disobeyed that advice. I grew up knowing a few people who still conversed in this patois or at least used isolated words.

The history of these territories demonstrates imperialistic determination and desire—*all for me!* Between Grenada in the south and St Vincent to the north is an archipelago comprising smaller islands, cays, and rocks called the Grenadines, of which Carriacou, at thirteen square miles (about eight thousand acres), is the largest. But the greater number of these islands belongs to St Vincent.

Indeed, it has always been said that the divisional line that demarcates these two groups actually traverses a small part of Carriacou at Gun or Rapid Point. For that reason, it was commonly stated that if one committed a crime in Carriacou, merely stepping across to the Vincentian side prevented an arrest from being made by the Grenadian authorities. It is my understanding that the line may have been redrawn to shift it northward into the open sea or that an agreement exists allowing Grenada to look over that small area.

No big deal!

One might think, expectedly so, that transportation between the major islands and territories played an important role. In my early years, this included regular air travel via the less common use of sea planes, which are still being used in the Virgin Islands. However, transportation by boat featured prominently. It still does, though now that time has passed, it's not as unrestricted as before because of sovereignty rights.

One must bear in mind that before the British territories were decolonised, their citizens were all British and had the freedom to travel from one British territory to any other and even to the United Kingdom.

Before these rights of autonomy became established and perhaps more forcefully enforced, particularly due to the attainment of independence, the sea form of transport was important for the movement of persons, the trading of goods and produce, the delivery of mail, and undoubtedly the plying of the illicit items, especially those of an alcoholic nature.

There is no doubt that to this day, boating still prospers. Perhaps because the islands are disposed in an archeologic chain and sailors were partly guided by the stars, travel from one land to another was readily accomplished. However, many a boat drifted out of contact, and for this, a pig was kept on board, for it was believed that if thrown into the sea, a pig would always head for land, wherever that was.

At that time, prior to the overriding concept of self-determination, it appeared that it was relatively easy to go from one island to another, irrespective of each island's colonial status. Indeed, for this purpose, boats were particularly useful. Necessarily, boat-building capabilities developed and prospered in some islands, and some became well known for that.

The boats ranged from the small ones that were primarily propelled by rowing or by outboard (Johnson) motors and were used for fishing or for travelling short distances to the larger sail boats, like sloops and schooners, some of which were also internally motorized.

Some of these larger boats from Carriacou plied to and from Grenville, the town of the Grenada parish of St Andrew, mainly to exchange farm animals and fish for agricultural produce. But the better-known vessels with regular schedules travelled between Hillsborough, the town of Carriacou, and St George's, as well as farther down south to Trinidad. St George's was and is the capital town of both the parish of St George and Grenada itself.

I can name, as my memory resurfaces, the following schooners: *Principal S*, *Lydinia A*, *Rhoda L*, *Lady S. Mitchell*, *Island Pride*, and, travelling at a later date, a bigger one built and owned by the Josephs of the islet Petite Martinique. All were built from wood. Much later came those with the names Alexia and Amelia painted on iron hulls.

The schooner *Rhoda L* (Lendore) was wrecked by hurricane Janet in 1955 in a bay called the Spout, which was a Tanteen extension of the inner harbour of St George's. The more adventurous boys would climb to the leaning, partly upright spars and then dive into the surrounding sea.

I don't think the following incident was directly related to the above, but in the bay where some of us swam on Saturdays or Sundays, a schoolboy of my age from Grenada, Ashley Bernadine, was said to have dived from the small jetty near to the boat and had his belly ripped open, maybe on a sheet of metal. With medical intervention, he survived the injury.

This unfortunate incident may have resulted from the direct dumping of trash in that area, or the tidal movements may have moved the trash there from elsewhere.

I wish at this stage to make reference to two matters. The first matter is that Ashley, whether before or after the above incident I'm uncertain, once came to spend the summer vacation at the home of

Mr. Hamilton Cyrus in my village in Carriacou and was picked to be on my team for a cricket match against another village. Many years later, when Ashley was the lawyer of my brother Nicholas, who I was then visiting, Ashley related how I was once his captain, to which Nicholas responded, "I'm not surprised. Anybody could captain you." The remark was demeaning in jest, but which person was it meant to demean? Did it apply to both of us?

On another note, if, perchance, one had plans for the day, one had to run quickly away if Ashley was espied, for his conversation, mingled with his deeds of kindness, could easily extend for hours.

What follows happened to me but only once. On a visit to Grenada in November 2001, I went to the office of a lawyer at about nine o'clock one morning. Ashley, whose office was nearby, saw my departure and beckoned me to join him. He then proceeded to converse ceaselessly as if he could never stop talking. Afterward, he took me to a Rotary Club luncheon meeting as his guest, then to his bank, then to his home, and finally back to his office, by which time it was just before 4 p.m. I managed to accomplish what I had first planned to do next that day, which was to go to the produce market, but I accomplished it almost at closing time.

I saw him several times after that, happily in more restricted situations, both in Grenada and once during a visit he made in 2002 to Freeport, Bahamas, my then place of residence. We last saw each other in Grenada when I went to my university faculty reunion in 2005. Sadly, Ashley died at his home in August 2018.

Ashley and author

The second matter relates to the parishes of Grenada, which I have already mentioned. All six parishes within the island are called by the names of saints—most likely those associated with the established church within each parish. One can therefore appreciate that the island parish of Carriacou, the exception to the above rule, was not always a dependency of Grenada. At least, it wasn't when the other parishes were named.

Strangely, only the parish of St George has a town of the same name, St George's. Perhaps that is because of the parish's importance. The others have towns that are called differently. I am uncertain whether or not the parish of St David has a town called St David's. If so, it may be just a square. It has always been my understanding that St David was the only parish without a town.

Of the European colonial powers other than Great Britain, France, the Netherlands, and the United States of America still possess or have special relationships with islands in the West Indies. As for the British Overseas Territories, all except for six (Montserrat, Anguilla, Bermuda, the Cayman Islands, the British Virgin Islands, and Turks and Caicos) have become independent nations, beginning with Jamaica in August 1962.

Trinidad followed at the end of that same month, the ceremony preceded by the often-cited witty words of the then premier Eric Williams, "One from ten leaves nought." This signalled an end to the ill-fated West Indies Federation of ten colonies and also the attempt to form the so-called Little Eight, which never materialised.

With independence and the incorporation of others, the attempts to unify these territories have continued with the formation of various entities, of which the best known are the Caribbean Free Trade Association (CARIFTA) and the Caribbean Community (CARICOM).

Grenada, often called the spice island of the west, has been independent since February 1974. It is often referenced, particularly internally, as the tri-island state of Grenada, Carriacou, and Petite Martinique, the latter two considered to be the sister islands of Grenada.

Petite Martinique and the nearby uninhabited isles, cays, and rocks, including Petit Dominque and Feta Rock, are visible from the eastern parts of Carriacou, as is the well-known Vincentian resort island of Petit St Vincent. Another island of St. Vincent, Union Island, is also within sight from other parts of Carriacou.

It is again necessary to emphasize that prior to independence and the sovereignty rights of countries, citizens freely travelled as necessary between the British colonies and their sister isles, as well as travelling to the non-British ones. Even now, perhaps because of the proximity, persons from Petite Martinique are transported daily, by understandings or agreements, to work on the resort isle, a part of St Vincent.

Understandably and as previously mentioned, Carriacou, like most other parishes and islands, was further subdivided into villages or districts. Within these, there were many smaller, ill-defined areas with gradually disappearing names that originated, I imagine, for whatever then seemed good reasons. So, for example, within the districts where I grew up, there was an area called Works, in which were the derelict remains of mechanical iron machines that were used in the past.

The area Quarry was and still is laden with large rocks, which were gathered by individuals to be pounded and sold for use in the construction of houses and roads. Other names that come to mind include Nehgah (Nigger) House, the Point (Tarleton), and Kainash, where I lived. Top Hill, another district, was on an elevated area overlooking the valleys, which extended from the seacoast inwards.

Carriacou is oft described as hilly. The hills arise from the flat coastal regions and slope, in my view, gently and gradually upward and towards the centre, unlike the steep rises in Dominica and Montserrat. But some hills do originate from the seacoast.

In addition to the retention of names, other existing evidence is reflective and reminiscent of the imperialistic past in Carriacou.

For example, scattered throughout the island are twenty-to-thirty-foot-tall block-like towers built, I imagine, by the slaves of those strangers who had captured the land. As time passes, some of these towers are gradually falling apart. These were said to have served as the foundations for the windmills that were needed to crush the sugar cane and limes that were grown for the value of their sap and juices.

Except for its more and more limited use on the boats, wind power is seemingly no longer needed in Carriacou, for after all, we now have the power that is derived from carbon fuel. Or could it be that the sun is just too hot to serve any useful purpose?

The two adjacent villages/districts of my childhood neighbourhood were Grand Bay and Mount Pleasant. There was broad acceptance of the separating boundary, and although it was possible to find out, it never really mattered to us young ones where that separating line was. They were commonly referred to loosely and interchangeably as if they were but one village.

North Hill, Mt. Pleasant, School, Petit Martinique

South Hill, Grand Bay

In this regard, although Grand Bay is more prominently displayed in most maps, Mt. Pleasant was the single name most used locally to refer to both villages. Indeed, my sister Alethea would occasionally have been heard singing, "Sweet vale of Mt. Pleasant, how calm could I rest?" even though the words applied to and were derived from elsewhere.

Purposely or not, people were being *brainwashed*.

Nonetheless, it had been indicated by word of mouth that the dividing line extended from the coast at the fort, through Tan Dorah's Junction, and continuing upward, between my parents' main house and the kitchen, towards Top Hill. One should bear in mind that in those days, the kitchen was always a separate structure from the house but was still within the owner's yard.

Tan Dorah's bungalow house, which was just about a hundred yards from the seashore, was on a property that had an open area on the west aspect. Continuing westward, this was separated by the main road from an open rocky area on the adjacent property. This resulted in the formation of a space sufficiently large and vacant to be often used for meetings, celebrations, or just liming by the boys.

The word *liming* just meant being in the open, usually as an idle group, but in a somewhat more positive manner than just loafing or doing nothing. Stories may be told, music played, and pranks exchanged in this light and fun atmosphere.

A Topographical Outline

Topographically, Carriacou was very hilly. Although there were hills within Grand Bay and Mt. Pleasant, these two villages were enclosed by two much more prominent hills that extended from the seacoast, one from the north and the other from the south. These two hills blocked sightlines between these two villages and the other villages, except Mt. Dor, Mt. Royal, and Top Hill. These three were more closely merged and were centrally placed at the eastern crest, where all hills tended to converge, above our lower and flatter coastal villages.

The northern Belair Hill or Belair Land, above Newland, which arose near the Point and Tibeau, separated us from the north-eastern districts of Limlair, Belvedere, Dover, and Windward, all of which were on relatively flat land.

Not far from the top of this hill, at its most central location, was Belair. That was where the hospital was located, as well as the residences of nurses, the medical doctor, and the administrative district officer. From this hilltop there was an excellent, though not totally panoramic, view of the town and the village and sea of Mt. Pleasant.

The districts just mentioned were themselves separated by another hill from west-central Bogles, Bousejour, the town of Hillsborough, L'Esterre, Lauriston, Harvey Vale, Six Roads, and other adjacent areas. All were on relatively flat land, but Chapeau Carre, the second highest hill in Carriacou, was somewhere in that area.

In essence, Newland or Belair Hill separated Mt. Pleasant from other eastern villages, like Dover and Windward, and these were separated by another hill from Bogles and, continuing north-westerly, Hillsborough, Harvey Vale, and others beyond.

The prominent South Teeblee Hill separated Grand Bay from Sabazan, Dumfries, Six Roads, and those places that we in Mt. Pleasant referred to as *below side*. These included Belmont and Bellevue.

Within Grand Bay itself was a low hill with a street running lengthwise on it. Visible from this street were the coastal estates of Kendace and Breteche, which were also on the eastern front between the street and Teeblee, as well as the cemetery and our land, which were more inland and closer to the street.

Children were scared of the spooky Teeblee Hill, as folklore led us to believe that it was the home of the evil spirits. Understandably, I personally never ventured near to it, especially as there was no reason to, except for one time at about age 18 when Wilcome, my closest friend, and I sought wood from there for making coals. With Wilcome's companionship and physical stature, one became daringly fearless. Let me add that most of the hills were wooded, with some of the wood prized for boat building.

There was another small hill beyond the above coastal estates that separated them from southwestern Sabazan and Dumfries and the adjacent Six Roads. While growing up, I was acquainted with the eastern villages and the town of Hillsborough but only later truly got to know the others. Those below-side villages seemed to have retained more of the old culture, such as the heel and toe and quadrille dances and the Big Drum Dance, also called the Nation Dance. By contrast, the eastern villages, despite the continuance of boat building, portrayed an image that they were more progressive in outlook.

Live and learn.

Having mentioned the Kendace Estate, I'm reminded of the constant warring over land ownership between two of the McIntosh's brothers—Cousin Moore and Cousin Toby (Tobias)—and my immediate neighbour, Charles Cayenne, who was married to a sister of the McIntosh's, Alexandrina, who was locally called Cousin Mammie or Dama. I recall that it was on a Sunday morning that Charles chastised Toby, who offered no resistance, with a broomstick near Tannah's shop. I suspect that this ended up in the courts.

And there was a time when Charles took Moore to court over the land but lost the case. This prompted Lincoln, a son of Moore, to compose and sing the following song:

> Monday morning in Magistrate court
> To see a learned man losing his case,
> For the Magistrate declared there and then
> He could not waste time on such a case.
> I know the Kendace plan, and we go whip them with that.

This leads me to say that there were other simple refrains with sexual overtones that were composed by persons not known to me. The first involved a girl who was caught stealing corn from a garden. It was said that on the approach of the owner, she laid herself supine on the ground and pleaded with him.

> Pet Blue in the garden hiding.
> Pet Blue in the garden stealing.
> The news come and reach me in town,
> The way how she lay on the ground,
> And she saying, "Grind me corn, Mister Gerald.
> Ah tell you, grind me corn."

The next had to do with words from a man to a woman.

> Open bam bam, ah me wey deh.
> Open bam bam down dey.
> Open la la, is me wey dey.
> Open la la down deh.

And finally, a taxi driver, Irvin Blaize, befriended a young girl from Mt. Pleasant. I'm not sure, but I believe that his Chevrolet car was named Sweet Sixteen, either reflecting the age of the girl or sixteen corner, located on the road to town, where he may have first had her.

All day, all night, she driving up and down. All day, all night, she driving up and down. Ah send me daughter to make ah message. She friend with the green-Chev man.

Home Sweet Home

Invariably, there were two main structures in the home property, the house and the kitchen. In Mt. Pleasant, the houses, and particularly the living or sitting rooms, were treated somewhat as sacred structures and so were rarely used willy-nilly. They were instead reserved for special occasions, such as for reposing in if ill, for entertaining visitors, and most always, for family gatherings, prior to sleeping at nights. Otherwise, one only entered as was necessary and quickly exited.

Original house with right extension.

However, not all followed this view, so there were a few homes in which we, as children, were allowed to play in the living rooms. In this regard, I recall the home of Cousin Leenus, located near a tract road to our land. She called me godbrother because she was the godchild of my mother. There was also the house of Cousin Wandalina in the lower part of the Grand Bay Hill, near to the seacoast, and Tan Dorah's house, playing within the realms of decency.

So except for the immediate neighbours' yards, in which we wandered and played, I, as a youngster, usually only went to other homes when sent to take or obtain messages and would usually just stand in the yard. Exceptions were when I accompanied my sister Alethea on her visits farther afield on Sundays.

Hence, the daytimes were most often spent outdoors, either working or just relaxing. Children in particular were supposed to be outside in the yard, especially if guests were being entertained. There they were to keep out of big-people conversation and business, barely heard and glancingly observed by the adults so as to ensure their proper behaviour.

One did not whistle in the house, and if, perchance, a child was whistling, it certainly would not be around adults. Even the meals were generally consumed outside in conveniently created locations in the yard, the exception being when the older siblings would arrive home from work in the evening or night and would eat at the dining table in the house.

The yard was the open area between the house and kitchen with variable extensions beyond and around the two. Not unusually, other smaller outbuildings were present in the yard. When not in use, the doors to most buildings were conveniently kept closed but were rarely locked. That applied even to the house, though less so. If, perchance, a fence existed, it would only be partly around the land and would be there to deter animals from entering.

Yes, the house was treated with great respect. It was even sacrosanct for some. However, one's, yard remained open and entirely approachable, but beware of the dogs for some would come after you without being sicced.

In our yard, there were a few trees, including two white cedars and two needle-leafed pines, as well as a flower bed in which were a red-flowering hibiscus, a no-named plant with purple flowers and milky sap (now thought to be an Indian rubber plant), and few evergreen shrubs. However, most flowers that adorned the house on Sundays or on any special day were obtained from Da Worth Noel's yard, near to the post office. I was often sent there to get them.

I suppose it was from then that I grew to appreciate prettiness. Nevertheless, later in my life, I have been known to say to my girlfriends that all ladies, like flowers, should be adored in their natural state, not picked, plucked, broken, or wantonly deflowered. I reiterate that the splendour of flowers should be appreciated on the plants, not cut off to be later reduced to dropped petals on a tabletop. But I accept as in Isaiah 40, that naturally, they also fade.

Said to have been bought by my father, either from a Cayenne or a Calder who may have been a doctor, our house was located on a small central plateau of a hill, with slopes on the north and south sides. Fairly typical for the island, it was wooden and elevated on wall and wood pillars.

The roof had an east-to-west A-shape at the north front overlying the east living room and the west main bedroom. A smaller, only slightly sloping south end extension overlaid the boys' east and girls' west bedrooms, which were separated by a wash-up area.

The house was south of the kitchen and was approached from the yard up four concrete steps to a platform that led to a north-facing double front door, one half of which was kept bolted closed from within. On the inside of this door was a shorter double door that opened inwards and was invariably open.

The outer walls of the house were covered with wood shingles, as was the roof, but the latter was changed to galvanized sheets in my youth.

In later times, what seemed strange to me was that whereas the house before had seemed large and spacious, as an adult, I could cross from the front to the back in five steps.

And yet, be it ever so humble.

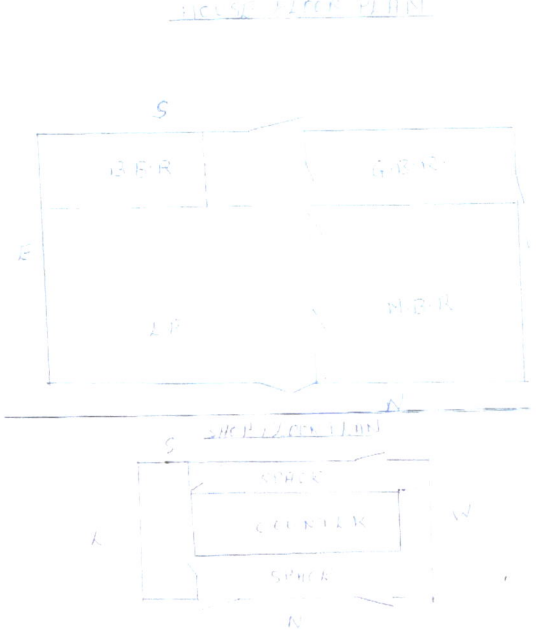

FLOOR PLAN

I will further describe the house in some detail, as it then exemplified a norm for the villages, although, of course, there was variation in size as befitted one's means.

A passageway led from the front door through the western part of the living room and the middle of the wash-up area to the back door. There was no ready access to or from outside from the back door because it was elevated from the ground, but there were horizontal wooden bars at the lower part to prevent accidental falls.

Especially at nights, the boys usually peed through the gaps between the bars onto the ground. If one were in that part of the backyard, one would note that it exuded the urinary aroma of ammonia. After I had acquired some height, I climbed up to or exited from that door many a time, though to what purpose I do not know, unless it was to obtain something without alerting others.

Well, with a door and bars being there, it must have been seen as a good thing for a boy to do.

The furniture and cabinetry were of cherished wood—mahogany artistically designed and intricately carved by woodcraftsmen. The fancy chairs, used mainly by sitting guests, had cane wicker seats with curved wooden, rattan, or bamboo frames.

The exceptions to this were the dining chairs and the two Morris armchairs, which were not fancy but just plain and sturdy. The armchairs were stationed in against the partition that separated the living room from the large bedroom.

At our nightly gatherings, we children would spread out, sitting on the floor of the living room, with the older ones in chairs. Especially with Alethea, I would play card games—gin rummy, search the pack, and one I remember as "sub-de-well" in which one attempted to match face-down cards. We provided our own forms of entertainment before retiring for the night, never later than perhaps eight or nine o'clock.

On crossing the threshold of the house, one would encounter a small vestibule that opened directly to the main living room. To the left, against the inner front wall, were a Singer sewing machine and the dining table and chairs, and on the inner east wall were the sitting chairs and a rocking chair of similar design. Against the partition that separated the living room from the boys' room were the *waganet* and a couple of chairs.

In the middle of the living room was a crafted, round-top centre table on which prettily coloured decorative articles, ornaments, and kaleidoscopic trinkets sat around a centrally placed, partly globe-like lamp. This consisted of a glass shade that protected the knitted, canvas-like wick, which extended down to the kerosene-filled receptacle.

The table top was supported by a central pole, also craftily designed, attached to three or four legs, similarly crafted and partly arched.

What we called the *waganet* was a credenza-like item of furniture. It was supported by four designed legs, which ran from the floor to the very top. At the bottom was a two-door cabinet, and above it were two drawers that contained cutlery. Above the drawers there was an open space separated bisected by a shelf. Glassware and crockery were placed below and above the shelf.

The origin of the word is not known to me. However, this item of cabinetry somewhat resembles a small wheelless wagon.

One of two partitions, which also bore craftily carved patterns, separated the south-eastern part of the living room from the boys' bedroom; and the other partition separated the western portion of the living room from the master bedroom, which was reachable via front and back doorways that usually remained opened.

Most bedroom windows remained closed at nights, and as the master bedroom was on the west side of the house, the nights were sometimes uncomfortably hot in it, especially if mosquitoes were around singing and biting, even though my mother whisked with her towel. The only comfort and rescue came with sleep, when I started sleeping there. To this day, I actually hate mosquitoes.

I am of the belief that in our villages, a small majority of the parents' bedrooms were located in the west of the house. This, perhaps, along with most windows being kept closed at nights, provided some measure of protection from illness-causing draughts of air and the evil spirits that wandered at nights. Also, by placing the living rooms to the east, the airiness could be better appreciated in the daytime, especially by visitors.

But my oh my, these western bedrooms were stuffy.

The boys' bedroom was separated from the wash-up area by a movable partition. There was a glass-paned window on the east wall of the room and a wooden one on the south, from which it was easy to exit onto the roof-top of the cistern and then jump down to the yard. My brother Godwin, the eldest child, told me that he used this route to escape at nights to go gallivanting.

The western girls' bedroom was separated from the wash-up area by an installed partition with a door. This room was south of the master bedroom and was separated from it by either a movable partition or a seldom used door. It had a south-facing wooden window and a west-facing double up/down exit door that was hardly used, except when there was a general house cleaning.

The children's beds were made of iron, and the mattresses were either home-sewn by knowledgeable persons, with the padding sometimes composed of straw from corns or unseeded cotton, or they were commercially bought. Each bed easily accommodated two persons.

The wash-up area was between the two children's bedrooms. Within it was the safe (a pantry cabinet), atop which were kept Saturday's baked products. The enclosed shelves were mainly used for the storage of food items, including fried fish and canned foods, like sardines or a tin of condensed milk in which were punched two holes on opposite ends. This tin had to be placed in a saucer of water to prevent what we called crazy ants from getting to it. I don't recall that cockroaches posed a problem.

In the wash-up area, there was also a table with a lower shelf for the ewer, and on top of that was an open surface in which was fitted the wash basin. On one side, there was a towel rack. On the back wall of the house, between the entrance to the boys' bedroom and the backdoor, there was a shelf upon which was an earthen goblet that contained the coolest water then imaginable. The drinking glass next to it was used by one and all at home and was seldom washed.

There was a four-poster bed in the master bedroom, as well as a trunk for storing documents and linen. On either side of the bed, on the west outer wall, was a chest of drawers with mirrors.

Its drawers contained articles of clothing and linen items. I don't remember the bed being canopied, although it was built for that. Moth or camphor balls that served as mould repellents and pesticides were kept within the drawers of the bureaus. Some items of clothing were hung from nails in the walls or from the bedposts. And on the floor near the head of the bed was Iah's clay chamber pot.

The mattress, from which we children teased out bed bugs, lay on removable slats. It was taken out on Sunday mornings, and we took turns knocking out the bed bugs. At times, we sprayed the bugs with kerosene, but more usually, they were crushed on a hard surface, leaving dark-red lines of blood from which emanated a most horrible odour.

Mention was made earlier of a shorter, smaller inner door with two halves. Well, behind one half of this door, readily reachable by my mother from where she sat on her Morris chair, were good-sized twigs or whips from our big tamarind tree, which today still exists. The twigs were used for disciplining.

Other items in the house included lanterns and searchlights (flash or torch lights). There were also articles of different materials hanging on the inner walls that depicted themes of significance. These included a framed photograph of my mother and her sister, my aunt Loonie, and clay plates painted with coloured pictures and etched with phrases like "Welcome", "Home Sweet Home", "Christ is the Head of this House", "The Unseen Guest", and "The Lord Is in This House".

One article that stood out was the framed speech of Winston Churchill, from which we children often recited the following extracted phrases--, "We shall fight on the beaches, we shall fight on the seas and oceans, we shall never surrender."

The house was well ventilated, at least in the daytime, because of the many windows. In general, the front rooms had paned glass windows; the top halves were fixed, but they could be opened by sliding the bottom halves upward. Decorative blinds or curtains were hung on the inside of the windows. In each bedroom, there was also a swing-open, double-door, wooden window.

There were no doors on the east and west outer walls of the house, except for a rarely used one in the girls' bedroom.

Always at nights, there would be flat-headed, dull, light grey lizards sitting on the inner parts of the rafters or on the ceiling. We became accustomed to them, even though they were not pretty to look at. Sometimes, there were also spiders.

Whether on hills or on the flatter coastal areas, most houses were elevated above ground on concrete pillars or wooden poles, partly, I imagine, so that the breezes could ease the discomfort or agony of the sun's heat but maybe for other purposes. Children played under houses, and dogs often slept there.

Later in life, I was led to understand that houses in Suriname and Guyana were also elevated from the ground but more so because the lands, being flat, were easily flooded by the heavy rainfalls and because huge snakes crawled the earth.

In Carriacou, the area beneath the houses allowed the construction of above-ground basements or downstairs areas, which conveniently created more usable space for the house. Most downstairs areas, including ours, were accessed through an outer door.

In ours, we stored cotton after it was picked and prior to it being bagged to be sold. There was ample space on the concrete floor for playing without getting soil dirty. There was a central post on which the mill for grinding dried corn seeds was positioned, but the green corn was ground in a portable mill that could be suitably attached elsewhere. Both mills were available for use by other villagers—for a fee, of course.

It does appear that the Amerindians, the indigenous inhabitants of the island, had preferred to live nearer the coast rather than on the hills, for we often discovered evidence of them in the form of different buried artifacts and portions of crockery, earthenware, or pottery, especially around Kendace but also elsewhere. They supposedly gave the island its name: *Kayryouacou* (land of reefs).

Carib relics

Beyond the house

The kitchen was a rectangular structure, elongated east to west, with three only partly separated main compartments. It was spatially compact and was situated about four yards north of the house. Like the house, it was also a wooden structure, but it was constructed directly over a concrete foundation. It served primarily for cooking, which was done on a constructed brick fireside, but had tables, shelves, and enclosures that were used for storage.

There were the usual crockery and cooking utensils, but the only cutlery we used for eating were spoons, of which that of my mother was special. There was a board window in each compartment, and each also had an outside door that faced the house.

The fireplace, situated against the western wall and built above the concrete floor, was rectangular and had an open front that was surrounded by a three-sided wall structure with a flat top, on which different items could be placed. The open brick area was where the wood fuel burned, and above that were iron rods, on which up to two pots could rest.

Between the back of the fireplace and the back wall of this compartment, there was a narrow passageway that abutted a wooden safe on the west wall and shelves for the eating implements on the northern back wall. It was in this space that I usually stood while my sister, Alethea, shared the food for me to put away appropriately and then either to eat or, more usually, to first take my mother's portion to the shop.

Another useful item was the portable coal pot with its removable grill, which was used for cooking, roasting corn, or heating both the ladies' curling irons and those used for ironing clothing. Sometime later, in my preteen years, a two-burner kerosene stove was located on a table in the middle compartment.

It was also not that unusual to cook in the open yard, with the pots placed on an assembly of three large fire stones.

The middle and fairly open compartment housed a brick oven, which stood against the front wall, between the west and middle doors. The oven had concrete sides and a flat top that was convenient for storing articles. A table for water containers and pots, containers for the pigs' slop, and small enclosures for storing items like the wood used for fuel and the garden implements were also in this area. I remember collecting the leaves from the calabash tree. The bread dough was placed on these leaves before being put into the heated oven. Cakes were baked on greased flat tin pans.

In many homes, the ovens were located outside but near to the kitchen, with the walls of some made from mud.

Like most of the larger kitchens of the area, ours had an overhead loft for the storage of shucked corn. It extended from above the fireplace eastwards and could be accessed by a ladder in the third compartment. This third compartment had an enclosure for storing pigeon peas still in their pods, but it was used mainly as a preparation workplace for baking.

Some walls and roofs of kitchens and even houses on the island were built from an interlacing of wattle-wood for the walls and roofs, especially if their owners couldn't afford anything more. The walls of such buildings were plastered with white clay, and the thatched roofs were covered with straw and palm fronds. But as has been put to song, be it ever so humble, there is no place like home.

I am of the opinion that limestone from the coral reef was collected and burnt in kilns to make quicklime, which was also used in the construction of the walls. Some of these kitchens may otherwise be well accommodated, while some were mere enclosed structures with only a cooking spot of large rocks on the dirt floor.

In a general sense, we used stout, dried logs that we collected and then chopped smaller to make strong fires and used the dried bramble of the cotton and pigeon peas plants for less strong fires. If the fire was being prepared in the outside yard and there was a lack of wind, we would fan the flames with any flat item, such as a piece of cardboard, or blow with our mouths to get the fire going.

Oh, but how the smoke got into and irritated the eyes!

Although we infrequently produced our own coals for use in the coal pots, it was more usual to buy them from others within the village. Kerosene was used as a starter fuel for the wood and coal fires in addition to being fuel for the lamps, lanterns, and stove.

Out of curiosity, I once unfortunately opened a gas lamp, which was brighter than the kerosene lamp it had replaced, and touched the woven light source only to have it disintegrate at my touch.

Some other items found at home and stored wherever seemed appropriate included a kneading tray for dough, a mortar and pestle, and a jooking board, which was hand made from wood until we obtained a commercially made one of thick glass. In addition, we had graters and garden tools, like cutlasses, axes, hoes, spades, and forks. An iron file was used to manually sharpen knives and cutlasses.

The smaller graters were used for grating ginger, coconuts, and cocoa balls, and a large one was for grating corn on the rough, punched-out side, and for sifting material from the inner, smooth surface.

There were crocus bags, which were used for different reasons that will be mentioned later and were readily located when needed.

A clothesline extended across part of the yard for hanging laundered articles, but some items were also spread over shrubs for sun drying. An occasional downpour would have us scrambling to gather them in. Usually, we had ample time, as the rain would invariably set up over the sea and wend its way westward over land.

Toilets or latrines were little outdoor buildings that were built over dug pits and would be moved as necessary when the pits filled up. In my early years, we knew nothing of toilet paper; instead, we used pieces from old newspapers sent from Grenada, portions of corn cobs, and sometimes leaves, especially from the cotton plants that were close by, to clean ourselves. Very rarely, in fading light, persons have been known to tear off leaves from an irritating plant—including the one we called zooty, a stinging nettle—resulting in dire consequences.

In the mornings, because of the bulky nature of our foods, we lined up to use the toilet. If one could hold no longer, one went into the adjacent garden to perform one's business and cleansed with the cotton leaves. It is alleged that the Mighty Sparrow, a known calypso king, intonated that in days of old when men were bold and paper not yet invented, he wiped his glass (arse) with blades of grass and walked away contented.

The story was told that as children, my brother Gilbert and his friend Boland Nelson once stole candies during a night affair in the village and were being chased by an adult. The friend partly fell into an incompletely dug latrine pit and damaged some of his teeth.

In some yards, like ours, there was an enclosed structure for bathing, but it was not unusual for baths to be taken in any location that was partly hidden from general view, including under the house. The usual weekly bath was performed using a bucket of water from the cistern which either had some boiling water added to it or had been left for a while in the sun for warming.

Until I was about age 8, my mother, when taking a Saturday or Sunday early morning bath, also bathed me. The water would usually be dipped from the larger container using a large cup, bowl, or calabash and then poured over the body, but sometimes, a wash rag was used. Any other daily washing was just of the feet, hands, and face. We would do that before venturing out, like when we were getting ready for school, or before retiring for the night.

Also in the yard were a fowl house (also called a fowl coop) and pig pens with adjacent troughs that were either hewn hollow from large stones or were concrete built. Holes were dug in the rocks of the yard from which the untethered animals would drink the added water. There was a large iron trough to catch rainwater for the animals.

Those who were financially able built concrete cisterns to collect and store rainwater that was spouted from the roofs of the houses. Others used drums or other containers for collecting and storing water. Rainwater was also distributed from the government cisterns via pipes, depending either on gravity or pumps, or else the water was drawn from the cisterns with buckets.

The storage of water would have contributed to the ever-presence of mosquitoes, well known for disturbing sleep. To mitigate this annoyance, some would use kerosene or an oil to cover the water surface, while others would place a removable cover over the container.

Particularly in the cisterns, a type of small freshwater fish, which we called millions (guppies), that fed on the mosquito larvae was used. If sitting out at nights, we sometimes burned green twigs to ward off these pests. And there was the hand-pumped spray can in which kerosene was put.

Our cistern, which was attached adjacent to a part of the southeast outer wall of the house, was accessed by steps that led to a window in the facing of the roof, through which the water was drawn. When one was really thirsty, this water, like that from the goblet, was ever so refreshing.

Our yard space was ample, except for a very narrow tract of land that separated our cistern from Say Doone's yard, which was just down the southern slope of the hill. Despite its narrowness, however, it nevertheless allowed us children to run races completely around the house.

Once, my brother Lysander, known to be somewhat bunglesome, missed the turn to this track and fell some five feet to the yard below. Say Beebee, the daughter of Say Doone, was alarmed, at first thinking it was some animal that had fallen.

Fortunately, except for a bruise or two, Lysander broke not a bone in his body.

Provided there were no inconveniences, my mother would lead some members of the family walking along the track road for a sea bath on some early Sunday mornings. We would walk past our immediate neighbours (to be later mentioned) and then lower down past Miss Queenie, where lived Donald (Dan) Jackson, who had sustained a cut from a flying piece of galvanised metal near his ear during hurricane Janet. We would go past Cousin Effie, whose son, Joe Landon, I met when he visited years later from New York and through Tan Dorah's Junction. We would continue on, passing houses on either side of the track, including that of Cousin Patient and her son, Arthur, and that of Miss Bee and Darteen, eventually making it down to the fort at the seashore, locally called the bay.

Then, on returning home, we would rinse off with rain water.

Indeed, this entire track, which was almost a straight line from our home to the fort, which itself jutted out seawards as coastal rocks, seemed to represent the line of separation between the two villages. With the jutting rocks into the sea, it also separated the northern Mt. Pleasant beach from the southern Grand Bay beach, both of which had greyish sand.

At some point in time, there was a house on the fort itself, and later on, it was refurbished or rebuilt by the Mills family and used on weekends as a nightclub. I suspect that this may have seen its time and exists no more. I cannot remember with certainty whether or not there was a cannon on the fort, but I believe there was.

Though I have previously noted, it is worthwhile repeating for emphasis that most houses and other buildings were built with wood. The larger parts of the roofs were A-shaped, and those parts merged with smaller, slightly sloping extensions. Most roofs were originally covered with shingles, but the shingles were eventually replaced with galvanized sheets. The exterior walls were also protected with shingled coverings. The entire outer structure of buildings was usually painted. Bungalow-type wooden houses also existed.

However, with the passage of time, concrete-block homes, constructed directly on the ground and no longer on poles, became more common. They were usually built by residents who had returned from working overseas or who, whilst still abroad, had sent home remittances for these constructions as well as for the support of relatives.

Patios, verandas and porches, present in both the old and more recent houses, always were at the front and faced the road. I am of the belief that in more sophisticated countries, they face the back sceneries.

This has continued to this day. These houses, some quite majestic, were not always occupied and indeed were sometimes vacant for long periods. This vacancy continues to the present, because many who return only spend a short time on the island or, being of an older age, die shortly after returning. Understandably, the children of these people only rarely visited. This was true irrespective of where born, but it was especially the case if they were born abroad. Such homes and some others specifically constructed for the purpose are now advertised as being for sale or for rental by visitors (Airbnb).

As if part of a natural process, it is not unusual to see the structures of one's youth lying abandoned, in disrepair, decrepit, dilapidated, collapsed, or completely destroyed, whilst scattered new edifices stand empty within fenced-in properties. Of course, this description is not one of all or none.

* * *

Throughout the Caribbean, complaints are often heard, particularly from those in authority, about the citizens leaving and not returning to contribute to their home countries. This often is in reference to what is termed "brain drain", especially when that brain has been trained at home.

However, for whatever reason, economic or other, I contend that human beings will forever seek a better life if circumstances permit. Let us therefore offer praises to those who have never left or who have returned to serve but belittle not, nor debase, those who have done neither.

It is up to the countries to adopt strategies and measures to encourage their citizens to remain or to return when still able to contribute meaningfully and not when retired—in essence, ensuring a brain gain. Easier said than enforced!

The bottom line, however, irrespective of what exists and what has transpired, is that human beings seem to be always capable of justifying whatever actions they may have taken or what they support or not. It is, at times, surprising to me how strongly and vehemently stated these defending views can be, even if seemingly meaningless to another ear, but no one wants to be considered an idiot. Each person is responsible for who he or she is and what he or she does, and if perchance that person dreams, so be it, as no dream is impossible to attain.

People are capable of doing anything, and in my view, once circumstances present at the right place and time, they will behave in a manner and do what seems beneficial to them at that moment. Without doubt, one looks after oneself.

It is my opinion that there were persons who had expected me to return to Carriacou. They could not have cared less about me being a pathologist—which is not a profession by which I could have supported myself there—but strongly entertained the view that a son of the soil, having become a doctor, should return to serve his people. Even in the larger Grenada, it proved difficult to meaningfully practise the discipline of pathology at the time that I returned.

As time passed and the population steadily declined, the zeitgeist of the old Carriacou gradually diminished, and perhaps some culturally different customs, not all newfangled, have evolved in its place. The robustness, pride, buoyancy, and joie de vivre that once stood for Mt. Pleasant and Grand Bay have been decreasing and are still being gradually eroded. And yet, it should be appreciated that although at any point in time, culture has identity, it is not a static phenomenon and may even prove undefinable, convoluted, and difficult to qualify.

The population of the island, which was 13,000 in the 1950s, has shrunk over time to less than 8,000. Although some aspects of our lives in this ethnographic microclimate still spontaneously exist, there is now the tendency to organise shows that demonstrate our culture to visitors, for we no longer live it. And as it is now said, it's just for show, man. Yet, life continues.

In deference to our culture, I pay homage to a former classmate of mine, against whom I have played cricket. For years, he epitomised the culture of old in his knowledge and behaviour and through organised performances, locally and abroad. Rest in Peace, Winston Fleary

Charles Darwin propounded a theory of evolution, particularly about living things, based on the survival of the fittest. But I extend it as questions arise: Whither goest, Mt. Pleasant? Whither goest, Grand Bay? Do provide some answers, Carriacou!

For I know not where to, but even empires died.

Primarily as a means to acquire wealth, Carriacouans, mainly the men, emigrated to different countries long before I was born. The practice continued through the period before I had developed any degree of understanding and appreciation, and as time has elapsed, it has continued throughout my adulthood.

In large measure, they went to Venezuela; the Dutch Antilles; Trinidad; Brooklyn, New York; London, England; and Canada. The Dutch Island of Aruba attracted workers for the Lago Oil refinery plant, Trinidad for the oil fields, New York for the building of the subway, and London for general labour. Canada originally opened for domestic workers, usually of the female gender, but it is now open to different categories of workers.

In those earlier days, wives and children were left at home. Later, they joined their husbands in New York, for example, whereas those men in Aruba tended to later rejoin their wives as they retired in Carriacou. I do contend that some of these latter men have indeed made significant contributions. The term *lay-off* was heard quite often, which invariably meant a dismissal for whatever reason and resulted in a return to Carriacou.

When England opened up in the late forties and fifties, young men emigrated, and when it was convenient, they sent for ladies from home for marriage. Those who became permanently settled applied for others—not only wives or immediate relatives but also friends.

Particularly with reference to the United States, one would hear in the village, "The papers come." It was then necessary for the person to first travel to the American Embassy in Barbados to begin the process of documentation for entry into the US.

At that time, in reference to England, one spoke of the Geest banana boat by which they travelled. This boat was primarily for freighting bananas from the Windward Islands to England, but it also boarded passengers.

In Grenada, the stevedores lived the life of the song "Banana Boat (Day-O)", popularised by Harry Belafonte but said to have originated from Jamaica, as they loaded the boats.

In 1956, the movie *Island in the Sun*, which starred Belafonte, James Mason, two beautiful Joans, and the attractive Dorothy Dandridge, had some of its episodes filmed in Grenada. Grenadians gathered at the shooting sites, but I remember just barely seeing a couple of the stars, as filming never started at the scheduled or advertised time, so one grew tired of waiting.

A young student, Jacobs, made an appearance in the film on his bicycle. Jack's Alley, through which I walked from church to the wharf for the Sunday boat to Carriacou, was the site of a murder in the film. A student, Jack Radix, adopted the hairstyle of Harry Belafonte, and the song of the movie's name became very popular. The boys' hairstyles in vogue then included a part on one side or in the middle and the use of a thick hair grease and prolonged brushing to produce waves.

But even when children had fathers who had not travelled, for different reasons, they seemed absent from home during the day. This, compounded by many men being abroad, had contributed to Carriacou being a place somewhat dominated by women in general and mothers in particular. Therefore, if a big child were to be punished, he or she might hear, "Just wait until yuh fader come home."

Fathers and other men may have had the final say as the rulers, but the females controlled the homes. Female empowerment!

People emigrated to seek a better future, certainly, but I would imagine that emigration from Carriacou was readily entertained as a means of gaining relief from the hard manual labour, the long waits for minimal financial returns, and the overall rigors and uncertainties of agriculture.

One must bear in mind that intra-Caribbean emigration also occurred. Many Grenadians went to Trinidad. Some of my high school teachers came from elsewhere, especially from British Guiana and Barbados. Some aspects of emigration are now considered illegal, as occurs frequently in the Bahamas.

Expectedly, as the population dwindled, the clearing of the land and tilling of the soil diminished, and Carriacou was fast being transformed into a place overgrown with many relatively useless but native plants, such as the zooty (nettle) shrubs and the thorn (cashee-picka) and common cherry trees.

Of mere unsightly annoyance now, some of these plants did offer some benefits when we were growing up. For example, the pods of the cashee-picka plant (an Acacia species?) and the common cherry both provided a gluey substance often used especially in the making of kites, and in times of hunger, we also sucked the sticky sap of the cherries. The hard wood of the picka plant provided good fuel, and the stripped bark of the common cherry was used to make rope to tie together the collected dried brambles to make for easier toting.

As an aside, we also made a paste from flour and water that was used for sticking paper and light wood surfaces together, but it provided less adherence than the above plant products.

In these modern times, these are things of the past. Time moves on and brings changes with it.

2

GROWING UP: THE FAMILY AND THE NEIGHBOURHOOD

Iah

When I became conscious of whom I was, there, outstanding as ever, was my mother—a no-nonsense, demanding, and domineering disciplinarian then in her late forties. Her name was Caroline Sophia Brathwaite, née McLeod. Her children and the vast majority of the villagers called her Iah, I imagine because the ending of her middle name, by which she was better known, was pronounced as the word *fire,* itself a suitable name for her.

I remained uncertain till my adulthood about the origin of her parental surname, and the same can be said for many other surnames. Speculations about the origins of surnames have been proposed. I add here, as has been told, that in the Bahamas, the slaves were identified by the landlords' names, and these names were retained after emancipation and the departure of the owners. So, a slave originally identified as Jack of Rolle (Rolle being the landlord) later became Jack Rolle. In this regard, many Bahamians, not only the former slaves but also children of the landlords, bore the same names, shared relationships, and could trace from which island of the archipelago the name had originated.

However, I have since been informed that her father was of Scottish heritage, even though he may not have emigrated directly from Scotland. My father was also said to be of a Scottish lineage.

When my mother issued commands, as she was wont to do, we children could reason and perhaps even argue, but it was unacceptable and ill-advised to mutter, grumble, back chat, or suck teeth or sstupps (a sound produced between closed teeth and pursed lips, said to mean "kiss my arse") within hearing. It was even worse to disobey, for then one would learn the meaning of respect the hard way—through the licks and blows that rained down on one so bravely foolish. And as the licks were being rendered, one would hear, "You must be hard ah hearing, come yaah. Whey ever you pick that up, go back deh and drop it."

I don't think she ever expressed sorrow after beating you, for I guess that in her mind, she was teaching you a lesson that you deserved. And yet, I and undoubtedly all her other children always loved her. It was a love that was eventually twinned with an admiration in thoughts that continue to be expressed verbally and with pride and adoration. To this day, others who had dwelled in her home, including children who had come under her influence, so express the respect with which she was and is still regarded.

Until I was about 6 years old, it was known and accepted that at every opportunity, I would nestle in her lap and even play with her breasts. Why this was allowed to happen, I would never know. As individual white hairs appeared on her head, she would allow them to be plucked from her scalp. She was also known to dye her hair black as the greying and whitening increased.

She was human.

Naughtily, however, we understood quite well that this stalwart lady—this bastion, this female stallion, one who was said to be able to live with snakes and lions—could control the day and the hour but certainly not every minute. So, we sometimes seized those rare opportunities when she lapsed and did whatever came to our minds, just skylarking, behaving waggishly, or delving into our shenanigans.

At times, the gentleness of her manner and voice would soothe any ache that plagued us, but low and behold, a stentorian shout or a holler or bellow of your name would momentarily freeze you and then melt your shaking bones as you pondered what wrong you would have committed. But I have never heard her to curse.

Her ten living children consisted of seven sons and three daughters, and I was the youngest. We were neither rich nor poor but fared comfortably well. Perhaps in this day, it would be referred to as being middle class or fairly well-to-do.

I knew not my father, who the much older siblings called Poopa and who had died on 29 September 1941 when I was 5 months old. His death certificate listed his occupation as "proprietor".

As an adult, I have reminded the older ones that our father, in seeking perfection, impregnated his wife fourteen times, resulting in three babies who perhaps did not see the light of day; a boy, Edmund, born in 1927, who died at age 9 months from acute enteritis (*marasma*, according to the eldest, Godwin); and the ten offspring then still alive.

I teasingly claimed that our father, after I was born, looked me over and looked into my eyes and, feeling fully satisfied that his quest had been fulfilled and his goal achieved, promptly departed this life. To him, at last, the best that he had helped to create pleased him. Hallelujah! Eureka (a la Archimedes)!

I must add that his patrimony was adequate. It included a large portion of just over fourteen acres of land in Grand Bay, a home, a shop called The Liberty Shop, and a name and legacy to be proud of.

He may have started what is now so common in the correspondence of social media, for on the title board of the shop was also written, "Thank U".

In addition, he made allowance for each child to receive 1,000 pounds when needed. However, I never received mine. I was led to believe it was used for some other purpose, presumably to further the education of an older sibling.

Iah has told me that it's her belief that I was born before 22 April, maybe about the 12th, but because of my father's illness, my birth registration was late, and the date was therefore advanced. If one followed the astrological signs of the Zodiac, then my birth fell either in Taurus (the bull), or Aries (the ram). I wonder, at times, as to whether one was representative of an also-ran and the other a champion.

I have always kept in mind what I read at a very early age about the Taurian sign: lucky in money matters but not in love affairs.

Ha, ha, ha! No other response from me.

With the uncertainty, and not knowing that I had a choice, I clung to the bull, for it mattered not whether one or the other. I admit that I'm now happy to be associated with the celebration of Earth Day, a day that I truly identify with. My favourite colour has always been green and, in general, the softer hues.

I add here that in my youth, most of us knew only a very few basic colours. Even pink would have been called red.

Thus arrived Alfred Fitzgerald, a name to which, sometimes and much later, Kempster and Alexander were added, one or the other chosen by me when my name was being given to a new girlfriend.

I am not sure why, but in the South Caribbean, the name Brathwaite is pronounced as Braffit—a pronunciation of British derivation, undoubtedly. I'm also aware of what seems to be variations of the name, some containing another *i* or *h* and some omitting the *h*.

It was accepted that my father was born in Barbados on 18 September 1881. As an adult, I sought and found evidence of it in the Department of Archives of that most eastern of the Lesser Antilles Islands, Barbados, which was British-ruled until its independence in November 1966 and which has always been referred to as Little England.

Not surprisingly, in the city's Trafalgar Square is a statue of Lord Horatio Nelson, who we learned in school was the one-eyed, one-armed Elizabethan pirate who, though having died aboard *The Victory*, was known for his defeat of the Spanish Armada and for his words, "England expects that every man will do his duty." To this I add, in the words of my school song, "For each has to play his role."

The telephone directory of Barbados teems with the name Brathwaite.

I was made to understand that a white man, Brathwaite, of Scottish ancestry emigrated to Barbados. With a slave woman, he fathered, among others, a son named Moses Brathwaite, born in the 1830s, who in turn sired my father. My paternal grandfather was of this lineage, but it is believed that my grandmother, Sarah Elizabeth, was a black woman, probably a field worker or housemaid on a plantation. Each name was passed on, respectively, to two of my sisters, and one of my first cousins, from Uncle Darrell, is called Moses.

I was later told that many ancestral given names, and not only those of the Brathwaites, either came from the Bible, as did Sarah, John, and Joseph; came from a historically admired or famous person, as did Alexander and George; or were the names of the parents, like David, II, David, Jr, or the patronymics Davidson (from David) and Fitzgerald (from Gerald). Examples of these will be noticed in the names of some of my siblings. But without a doubt, mine was from Alfred the Great. Ha, ha, ha!

I have also been told by both Iah and Godwin that my paternal grandfather was considered to have been a cruel man. The story goes that on a Saturday morning, he sent his 12-year-old son to the market with a cart laden with produce, including eggs. For whatever reason, the mule bolted, and the cart tumbled over.

The youngster, knowing what to expect if he returned home, left everything on the road, went to the harbour, stowed away on a vessel, and ended up in Grenada, where he was taken in by a woman.

Charles DaCosta

I do not know how he got to Carriacou or with whom he stayed. That young boy, named DaCosta Alexander in the archives, became Charles DaCosta Alexander Brathwaite, known locally as Charlie Braffit. Gilbert, one of my brothers, was named after him. Godwin, meanwhile, named his first son after himself and his father but also acronymically after the zodiac sign of his birth—Charles Raphael Algernon Brathwaite (C. R. A. B.).

At a reasonable age and like some others, my father went to the mines of the "Main" in Venezuela and eventually returned to Carriacou with a reasonable sum of money. After this, he worked in Cuba as an overseer of an estate. The story then differs. Some claim that he took time off, returned to Carriacou to marry my mother, then Caroline Sophia McLeod, and then left by boat for Cuba, accompanied by his pregnant wife, to resume his job.

On the journey, when they arrived in Trinidad, my mother was near death from sea sickness. She asked him one question: which was closer, Carriacou or Cuba? Thus, they ended back in Carriacou to finally settle.

In another account, he was on his way back to Cuba alone and not yet married when he met an adult known to him from Carriacou. This adult chastised his ungratefulness and urged that he should return and settle in Carriacou. And this he did.

Not all has been told, but to me, the former story seems more credible and, as far as I recall, was supported by my mother.

The stories told about him were indeed legendary. He was an astute businessman all was not merely business as usual for him. He started the shop, and the business thrived due to his ingenuity, accommodating manner, and salesmanship. Let's say, as an example, that your money was not enough for the minimum ounce or pound. He would give you a proportionate amount of goods anyhow. There may also have been some aspect of trading, like butter or sugar in exchange for eggs. His bargaining abilities may have continued in my mother after his transition from this life.

The Liberty Shop—Thank u, from little comes much

Iah at the shop

It is my understanding that the shop was originally located in an area called Tan Dorah's Junction but was moved on rollers about thirty yards to the southwest to its present location, where I found it.

During my childhood, the shop was opened every morning from Monday to Saturday near seven o'clock and, with rare exceptions, was manned by Iah until about seven or eight o'clock at night, depending partly on when nightfall came.

On Sundays, it was opened a bit later and closed earlier, in the late afternoon. Only the back door was open for transactions on this holy day and on holidays, and if my brother John was not away from home, he would often act as the man of business on these days. After some time had passed, Iah tended to remain at home, and he eventually took full control on those days.

On some days, when most people were attending other events, most village shops would remain closed. If the event was in the village, I was given a glass jar of candies (sweeties) to sell. I do, however, believe that on Christmas and New Year's Days, it was fully opened, as sales were good. This also facilitated the exchange of greetings and felicitations for the season, as many people just wandered about on the main streets in new fineries.

It is true to say that on regular days, buying generally occurred throughout the day but with spurts in the early mornings and late afternoons. In the early mornings, children and women would shop for food items before school started, and in the late afternoon, they would shop for dinner ingredients.

The men would gather after work and stay into the night to buy their rounds of drinks, which usually was the Jack Iron rum. This would be served in a container appropriate to the volume of the order and placed on the countertop, alongside another container with water.

When taking a shot, each man would pour rum into his glass, and after a word or two, they would all simultaneously imbibe, though they held it in their mouths to await the pouring of the water to chase the strong drink down the throat.

Iah ruled supreme in the shop and would no longer serve if she felt someone had had enough.

It was in the shop that I first heard the words *demijohn* and *gallon* and ordering terms such as *drink, shot, pint, eighth*, and *quart*.

Especially on Saturdays and on weekdays during school vacations, working in the shop also allowed me to become acquainted with weights, and I came to know how much of an item amounted to an ounce (e.g., of butter or lard) or a pound (e.g., of sugar or flour). In idle or inactive moments, I would fill the one-pound paper bags of the latter items to await customers. The currency then was British pounds, shillings, and pence. (The monkey ran up the fence. He scratched his tail on a rotten nail, and it's pounds, shillings, and pence.)

Furthermore, helping in the shop proved somewhat easy, as I was good at arithmetic and was generally considered to be a bright boy. That meant that adding up the price of the purchases and rendering the change was relatively easy. Not too often, I would be left alone in the shop if Iah was making a short visit elsewhere.

On two occasions, I bested George, my brother three years older than me. When questioned by the police after the shop had been broken into, he referred to the corned beef as being Bentos Fray brand instead of the reverse wording; and on a second occasion, in the presence of teacher Cuthbert Simon, he spelled the crackers that we sold as b-i-s-k-e-t. Feeling the proud champion, I, with aplomb and full of bravado, gave the correct answers.

The shop, a short rectangular structure, was fronted by the main street to the north. A counter ran almost its length east to west, but an eastern entrance led to a private east enclosure. From here, one entered through another door to the back of the counter.

On the floor at the back of the counter were placed the barrel of sugar and the flour, usually in its bag but sometimes in a barrel. Other items on the floor included containers with corned or salted beef or pork and coarse or unrefined sea salt. Kerosene was kept under the counter in its large tin container.

Atop the counter at the east end were the tins (possibly five gallons each) of lard and a reddish type of salty butter and a tin of biscuits, which at first were Crix from Trinidad and were later Wibix from Barbados. At the other end of the counter were candies (sweeties), like extra-strong peppermints and a variety of coloured ones, in two large, covered glass jars. In the middle of the counter was the one-pound sliding scale. It was further subdivided into ounces, and there were additional separate weights from one to maybe four pounds near to it.

Also on the counter were large sheets of wax and wrapping paper. I am not sure, but etched along the back edge of the countertop, there may have been a yard length of ruled inches. Whether or not we sold string, twine, or rope, I don't remember. There may also have been a hanging type spring balance somewhere.

On shelves on the back and two side walls were bottles of sweet drinks, Tennent's beer, and milk stout. I am uncertain, but I seem to remember that the stout we carried bore the names Tennent, Mackeson, Guinness, Royal, and Watneys. Iah often made a delicious eggnog with stout as one of the ingredients. There were also a few bottles of some more exotic liquors, of which vermouth, crème de banane, and crème de menthe come to mind.

The shelves also held miscellaneous items like tins or cans of sardines, corned beef, and condensed milk; cigarettes and matches; starch and cubes of blue for laundering; a type of bluish-coloured washing soap that came from a factory in Tempe, Grenada; and cooking and olive oil. I can picture the olive oil in a small, rectangular bottle and sense the aroma and flavour that it gave to a salt fish dish.

There was ample operating space between the back of the counter and the shelved walls.

Although cigarettes were sold, I don't think that too many persons smoked, and those who did usually bought just a single one or two of the Phoenix cigarettes that were made in Grenada by the Caribbean Tobacco Company. They would also request a light from the ever-present box of either Three Stars or Three Plumes safety matches, and light with a flick of the wrist.

Essel "Bocos" Lang, who walked the streets, comes to my mind as such a smoker. Maybe a few men would have purchased as much as a pack, and even fewer smoked tobacco rolled in paper. Tobacco was also stuffed into short-stemmed pipes, especially by elderly women who enjoyed their smokes at home.

As boys, perhaps because we'd seen it being done, we excavated the soft centre of a piece of corn cob to serve as a bowl, stuffed the dried female flower (purport) of the corn plant into it, attached a tube, and smoked. The tube may have come from the long stem of the pumpkin leaf, which we also carved and cut holes into to make a flute.

I believe it may have been as a Christmas gift that I got a real child's plastic flute with six holes at the front and one at the back. I practised on it and taught myself my first song, the lyrics of which began "John 3:16, John 3:16, for God so loved the world". Eventually, I gained an appreciation for chords. I played quite well but never followed up after leaving home to attend secondary school in Grenada.

I was never able to play the mouth organ (harmonica), never knowing when to blow or to inhale, but my brother George did play and quite well indeed. There is an ear for music within me, but try as I might, my dream of being a piano, bass guitar, or steel band player never materialised.

Even my children, despite going to schools of music, never maintained or retained an interest. The saxophone that I bought for Dax as a Christmas gift in about 1988 still remains in its case in my home, never having been used.

The small eastern private room in the shop was for the changing of one's attire and for cooking and eating. There was also a rather small alcove at the southwestern end of it with a table and shelf where the rum was kept. Few men would be allowed in this room to have their drinks or, more rarely, to share a meal.

The spacious area between the front of the counter and the shop's north front opened to the street by two doors. The west door served as the main entrance to the shop. The east door was guarded by Iah on her small bench with her stout stick nearby. There were benches in this frontal area that provided limited seating for patrons.

The story goes that some women were annoyed with her and angrily approached the shop. Iah seized her stick, stood, and challenged, "Ya'll come, but one by one."

What we called a sweet drink was referred to as a soda in some other places. Soda, for us, meant soda water. Our sweet drinks came in different flavours and were obtained in crates or boxes of twenty-four either from Stroude's factory on the Carenage in St George's,

Grenada, or from Cannings factory in Trinidad (purchased locally). Persons ordered their favourites—ginger ale, aniseed, cherry, orange, cream soda, cola champagne, and so on.

Much later came the other brands, like Solo, Juicy, Red Spot, and Fanta which came out of Trinidad. Those also came in different flavours. In those early days, there was no ice, and drinks were served at room temperature, which was acceptable and not a problem then.

Also in those days, the glass drink bottles were recycled, and if one returned an only partially full crate the next time one made a purchase, an extra charge was levied. Therefore, customers would bring a replacement if they intended to take away their ordered drinks. So, my question is, from where came the first replacement? This system likewise applied to visits to the doctor, for if a prescription was given for medications, it was necessary for the patient to produce a receptacle for the pills or a bottle for the liquid medicine.

So, like we abandoned wind power, we have since abandoned recyclable bottles in favour of plastics, and now, plastics are the culprits that harm the environment.

The more we change, the more we change—for the better, it is claimed.

As an aside, the government dentist, Dr John Radix, brother of the locally stationed physician, only visited about once a month from Grenada, and as far as I remember, he did his extractions either completely without or with sparing use of a deadening agent, especially for caries or complaints of toothaches. By the time he arrived, the ache may be no longer present, but one still sought attendance. The dentist would ask the patient to point to the problem tooth. Many a time, the wrong tooth was pulled.

Although they were troublesome when they became shaky, we children were nevertheless glad for having milk teeth that could be easily pulled by him. That was less frightening than the method of attaching one end of a string to the tooth and the other end to the doorknob and then waiting expectantly, knowing that someone would snap open the door but not knowing when.

We have indeed come a long way, for I remember that when I was in school in Grenada, at the bottom of Church Street was the office of a dentist named Dr Lindsay, a big white man who never seemed to know about deadening the mouth. All one heard from the waiting room or even outside on the street was the sound of a drill and a cry of agony.

At first, hurt not—an oath.

It was always possible to order ice in hundred-pound blocks or portions thereof from the factory in Grenada, usually for an event such as a concert and dance. It would be shipped by the scheduled boats and arrive for that same Saturday. I remember that once, when the shipment was missed, the soft drinks were placed in a tub of water or in a cistern for hours prior to the event. I don't know if that made a significant difference.

Some persons ordered ice for private use, such as for the making and selling of ice cream, or just for a small function or celebration. Mainly because ice was not readily available, most burials took place as quickly as possible after death. However, if there was a reason for a short delay, the body would be placed on ordered ice. Embalming was not yet available in Carriacou and perhaps also not yet in Grenada.

Eventually, ice was made more readily available for home or more limited private reasons and could be bought within the village and stored in a thermos flask. One of the early suppliers of home-made ice was Cousin Philbert Isaac, who had returned from Aruba, I think, and had installed a kerosene-operated refrigerator in his recently built house.

At the time, it had seemed strange to me that a similar flask could also maintain the heat in hot liquids, but this was truly appreciated, for otherwise, just having a cup of tea would have necessitated the lighting of fire.

I'm digressing again, but I always found it strange that, especially in a dance, it was expected that a fight would break out between two men. Somehow, a woman would be the apparent reason for it, sometimes based on a previous grievance. In countries like mine, some traditions were culturally ingrained, and if and when they were not adhered to, thereby challenging a man's ego and machoism, it could lead to a more serious entanglement.

As an example, a lady who was invited or brought to a dance by a gentleman would provoke vexation if she allowed herself to be approached by or, worse yet, danced with another man who had not first sought the permission of the first man. But who knows? Alcohol may also have played a role in such encounters.

But grievances must be settled.

One night, we in the village awaited word about Clinton McIntosh, the son of a close neighbour, who, it was said had been stabbed at such an event and had been taken to the hospital. He turned out to be OK, but I never knew or at least cannot recall what eventually became of him.

As I recall, my first formal dance was at the hostel of the Grenada Boys Secondary School in a controlled atmosphere. In attendance were senior boys from GBSS and senior girls from the adjacent Anglican High School. I tentatively approached and requested a dance—a waltz—with Gloria Payne, and she accepted. In a waltz, one was supposed to dance around the floor anticlockwise, which I did.

On Facebook recently, I saw her dancing at home in celebration of her birthday. I also remember that in Grenada in the 1950s, a group of us went to events, like football, together, just as mates of the same age. We were young people up to just being friends.

She was on the university campus at the same time as I was and performed on stage at some events in the dance style of her Jamaican friend, Maud Fuller. I feel honoured to have walked the same path as these two ladies. It is my understanding that Maud, known for her love of and dedication to our university, has departed this life.

Without question, the most notable liquor of Carriacou was strong rum, especially the brand called Jack Iron. It was obtained legally at first, but with the ready availability of Carriacou boats, it was later smuggled to escape the tariffs, together with other items such as cigarettes and French liqueurs from the more northern islands. Even if the smugglers were apprehended by the police or, later, the coast guard, the endeavour must have proven profitable, because it has continued.

This led to Herbert Blaize's government issuing an ill-fated declaration, perhaps in the 1980s, that crew and passengers must provide customs declarations on arriving in St George's from Carriacou, and this included searches of the boats and personal items. The thinking was that Carriacou's smuggled products were being brought to be resold in Grenada.

By and large, all shops of the village sold similar grocery items, and as far as I knew, quite a few sold rum. If one started from the upper part of the main street of Grand Bay, the shops, which were all along the main roads, included (in order) those owned or operated by Sidney Cayenne (the man who owned a gun); Cousin Fred Samuels, who was from Top Hill area; Cousin Herbert Alexis, who built it after returning from Aruba; our family; Tan Dorah, at the junction; Helena (Tanah) John, a stronger competitor in rum sales; and almost opposite, Bert Cyrus. Much later, in Tana's old spot, there was a concrete shop run by Alfred Quashie.

Continuing on, next came Da Worth's shop, which was in the same small building as the post office. Da Worth repaired shoes in his shop, which only retailed small items, including home-made products. On the opposite side of Da Worth's was the store run by Cousin Irwin and wife, Miss Nora, and on this same side within twenty yards was one run by Cousin Hamilton Cyrus, who I think had built it after returning from Aruba.

There were two junctions on the main road of Mt. Pleasant, one near to the school and the other with a split either to Quarry or to Works, where the shop of Cousin Darelia was located. Further along, on the way towards Works, was the home of Robbie Simon in the downstairs of which was a shop. Robbie was a brother of Cousin Basta, of whom more will be said. In more recent times, a shop has been opened in the downstairs of Ken's house, near to the school.

Now that time has passed, some shops no longer exist, and a new one or two have since popped up.

Perhaps in the 1950s, Joyce's mother, Tan Faith Charles, who had also returned from abroad and lived in a newly constructed wall house, introduced weekend dances in the downstairs of her home, which was opposite but not directly across from Robbie's. Joyce was one of the girls that I had feelings for. Iah was never happy with Gilbert's attendance at these dances, but then, that was Iah, the worrying warrior.

Even in what we would now term adulthood, permission had to be obtained from her, especially by the girls, long before one intended to go out at night to a specific event. When any child, adult or not, was out, Iah slept not. She would worry and was known to awaken me to go with her to find the young ladies if what she considered curfew hour had passed.

Robbie, mentioned above, once visited from Aruba and introduced a fitness program to accompany the art of boxing for the young adult men of the village. Daily, in the late afternoon, they would trot up the hill of Nehgah house to Top Hill and back down to the village via Grand Bay Street, an up-down loop, before beginning the boxing lessons. Before he returned to Aruba, he organised a boxing contest in the school. A name that comes to mind is Bristol "Coonyawh", who squared up but was totally outmatched against teacher Sammie in the show.

I would have been in school in Grenada when my brother John married the daughter of Robbie. She moved with him into our house but was sent packing in little to no time, because it was said that the marriage was based on a lie. It was because of this that those women mentioned above were angry, one being the mother of the girl.

John did not take kindly to nonsense, nor did Iah.

Permit me, however, at this stage to focus on the first son of Iah and Poopa and some of their other children.

The Alpha: My Eldest Brother

Alpha and Omega

In his late middle-age years, Godwin told me that our father had died intestate and that it was our mother who had commanded him, the eldest, to write a will dictated by her. The property became generational so that any one of us could come back from wherever to reside there, but now, only a niece, Betty, the first child of John, lives and takes care of the house, the shop, and the surrounding lands on which they lie.

New house

Whilst Iah was still alive two bedrooms were added to the front of the house under her guidance and without Godwin's involvement, partly to conveniently accommodate the younger relatives who were taken in to live. After her death, there was an almost complete but gradual remodelling of the house that included adding a bathroom and a kitchen and converting it from a wooden house into a concrete structure. That was organised by my sister Alethea, my brother Lysander, and Betty, with small contributions from me.

They also arranged for water to be pumped electrically from the cistern to overhead tanks and from there piped to the house through the force of gravity. Although one could now take a shower within the house, it was not unusual for me to continue bathing outside from a bucket on my visits.

They had come a long way, even without emigrating.

Since the death of Iah, Godwin has divided the fourteen acres of land in Grand Bay into lots for the ten of us children. This was done legally but was perhaps a bit highhanded, as it was done without full consultation with all the others.

Godwin, the trustee or executor, had spoken and acted.

To all intents and purposes, the main land now lies completely abandoned, but the taxes are paid annually by the owners or their offspring.

It is my understanding that Godwin, expectedly so, was the one Iah depended on for decision making early on after Poopa's death. But he lost his influence as the others attained adulthood, partly because he was no longer around as often.

Being then too young, I don't remember him ever living with us, but later, he only visited the home, even when he resided in Mt. Pleasant. At the times when he visited, my job was to shine his shoes to a glowing sheen, as was the expectation in those days—one cloth to polish and another, with some spittle on it, to shine.

Our relationship grew stronger when for a short period we both resided in St George's, he working for the department of education and I attending the Grenada Boys Secondary School. Every early morning, he would take me to the village of Morne Rouge in his car to teach me how to drive. And when I moved to Jamaica, he took out a special term life insurance policy for me with the Chasley David agency, which came in handy when

I surrendered it years later.

Chasley was one of the friendliest, most decent, honest, and helpful men I have ever known. After my return to Grenada in 1974 as a pathologist, he willingly and very pleasantly assisted me in settling down. And even after I had left Grenada and was only just visiting, he would offer me a motor vehicle from his rental agency to use, free of charge. It is my understanding that he died in 2020.

He was the godfather of my son, Ricio "Dax" DaCosta. He was also one of my referees.

Between 1967 (after my graduation from university) and 2018, I often visited Grenada and, of course, Carriacou, and quite often, I stayed with Godwin at his permanent residence in Old Fort. But even before that, I had also stayed with him in St Pauls at the head teacher's residence, and in a house next to the prime minister's residence in Sans Souci, and elsewhere.

In Old Fort, he reared pigeons, which in the hands of his wife became delicacies at breakfast, and he loved gardening. Much of his produce was served at home, but it was also sold to shops and hotels. I am sure he missed not being active as he aged.

His wife, Bonace, tended her garden of flowers well, winning many a floral competition, especially with her prized orchids.

He was a jealous man and so was not too happy when I stayed alternately with Nicholas in my earlier visits. Godwin's position was that it was his due, as the eldest, that I should stay with and report to him. So, in my later visits, I always resided with him, with Nicho's ready concurrence.

As if I needed to be cared for.

Even when I lived in the Bahamas in the late 1970s, he took on the responsibility of selling a portion of land in Grenada which I had long before bought from Pearl De Lamothe, who, through Vivian, my wife, had become a good friend of my family.

In truth, many were our conversations and experiences, from just going driving, encouraged by him, to our talks about the ladies. He discussed with me his journey from being an Anglican, which he never took too seriously, through being a Catholic with his religiously dedicated wife, to eventually becoming a staunch Seventh Day Adventist. For personal reasons, I adopted its school in St George's for small donations.

He was a serious student of the Bible, accepting its truth and its magnificent portrayal of good. Strangely, some years later, as he was obviously ageing, he asserted that it was a questionable document and full of nonsense, or so I believe he meant. There was no argument from me.

He wondered why people built large bathrooms in their houses and even spent lengthy amounts of time in them, considering what they went in there to do. As he progressed in age, he added on a separate bedroom with a small bathroom for himself to his home; it was adjacent to the room I occupied on visits. I would think that he never luxuriated in the warmth in a bathtub.

He, more than once, claimed that there were three words starting with the letter *p* that he always had trouble remembering. I think they were *paradox*, *paradigm*, and another one, which he himself could not remember. Strangely and likewise, I have always had difficulty remembering the word *polarised* when speaking of sunglasses. The word *serendipity*, which I first encountered as the name of a bookstore in Tortola, I could never remember the meaning of.

Never end a sentence with a preposition, as I just did.

Ask this of Sir Winston Churchill, well known for his witticism "up with which I would not put." It has been said that a lady of the opposition party once said to Churchill that if, perchance, she had been married to him, she would have poisoned his drink. Churchill replied that if such would have been the case, he would have drunk it.

Godwin introduced me to the author Andrew Greeley, some of whose books I have since read. So often, he related stories of his life in London and of being trained in education, together with Felix Deleveaux from the Bahamas. He claimed that on one occasion, departing London by boat, he met a beautiful lady from the Bahamas who promised to see him on the last night. She never showed. From the boat, his only view was that of the pine trees in Nassau, he claimed. I have since found out who this lady was. He also was the recipient of a visiting Fulbright scholarship to study in the United States at, I believe, Stanford University.

Although most often a rather pleasant and amusingly entertaining man, Godwin nevertheless projected a somewhat superiorly aloof image and was quick to get annoyed. His manner was such that his opinion was always the right one. He had a tendency to shout at people who did what he disapproved of or could not properly do what he wished, calling them "damn stupidees" and "jackasses" to their faces and referring to each as "that no-good nastiness" when they were not around.

Notwithstanding that his emotions all seemed to stem from his heart, he was a sharp thinker, solving Agatha Christie's mysteries before reading halfway into the books. I, on the other hand, had to read to the end of the many books of hers that I had read.

It is my belief that he started his career as a primary school teacher. Following that, he was successively a supervisor of junior teachers, an inspector of schools, an education officer, the chief education officer of Grenada, and finally, a cabinet secretary, the highest post of a civil servant, in the government of Eric Mathew Gairy. He also held regional advisory positions. His honours included a CBE and an OBE given by the queen of England.

The last time that I saw and stayed with him was following my attendance at the 2017 annual conference of the Caribbean Public Health Agency (CARPHA) in Georgetown, Guyana. Brought by my brother Nicholas's son, Benedict, from the Maurice Bishop International Airport in Grenada, I arrived at his home on 30 April. He recognised me not, asking who was this strange person, even though I had last seen him just the year before, when all had seemed quite well.

He obviously had developed dementia, perhaps from senility but bordering on Alzheimer's. But for a week, we spent some quiet and most enjoyable moments together, especially at seven o'clock in the mornings, when I made coffee for both of us to enjoy with crackers as we awaited the arrival of Jean, the maid who, after the death of Godwin's wife, took over management of the home.

His mental condition varied from being lucid to being totally out of it and suddenly annoyed, not only with others but also with himself for being out of his normal control.

He had avoided coffee for a rather long time, having long before read a book that dismissed coffee as being bad for the body. However, on the first morning of my visit, upon smelling the aroma and seeing my obvious enjoyment of it, he quickly requested a cup. He then drank an early cup of coffee every day for the rest of my stay.

One night, he really caused me to laugh. He, his evening aide, and I were watching TV. For some reason, he thought that the characters of the show had invaded his home.

"Who are these people?" he asked. "I did not invite anyone here. Boy"—he did not know my name—"go and look below the house for a piece of wood and beat them out from my house. Get rid of them. Call the police."

I, in response, said that I was not messing with those people because they were carrying guns, and as a matter of fact, I was going to go to my room and would lock the door.

He quickly said, "Take me with you."

I had made arrangements to see him again in July 2018 before going on to St Lucia for the University of the West Indies Medical Alumni Association (UWIMAA) meeting. But at age 95, having entered this world 12 July 1922, he decided on 8 February that he wished to wait no longer to pass on, and God granted his wish.

I recently read one of his letters to me when we corresponded during his glory days. His words were, "In timing and mode of expression, you are hard to match."

It is my understanding that Poopa fathered two sons outside of his marriage, one obviously so and acknowledged and the other dubious. Most of his sons with Iah bred children before they got married, with the well-endowed John being the master at this. So, when in later years I would visit Carriacou, it was not unusual for children to approach and address me as uncle, and respectfully so.

John was born on 1 January 1934, and his birthday was the only one celebrated at home, with sweet drinks and a special home-baked cake. More usually, our cakes were basically either buns or softer and larger sponge cakes, with eggs used in the preparation of the latter. A piece from a chocolate bar was a rare treat.

I doubt that we ever had ice cream in those earlier days, though we eventually got the hand-cranked mixer that required ordered ice, plenty of salt, and manual labour. It was all worth it, especially if you first received the central blades for licking.

It should also be mentioned that two of Poopa's daughters had premarital relationships. My sister Balvina's widening condition was unknown to Iah until it was reported to her one day in the shop by Cousin Lovie Cyrus. The way of life in Carriacou, especially if a father felt ashamed, would have led one to expect that all hell would break loose, and Balvina would be kicked out of the home.

Iah sent me home to summon Balvina. All I understood was that after the visit, Iah said something to the effect of "They expect me to put her out, but that will never happen to my child." And remember, in this home, there was no longer a father to overrule her—as if anyone could have ventured so to do.

I became aware that she next summoned the supposed impregnator of her daughter.

Balvina, attended by Tampish, the village midwife, gave birth to Alma Elizabeth on Iah's bed in 1949. During the labour, I once walked into the room and was chased out by the midwife, but Iah said to leave me be. Surprisingly, Iah could be so unexpectedly understanding at times, as she was this time. Bear in mind that this action perhaps stemmed from her already being aware of my desire to be a doctor. So, perhaps she was also thoughtful—or as I have said before, human.

I buried the afterbirth and navel-string in front of the kitchen in a soft area of an otherwise rocky yard. In the future, if ever I craved or demanded respect from Alma, in the words of the village, I would only have to say to her, "I know where your navel string is buried, Jean." I was told by her mother that it was I who first called Alma by the name Jean, and that's how she was intimately called for the rest of her life.

Balvina got married to Earl John Noel, the father of the child. He was a teacher at the village primary school and lived with a Sunday school teacher, Meemee, who was taking care of John's grandmother. He left Carriacou first to join his parents in New York, and then Balvina and Jean followed in 1950. They have permanently settled there.

Jean visited Carriacou and Grenada as a preteenager, but I did not see Balvina, now called by her first name, Sarah, again until 1962 when I visited for the summer vacation from the university in Jamaica and stayed at her home on Sterling Place, Brooklyn, New York 11213. It was during that visit that her son, John "Junior" Wesley, said that the hair on my head felt like steel wool.

During that visit, I followed the games of the Yankees baseball team with players like Mantle, Maris, Ford, Downing, and the philosopher, Yogi Berra, who supposedly, among his oft cited quotes, once said, "When you come to a fork in the road, take it."

Many a time, as life presented its confusing twists, I stood hesitantly at a junction, as each road from there appeared equally travelled by, or not at all travelled, perhaps too straight and narrow.

And how well do I remember hearing on radio the popular song "Beechwood 4-5789" by the Marvelettes, the jingle "Seventy-seven, WABC", and the advertisement for Palisades Amusement Park.

I was introduced to pizza, dough topped with cheese, in an open-air pizzeria on St John's Place, where the dough was tossed in the air and caught around the elbow by the aproned man. I enjoyed the burgers of White Castle—no more than two or three bites to finish one.

In 1964, I again visited Sarah for summer vacation, and then, between July 1969 and June 1971, I lived in Brooklyn while undergoing residency training in pathology and visited Sarah very often, especially on weekends, to enjoy a tasty meal.

Sarah and sister Ade.

She was a wonderful cook. On 3 July 2020, this gentle soul celebrated her ninetieth birthday. After that, we spoke often on the telephone. She usually called me in Freeport, Bahamas, where I have resided since 1985.

I remember her at home in Mt. Pleasant when I was a child and also remember her as a teacher in the school, but I remain uncertain as to whether or not she taught any of my classes. However, I do remember that as a fielder in a cricket game in the school yard where the men played against the women, she allowed a ball hit by Charles Cayenne, our neighbour, to go through her legs (an error), allowing him to score a run.

Prior to becoming a teacher, she, and most likely Alethea before her, attended special classes at Simmonds House taught by Mr. Campbell, an inspector of schools from Grenada, and passed the qualifying exam to become a teacher. When she moved to New York, she became a nurse and worked in a Brooklyn hospital.

Sometime in the 1970s, she developed cancer of the breast and was obviously cured. But that nasty disease recurred in 2022, and my dear sister, who was highly religious, refused therapy and peacefully departed this life on 19 August.

Sarah and husband

* * *

Switching gears somewhat, it was during my 1962 vacation in Brooklyn that I first met a young lady named Merle, who was originally from Aruba. She was living with her parents and helping at the shop of Sister Anita. Sister Anita, so originally called, was originally from Carriacou and was related to Tan Dorah of the eponymous junction.

Merle and I developed a close relationship. I again visited in 1964, during the university's summer vacation, but this second visit was not so much to see her but to see Rhoda, my girlfriend from the days of my youth in Carriacou. Rhoda was visiting Brooklyn from England, and I was hoping to reignite what once glowed between us.

It was at this visit that I also met Yanks John, who was from Carriacou, and his wife, Gail, from St Lucia. They were living next door to Sarah, and I developed a lasting friendship with them. They returned to Carriacou and established a home in Belmont, which I visited whenever in Carriacou. The friendship has continued with Gail and her daughters, even after the death of Yanks.

I advance my story to my relationship with Merle during and after my visit to Brooklyn in 1964. She was extremely affectionate, nice, and kind to me, even giving me spending money and taking me to the World's Fair in Queens. However, she liked to pinch me, which was annoying.

One night, Merle and I went to a West Indian–organised boat ride. Rhoda, who I had already visited where she was staying with her relatives, was on the boat. She paid me no great mind from then on, perhaps after seeing Merle and I arriving together.

Anyhow, I also understood that she was in love with Winston Simon, and maybe she avoided me because her granny had cautioned her to stay away from the Brathwaites. On her return to England, she joined Winston at the altar. More will be said about Rhoda and me, but at this time in Brooklyn, I wondered "where love had gone", to paraphrase the title of a Harold Robbins novel.

Having returned to Jamaica after my vacation, I learnt that Merle was pregnant. She called me often—embarrassingly to me, at times—to seek marriage, which I had no intention of considering as a student. I may have made promises about our future after my expected graduation in about three years.

One Saturday morning in my room on block B of Chancellor Hall, I was informed that I had a visitor. It turned out to be a very pregnant Merle. She strongly proposed that we should get married, and after my refusal, she introduced me to a lawyer who had travelled with her from Brooklyn and was said to be originally from Grenada. He, with his self-driven car, outlined the issues as he took us driving. We may have had lunch.

Along the way, we encountered my so-called "half-brother", David "Jack Buffang" Radix, on the ring road around the university hospital, and Jack wanted to take me away in the car he was driving—our car, a Cadillac, that Dennis Toppin, Jack Radix, another person, and I had bought together, each contributing ten pounds for its purchase. However, I told him no, because the situation was under control. Jack, a fellow student at the university, features in my journeys, but more on that later.

Once we got back to the hall of residence, the lawyer produced a multipage legal document for me to sign that committed me to providing plenty, plenty of money, including child support. I tore it up. Nevertheless, I invited them to the students' union that night to have some fun. They came and, as far as I know, left for New York the following day.

Some persons have believed that I didn't marry her because of a slap I had received to the back of my head when we were kissing in the corridor at her home in 1964.

Merle gave birth to Tony, and she and I kept in touch. But I became very bitter when I was made to understand that someone had written to the university, probably with the hope of having me either expelled or forced into marriage.

One cannot fathom how difficult it must have been on this decent teenager to be unmarried and have a baby.

It is my belief that Professor Francis "Bobo" Bowen, the warden of Chancellor Hall, stood at the university council meeting and defended me, and I thank God for that.

It was not long after that that he told me I was wasting my father's seed and moved me from block B to the Nunnery in November 1965. I was somewhat unhappy, for I had just been re-elected as the block representative for block B in Chancellor Hall for a second year.

I remained in the Nunnery until my graduation in 1967. Let me say here that in the Nunnery, it was my habit to go to sleep early at nights and to wake up between midnight and 1 a.m., having set the alarm bell of my wind-up clock, to study for the rest of the night. On the day that I received the good news about having passed the finals, I still set the alarm that night, and when it went off, I got up, laughed loudly, and then went back to bed. This was the end of one period. I was a champion with a stepping stone towards a new stage in life, for which I was ready.

The journey would be continued, but the destination, if ever there was one, was as yet unknown.

But continuing with Merle, during my residency in pathology, which first began in 1969 in Lutheran Medical Center, South Brooklyn, New York, Merle and I made efforts to reengage. We did so again during my residency at Brookdale Hospital Center the following year. Although we remained decently in touch, there was no longer any spark to our relationship.

I was seeing Tony, my son, fairly often. Once, just before Christmas, we all went to Manhattan, where we walked along Fifth Avenue and bought hot pretzels and roasted chestnuts. Even after I later got married, Merle kept me abreast of Tony's doings, particularly about his progress with playing the piano and even about his solo recital.

I do believe, however, that Tony gave up music and may have become somewhat unruly. I was out of contact with him from about 1971 until about 1979, when we reconnected. He even visited me in Nassau, where I was then a resident. When he got married in New Jersey, my son Dax and I went. He would call quite often, but in no time after fathering children, he was divorced.

We saw each other again when his eldest child, Anthony, graduated college in Henderson, North Carolina. Vivian, my wife, accompanied me to the ceremony. As expected, Merle was there, and she sponsored the post-graduation lunch. Since then, Tony and

I have been in constant touch. Through him, I have grandchildren, the eldest two of whom I have met, and great-grandchildren, whom I have not yet met.

In 1972, when I was married to Vivian and in Ottawa, the mailed envelope with the small financial contribution I was making to Merle was returned. Vivian, who knew of Tony, opened the envelope and learnt that I had had another son, Raymond, born the year before, also in Brooklyn. In her written comment, Merle said she thought that I needed the money to support my other child. I got mad with Vivian for opening my letter.

How strange do men behave, even when they are in the wrong.

*　*　*

Returning to my siblings, as a child, I did not know Adeline, the second child of my parents. She did not live at home and visited only once. She had moved, or more likely was sent by Iah, to Grenada, at first to Mt. Moritz with Godwin. Later, she moved to St George's, where she became well established as a seamstress but was better known for her skills in crocheting and embroidery.

Whilst in St George's, she, then pregnant, got married to Martin "Cheese" Lashley. They resided on Bain Alley, a short connection less than a hundred yards in total length from Tyrell Street steeply upward to Green Street. That was where I lived when attending GBSS. More will be said of her later.

Alethea, my second sister, was born on 4 September 1928. Before her marriage, and in my mind for I was in the general area, she was either assaulted or willingly succumbed to the determined pressure from the son of a neighbour, who was then visiting from Aruba. Days after, the incident manifested itself in the form of tiny bites in the area of the mons Veneris.

Alethea taught me at school in Mt. Pleasant. Other than Iah, she was the only one who sometimes beat me at home with a whip. Iah was never too happy when that happened and I complained.

Once every month, this dear sister would get very sick, staying in bed, unable to attend school to teach. Eventually, many years later, she had a hysterectomy, which eased her condition, I was told.

She was the one sibling who was always at home, controlled by Iah, and must have contributed heavily towards financing my education. She was perhaps the only sibling who persisted in calling me Ned.

We got along very well as adults, and she especially would give that extra effort during my later visits back home to Carriacou to make sure that I was happy.

Before and after retirement she was highly religious and was a faithful member of the Anglican church.

Whilst I was working in Freeport, Bahamas, her health was deteriorating, and we spoke fairly often, with me offering medical advice. In her final call, her last words to me were, "When you coming?" She died shortly after on 14 August 2003 at age 74.

I should have gone to the funeral but was not able to. A good and precious soul had passed on. My tears flowed freely when Betty, our niece who lived with her, and I were on the phone.

She ended her last letter to me, dated 14 April 2003, with the words "from your dear sister, Alethea". On 18 August, I penned these words in her memory:

Sleep well thou sweet and gentle lady. Sleep well! I will see and talk with you again, if not in the kingdom of thy Lord, then you will find a way to quench my thirst, elsewhere. Sleep well!

The Grand Bay Land

As I recall, Carriacou had ample flat and sometimes even swampy coastal lowlands that seemed gradually to evolve into or merge with gently sloping hills. The hills appeared to crest towards the central parts of the island, and this, as I have intimated, contrasted with the steep, precipitous rises and cliffs of Dominica and Montserrat.

There were no mountains in Carriacou, but two hills, Chapeau Carre and High North, the names of which always came up in general knowledge questions, were over 900 feet in height. Most of the hills, beginning at different distances from the coast, ridged centrally, but many had ample plateau areas. On both sides, the slopes ended in valleys or gullies.

So, Carriacou, in my opinion, was topographically composed of coastal flat land that blended into hills that were separated by valleys.

There were no rivers in Carriacou, but folks referred to fast-flowing waters in gullies after or during prolonged rains as such. As a result, swamps and long-lasting puddles were created in the lowlands.

There were freshwater springs and many ponds. The ponds varied in location; there were the salt water ponds adjacent to the sea coast, brackish ponds more inland, and other ponds in the hills. I have known persons to place portions of the poisonous manchineel tree into the salt ponds, killing the mullet fish, which they then gathered for food.

Animals, and sometimes extremely thirsty humans, drank from the less salted ponds, first scooping aside the green algae on the surface. Birds always seemed to be nearby. We boys, in acts that now seem like wickedness, pelted them with stones. The killing of those we called blackbirds, perro birds (sparrows), pippiree birds, and seesee birds now seem so senseless. We, however, never harmed the hummingbirds. They were never still, anyhow.

But some others, which we killed by stoning, by using slingshots, or by ensnaring them in our traps, served as food. The edible ones included ground and mountain doves, pigeons, and ramiers—our game birds, though small.

In the mornings, flocks of birds traversed the sky to their feeding grounds, and they made the return trips to their tree roosts in the late afternoons. These were resident birds. Occasionally, we saw scissor-tailed birds and those with talons, from which we had to protect the baby chicks. There may have been cobo (corbeau) and coastal birds as well. Some of these birds were most likely transitory, visiting, or migrant, especially the seashore ones.

There were no large wild beasts in Carriacou, though some men were thought of that way. Two small wild animals were the manicou (opossum) and the iguana, both of which have become increasingly popular as food delicacies and, in this regard, have joined the tattoo, which is an armadillo in Grenada, and sometimes the turtle on the list of wild meat consumed on the island.

There were small roaming ground or tree animals, including lizards and the bigger ones called zandolees, as well as nonpoisonous grass snakes. I have heard that there were also techeers and mabouyas. There was a tendency to refer to larger snakes as serpents, as if in reference to that very first garden in the Bible.

Although now apportioned, our land in Grand Bay, about a half mile from home, was and remains a continuation of flat land that extends just less than 200 yards from the eastern seashore. It has been said that originally, most of Grand Bay estate was owned by the Mills family.

Our portion was bordered by hills to the north (Grand Bay) and south (Teeblee) and by the beginning of the hill to Mount Dor at the west. On the eastern boundary was the Grand Bay Cemetery (burial ground, to most of us, and to the south were the lands of two other persons, Scipio John and Freddie Nelson. Separating the northern and western borders from other lands was the fairly large estate-type road.

A government pasture encroached from the north road southwards, and there was a well—long well—in it that was open for public use. The villagers brought their animals for water, which when drawn was emptied into a copper trough. Because of the overgrowth of trees and shrubbery, I recently had difficulties in locating this well, ultimately finding that the well itself was overgrown by the bushes, both outside and within it.

Some portions of our land were identified by different names that I always had difficulty remembering, but I can think of two names now: Faithman and Maggie. It was not unusual for certain crops to be grown in different portions of the land, and there was ample pasture space available for the farm animals—cows, donkeys, sheep, and goats. A small shed was present for resting from work; it provided shelter from rain and, yes, the sun.

Some persons who did not own land would lease portions from us, allotted by a ten-foot measuring rod or pole, and usually, the agreement was that they would repay us with part of the harvest. The use of the pole also helped me to appreciate longer lengths, as the twelve-inch ruler did for shorter ones.

Once in school, the teacher held up a pencil and asked for its length. I was the only one that came close. I answered that it was seven inches, but it was six and three-quarter inches. So, although placing first in this exercise, I was, in the words of the demanding Queen Iah, "still not a hundred per cent".

But first place does not automatically equate with 100 per cent, only with the best at the time. And with my persistence, champions may be individuals other than those in first place, and merely for argument, as already stated, champions may become also-rans.

There comes a time to retire.

In those days, though not too often, we went to and from the land via the main big road, but it was more usual to traverse the meandering track roads, of which there were quite a few. They ran first down the declivity of our hill to the flat, then up Grand Bay Hill, and finally down to different parts of the land.

The shop was closer to home, also on flat land, perhaps just under half a mile from the bay of Grand Bay Village. Because they were located in the flat, the heat of Carriacou was more intensely felt on the land and at the shop than it was at home, but the occasional breath of wind eased the discomfort.

It has been said that when it was colonised, Carriacou was mainly agricultural, with the primary crops being cotton, sugar cane, and limes in those torrid days of slavery. In the time I grew up, it was still agricultural, but people grew different products, more of which were consumed at home. These included, among others, Indian corn (maize, mainly yellow), pigeon and black-eyed peas, beans (boocoosoo), ochro, melons, pumpkins, sweet potatoes, yams, and groundnuts. In addition, on our land were lime, mango, and sapodilla trees.

When the growls of hunger grew painful, raw potatoes came to the rescue.

Generally, the land refurbished itself when it was left fallow, but very rarely, we gathered seaweed from the beaches to fertilise some areas. Some portions were ploughed in the off-crop dry season as the planting time neared, and this provided an income for some workers.

It was truly amazing how the landscape transformed from being brown and dusty in the dry season to being lush and green in the wet season. The big fields would be dominated by the tall corn (maize) plants with their added colours of efflorescence.

The corn is so high, it's above any man's eye, but it never quite reaches way up to the sky, to paraphrase the musical *Oklahoma*.

There were two other wells in our districts: Pond Well, adjacent to a pond very near to the seashore in Grand Bay with brackish water from which the animals drank, and Petit Bin Well in Mt. Pleasant, also not far from the seashore. Once, a calf fell into the latter but was successfully recovered by men. Something like this was a big event and provoked a turnout from the villagers, there perhaps not only from curiosity but to assist or to advise.

In my teenage years, the government dug wells with attached pumps throughout the island, including one on our land, but I don't think they ever worked well or lasted.

The Days of Labour: Gritillia Commands

My duties at home included sweeping the yard on Saturday mornings. I shared this duty with my three-year-older brother, George Benjamin. The brooms were made from the large twigs of a hardy shrub less than three feet in height that grew in the rocky slopes and had leathery, greyish-green leaves that were not easily detached.

There was another plant that we rooted and used as a broom for the kitchen floor. It was softer and blossomed with a white, bud-like flower. In addition, we bought imported brooms for use within the house, and craftsmen often came around with straw brooms made from palms. These latter had long handles and especially useful for the ceilings.

Early in the mornings on most weekdays, George or I went to the land primarily to fetch the cow's milk, when such was available, to be used in the breakfast tea. Of course, since we usually had only one or at most two cows at a time, most of our milk was purchased from other farmers. Every hot beverage at breakfast, no matter from what it was made—canned Ovaltine or Milo, local plants (bush), and so on—was called tea.

On the previous night, the calf would have to be hidden or isolated from the cow so as to assure a good supply of milk the following morning. From the side of the cow, the nipples were manually manipulated to express the milk. This act created a froth at the top of the container, which we children skimmed and slurped using a partly folded common-cherry leaf as a scoop.

At home, the surface cream of the milk was separated and stored. This was later churned into butter, whilst the whey was sweetened to make a sour-milk drink. Yoghurt reminded me of this.

On writing about milking from the side of the cow, I remembered learning about this the hard way from one of our donkeys. I was aboard the animal but was unable to control it, so I slid off from the back of it. *Boop* was the sound of its hoof on my chest as I fell backwards.

Strangely, a man approached me years later at a party that I was attending in London and asked if I remembered him, but I did not. He was annoyed, claiming that he was the person who lifted me up after the donkey had kicked me down.

Always dismount from the side of the animal.

In addition to what else they had to do, the older brothers, John Albert and Charles Gilbert, would bring home the produce they had harvested later in the morning. Of course, one ought to appreciate that what occurred on mornings depended on the ages of the children, whether they were still in attendance at school or had a steady job.

Other quotidian tasks included just being an errand boy and gathering firewood and the parts of plants used as food for the pigs. The pigs particularly enjoyed a thick-green-leaved, reddish-stemmed ground cover-plant that we called "fat pork". I have since recognised and eaten this edible vegetable, which is called purslane. It has now taken over my more preferred vegetable beds in Freeport, Bahamas, as a weed.

Irrespective of what task we had done, my mother, always hoping to be prepared for any eventuality, would send us back to repeat the task, especially when it came to the gathering of hog meat and wood collection. This was because, in her view, tomorrow was another day and should not just be taken for granted, for no one knows what tomorrow may bring. For example, in her mind, it may rain. It was as if Carriacou was favoured to be affected by these unexpected happenings. Or, in a reverse way, she thought we should be saving for another dry day.

Other children at home—Laca, Betty, Floyd and Clifford.

At times, Carriacou seemed so humdrum. Somehow, though, the sun would always still shine brightly the following day. This source of vitamin D seemed always to be present. "Tomorrow, tomorrow … only a day away."

On Saturdays, we also assisted with the preparations for baking. I never understood why the kneading tray remained uncleaned until the following week, when it would be a task to scrape off the adherent hardened dough remnants, which needed to be first softened with water. In those days, a portion of dough was sometimes left over to be used as leavening the following week.

Hence, there was always work to be done; my mother made sure of that. This, in a reverse way, always reminds me of the comic-strip character named Andy. When asked by his wife, Flo, what he was going to do that day, he said, "Nothing!" "But that's what you did yesterday," she replied, and he responded, "Yes, but I wasn't finished."

I must admit that, when appropriate, I am a master at doing absolutely nothing for hours. Doing nothing is not the same as resting or dozing; it's a state of positive blankness.

In my youth, there was a feeling of sameness to each day, so that when the day had ended, there was the happiness of relief. And yet, that relief was sometimes bolstered by the satisfaction of accomplishment, a contentment within one's being, jobs well done.

We did have ample time for playing, allowed by that woman called Iah—that woman who invoked fear, that woman of fire, that woman who some village folks referred to as Gritillia for a reason not really known to me but thought to be derogatory. The nickname was given her by a woman who was at loggerheads with Iah's mother, Ansay, I have been told. It was spoken in referring to her, yes, but she was never directly addressed as such.

I suspect that she enjoyed being in control, for as she gradually began losing this ability with her own children, she began inviting in or allowing others, particularly some of her grandchildren from John and Gilbert, to reside at our home.

We, the younger children, certainly like the older ones in the past except for, perhaps, Lysander and the girls, also knew about work that was related to gardening. This included the picking and shelling of pigeon peas and beans, the picking of cotton, and the weeding and turning over of soil around the young plants—all of this usually in the house garden. But as we aged, we graduated to the larger field in Grand Bay, that we called "the land".

To the above was added the occasional picking of limes to be crocus-bagged and taken by donkey to the factory in Craigston for sale. I don't know if the limes were fully processed there or if they were shipped to the lime factory on the Carenage in Grenada. This factory was located on the wharf and was run by the Shillingfords from Dominica, a surname also associated with a pharmacy. However, in the village of Dumfries in Carriacou, there was also a lime factory, although whether it was then still functional or not is uncertain.

After being picked, the cotton was stored, in our case, in the downstairs to be later compacted in crocus bags to an approximate weight of 100 pounds before being brought to the main road to be collected by trucks and transported to the gin factory.

The cotton we grew was the Marie-Galante variety, not the shorter Sea Island variety that had been introduced to St Vincent.

I thought then, and still do, that the picking of cotton in the hot sun was a punishment for crimes committed, crimes unknown, a legacy of bondage. No wonder agriculture in Carriacou has waned over the years. I now strongly believe that cotton is no longer grown in Mt. Pleasant, Grand Bay, or any part of Carriacou. It is not welcomed anymore "as time goes by"!

With age, travel, and general life experiences, I have realised that many other places in this world are as hot or even hotter than Carriacou, but I never had to pick cotton in them.

Between attending high school in Grenada, being supplanted by younger relatives who came on the scene, and perhaps growing in defiance and rebelliousness with age, I and others eventually escaped from some of these burdensome tasks. As already said, Iah could not control every minute of the day or night, and so when opportunities arose, we demonstrated mischievous behaviours unknown to this iron-willed woman. Rarely, one achieved selfish aims through gentle persuasion, as the turning of her ageing world more readily induced sleepy tiredness.

Without doubt, as she aged, she became less imposing and gradually more accepting. She welcomed advice but never yielded to unjust orders.

But as already mentioned, she could not be aware of everything. Godwin has told me that as a boy, he climbed through his bedroom window to the cistern top and from there to the yard when he wished to go out secretly at nights; and when he wanted to escape a taxing chore, he would pretend to be otherwise occupied.

There were certain jobs that I gladly performed. If I was not busy working, I often got involved in parspartu (passepartout), usually of documents. Without being asked, I also volunteered to replace the old shingles of buildings and then paint them.

As far as my mother was concerned, all her children were to be educated, and she was dedicated to ensuring that this happened.

Of course, to her, this simply meant attendance at the local primary school. Further advancement depended on the ability of the child. Of course, further entry into secondary or high school, though worthwhile, could prove an inconvenience, as it entailed expenditures for residency in Grenada and for the education, as well as a loss of earnings from a potential worker. And yet, in our case, four of her boys attended secondary school in Grenada.

It was therefore not unusual in these parts for all efforts to be concentrated on getting one of the bright boys to go upward and the others to hopefully work and contribute towards the expenses. Apprenticeship in a trade or some other avenue of advancement in life remained a possibility.

People were resourceful, and in the then absence of banks in Carriacou, one always heard of the moneys being kept under the mattresses. Iah made her money mainly from the sale of cotton, the contributions extracted from the children who worked but still lived at home, and shop sales, and it was somewhere in the shop that she hid it. The shop functioned as the immediate source of food for the family. The sales made possible the further purchase of supplies.

For a period of time, we, the four youngest boys of between 6 and 13 years of age, all simultaneously attended at the local school, Mt. Pleasant Elementary, where two of the girls, Sarah Balvina and Alethea Sophia, were already then teaching, or at least were in training locally to become teachers there. I did not know them as students.

Like us boys, however, they too were bound to perform their usual house duties, such as cooking, baking, laundering, ironing, and sewing. Despite this, it seemed that we always had a maid to help with these duties, a person who was treated just like any of us, except that she got paid.

I do not recall the name of the end-of-year turning-out activity in the school—probably "Parents' Day"—but it always included a concert, followed, at times, by a dance. I do remember that my brother John, then in his last year, performed in a play. Stocky and strong, he, dressed as a pirate, strutted as one of the "fifteen men on a dead man's chest, yo, ho, ho, and a bottle of rum".

That same night, Gilbert, with a face more of innocence than wisdom, sang with two others to the baby Jesus of his gift of myrrh—"Star of wonder, star of light … guide us to thy perfect light."

At this function, there would also be the usual speeches and distribution of prizes. Students could quit school at any time. The decision was in the hands of the parents, for I'm not sure if there were regulations or laws to prevent that from happening. Standard six was the last class for me, but I gather that a student could have continued for another five or six years and, if required, received special lessons towards taking an examination so as to receive a useful document—a school leaving certificate.

During the mid to late 1940s, the eldest siblings were not at home, being educated or otherwise occupied elsewhere.

The eldest son, Godwin (Darwin) Algernon, I first remember as the head teacher at Mt. Moritz School on the outskirts of the capital town in Grenada. Living with him and taking domestic care in the government-provided house was the eldest daughter and second child, Adeline Elizabeth. Also with them was the fifteen-year-old son, Joseph Lysander, who was then attending GBSS in the capital.

In this time, the third child, Nicholas Alexander, may have been in Trinidad attending a teacher's college. I later understood that prior to that, he also attended GBSS, the new name for the grammar school. With Poopa's death seemingly eminent in 1941, I understand that he returned home to his dying father, whose last words were allegedly to him, advising that he must certainly return to complete his schooling in Grenada.

I remain uncertain of his exact location after finishing school but do recall that he was a trained navigator and was always attracted to the sea. It is my understanding that Godwin had preceded him in also pursuing teacher's training in Trinidad. Prior to being the head teacher in Mt. Moritz, it is my understanding that Godwin had first taught in the Hillsborough school in Carriacou.

Keep in mind that a son, Edmund, had died in infancy on 24 November 1927.

My mother was slightly bow-legged—a trait she passed on to some of us—and not physically big, yet she projected an image of a woman of no mean stature. Dominating? Yes. Domineering? At times. But draconian? Never. And as I've said, she was willing to listen to advice but not obliged to accept it.

She, with great pride, ran the shop and ruled supreme over all at home, a dedicated shepherd in control of her flock. The man who she married on 28 August 1921 had died, but she proudly took over the reins, and woe betide anyone whose actions showed an ignorance or defiance of this fact and what it stood for. In this regard, I never missed not having a father in my life. That never seemed to be an issue.

Usually at nights and when we were all settled at home, she would give instructions which were to be implemented or acted on in the days ahead. She also dictated to Alethea the responses to letters which had been received that day from the post office but were only then opened and read to her. In her view, one's mind should be at ease and untroubled before the reading of letters, particularly because the news therein may be unpalatably bad.

Other than on being always prepared, she handed down lessons on how to be careful and how to avoid accidents and embarrassments. Pot handles should not extend beyond the table or stove top, especially if toddlers were around. Don't hold a pointed sharp implement in front of you when walking and definitely not when running. And don't offer a visitor a liquid drink in an overfilled glass, for it just doesn't look right.

When the opportunity arose, she would share stories about herself, including about how in her youth, she may have had certain intuitive or visionary skills which had, with time, become significantly diminished.

For example, as a girl at home she was sent by her mother, Ansay, to the yard one early night to bring in some water. She, on re-entering, asked something to the effect of "How could you all say this woman was on her death bed when she just passed me in the yard?" Ansay slapped her three times for that, which Iah said resulted in the loss of some of those skills.

There was a general understanding that, with impending death, persons retraced the paths they had taken in life. It was for this reason, it was said, that the dogs howled like wolves, especially at night; they were seeing or scenting these apparitions.

She related another incident that occurred when she was also a young girl. She left home and was on her way to the field to accompany some others of her siblings back home. As she approached them, who were already on the road coming towards her, she saw a man pursuing and trying to hold on to the shirt tail of Powell, her youngest brother.

They could neither hear what she was saying nor appreciate her warning signals; but once they had closed the gap between them and her, the man ran through a bushy track towards the sea.

Later that day, the dead body of a villager, who perhaps had been roasting either corn or sweet potatoes on the side of the track, was discovered, believed to have been struck dead by an evil being.

She also predicted the death of her husband, for in picking cotton, whenever she reached for a ball of it, it seemed to vanish and was replaced by his image.

It is claimed that she also had special skills to handle evil, an example of which was her intervention to rescue Betty, her grandchild, from a spell of *mal jo*.

So ingrained in me were these tales that I never determined to prove her wrong on any issue, and when she once said, "You will never get a hundred per cent," that remained with me, within my very being.

In another vein, each village, each country, and each region had some form of traditionally established lore, which was generated, circulated, and cited by the older folks. Mt. Pleasant, Grand Bay, and Carriacou had their myths, legendary sayings, fables, and what may be called adages like anywhere else, usually with some degree of similarity to those of other places. I would well imagine that most had their genesis elsewhere and were merely handed on.

There was a myth that when one's palm itched, it was a signal that news or some kind of communication would soon be arriving, usually through the post office; ringing in the ears, meanwhile, meant that a conversation about you was taking place somewhere else.

And continuing in this vein, if one was in a liquor-drinking group, one could not leave having had just one drink, because one couldn't walk on one leg. A nauseous, squeamish, or queasy feeling during or after an experience or an event was aptly described as "it making me stomach sick". Another adage, still generally heard and perhaps logically so, was that one shouldn't go swimming shortly after eating. It was also said that you shouldn't point a finger in the cemetery, for it might rot and fall off, and if it rained when the sun was still shining, that meant the Devil and God were fighting.

I don't recall that she spoke about her education except that she did attend primary school, but for how long, I don't know. She did relate how she won a race at school. At one end of the track were placed limes and at the other, buckets. At the starting, each runner had to take one of the allotted five limes, run, and drop it in the bucket at the other end. Then they had to run back and repeat until all five were in the bucket. She, when five feet from the bucket, tossed her limes in, ending up with an advantageous lead not to be relinquished.

My mother did what she thought was right, and in this regard, she never claimed to be religious but rather practical and Christian-like in her dealings, except for one incident that I became aware of. I don't know that she doubted the existence of omnipotence but rather the way in which it was being portrayed.

However, sometime in the late 1940s, before we knew that hurricanes were given names, we were assailed by such a storm without warning and during the night. It was the first time I saw my mother not only seemingly frightened but also pleading with Alethea to read from the Bible. I'm not sure what was read.

We were all frightened, because it was our first experience of something so terribly dreadful and because Iah was seeking assistance from an entity she had not encountered before who had a power greater than that which had been granted to her, a power capable of wreaking havoc and destruction.

That late afternoon before the storm, a plate not yet completely empty of food was blown away from one of us children, but we knew not what that portended.

I think that it was that same night that our neighbour, Flora, and maybe her mother, Yahyah, spent the night with us. Very early the next morning, she went to their badly damaged bungalow and retrieved a pint of rum. Our house received only minor damage. The image of God as an almighty being watching and controlling our every action was unacceptable to Iah. She expounded that God dwelled within each person and that it was up to each to act accordingly in this life. What she believed may have even boggled her own mind, and if her views changed over time, it was not known, not by me. In my opinion, she believed in an almighty power that controlled what happens around but not within man. In some form, in ancient times, the Greeks and Romans had multiple different gods for that same reason. These gods now exist only in tales and the Christian God only in faith.

As she often said, "When you dead, you done."

If there is a fight between God and the Devil, it's a fight within each of us and between each of us, whether individually or multiplied to man versus man. If there is a heaven, it is right here on earth, just as hell is. Such were her thoughts, as I thought. Somehow, she created a blend of God with humanity.

A story goes that a man inherited or bought a portion of land in the boondocks. He laboured and transformed it into a prized agricultural property. A priest, on passing by, said to the now proud farmer that God had indeed blessed him with that wonderful land. The farmer responded, "Yes indeed, but you should have seen what it looked like when he had it all to himself."

That's what my mother would have said.

Nevertheless, and irrespective of what she believed, as far as I understood it, she sent all her children to Sunday school in the Grand Bay Gospel Hall located on the upper part of the main street of Grand Bay. I think this was to ensure that we learnt the basics of good and bad. In my youth, Teacher Meemee ran that church, assisted by Tan Fan.

John Noel, who married my sister, Sarah Balvina, lived with Teacher Meemee, who was caring for his aged grandmother, before he left to join his parents in New York.

Occasionally, there were leaders who visited from the church in Grenada. I recall Miss Tyson, who, when she came, always distributed spiritual pamphlets, magazines, and booklets. I wondered later in my life if she was related to Cicely Tyson, the actress in the movie *Sounder,* who, it was said, had origins in Nevis, an island in the Caribbean.

I have had the opportunity to visit Nevis on more than one occasion and was impressed by the fresh lobster salad from a beachside restaurant, by the loose goats walking the streets, and by learning that the noted statesman Alexander Hamilton was born in a house now on display for visitors and that the British naval officer Horatio Nelson was once stationed there and married a Nevisian.

There was a white man who sometimes accompanied Miss Tyson and who held magic lantern shows at nights. I remember seeing one based on *The Pilgrims' Progress*, by Bunyan. Children enjoyed these shows.

To my delight, in Grenada, the head church was on Tyrell Street at the foot of Bain Alley, where I lived with my sister Adeline during my attendance at GBSS, and I sometimes attended the shows on Friday nights.

In Carriacou, the more established churches were in the town of Hillsborough, which was some three miles away and therefor considered too far to attend. Now and then, a service was held in the villages, maybe in the schools, though later, attendance in the town was facilitated by the onset of regular bus transportation. School buildings were always available for different functions and events, serving as a community centre.

We, the Brathwaite children, were all christened as Anglicans.

When I started sleeping in her bed, Iah always insisted that I say my prayers, kneeling on the bed, before falling asleep. Some prayers were meaningless to me because some of the words sounded like gibberish until I understood them later in life. The following are excerpts from two of them:

> As I lay me down to sleep, I ask the Lord my soul to keep. If I should die before I wake, I pray the Lord my soul to take. In my little bed I lie. Heavenly Father, hear my cry. Lord, protect me through the night and bring me safe to morning light.

* * *

> Gentle Jesus meek and mild, look upon a little child. Pity my simplicity … In the kingdom of thy grace, give a little child a place … Day and night my keeper be; every moment watch round me.

Speaking of hurricanes, the next one that I encountered and that severely damaged Grenada and Carriacou was Janet in 1955. At that time, I was in Grenada attending GBSS. There was obviously a warning, for we were sent home from school earlier than usual. I went to bed rather early and slept undisturbed throughout the night.

When I awoke and looked out the window, I realised that something was amiss. There was an uncanny, quiet emptiness, and my view to the lagoon was strangely unobstructed. That was because the warehouses on the pier in the inner harbour were completely destroyed.

There was an overall numbness in the atmosphere, and the first report from the planes that reconnoitred the region that Carriacou could not be found worsened the feelings. However, by the next day, the island was located.

People roamed the Carenage and the downtown centre in their search for items from the warehouses or the damaged stores, later eliciting jokes about, for example, someone carrying away a washing machine, thinking it was a fridge, and taking it to his house quite far from any electricity supply. I gathered many lead pencils on the seashore of the Carenage. GBSS suspended classes and was closed for three weeks, which I spent in Carriacou, selling the pencils from the shop.

Mt. Pleasant Beach in Carriacou was destroyed because a flotilla of trees from Grenada had washed ashore there. The only saving grace from this was that many palms were laden with coconuts in varying stages of development. Other fruits were also present, and eventually, wood was obtained to be used as fuel.

The coconut tree and its fruit are well known for their wide benefits. In Carriacou, we primarily used the dry "nut", as the milk from the grated flesh added a treasured, unique flavour to certain foods and the meat could be used in baked goods.

In Grand Bay, a house that was built on wall pillars was turned 360 degrees but remained on the pillars, so the entry to the house was through the back door. Also, in his house atop a hill, Mr. Wilson gathered his family together. The house was uprooted, flew through the air, landed in the valley, and burst open, leaving the huddled family on open ground. In the words of Mr. Wilson, "Safe landing."

My aunt Polina, who lived in the village of Dover, died in that storm.

Strangely, there was some degree of excitement in post-Janet Carriacou. It was always customary for families and relatives who lived abroad to send supplies home in barrels, but after Janet, they sent more than the usual. In that same vein, relief supplies came from different sources and were distributed by government workers. Whether fairly or not is not the issue here.

Among other things, there were items of food, and I ate many ready-to-eat puddings, jams, and cakes in flip-top tins from the US and British armies and navies. Also remaining in my mind was the powdered milk, which I did not like, as when mixed with water, it had a peculiar taste.

Say Farm, a lady older than Iah who normally received poor relief from the government, lost her little house, which was located near to our shop. The aid included prefabricated one-bedroom houses, perhaps from Suriname, and she, like others, was given one of them. These were called OPL houses, which meant that they were obtained from other people's labour. After that, a young boy from Grand Bay, Alwin, who we called Puff, moved in with her as a helper. He was maybe not yet a teenager.

I return now to the incident with Iah that I have alluded to. I was just a little boy and just innocently and partly aware of the happenings. A man came to our house, accompanied by my brother John, with a machine to make paper money, having been paid by Iah so to do. All that I can recall is that no money was made, that the man disappeared, and that Iah realised that she had been had.

* * *

As they come to mind, I now relate different aspects of life in my village as things were in my youth.

Many of the villagers reared farm animals. In our case, most of the farm animals—cattle, donkeys, sheep, and goats—were reared in the main land by my older brothers, but the pigs were reared at home or in the adjacent land at the back of the shop. Also at home were the fowl, dogs in the outside yard or sleeping under the house, and cats either outside or in the kitchen. The latter were well known for their screeching at nights.

I wish here to slightly digress to divulge that someone once put rum in the drinking water of the fowls. This resulted in laughter on seeing the unsteady, high-stepping walk of the poultry. The fowl cock never needed rum to high step, for he proudly did this, flapping his wings, after each conquest of a hen, especially a pullet, and issuing a crowning crow. It being daytime, he probably crowed more than thrice.

In addition to the slop made from peels and food remnants, I also, as previously stated, had to go to the bush areas to obtain plant material for the hogs for the next day's feeding. My never-be-unprepared mother, however, would send me out to do this a second time, especially if it looked cloudy.

Before the onset of the dry season, some families macheted grass to be stored for feeding their farm animals; otherwise, the larger animals were just let loose, often proving a vexing annoyance for farmers who had not yet completed the harvesting of their crops. Somehow, in the absence of what is today taken for granted, we were rather fortunate. It may not have seemed important then, but there was no organised or controlled system for the disposal of garbage or trash at that time. Tins and bottles were gathered in a heap behind the kitchen and eventually were buried, sometimes in the latrine pit on changing its location. Some stuff was just put under an area of the house.

Except for the very small bones from fish, every unused meal was fed to the animals. Our mongrels (called "potcakes" in the Bahamas) were adept at eating most fish bones without harm.

It's amazing how many times we were stuck or got injured by items like rusty nails, pieces of metal, and broken bottles but, except for developing leg sores, did not suffer a more serious condition, like tetanus.

Nothing to do with garbage but more so as an example of our lucky fortunes, one may go to bed with a fish bone that was stuck in the throat, undisplaced even after swallowing pieces of bread, and when one awoke in the morning, it was no longer there.

One would believe that something, someone, some being, somehow favoured and protected us, as has been portrayed in film *Somebody Up There Likes Me*.

Some poorer families, who cooked on firestones and who never had sufficient firewood, somehow produced food that tasted quite delicious if not well done. If a neighbour's child was in the yard, they may be asked, "You want a piece ah food?" "Yes, please, ma'am," was the usual response.

The most well known for this was Say Farm, the OPL older lady who had lived alone for a long time. Sometimes, Iah added something extra to Say Farm's groceries so that we could benefit from what she had cooked. Even though still not fully cooked, her food was never ready before nightfall.

I doubt it, but maybe that explains why to this day, I do not particularly enjoy a too-well-done meal, especially rice. In particular, I prefer a medium-cooked steak, unknown to me then.

Say Farm was known now and then and in a certain phase of the moon to throw a penny or a "hapney" (half penny) backwards over her shoulder into the bushes. I'm not sure why. Maybe it was for good luck for the home or for anyone who by chance found it.

Within and between the villages were the main streets, usually pitched or concreted. Occasionally, one would see the road crews at work on the main streets, cleaning the drains, opening up the culverts, or cutting the shrubbery. They would be overseen by a foreman, and someone else would be tending the steaming pot that rested on three rocks. Expectedly, the jobs of planning, maintaining, and repairing the roads were under a higher or more expert supervision by, for example, a road officer who paid the necessary supervisory visits, maybe when the food is about ready.

In addition to the main roads, there were less-maintained dirt roads to accommodate the farms and estates and to provide access to public places, like the beaches and cemeteries. There were also track-like trails or paths. These latter were uneven, rocky on the hills and more grass-covered in the valleys. They linked, intercrossed, and also connected the homes. Locally, all the above terms were used interchangeably, and the word *road* was applied to any pathway, no matter its size.

The houses were close together in clusters, in lines, or rarely, far apart, and they were linked by these paths, with some even sharing what seemed to be one yard. This created identifiable neighbourhoods with their own names. Kainash, where I lived, was one such.

The more modern style these days is for newly built homes to be sprawled out, more widely separated, and even isolated, and the attached properties are bigger and more usually enclosed by fences.

The neighbours were generally sociable and friendly, and neighbourhoods showcased conviviality. Of course, as expected, disagreements arose. There were gossips, and one would occasionally hear that, because of such-and-such, so-and-so had a falling-out with this other person, and they were not speaking to each other.

Thrown at each other may well be taunts like, "Shoo fly don't bother me. I'm a better woman than you."

Once, in a dispute, a young woman said to another that all her children were for married men. The older woman responded that, yes that is true, but look at you. The first jump you make is for a married man.

And no young girl ever wished to be called a jamette, a Jezebel, or a jagabat—all derogatory terms. The following was once asked about a non-Carriacouan woman whom we will call Nobody: "What is the difference between Nobody and the flu?" The answer: "Not every man has had the flu."

Obviously, sexual intercourse did not await marriage and resided not just within it. My father, Charlie, and my neighbour, Charles, were prime examples of that. Hell's fury was manifested in the exchange of words by the women and in the use of fists by the men.

A related story involves a married woman whose husband was away from home for long periods, probably as a sailor. Another man of the village took care of the business at the sailor's home. Unexpectedly, the sailor had returned and was at home. The moon was brightly shining. As the other man was nearing the house, intending to take care of the business that night, the wife went to the open door and shouted, "Moon ah shine like ah go back, he dey." (The moon is bright. Don't come. He is at home).

Curse phrases from one to another included "kiss me kaka hole" and "son-of-a-bitch". Although the latter was often loosely used, I only fully appreciated its meaning after its use once resulted in a fight, and I hardly ever used it again afterward. One boy, in response to another, asked, "You calling my mother a bitch?"

Fight broke out.

For my mother, the two women who had affairs with my father that resulted in births were off her friendship list. And my mother was always in a petty war with Cousin Jane Ann, wife of Amos, son of Say Doone, over the boundaries of land near to the shop. A calabash tree, the gourds of which I prepared to be used as containers, was claimed by both. Yet, I was told by one of Jane Ann's daughters, an everlastingly close friend of mine, that once, when there was a fire in the shop, Jane Ann was a most prominent person in the bucket brigade.

It was said that the fire had started because a rum drinker had thrown his cigarette stub on a pile of crocus bags that was kept in the shop. Crocus bags, used more usually to transport different things, were also readily converted into raincoats when necessary.

This leads to another story told to me. Semmie, a son of Cousin Jane Ann who was then maybe in his forties, walked the roads daily despite having a chronic leg ulcer, which as far as I know, he had sustained from a hot water burn. He used that ulcer as an ash tray for his cigarettes.

When visiting, I usually saw him and exchanged greetings, and though some have said that he was off his head, my only thought was that he was reserved. He died suddenly at the back of our shop in November 1995 at age 51, and when my brother John saw him, he left him where he was but called the police.

Verna, my brother Gilbert's wife, saw this from her nearby home on a visit from London and refused to talk to John from then on, her reason being that John should have removed Semmie, though dead, from the hot sun. Nonetheless, on the day of the tombstone feast for Gilbert, she made certain that John was sent his share of the cooked pig's blood on that morning. Yes, but he did contribute a sheep, which Gilbert's sons, Floyd and Clifford, and I had to chase to capture, it being loose in the pasture of our land. Did she forgive John?

Water flows away quickly under the bridge, and blood remains in the veins of families. Or, as otherwise said, blood is thicker than water.

John preceded his brother Gilbert into this world by two years.

I will always remember Mavis Scipio from Grenada, a close friend of the family, who, as a price control officer, took my mother to court for selling a box of matches above the listed price of a penny. Pleading guilty but with explanation, my mother was charged twenty dollars by the magistrate. I don't think that my mother, though saying nothing, took kindly to what Mavis had done, and I didn't either—especially years later, when that same lady received medical attention from me and, citing family friendship, refused to pay my fee.

Cited, in this instance, not through blood but through friendship for freeness.

At this point, I would like to mention the homes that were between our house on the hill and the shop, which was located on the main village road in the flat.

In general, as indicated, tracks led from house to house to house, and we children traversed them many times a day, up and down. Being always afraid of dogs and on the lookout for them, we sometimes held a stick to ward them off.

If bitten, the treatment included giving the wound a good cleaning and then applying a paint of iodine, a wad of the dog's hairs, and a cloth bandage cover.

At home, there were always anodyne items like iodine and Canadian healing oil. Other items of a medicinal nature were Vicks VapoRub, Eno's Fruit Salts, Milk of Magnesia, Epsom salts, castor oil, Limacol (the freshness of a breeze in a bottle), an enema bag, and a hot-water bag.

The track led from our home to the Cayenne's and then the McIntosh's, all close together. Jimmy McIntosh, maybe of Portuguese origin, was a fisherman. The family consisted of his wife, Cousin Millicent (Missent); sons Sherbotan, Dennis, and Clinton; and daughters Vida, a teacher, and Ometta, who was more at home.

They made some money from the goods they baked on Saturdays, and Ometta was usually the one walking the villages, selling sugary-sweet items like buns, coconut tarts, drops, and groundnut-sugar cakes.

The next house was that of Cousin Tahnee and Cousin Aga. I think that Tahnee was the lady who was said to have delivered one of her babies whilst hoeing in her house garden—in local talk, the baby drop. My brother Gilbert married Verna, née Quashie, who was of that house. Verna's cousin, Mathew, who seemed to be always sniffling with *fresh cold* in his nostrils, also grew up in that home.

Continuing down the Grand Bay slope of the hill, there was an abandoned house, then Say Farm's, followed by that of Mieye and Cousin Helen, which was adjacent to the main road and not far from the shop. Just above the shop but on the other side of the road was the home of Cousin Matill.

Cousin Helen would normally call me *Fe feh fed;* I always paid my respects on visiting Carriacou. Her son, Jerry, and I were good friends in Carriacou. Like many, he emigrated to New York, where he presently lives. We converse occasionally, especially about the old days.

It was possible to take another route that started from just below our house and also ended on the main road, passing the house of Say Doone and Cousin Beebee and then that of Cousin Tano and Cousin Vero, whose daughter Hilda and granddaughter, Nellis, lived with them.

It was said that Cousin Vero was one of the biggest eaters in the village, even though that may only be applicable to her main and only meal, after breakfast. The word that stuck with me was *tureen*, her eating utensil.

As far as I can remember, I have not seen any significant degree of obesity in Carriacou, except perhaps in those, pleasantly rounded, visiting from abroad. People tended to have well-defined muscles with outstanding tendons, except for the limited fatty curves of the women folk.

Cousin Tano, a son of Cousin Jimmy, was a seafaring man, but he also fished locally. He was perhaps best known for building a schooner in Grand Bay beach near to the fort area. In Carriacou, however, the villages of Windward and Harvey Vale, the latter a part of the area that we easterners referred to as below side, were better known for their boat building.

The launching of a boat was one of the well-known ceremonial events in Carriacou and usually had good amount of participation, widespread attendance, food, and drinks. It consisted of the blessings and the naming and had an overall brouhaha atmosphere. The first such launching I attended was that of Tano's boat *God Give Glory* (*GGG*). The *GGG* lasted only a few months, crashing on the reef off the Grand Bay/Mt. Pleasant sea as it attempted to navigate an entrance through the reef to the bay so as to gain anchorage nearer to the coast.

Cousin Tano also made play boats out of gommier wood for me. I sailed them in the sea when it was calm or in the adjacent and more tranquil salt water ponds. The ballasts were made from molten lead. At first, I didn't know where the lead came from, but I later gathered that it was obtained from lead batteries. Sometimes, we children used the barks of dried coconuts also to make play boats that we just sailed in the sea or raced in playful competition in the ponds.

I have not counted, but despite the building of a few new homes, I believe it's correct to say that of all the homes that I have mentioned that surrounded the area of my youth, over 90 per cent are no longer standing. In essence, on my last visits to Carriacou, in Kainash, there were no immediate neighbours.

As I think of how we school children played and sang, "Leh we go rong the mulberry bush; it's so early in de morning," and "Ring around the roses," I'm reminded of the four government primary schools that were then in Carriacou—Hillsborough, Harvey Vale, Mt. Pleasant, and Dover. Regular competitions, mainly sports related, were held between them.

Some head teachers' names associated with the schools over time included Mr. Harry Noel of Hillsborough, Mr. Cox and Godwin Brathwaite of Dover, and Nicholas Brathwaite and Mr. Bascombe of Mt. Pleasant. The names associated with Harvey Vale school included Mr. Willis, Mr. Duncan, and Mr. Languy, I have been told.

It is my understanding that prior to Mr. Noel, a Mr. Charles was the head teacher in Hillsborough, where my brother Godwin was a junior teacher. Apparently, a lady contrived with someone, maybe a student, who claimed that Godwin had stolen a watch.

The head teacher came to Iah at home with the false accusation. Iah, with her stick, threatened him and chased him from her home. Her children's honesty was sacrosanct. Anyhow, Godwin was taken to court, where the falsehood was uncovered.

Don't you ever mess with Gritillia's children.

I guess that it was at about age 6, in 1947, that I first went to the school in Mt. Pleasant, which catered not only to the two main villages but also to the neighbouring ones, like Mt. Dor and Mt. Royal. Rarely, a few children even came from farther afield.

Following the washing of hands, feet, and face from a basin, we changed into our nonuniform school clothes, boys with their shirts tucked within belted short pants that were worn for the week and girls in simple dresses. All of us were barefooted. The children wore shoes for special occasions, but there was no big surprise if the shoes were tied together and looped around their necks, either because it was raining or because their feet were not yet accustomed to shoes.

Some shoes were dressy, of a shiny, synthetic plastic, and some were washikongs. When the latter were worn for too long and too often, on removal, they emanated the odour of "toe jam will kill you", as is said in the Bahamas.

Most adults dressed appropriately for their jobs, professions, or status. Generally, but not always, the attire for boys and men would have included caps or hats, one worn regularly during the day and another as part of dressing up. Continuing into adulthood, men applied hair pomades, brand names of which included Vaseline, Brylcreem, Brilliantine, and Vitalis, and of course, a touch of powder on the chest and a dab of perfume on the neck. Old Spice became a popular deodorant.

Likewise, the girls and women donned hats, which provided some shade from the sun. Some were made of straw, and others were more dressy-looking ones for going out.

The women wore colourful head-ties for festive events but also had those that were not as fancy and perhaps made of a coarser material. The latter were worn more regularly, particularly when the women had to carry loads on their heads. Especially if it was necessary to put loads on the heads of children the heads would be protected by nests of intertwined soft twigs with attached leaves or by a folded cloth material, atop which the loads were balanced.

We carried laden baskets, bags, or boxes; tins of water; and wood for use as fuel. After we had gathered the portions of bramble-wood, they were bunched and bound together by rope or the strip from the barks of plants including cotton, common cherry, and black sage, all of which were pliable and strong.

* * *

Prior to my entry into school, the old main dormitory or barracks-type building was demolished and replaced by a long, more modern appearing and environmentally friendly one. I wonder if perhaps the old building had received some damage from the storm that I had first experienced in Carriacou.

All in all, I have experienced first-hand some eight hurricanes and have seen the effects of others on another two islands, David on Dominica in 1979 and Ivan on Grenada in 2004.

In this new building, the staff room was at one end, and in it was a desk for the head teacher, so situated that the corridor that ran the length of the classes was visible. There was a long table for the other teachers, and there were even books on shelves in a cabinet used as a library.

An open, sheltered space was adjacent to the staff room, and through, it one entered a southern corridor that ran the length of the building. Next to the open space, was a stage that was used both as the classroom for standard six and for concerts.

Continuing eastward, there were four lower-class rooms separated by movable partitions, which when removed created a large community centre. Standard four was next to the stage, and standard one was at the eastern end of the building, with two and three in between. Standards five-B and five-A were in another building.

The entire building was of wood but was constructed, along its outer two lengths, on an elevated concrete foundation, which supported the floor of the school and had a space between the floor of the school and the ground. Along the outer north wall of the foundation, there were four square openings, equally spaced lengthwise, created perhaps to provide a cooling effect on the classrooms.

When we played cricket, the ball sometimes went through these openings and therefore ended under the school. Only a small boy was able to enter through these into the crawl space to retrieve the ball. Many a time, that boy was me.

In the compound, at a slightly lower level to the south, was a separate but similarly constructed infant school in which was a kitchenette. Just east of this were two new gender-based latrines with pipes that inconsistently supplied water to the wash basins, and further east was a new head teacher's residence.

Between the main road and the new main building was an older, thick-walled building, probably of stone and mortar, that still exists. It was called the corn house, and it housed the two standard five classrooms. Very close to it was an above-ground cistern that was adjacent to but separate from the main building. It supplied the basins in the latrines with water by gravity via pipes.

I recall that when the latrine pits filled up, men whose identities were unknown to us children worked at nights to empty the material into previously dug craters. So, whereas the latrines at home were moved when filled, the two at the school remained in place. I have no knowledge of what was done for the one in the head teacher's residence.

Near to the head teacher's residence, between it and the main school, was an underground cistern that had a concrete catchment area but was also supplied with rainwater from the main school building via spouts. Though administratively controlled, the community was allowed to obtain water from this cistern, either by pumping it or drawing by buckets with attached ropes.

I can think of two other similar cisterns in the villages. One was in Nehgah house in Mt. Pleasant in the compound of the stone and mortar, former estate house of a Mr. Simmonds. The other one was in Grand Bay just above Cousin Wandalina's house. From these two, water was obtained via pipes through gravitational force.

A small post office is now located in the compound. However, in my school days, the village post office was within the yard of Da Worth Noel, from whose yard we obtained flowers, and was run by that family.

Twice per week, coinciding with the mail boat trips to and from Grenada, we either posted or received mail. On the days of reception, we would either gather as the names on the mail were orally announced or stop to obtain the mail on the way home from school.

In this small building, there was a wall telephone with a wind-up dialling handle. It was only connected to the main phone in the town of Hillsborough, where it was received by Mrs Mends, the operator, whose functions included receiving the transmitted messages, answering questions, and, it seems, carrying out the wishes of the caller.

All in all, the surrounding ground space of the school compound was ample for outdoor activities, which included mainly sports and games, and had a small area for farming.

I do recall that during the construction of the new school, the contractor and maybe architect was a Mr. Templeton(?) Keens-Douglas from Grenada, who was a close friend of the Brathwaites, and who, I think, had lunch with us during that period.

He gave me my first Christmas gift that was other than the usual balloons. It was a set of wooden cubes he had created on which were the inscribed painted letters of the alphabet and the numbers zero to nine. There were ten of them, each with two or three letters, capital and common, and one number. These were kept in the downstairs, where I played with and learned from them.

I believe that it was near the end of my first year in the infant school but before vacation that I had travelled with Iah to Grenada to visit her friends, the Louisons, in Grand Roy. My trip was extended to spend time at the residence of Godwin, who was then the head teacher in the village of Mt. Moritz.

This may explain why at the start of the new school year back home, when the teacher pointed to the children who were to move up to standard one in the main building, she never pointed at me. I went up anyhow. It must be pointed out that I'm not sure whether or not the infant schoolteacher, maybe Teacher Adelaide Blaize, Teacher Gracelyn, or Teacher Louise, knew what had transpired. Whether or not anyone did, she dared not stop Iah's boy.

In standard one, at the end-of-year ceremony, my name was announced as placing first to advance to standard two. I don't recall taking an exam, and though I had not previously been aware of this, I felt rather proud, because my sister Adeline was visiting from Grenada and was sitting next to me. My head was held high as I marched to the stage. It was the first time I had met this light-skinned, pretty lady, my sister.

My prize? I don't remember receiving anything, but there must have been something other than a handshake or a tap on the shoulder.

I remain ignorant of how I received the nickname, Ned. Iah never called me by that name. Some of my siblings did rarely, with Alethea being perhaps the guiltiest exception of the lot. But quite a few older villagers routinely referred to me as such, some as "Little Ned". Somehow, people were kind and tended to protect Little Ned as they reminded me that "Ned, Ned, the donkey dead; it died last night with a pain in the head."

I recall two other events related to my nickname that involved Adeline, who may have given me that name. They took place on her visit from Grenada. One day, she took me to the beach and beckoned me to swim to her beyond my height. "Come, Ned. Come, Little Ned," she encouraged as she either came closer or drifted farther away while I tried swimming to her. Somehow, I never became a strong swimmer.

The other occasion was when my brother Gilbert, on the bed of the older boys, dropped his pants, got on his hands and knees, and said to me, "Ned, umell. Umell, Ned!" of course, asking me to smell his bottom in his immature pronunciation. Adeline appeared and smacked him on his small buttocks.

When I refer to the bed of the older boys, I mean that of Gilbert and John. The younger boys, George and I, slept on rags on the floor of the living room until we no longer peed in bed. Somehow, on waking, we always had yampee clouding our eyes.

Subsequently, I moved into Iah's bed, a four-poster of mahogany wood that, as said already, harboured bed bugs in the slats and in the mattress.

What a choice: mosquitoes or bedbugs *and* mosquitos.

So, to put things in perspective, while I was between 6 and 8 years old, those at home included Iah, who slept in her bed; Alethea and Balvina, who slept in the girls' bed; John and Gilbert, who slept in the boys' bed; and George and I, who slept on the floor. My brother Lysander was then attending GBSS, and when at home on vacation, he slept in Iah's bed.

I do recall a third situation that occurred in my sixties. Walter McIntosh, whose favourite expression was "Whohpah" and who became my trusted friend and always made sure that I had whatever I needed whenever I visited Carriacou, once took me upstairs in his home to meet his mom. His father, Toby, the man who had been once beaten by Charles Cayenne, had already died, but his mother, maybe in her late nineties, was still alive. On the visit, he introduced me as Alfred, Iah's last boy. Cousin Leenie remained perplexed.

Then he said, "This is Ned. Ned for Iah." And her face brightened with recognition.

Family at home with Laca circa 1952

Maternal Relatives

As already said, I never knew my father's relatives; he supposedly severed all ties with Barbados, where he was born. However, at my very early age, a big white man once came to the shop and said that he was my father's brother. Nothing further came of that.

St Phillip was supposedly the parish in which his family was established, but after fire destroyed the Anglican church, records were no longer available. However, in my adulthood, I met a lecturer named Brader Adaleine Brathwaite from within the Eric Williams Medical Complex in Trinidad who was a Barbadian, and we both felt certain from the histories and our features that we were related.

I did know some maternal relatives. Stories were often told of my Carriacou grandparents, who died before I was born. It has been said that my grandmother, Ansay, came to Carriacou from one of the Vincentian Grenadine islands but had closer ties with people, including the Caesars, from one of Grenada's sister islands, Petit Martinique. I have also been told that my grandfather, "Dada Mack", a McLeod, was from Scotland, as was my paternal great grandfather.

I also knew uncles and aunts and their descendants.

GROWING UP: THE FAMILY AND THE NEIGHBOURHOOD

The eldest was Uncle Darrell, a fisherman, who in my youth lived in the area called Works with a woman, Cousin Thelma, who was once our washing maid, and his two sons, George and Natty (Nathaniel). As far as I know, Darrell had a wife somewhere in the USA who had not accompanied him when he had returned to Carriacou from there.

I always knew a cousin called Casper, who became the gatekeeper for the Lauriston Airport in Carriacou. I am uncertain of his relationship to Darrell, but I believe that he was a son of Darrell with his wife.

Other than the above children, this uncle had fathered a girl child, Iola, with Tan Florrie from Nehgah House, and another younger one with Cousin Matill, who lived close to the shop. This child, Aylin, was also locally called Soorie.

We visited Darrell fairly often, because on his land were many sugar apple and guava trees. My sister Alethea made jam and guava cheese from the ripe guava fruits, and we boys ate some of the ripe or half-ripe fruits but brought the full but unripe sugar apples home to ripen. As the hiding places were few, it was not unusual that some vanished.

There was a scarce fruit that I liked, but the one tree that I knew of was not on Darrell's land but somewhere above Kainash. Its fruit was called locust or stinking toe.

Another uncle was Abraham, who we called Deeclo. He was mainly confined to his house because he was diagnosed with what I believe was leprosy. I have no idea how that diagnosis was arrived at.

He lived with his wife, his two daughters, Maude and Rebecca, and his two sons, David and Abraham, in upper Grand Bay. The stories indicate that he was the rowdy warrior within the family who once attacked Darrell over a land issue. Darrell was defended and rescued by Iah from what would have been a severe beating. Darrell did always seem to be unsteady of leg.

The youngest and *baddest* of them all was Uncle Powell, who lived in the old homestead, which was close to our house. His wife,

Exeter, who we called Nennen, was Tan Dorah's niece. She had moved to Tan Dorah's house with twin daughters, Veda and Valda, to whom I gave lessons on Saturdays and during school vacations.

In that homestead, there was a tall gramophone that we played records on. I remember the huge logo of a dog and the name His Master's Voice on its cover.

Powell was strong, a no-nonsense man who I remember as giving sound advice to me, but he later started drinking the hard stuff and gradually became somewhat unsound of mind. It is my understanding that he had worked in Panama and sent money home to a brother for safe keeping, only to learn on returning that there was no money. From then, it has been said, his mind became troubled. His livelihood was then partly earned from fishing.

In the shop, where men gathered to drink at the end of the day, mainly Jack Iron rum, Powell would palm and shield his glass enabling him to pour more than the usual shot. His glass would be not half empty and not running over but more than half full.

There were other things I remember about him. At one time in the night, our shop was broken into. The next day, my brother George was sent to Mt. Royal to see a seer lady, who told him that a young man from a house neighbouring the shop had done the deed. Powell got hold of Moore, the son of Cousin Matill, and put him under the third-degree clinch, attempting to dig out his liver. I remain uncertain as to whether or not the young man had confessed.

The same seer also told George that his younger brother would become a doctor. That perhaps strengthened my already expressed intention, for I imagine that that seed was already planted in my mind.

Another incident that I partly witnessed involved a fight that broke out on the road between the shop and Tan Dorah's Junction. It was between Deeclo's son, David McLeod, and David Arthur, the son of a family who lived just downhill from Uncle Deeclo. There was the supposition that this other David had a knife. Powell separated the fighters and must have retrieved it. Then he declared that the two could now fight, and indeed they did.

Why did they fight? What was the outcome? Was there a victor? Don't ask me.

And a third incident involved Bastapool, who we called Cousin Basta, a son of Da Joe and Ninnie. Billy Nelson, a taxi driver who lived in town, had visited his girlfriend in Grand Bay on a holiday, maybe Christmas or Boxing Day. Having left her house, he was walking towards Mt. Pleasant, obviously drunk, and when he came near to our shop, he accosted Basta and tore off his shirt.

Powell, having seen what had taken place, got hold of a sizable rod and began approaching Billy, who himself had pulled a screwdriver from his pocket. Although backing away from Powell, Billy seemed to be waiting for the opportunity to pounce.

Iah went behind Billy and began hitting the right hand that was holding the weapon with her piece of wood, which she always seemed to have at the shop. She dislodged the instrument from Billy's hand and declared, "Powell, I got it." Powell then stoutly advanced and released his anger in the form of blows with the rod on Billy, who broke off and ran into the garden behind the shop.

In a short while, he came back out and passed out near Cousin Helen's gap. Shortly after, Basta's brother, Blackie, appeared on the scene and, on being told what had transpired, took a big rock and threw it at Billy's head. Luckily, it missed.

Two houses removed on the upper side of ours was the home of Bro Simon and his wife Edna. Bro was the godfather of my brother Lysander but was usually abroad, perhaps in Aruba. Edna Simon, née Simmonds, came to Carriacou from Bequia of the St Vincent Grenadines. There were three children, all girls: Celestine, Josephine, and Venus. Celestine was known for her shooting skills in netball. Blackie, who lived with his parents, as Basta also did, was known to visit Edna very often.

For whatever reason, Blackie and his sister, Peetette, never got along whenever she visited from her home in Trinidad, and she also stayed in the same abode.

On one of her visits, Peetette brought her husband, a huge white man. The war continued. On this particular day, Blackie was in Edna's yard when Peetette and her husband came on the scene, she armed with a long piece of wood.

A fight started between the men. The husband once pinned Blackie against the leaning trunk of a plum tree, but Blackie's right arm was around the man's back, attempting to throw him off. The wife laid blows with her rod on this forearm. Despite that, Blackie succeeded and threw some telling blows on both before running away. Peetette and her husband returned to Trinidad, and I really don't know what ever became of Blackie.

It was said that Cousin Edna became mentally unwell. One day, she ran to Mt. Pleasant Bay to drown herself and had to be rescued by men. This I witnessed. Bro returned home at some point in time and, at an old age, ended up in the old folks' home in Top Hill.

It became obvious, maybe years after, that Powell was becoming a different person with the deterioration of his mind. On more than one occasion, he was arrested as being insane, transported to Grenada, and detained at the crazy house in Richmond Hill in the capital.

There may have been a house, but his confinement was in an underground cell in a cave within the hill on which was located Fort Frederick. Perhaps this was for those considered potentially violent.

I feel certain that these created caves were present in other forts in St George's, and word was that two forts were connected by an underground tunnel. Indeed, as schoolboys, some of us ventured into one in Old Fort, having tied a string to an outside tree and travelled inwards with it. I never went too far in.

Once or twice, when he was so incarcerated and I was living in Grenada in attendance at GBSS, I visited and took him food items, such as biscuits, oranges, and bananas. As a young boy, I was scared, because I had to pass other occupied cells to get to his. But the cells all seemed to be locked. Maybe that was why no officer accompanied me.

It has been said that on one occasion in Carriacou, Powell went to the town. Why, I don't know. Nonetheless, the story was that he was drunk, and with stupid bravado, he got into a fight and was soundly beaten by a government employee from Grenada, who was stationed on the island as the officer in charge of the services within the revenue and post office building. He was one of those who we would have called white, a man named Andy Mitchell.

Sadly, when home on vacation from high school, I witnessed the death of Uncle Powell. This was linked to another uncle of mine, Griffith, who I visited sometimes in 1962 and 1964 when I went to Brooklyn from Jamaica to spend the summer vacation. He lived alone.

He was a good cook of creole food, especially pig feet, and he would feed me when I visited him. If he had won the numbers that day, he would give me some dollar bills before I left to return to my sister, Sarah, with whom I was staying.

At that time, Uncle Griffith did not seem to be a happy man, partly because of the lousy performances of the New York Mets baseball team but more so because he continued to mourn the loss of his son, Donald (Donny), a policeman who, on a casual visit to local grocery store, had interrupted and attempted to foil a burglary and had been shot dead. So, I was led to understand.

Before my trips to New York, he had once visited Carriacou, I guess in happier times. It was in September 1957. During the visit, he and Powell would be drunk daily, as he, coming from America, was able to purchase the drinks.

On the day he was leaving to return to New York, despite disagreement from Powell's family and Iah, he encouraged Powell to accompany him to town, where he was to catch the boat to Grenada for the plane onwards to New York.

It was understood that they drank heavily before Griffith departed, and Powell continued even after that. It's possible that this occurred on the same day that he was beaten, as related above.

Well, into the night, Powell still had not returned. I'm not sure how he was brought home—by car, maybe—but he was placed in a bed in Tan Dorah's house, unconscious. With nary a pause, he made a gut-growling, grunting sound not unlike that of a stuck pig at Christmas when the blood gushes from its heart.

The doctor was called but did nothing, really, except sound him. Powell died in the early hours of the next morning at age 55 because, in the words of some, "alcohol had cut his liver".

This sudden death was never investigated, as far as I know. As one would say, the doctor did everything, *sounded him,* but could not save him.

No matter which part of a person's body was unwell, it was believed that it would not recover unless the doctor placed the stethoscope in that area—sounded it. If not, he was not a good doctor. A visit to the doctor necessitated the use of the stethoscope.

I remember how they prepared and measured him. They bought the lumber from town to build the coffin and also the purple cloth to drape it. Despite the measurements, his grave, or perhaps it may have been that of another person, had to be embarrassingly widened at the time of the burial.

Cousin Basta, the grave digger, was blamed. But as expected, the grave was six feet deep.

From dust to dust the body went, but I never fathomed what *ashes to ashes* meant.

As an older man, Griffith retired to Carriacou. He got married to Cousin Ethel, a Carriacouan lady who had also returned from abroad, and bought a home near Grand Bay's main street. Prior to his death, I understand that he had become quite sickly and even had an amputation of one of his legs because of diabetes.

After Powell's death, maybe on the ninth night, the rite of worshipping took place. The specially prepared food was left unguarded overnight at the then abandoned residence of Powell, where he had lived alone for a long time.

Well, my gang of the time invaded and ate quite a lot of the food. The doors were locked, but we were able to hoist Gordon, the smallest, through a window that we had forced open.

Of course, the next morning, there was much less food than had been placed there the night before. Exeter (Nennen), Powell's wife, without doubt knew that Powell had not eaten it, but although she was told, she never believed that her dear little Ned, who by then had outgrown that name, would have had anything to do with that raid.

Before his mental status started to deteriorate, I admired Uncle Powell, as he seemed to know what he was about. I admired him so much that my thesis in 1978 was dedicated to him, as "an uncle who promoted ambition".

I heard stories of but never met or knew an uncle called Nash, who was the husband of Tan Dorah but who had left for Maracaibo, Venezuela, and had never returned. But there were, and here my memory is vague, a son and daughter of his who were sent from Venezuela, where they were born, to live with their grandmother, Ansay.

The daughter, Cousin Louisa, and her children, including one called Sonny McIntosh, eventually lived in Montinelle, a settlement that was located above another one called Along and that was on one of the walking routes to get to the hospital from Mt. Pleasant.

Another way to the hospital from Mt. Pleasant was via the road through Quarry, which, unlike that through Montinelle, could have been considered motorable. Quarry road was on the Mt. Pleasant side of the large Newland or Belair Hill, on the other side of which but more eastwards were Dover and adjacent villages already mentioned.

There is a story repeatedly told about Nash's son, Malco. One of Malco's daily duties was to take the hogwash to a pig that was kept in the garden in Newland Valley, which was near the area called Works. Whenever he was asked how the pig was doing, I'm told that his response was always to remark how fat the pig was. "Fat, fat, fat."

When they went to get the pig for the Christmas slaughter, all they found was the chain lying within a set of bones. No one knew whether or not he had consumed some of the pig's slop or had just thrown everything away to have time to play his games. For good reason, in Mt. Pleasant, Venezuelans got a bad rap because of him.

I now wonder how it was that no one ever reported a stench.

The land was probably too far removed from houses or the road.

Iah had two sisters. My auntie Polina lived in Dover with her daughter, Inez, and her son, Michael. I met Sheila, daughter of Inez, in Grenada in the 1970s. Further on, I will relate how Polina's cow once attacked me in the school yard. As far as I know, she died in hurricane Janet in 1955.

There was a framed picture in our living room growing up of Iah and Loonie, the other aunt, who had left her husband at home before I was born and headed for the USA to join Father Devine's group in New Jersey or New York. It has been said that a local song was composed about this.

She had a house, which was abandoned, located just below ours and near to that of her parents, in which Powell had lived and where the ceremonial plate had been left after his death.

Bats lived in that dilapidated house, and as boys, we caught them. I don't recall why.

It was in that abandoned house that I, between ages 11 and 13, experienced what I would consider my first true sexual encounter.

Open la la!

Over time, I have met my godparents. Fred McIntosh lived in New York but visited Carriacou. He once gave me money. Cousin Erwin, I think, worked in Aruba, and he also gave me an offering when he once visited. Cousin Eta "Nennen" lived in the area called Along in Mt. Pleasant, and in my youth, it was customary for me to visit her. I knew of Cecilia Quashie, but I don't remember meeting her until after my middle age years when she moved from abroad to the Westerhall residential area in Grenada.

3

AND THEN THERE WERE MEN: VILLAGE CHARACTERS

As said before, Carriacou, like most other places, had its share of beliefs, folklore, fables, superstitions, and legends, all varying in detail, generally unproven, and usually handed down orally within the community. Mention has already been made of ringing in the ears meaning that people were talking about you and an itch in the palm meaning you should expect news. And rain and sunshine at the same time meant the Devil and God were fighting.

Sometimes tales arose because of pranks having been played. A story goes that a head teacher of Mt. Pleasant school had his drinks in a lower part of the village at nights before climbing the hill for home. Some boys built a coffin, placed it in the middle of the road, hid in the bushes on either side, and moved the coffin from one side to the other by attached ropes. Imagine the consternation of the teacher when he approached this spot. It is said that he eventually turned his cap backwards, jumped over the coffin, and raced home. He was certain that this was some form of a spirit in action, and this became his story.

Mythical and mysterious but clearly unknown entities were said to exist and, in Mt. Pleasant, Grand Bay, and the surrounding areas, were identified by names that were at times unclear and dubious and sometimes similar but were as likely to be different in their meanings when spoken of elsewhere within Carriacou or further afield.

However, in my village, I understood as best as possible what the terms *la jabless*, *spirit*, *witch*, *jombie*, *ghost*, *loogaroo*, and *mermaid* referred to. In a general sense, these terms were applied to spectral or phantomic entities, even though with different names. They were all up to no good, though they used different means to accomplish their missions. Some were magical, some alluring, some mystical, and some, out and out, just plain wicked.

Spirits and ghosts may have human forms, alive, dying, or dead and visible to some but not to all or may be phantasmal. Funny, but some of these names were not only attached to but even fitted existing persons.

A story that I recall hearing involved a man named Dartan, the husband of Baah. Dartan was said to have once invoked spirits from Grand Bay Cemetery for a reason not known to me. He had to fight them off with a broomstick, fully aware that to get to safety, he must never turn his back on these apparitions. He was able to fend them off until he reached his home, which was only a few minutes away.

This is somewhat not unlike being warned as children about never showing your back to barking and advancing dogs, especially by running from them. If done, a bite would surely ensue.

As an aside, Cousin Baah and Dartan's last son, Gift, was said to be one of the few that had survived a premature birth. He was, however, of small stature in growing up.

Some individuals claimed to have seen mermaids on rocks in the sea, but that was it, nothing else. I'm not aware that manatees or sea cows inhabited our shores.

Most witches were women. The term has been applied in a derogatory sense to either sex but more so to women by other women when they were having a go at it.

"Shoo fly, you ole witch. Don't bother me. I belong to somebody."

These orally transmitted paranormal tales, when told to us children by adults, induced weird, uncanny, eerie feelings, such as a crawling tingling of the skin and unease in one's body, and at times created a frightening aura.

It was known that some of the adults who believed in these stories would safeguard themselves by sometimes taking preventive and protective measures.

A loogaroo or soucouyant was like a vampire. It could fly and change its skin and would seek to enter a home to suck its victim's blood, particularly at nights. Therefore, some people protected their homes by placing a container of sand over the threshold. An unwanted night visitor was expected to count each grain of sand so as to be able to advance further into the house. It was also said that tracing a line of ashes across a track road prevented a loogaroo from walking over it—an identity test.

One night when I was in Iah's bed, I saw the light of a flame through the glass window moving from a house on a hill to one in the hollow. The next day, a lady from the second house exposed a blotch on her thigh to Iah in the shop, claiming an assault by a soucouyant or a loogaroo.

Whereas Count Dracula was made to act as a suave gentleman, the loogaroo was more usually portrayed as a monster that, at times, had a little charm.

But during and at the end of the night, they both still sucked blood.

For the following incident, I was actually present. One early but dark night, a few of us children were sitting as usual on the front steps of Dama's house. Dama was our immediate next-door neighbour, and there were no obvious separating boundaries between our two yards.

Cousin Maymay, mother of Charles, the man of the house, came from within the house and went around it to get drinking water from the cistern. Dunstan, an outside child of Charles who was a few years younger than me and lived with his grandma a little way farther down the hill, was sitting with us. He followed his grandma, as he also wanted a drink.

When she passed to go back in, Dunstan was not with her, and we all knew that he would never wander off alone in the dark. We called and searched but did not find him. Well, when we were still unsuccessful after some time, the village was notified.

The villagers responded and searched, blowing conch shells in a manner reminiscent of the biblical blowing of horns. It was not until the next morning that we children learnt that he was eventually found late that night under a big rock. We gathered that on being questioned, he said that all he knew was that he'd kept following his grandma. The general feeling was that he must have followed or been beckoned by a spirit.

I feel certain that he was not sleepwalking. However, the story seemed incomplete at the time and has remained so.

And to think that sometime in the past these supernatural beings did not exist in Carriacou. There was a strange story that was tossed around within the community indicating that they had arrived by boat from the town of Grenville (La Bay) in the parish of St Andrew in Grenada. They, as ordinary people, had given the captain a bag of money to take them to Carriacou. On landing, they disappeared. When the captain reopened the bag, all he found in it was cow shit.

Did they move to and take up residence on that hill called Teeblee? Uncanny, isn't it?

Although there may be a basic similarity, especially within the Caribbean, between aspects of culture, beliefs, and certain customs and practices inherited from Africa and Europe or uniquely acquired, Carriacou had its own native twists to some of them. They are exemplified in the activities associated with certain events.

Thus, although an event may be the first for a family, the activity would have followed a similar, established pattern. For example, the building of a home or any other event of newness required a blessing rite or wetting of the ground either to protect from evil or to plead to God for good outcomes.

This varied from a fairly elaborate dancing rite for special invitees to the mere pouring of booze, more than likely Jack Iron, followed by water or a sweet drink on the floor or ground. This would be done together with a short prayer or a mere recitation of just a few words in the presence of immediate relatives and friends. In some instances, there were specially invited guests.

However, some of these activities have evolved into much more grandiose ceremonies such as occur at the launching of a boat, the dancing of the cake and flags at weddings, and saraccas and maroon festivals, which are all usually open to all and sundry to partake and enjoy.

Come one, come all! *Bomennaire*.

I hope to now identify a few real older persons who, for different reasons, may have unintentionally helped during my youth and even after to influence or shape the person I have grown to be.

It was customary, expected, and often dictated that all adults were to be respected in the village. Whether closely related to or not, most adults were called cousins when approached or spoken about, and many were known by dainty, respectful adjectives such as Tan, Say, and Da, which preceded their actual or the local versions of their names.

A child could not pass an adult without saying a respectful good day, for otherwise, it would be reported as a display of bad manners or rude behaviour or described, as is said in the Bahamas, as having no *brutupsie*.

On one occasion, I, a grown man, a doctor in my thirties or forties, was in the shop having a drink and conversation with my brother John and a seventy-plus-year-old man who, during the discourse, I called Harbin. He immediately chastised me, stating that he and I did not grow up together. He insisted that to me, he was Cousin Harbin.

* * *

In referencing persons, my discourse includes factual things, stories told to me, and my own impressions.

Of the living characters in my time, the first that comes to mind is the already mentioned Bastapool, the man who was assaulted by a taxi driver on or near Christmas Day. He was Cousin Basta, but sometimes behind his back, we called him Bastafool. He was a son of fairly close neighbours, the Simons (Cousin Ninny and Cousin Da Joe, a fisherman). Cousin Ninny was the sister of Jimmy McIntosh, who was of Portuguese descent.

Basta was known locally as perhaps the best person for castrating animals, but he was also known as a butcher, a grave digger, and a fisherman. And rather respectfully, he was Iah's "man of business".

Especially when drunk and being teased, he would either use strong cuss words or respond with, "*Nunca falta*," having spent some time working in Venezuela, like so many others from Carriacou. When not drunk, he was a very humble individual, and no matter how drunk he got at nights, he was always up early and fully functional on the morn and remained so until it was time to drink again after work.

I respected him for this trait.

However, it was known not only that he could not hold his liquor well but that he was also a bit simple minded or dim-witted and could not read. So, when he helped unload the sweet drinks from the crates so we could place them on the shelf in the shop, he would attempt to show off by looking at the names on the bottles. However, he only identified them based on the colour of the drink. So, when he called out cream soda, it would be a cola champagne or an aniseed label.

One night, he was too drunk to get home, so someone placed him among the pigs to sleep it off.

Oh, my naughty brother John!

When I was older and home on vacation from high school, I began accompanying him to the sea to raise the fish pots, built to entrap the fish that entered them. A floating log was attached by rope to the pots. Customarily, two persons manned the row boats, but a few individuals, like Cousin Shepherd, Johnathan Dick, and maybe Uncle Darrell, went out alone. Somehow, Basta and I never seemed to catch too many fish. But when I took some home or bought fish from others, my job was to clean and salt them.

It was understood that one had to be able to locate the set pots when one returned, usually the following day, to raise them from the seabed. Because the land curved around the bay, it was usual to use a right-angled marking system that was directed at two landmarks so as to pinpoint their location. It is said that Basta once used a cow as one of the marks. The next day, he experienced some difficulty in readily locating that pot, as the owner had moved the cow the evening before.

In the village, those on the hills would look out for the fishing boats on their way in and would alert those in the flats. Then they would all head to the shore to make their purchases.

After my departure for Jamaica, I don't think I ever saw Cousin Basta again. I was led to believe that he ended up in Trinidad to live the rest of his life with his sister, Peetette, the lady at loggerheads with Blackie, their brother.

Basta may not have been thought of as a champion, maybe not even an also-ran, but he knew his trades, was no jackass, and above all, was a reliable man.

Somehow, I don't remember him being in a sexual relationship with any other person. No one believed and he was teased about the three children he claimed to have fathered in Venezuela—Live, Livelight, and Job.

I liked Cousin Basta—a simple, honest man. He was a jack of all trades who mastered the neutering of animals, even though mainly castrations.

* * *

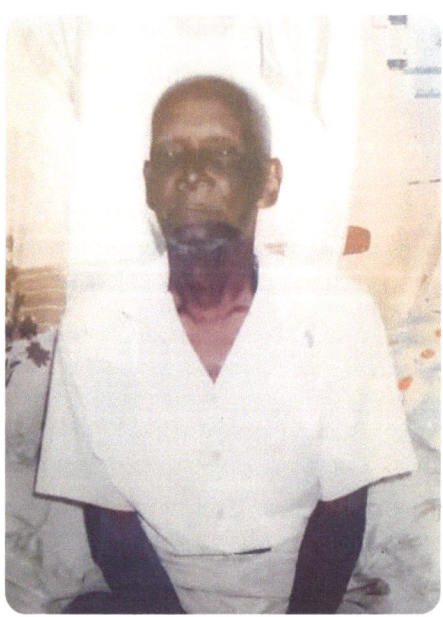

Da James

Another well-known person was Da James, Cousin Delfina's husband, who was readily associated with and was apparently never without his donkey. It was well known and expected that he would descend on late afternoons from his home, which was just off Grand Bay's main street, to the shops in the valley, going either to ours at the end of Grand Bay or further northwards to another in Mt. Pleasant.

When it was time for him to return home, as drunk as ever, he would mount his donkey, normally a spritely beast when coming, and it would, without further guidance, slowly and carefully take him straight back home, the two in quiet harmony.

Once he fell whilst attempting to mount, and his excuse was that the animal had shied from something. I always teased him about that, and he would just laugh. On passing by, his favourite response, when hailed, was "Whapes, again," not unlike Walter's "Whohpah". I never knew if there was meaning to these words. It was always a pleasure to have a short, teasing chat with him, for he always exuded happiness—a most effervescent character.

It was usual for me to see him whenever I revisited Carriacou. The last time was when I walked to his home, where he was more or less confined because of senility. This was many years after I had left Carriacou, and I was just paying a short visit.

In offering him some money, I suggested that I would prefer to wait for Cynthia, his daughter, to return, as he may lose it. He, with a look of mischief and the hint of a smile, insisted that I should give it to him, claiming that he was not yet dotish and that Cynthia may keep it to herself.

He knew what he was about and approached it seriously, but he created and enjoyed the lighter moments in his life. It may or may not have been him, but because of him, I remember a time when a man placed a pint of rum in his pants pocket to take home from the shop and, on mounting his donkey, was told that he should be careful as he may drop his pint. His response was, "You ever see a cow kick its own calf?"

Da James and his children had dark, narrow features, and the girls were quite pretty. The best known in the village was Cynthia, a tomboy who played a better game of cricket than many boys but also, if disturbed, would use the choicest of cuss words and would even lift her dress to bare her middle front.

Whenever I visited Carriacou, I normally sought her out to get my triple hugs of friendship as she gladly accepted a small gift from me. The last time I saw her was at a fair held by the school in the school yard in 2018. She came when I beckoned, but I don't think she recognised me. A pleasant soul she was, but a terror if angered.

Her father was never a terror and was one who portrayed an image of having no desire to be more than what he was. Napoleon, his son, allowed me to have his father's photograph.

Da James lived to the enviable age of 103 years, dying in 2003, perhaps with his final word being "whapes".

* * *

In terms of physical stature, no one fitted it so inimitably well as my next character, George Dudley Porter (GDP), who was perhaps of Portuguese origin. This imposingly towering man was always well attired as he resolutely strode the street from his place of abode to Mt. Pleasant, head held high, certain of his destination. He came no further south than the shop of my mother—or more rarely our home—at least twice a week. It was not unusual for him to share my mother's meal in the shop, and it was even thought that he had feelings for her.

He was a shoemaker who lived alone in another village near Belvedere called Bayaleau, and it was he who made my first pair of a very stiff leather sandals when I was leaving for GBSS in Grenada. I barely wore them because I developed corns on my heels, the right more than the left, from them.

However, they proved to be very handy when I sliced my right big toe on a seashell whilst bathing on the seashore termed the Spout in Tanteen, St George's, Grenada. After the toe had received its daily morning cleaning and dressing at the health centre on the esplanade, it was not possible to wear shoes. It proved more practical to strap the entire right sandal under the foot.

I wish to add here that I always believed that my right foot was slightly larger than the left, but the left leg was the longer of the two. This caused me to have a special, recognisable style to my walk.

GDP was also known to associate with the men of the village, particularly when they gathered to play board games, such as all fours and dominoes, at the school's residence, where Godwin, my eldest brother, was once resident, perhaps as a school supervisor. On such days, Teacher Cuthbert Simon was the cook. He would use rather big pots, and they would all consume large amounts of food and booze.

One late night or early morning after a Saturday or Sunday when the food had been of rice, provisions, and turtle meat, it was cried out that Cousin Irwin Noel, who was at that affair, had died. George Dudley, being the well-spoken man that he was, later declared with seeming profundity and aplomb that Irwin had died because he had choked on his balls scrotum. That was a little educational but very dramatic sounding when told to me by Godwin. I now, at times, wonder if Irwin may have had a scrotal hernia.

This event must have happened in 1950, for I was then beginning to get acquainted with international cricket, which was often a topic of conversation for the men. The West Indies team had just defeated England in England, warranting Lord Beginner's calypso: "Cricket, lovely cricket, at Lord's where I saw it … with those little pals of mine, Ramadhin and Valentine."

George Dudley Porter was indeed a man that I admired for his upright manner, which earned him the respect of others.

I cannot remember why, but the school children were assembled and lined up by class to march to and attend Irwin's funeral service at the graveyard in Mt. Pleasant cemetery. I strongly believe that it was because one of Irwin's sons, Kenneth, was then a teacher at the school.

Nuff respect!

In those times, and especially in the out-of-town villages, it was not usual to have a church service.

I wish to say here that Teacher Cuthbert, one of the village barbers, was the one to whom Iah sent us with our picky heads. He would roughly uncoil our knotty strands using the smallest of combs and use either a razor that seemed dull, though occasionally stropped, or the sharp edge of a broken bottle to shave our napes. For days after, we would suffer the pain from the skin bumps of in-grown hairs.

* * *

Although these three men stood out to me, some other persons were characters for one reason or another, though I perhaps did not know them as well. These other persons will be mentioned elsewhere as appropriate within this composition. However, I identify a few who, for whatever reason, stood out.

Mr. Fortune Simon lived in a large fenced-in house and was seldom seen away from it. He was distinct in stature, and in his dark attire, he looked like an undertaker and, indeed, somehow engendered fear. He made and sold the headstones for tombstones.

Cousin Amos Nedd seemed to prefer being alone and could usually be found either at his home near Tan Dorah's Junction, at the home of his mother, Say Doone, or on the track road in-between.

Mr. Theophilus Baptiste jealously protected his girl children, so there was no playing around in his yard.

Mr. Adolphus Quashie, whose estate-like big bungalow house stood prominently atop a crest, was held in great respect in the village, especially when riding his horse. Someone related to him—maybe his son, Alfred—on returning from abroad, built a shop where Tanah's was.

I also remember Boye, or Pallard, who was conspicuously present whenever a food festival took place and who found it convenient to stay all night at the home of the organizer.

Eustace was also known to go from village to village, seeking sustenance. He died in the mid 1970s as a pedestrian in a bus-related accident, and I performed an autopsy on the body in Carriacou.

A few individuals were thought not to be altogether in total control of their minds. They included Valentine, from Nehgah house, Claudius, and Da Jim, a son of Moore McIntosh. I cannot recall associating violent behaviour with any of them.

Let me also admit that in Grand Bay and Mt. Pleasant, and in Carriacou as a whole, there were certainly few who behaved differently. Some appeared to be of a different sexual orientation, some were dudoyes or stupidees, and some were known to be thieves.

In these present times, and particularly in some other countries, thieves are daring and brazen, even venturing into homes when people are expected to be at home, but fortunately, in Carriacou, they always were and still are a bit more cautious, though this may be changing.

Nobody broke foot faster than a Carriacou "tief" if he perceived that he may be caught in the act. But the opportunities for "tiefing" are becoming rife, as there are fewer persons around to see the culprits and, as stated before, many houses are conveniently isolated and vacant.

In a general sense and as expected, there was some degree of bias in how people were treated. So, for example, when there was a falling out, one of brown complexion may refer to another darker-skinned person as being "black as coals" or to a pale, red-skinned one as being a "bakenegg". But respect went to all, though perhaps a bit more to some than others.

Some are firsts among equals.

I will write of a few more, for it took all types to make a village, as they say.

* * *

I now speak of my brother John, who was, without a doubt, a character of note. He ran the shop on most Sundays and took full charge after Iah died. It was said that due to a falling out at home with our sister Alethea, who I gather he almost choked to death but for Charles Cayenne's intervention, he built an apartment attached to the shop and moved out of the family home. The falling out was because John was bringing his women to Iah's house, which Alethea resented. She openly and loudly broadcast her complaint to the public.

He became the caretaker not just of the shop but also of the land, where he reared his animals, and of his women. Taking domestic care of himself was nothing new, as he had done so before when he had been relocated to the town of Victoria in the parish of St Mark in Grenada. This move was for a government job as a road officer.

I visited him at least once then and sampled the tasty lunch that he had prepared.

After Iah's death, within what was now his shop, he stood always ready to start or defend any argument and loudly so. Many persons wondered how, though he seldom went out, he yet seemed so well informed, particularly about happenings from all parts of the island and further afield. Some would stop to seek his advice or just begin a conversation with him—with Braaf, as he was affectionately called.

He must have taken great delight in breeding women—and, I imagine, not massaging but pounding their mortars with his pestle. In my mind, I hear the refrain, "Grind me corn John Braffit. Ah tell you, grind me corn."

The rum in his shop was said to be the best, never diluted, and it was delivered without the import duty of customs by his and my very good friend W (Winston Stewart), a boat owner and captain.

W Stewart

Switching gears, W was very proud of me and at every opportunity boastfully made that known. He visited my private office for minor medical issues after I had returned to Grenada as a specialist. He was then an engineer on a boat, but sometime after, he acquired his own. The first time I visited him was in his shop in Dover. He was called from the adjoining field by his wife, and when he saw me, he called in all his workers, declaring that there was no more work for that day because the pathologist was there to see him.

I always visited him at his shop whenever I happen to be in Carriacou and always left with my choice of a bottle of good liquor. This continued after his death through his wife, Evelyn. I think well of their son, Emmanuel (Manny), who is making a name for himself as a regional junior cricketer. Their daughters are very attractive ladies.

I remember that W once took Vivian, my wife, Nika, our daughter, and I on his boat and anchored off a sand bank between Windward and Petit Martinique. As Evelyn prepared a meal, he and I drank.

Once, on a visit to Carriacou with Dax, my son, W calmly met me at the jetty and handed over the keys to his van, making it available to us for the duration of our stay. Dax drove, as I was no longer keen to use a standard shift vehicle, and we got involved in a minor accident on our way to Mt. Pleasant.

W always promised to sail to Freeport, my last place of residence, to spend some time with me, but that never happened. He did call me once when he had developed serious problems with his hip. In Carriacou, I would occasionally visit his tomb on the property at the back of their shop.

In his late teens, John was a few weeks away from qualifying to be a druggist through the apprenticeship programme when, without any explanation, he called it quits. During that apprenticeship, he once brought home potassium permanganate to be used on my face and chest, after it had been left in the dew overnight, to treat my lotta or shifting clouds, and the treatment was successful.

I know that he got a job in town and was in Victoria years after that as a road officer. He ended his career back in Carriacou as the chief road officer. I think he resigned, probably shy of the retirement age, when the Maurice Bishop led the New Jewel Movement coup-d'état that dislodged the Gairy government from power.

I further remember John for some of his sayings, such as "I've lived to see that my last brother is a doctor, and now I can die," and "One can sip a glass of water and successfully imagine it to be wine."

This leads me to a lighter moment. A priest was very often in a bar where he would consume his favourite wine. On one occasion, the bishop unexpectedly and surprisingly entered and expressed his dismay. The priest looked at his glass and asked the bishop, "Are you responsible for this? A second ago, this was water. Bless the Lord. Bless you." There was no Mary in this story.

I understand that during his active life, John had made arrangements for his death. His body was to be cremated and the ashes scattered in the sea at the Point (Tarleton) in Mt. Pleasant. When he did become very ill, he fully rejected any effort anyone made to get him to seek medical attention and possible treatment on a larger island. I am led to believe that, so far, we Brathwaites have accepted the inevitability of death with calm resolve.

In his heyday, he espoused the belief that Godwin was a real man, but Nicholas was a coward. And yet, on his death bed in the hospital, he told Godwin off because Godwin had not deeded the land and shop to him.

John Albert, indeed, a no-nonsense man, died 24 August 2004. I always felt good in his presence and was proud to know him as a brother.

THY DAILY BREAD: LET US EAT

Even though there were other industries, most English Caribbean islands, Carriacou in particular, were primarily agricultural in those days of my youth. The rainy or wet season usually started after April, usually in late May into June. It was not predictable in arrival and had changeable patterns, but it was eagerly awaited every year.

The elder experts of our village would sense or prophesy its onset and would loudly proclaim, "Season come," or "Season start." Woe betide the family who, without that sage advice, was misled by the first rains, planted all their seeds, and subsequently lost their wilted crops in the sun-dried soil.

Most produce was harvested between August and September with the onset of the dry season. During this time, many an animal, though never the pigs, would be let loose—we would say, "Lehgo animals"—to forage for their own food. Too often, they would cause annoyances and problems for those farmers who had not yet reaped.

I seem to recall that the Roman Catholic and Anglican churches would have so-called corn harvests to coincide with the reaping of the corn during which parishioners would make contributions to the churches. Their purpose was to give thanks but also to raise funds. They also held fairs and bazaars. Thanksgiving was in the air and may not have been based on a specific date, like in some other places.

Grenada was much more fertile than Carriacou, and we depended on the supplies that relatives or friends sent us from there or that were imported and sold in local produce stalls. Eventually, the Grenada Marketing Board established an outlet store in Carriacou—that land of ours that, despite having ample arable land, just seemed drier because of receiving less rain and because of that hot sun.

Our meals were prepared from locally grown goods combined with imported ones. The imported goods included flour, rice, sugar (mainly brown), onions, and preserved foodstuff, such as corned beef, salted pork and beef, and salted fish (codfish).

Some of the adjectives we used to describe meats in the local talk were shortened. So, for example, the word *salted* became *salt*, and *corned*, *corn*.

The local foods were primarily grown in gardens from subsistence farming. If there was a bumper crop, the extra dried corn would be stored in the loft of the kitchen to be grated when needed so as to extract the seeds. The pods of dried pigeon peas were stored in an enclosure in the third compartment of our kitchen.

When it was time for them to be used, the required amount of pods would be put into a crocus bag and beaten with a log to pop open the pods and loosen the pea seeds. The mixture would then be sifted in the wind by holding one basket containing the pods and pea seeds up high and transferring them to another basket or large pan below.

The cooking utensils were primarily made of cast iron, and there were several of different sizes or styles that were appropriate to suit their functions. A few were of aluminium. Plates and cups were made of enamel, but some that we called pan cups were made of tin. Every so often, a tinsmith would visit the villages to repair cups by soldering or to sell new ones.

Besides the fireplace, as already mentioned, there was another useful item—the portable coal pot that used coal for fuel. The coal was obtained locally. To produce coals, persons collected still partly green logs and placed them in a dug pit. They would then set them alight, cover them with earth, and allow them to burn slowly for a few days.

One implement that was present in most homes and shops was a multifunctional opener that was needed to punch holes in cans, cut open sardine tins, pop open drink bottles, and unscrew corks. Modernisation has since made life easier, what with flip-top cans and tins and bottle tops that can be easily unscrewed. However, most corned beef tins seem to have retained the roll-around keys they have always had.

When I think of technological advances, my mind returns to the zipper that replaced buttons at the front of men's pants. God help you if you weren't wearing underpants and, on pulling your pants up after peeing, the zipper caught on something with lax skin. Woy, waie, woieee! I have uttered such more than once.

Breakfast, the meal itself, was also called tea and was served at about eight o'clock in the morning. It included a cup of tea, a term which was applied to any sweetened hot beverage that was made from molten native cocoa balls (flavoured with tonka bean); cinnamon bark or bay leaves (borden leaves) from Grenada; or plant matter obtained from the local and native plants, such as the leaves of lime, black sage, or soursop trees. Beverages made with the latter we referred to as bush tea. Rarely, the local pod-bearing, wild coffee plant provided a mild coffee flavour from its crushed seeds.

The term *tea* also referred to hot beverages made with commercially obtained items, including the canned chocolate drink mixes, Ovaltine and Milo. At times, the tea could even just be some milk added to water, heated to boiling, and sweetened. If cow's milk was not available, we substituted s sweetened condensed or powdered milk. After Hurricane Janet, we used the distributed powdered milk, but Klim was always available.

Instead of this primarily liquid beverage, the tea may have consisted of bon pat (burned pot) from the previous day's coocoo, which was purposely partly burned at the bottom. For breakfast, this was scraped off the bottom of the pot, added to water and milk, sweetened, and then recooked, resulting in a form of porridge.

Coocoo was a paste-like food that we prepared from corn meal cooked with water and salt. We were not into the coarser grits popular in the southern United States and the Bahamas. We also made porridges from boiled rice, from either green or dried corn meal, from oatmeal, from Cream of Wheat, and from flour (flour pap). The brown sugar that we used may have come from Grenada or another island in the Caribbean.

Whatever the tea, it was served from Sunday to midweek with bread that had been baked on the preceding Saturday. On subsequent days, instead of bread, the tea came with fried or roasted bakes that were usually prepared on the same morning or with some other solid food, including boiled green-corn dumplings and rolled coocoo (leftovers from the previous day's dinner), both of which may be slivered and fried. At times, biscuits were sent from the shop to be served with the tea.

A serving of some kind of meat would go along with the above. This could be sautéed codfish, fried eggs, salt fish cakes, fried local fish, or canned meat, such as corned beef or sardines.

The names of the locally caught fish that I remember are grunt, jack, maryann, doctor, hind, and cacabarry. Cacabarry heads, the flesh of which was rather soft, were Iah's favourite.

I once had at dinner roast bakes together with the tasty, sautéed meat of a stingray prepared by my nephew Jeffrey, a son of John, and had the same meal on another occasion at a restaurant in Anguilla.

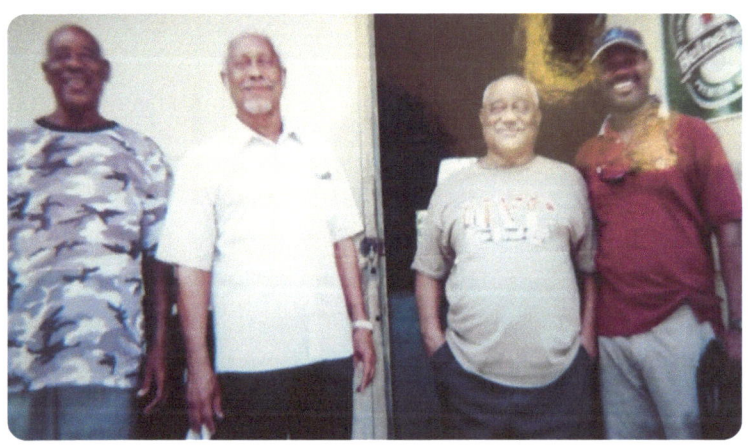

Brothers Lee, Alfred, John, and Jeffrey.

For me, a breakfast treat was the occasional bit of sautéed minced shark meat, sprat, or pisket. Pisket was probably the young of a fish, about an inch long, that swam in large schools near to the shoreline in the calm waters of summer. They were easily gathered with a basket and were rarely used to make fish cakes. This fish was probably the same as what Dominicans called *titiwi*.

Sa ka fete, Dominica!

As far as I recall, no one set out to purposely catch sharks, but they sometimes became entangled in the nets that were set to entrap turtles. We tended to mince the flesh of the shark and sautéed it for breakfast. In Trinidad, I have had filleted shark that was served as a sandwich (shark and bakes) at Maracas Bay, but it is also available at events or throughout the day in roadside shops. It may now be considered strange, though it was not so then, but fisherman would give children lobsters and a box-like fish called cuffs that resembled coffins whenever they were caught. These would then be roasted in an open fire by the young boys.

This is not done anymore, and they are now rather expensive items. The last time I ate cuff was at a get-together at a home in Tortola circa 2007.

Other than being caught in the nets, turtles were occasionally captured when they came on land to lay their fertilised eggs in the sand. When caught, the turtles could be slaughtered and sold locally, but they commanded a better price when exported.

The fertilised eggs were enclosed within a soft white shell. The unfertilised were yellowish and round but had no shell; they were obtained from within the turtle. When collected, both were usually boiled in salted water and consumed as snacks.

When I was stationed in Suriname in the late 1970s, I went with my family and friends, including Paul Yvel and his lady, on a weekend visit to French Guiana, and we were served fried turtle eggs at breakfast. An extremely severe case of gastroenteritis ensued the following day.

In speaking of meats, as mentioned before, we referred to salted or corned meats as *salt* or *corn*, dropping that *-ed* ending. A favourite meat of mine was, and still is, salt fish (salted codfish).

Much later in life, after I had spent two weeks in Newfoundland, Canada, as a young doctor, it was joked when I returned home that I was the only Grenadian who had ever seen a salt fish head. That was because salt fish was exported without the heads.

Before its preparation as a meal, the salted fish, locally prepared or imported, first had to be desalted by soaking it in water. It could then be used in different ways. When sautéed with onions and sweet peppers in vegetable oil or butter to make a souse, it would be served, especially with bakes, as the breakfast meat or as a midday meal, together with provisions or rice. Sometimes it was served at dinner. It was also just used as the meat in soups.

Sautéed salt fish mixed with boiled eggs is part of brunch on special occasions in some Caribbean islands. In this regard, the islands of Bermuda (which is not Caribbean) and Dominica stand out prominently in my mind.

The provisions included underground tubers, such as yams, sweet potatoes, tannia, and dasheen, as well as green bananas, breadfruit, and bluggoe, which is a type of banana that in some countries is called a hog banana. Not all families ate bluggoe, as it was thought of as a poor relative of a plantain fit only for the hogs. Presently, I consume lots of it from my backyard in Freeport.

Other forms of preparation, especially for dinner, included stripping the desalted salt fish into small pieces, and seasoning them, and serving them with stirred-in olive oil without further cooking. I have since had it minced and prepared as a patty. And my, my, salt fish cakes composed of the shredded fish mixed with flour and herbal seasonings and deep fried are absolutely delicious.

Salt fish and breadfruit were once considered poor man's food, but now they are rather expensive items, especially the salt fish. Fortunately, breadfruit is fairly abundant, coming from Grenada.

Both are ingredients in oil down, the national dish of Grenada. We should be thankful to Captain Bligh of the HMS Bounty for bringing the plants from Tahiti to the Caribbean to use the fruit as bread for the slaves. I am of the view that sweet potato was preferred over breadfruit in Carriacou.

It is now customary to obtain salt fish as a souse in local restaurants or as a sandwich at the roadside, especially at crowded events. In that, it is somewhat reminiscent of the hot dogs more popular elsewhere, like Coney Island in New York and at baseball stadiums in the USA. In recent times, a lady has begun selling this meal boat side near the *Osprey*, the scheduled boat between Carriacou and Grenada, before its early-morning departure from the wharf in Grenada.

For our lunch, imported foodstuffs were supplied from the shop and included flour, which usually came in Robin Hood bags (flour bags); rice and sugar in bags; and corned or salted meats, such as beef and pork, in large tins. Of course, meat from our locally slaughtered animals and fish was salted and sun-dried as well, and every so often, one would spot the larvae of house flies in the cooked food.

Therefore, our meats included those that were primarily imported, preserved in tins or salted and dried; fresh or salted meat from our farm animals; and the meat of sea creatures. We had conch, eel, and sea egg from the sea only rarely and the odd piece of porpoise more rarely still. Sea eggs were much more popular in Grenada as a part of breakfast.

The St Vincent Grenadine Islands were known for the harpooning of whales, and we sometimes got whale oil from them. I do not remember what we used it for, and neither do I recall eating the meat.

Though not always, the meats were usually steamed or stewed in well-seasoned sauces that were prepared with varied items, like onions and ochroes, the later fresh or sometimes sun-dried or parched and then ground. The meats, especially if tough, were parboiled, seasoned, and put away safely for the next day's meal.

It was my understanding that the rice we bought was imported to Grenada from British Guiana and sold in the local stores in town. Not all stores carried the same items, but the main business stores in Hillsborough were W. E. Julien and Granby's, both branches from Grenada, and the locally owned S.C. Jacobs and Joseph Brothers. The Joseph brothers, Innocent and Garnet, will be mentioned again.

In the imported rice, it was usual to find many small, broken, partly blackened grains not unlike cariously eroded teeth. Those who cared picked those out and washed the rice before cooking. Some persons couldn't care less.

Not unusually, we children would say a thank you for Uncle Ben's long grain rice, just as we did for refined granulated white sugar.

Lunch was prepared and ready by the 12 p.m.–1 p.m. school break. As boys, we ate perhaps hurriedly, hoping to return to play games in the school grounds before the afternoon sessions began. Ours was always a cooked meal and was, as indicated, made from a combination of local and imported produce. It provided the needed carbohydrates, proteins, fats, other nutrients, bulk, and fibre for nutrition and good bowel movement.

Some items were cooked either separately or combined—for example, rice and peas (known as "peas and rice" in the Bahamas), coocoo and ochro, and coocoo and peas (coocoo poi). Beans were substituted for peas as was convenient. Sometimes most items would be cooked together in soup or as a one-pot meal. Although the dish was not as popular in Carriacou as in Trinidad, we occasionally had chicken mixed with rice and other ingredients—a dish we called pelau, a cousin of paella.

When Godwin and Nicholas in particular lived, at different times, in Mt. Pleasant, we younger ones took home-cooked food to them, either to the school's residence or to the Simmonds estate house in Nehgah Hill. For the latter, we would cut through the periphery of the Mt. Pleasant burial ground, maybe with haste but never truly in fear. If the food was tasty, I expected them to leave a small portion in the dish for me.

It was on one of my visits to Simmonds house—on a Saturday, I think—that I first ate oysters, which grew on mangrove tree roots in the coastal sea of Harvey Vale. Someone had brought them to Godwin, and he kindly allowed me to have a few with a squeeze of lime juice. I enjoyed them.

Lunch would be cooked early when Lysander, John, or Gilbert left in the mornings for work. They took the food with them in what we called stacked carriers and ate at a friend's house near to the work site.

My sister Balvina (Sarah) once told me that when Godwin taught at Hillsborough School near to the town, she, then a young girl, would carry his lunch during her lunch break at Mt. Pleasant School, running all the way up Top Hill and then down the houseless, wooded north side of the Belair Hill. I believe that that occurred before I was born or when I was only a baby.

Rarely, between lunch and dinner (supper), we had a prepared sweetened beverage—now and then, Iah's eggnog—a bottled sweet drink with a cracker (biscuit) or piece of cake, or even a fish broth. On Saturdays, if I was hungry, Iah would put some sugar in my hand and offer a biscuit or two dabbed with butter. We did not have, as I later experienced in Grenada, an expected tea at 4 p.m.

High teas were welcomed ceremonies that were usual in Grenada. They were organised by different groups, primarily to raise money, and dress was fashionable, with the ladies in hats and gloves. I also experienced them as run by churches in the Bahamas and at tourist sites in Jamaica. My last high tea was in 1998 at a resort called Strawberry Hill in Jamaica.

Dinner was a scaled-down version of lunch but was a separate cooked meal, except on Sundays, when more than enough food was prepared at lunch so as to have some for later. It ought to be appreciated that leftover food was kept at the fireside so that it remained a bit warm, but invariably, such food was eaten cold. It was most unusual to light another fire.

On Sundays, later in the evening, one might have been offered a sweet drink, juice from canned grapefruit or orange concentrate imported from Trinidad, or fruit cocktail served with a piece of cake from Saturday's baking. As said, a small piece from a milk chocolate bar was always appreciated.

During school vacations, the older boys would pick limes and juice them for a drink, especially after returning from working the land in the hot sun. The drink ought not to be too strong, for otherwise it would cut their nature, or so it was said. Locally, we referred to these as juices rather than drinks or fruit-ades.

When any food was delicious, it was not unusual to share Iah's, even if one had already eaten. At times Iah shared a bit reluctantly, but the food on her plate always seemed to taste even better. On the other hand, if she became aware that I had given the dogs most of the food I did not like, she would then force-feed me hers. Her spoon was a special one which that been found washed up on the beach with the letters *USN* engraved on the handle.

Back then, whether one liked a meal or not, one was coerced into eating it, especially under Iah's influence. No other food would have been available anyhow. Somehow, I think one of my adult male siblings received special meals other than the main one but only for a spell, maybe because he was ill. My memory falters on this.

Iah was an excellent cook, and Alethea was not too bad. When we went for a long period without a maid or servant, Iah prepared the lunch in the shop using a two-burner kerosene stove. And if the elders were out, Iah would occasionally send me to the house from the shop in the interest of time with what was to be cooked for dinner, first giving me explicit instructions on at least starting the cooking.

Iah was known for making a delicious eggnog with milk, eggs, and stout sweetened and garnished with nutmeg and a little added rum. She would serve it as a post-lunch beverage. I was led to understand that later in life, she drank a bit more of the Jack Iron, which she had begun keeping at her bedside.

In spite of everything, with some meals enjoyed and some forced-fed, I was not considered in those days to be a big eater, and my body was physically lean. As was said locally, I was pooro (skinny). I offer the following as a form of explanation.

As noted, it was not at all unusual to be bruised, stuck, or cut by sharp items such as broken glass bottles, nails, bits of metal scattered around, and picka (thorny) plants. That caused some of us to develop sores and ulcers on our feet and lower legs. Particularly so affected were Balvina, Lysander, sometimes George, and definitely me.

I now wonder whether or not this made us, especially me, sometimes sickly or may even have contributed to a weak appetite. Dependably, Iah would attend to these with daily cleansing and dressings with aloes, among other stuff.

As a kid, there were some meals I did not enjoy at home, including coocoo and ochro (okra). I also had no great liking either for rice served with the steamed local fish. I did not enjoy coocoo, for to me, it was tasteless, and the accompanying ochro (swivel-stick) sauce was too slimy. But later in life, after I had left Carriacou, I grew to enjoy coocoo served with the separately cooked steamed ochro and flavoured with fresh or salted fish or salted beef, particularly if this was prepared by my sister Adeline. In Grenada, when Adeline cooked, even a simple dish of white rice was so tasty that it could have been fed to me daily. Now, no matter who cooks it, I can eat boiled white rice every day.

Permit me to restate that coocoo was a meal made from finely milled dried corn, which, like the ground green corn, was also used to make porridge for breakfast. The coocoo was usually served paste-like but was, on occasion, served rolled into balls. As mentioned already, when done at home, the balls were saved for the next day to be sliced and fried for breakfast. Otherwise, the partly burnt coocoo remnants were scraped away from the pot's bottom and combined with milk, water, and sugar to make bonpat (burn pot) tea, a form of cereal, the following morning.

The corn meal was also used to make corn bread, and when combined with other ingredients to make a congealed pasty mix, it was wrapped in portions of banana leaves and steamed, produced a sweet-tasting snack named conkie.

For festive or other particular occasions, the coocoo and rice were both served rolled into balls. Altogether, people were inventive. Some improved the coocoo by cooking it with pigeon peas to give coocoo poi, while in Barbados, it was cooked with added ochro and served with their famous flying fish. Flying fish was also present in Grenadian waters, and in flying, they sometimes landed in the row boats.

As said, I eventually grew to enjoy the coocoo meals, but I was always a lover of soups—any soup, especially with peas or beans—with ground provisions and, as a must, dumplings, whether they were made only from flour or from flour mixed with corn meal. The watery soup called san coach (in Latin America, *sancoche*) was also a tasty favourite of mine. Any day now, I can be fed ochro soup with salted meat and dumplings (called dough in the Bahamas), and I will eat it with absolute, total delight and enjoyment.

We made three types of dumplings: a long, finger-like dumpling made by rolling the dough in the palm; a round, ball-like one; and a broad duff, spread and flattened by the fingers and palms. Everyone expected at least one broad dumpling in their serving. It had a resilient consistency on chewing it, and the tougher the better. It filled one and caused bloating but was enjoyed. Don't look for the dog when borborygmi and its foul gaseous discharges followed; the dog is under the house. So, each person looked around and at each other if it was not obvious from whence the stench originated.

The Bahamian dumpling tended to be a flat, shapeless, and a rather soft mass. The word *duff* may have been a variation of *dough* but, in an oft confusing handed-down or passed-on language, was pronounced as one would the word *rough*.

It is just as confusing as one house, two houses, but one mouse, two mice. What about driving on the parkway but parking in the driveway? I oft wonder why my grandparent is older than I but all my grand nephews and nieces are younger. Is grand both great and minor?

It must be appreciated that what I have described was not the norm for all families, as there were, of course, variations depending on occupation, work schedule, and financial capability. Cousin Flora (Fowah), our immediate uphill neighbour already mentioned in the hurricane story, usually left for her fields before daybreak and returned after about 4 p.m. or even later, for the probably primary and maybe only meal of the day.

I must admit that if I ever did enjoy the dish that was normally distasteful to me in my youth, coocoo with fish and ochro, it would have been when it was prepared by that family. The older lady, Yahyah, the primary cook who ate from a calabash with her fingers, must have had a special touch.

The day for some villagers began with going to their gardens after the third crowing of the fowl cocks. Breakfast, prepared by others at home would be brought to them. At times, persons were fooled, mistaking which crow it was and leaving home too early, especially if a moon brightened the night. That resulted in longer work hours.

Not unlike elsewhere, sugar and salt were perhaps our predominant tastes. Consequently, other than cancer, the main medical conditions that we heard of were high blood pressure and sugar in the blood. With cancer, whatever its cause and whichever organ it grew in, it seemed that when someone was diagnosed, the doctor's prognosis was that the person had either three or six months to live. Perhaps with this on the mind of the patient and caretakers, the prognostication was often allowed to be proven correct.

An old joke went that an ill-nourished man was told by the doctor that he lived too far from the kitchen. So, he moved his kitchen closer to the house—LOL.

When death came, the person was invariably at home. If a person went at all into the hospital, the illness would have been of short duration. There were no nursing homes or hospices. But at home, one was not alone. Family and neighbours were at hand, and friends visited more often. It was then that one made post-death plans. Occasionally, the doctor would be requested to make a home visit, at a standard cost.

I feel certain that there was a poor house reserved for the destitute, but most families cared for their own and even others. It is my understanding that there is now an old folks' home in Top Hill.

Life was moving smoothly along, but at some stage of my early youth, I became aware, mainly from hearing it at home, that things were becoming tough. I somehow gathered that this resulted from a war, wherever that was taking place.

But as previously noted, on the inner eastern wall of our home were two framed objects, one being a photograph of Iah and her sister Loonie as young ladies and the other, of greater relevance then, being the speech by Winston Churchill. "We will fight on the seas and oceans … we will never surrender."

We reread it quite often. Hooray for Great Britain in the war. That was our country, even if not "my own dear land, where'er my footsteps wander … dear land that gave me birth."

But in Carriacou, the pinch was being felt. For example, dinner was no longer a separate cooked meal but instead consisted of leftovers from lunch; alternatively, the food may have been cooked later in the day and served as the only afternoon meal.

What seemed before to be the usual for others now befell my family, as we began using flour bags to sew underpants for the bigger boys. I cannot remember at what age I began wearing underpants and socks—most likely as a teenager in high school.

Not by bread alone!

Nevertheless, some fished, most farmed, and everyone ate.

During the day, it was not unusual to see these strange large objects that we called Zeppelins. They flew very low in the sky, which enticed us children to pelt stones at them, but we stopped when we were warned in the village that the soldiers in them may shoot at us.

Although not fully understanding, I became aware that there was an explosion in the village of Windward around that same time. Eventually, the story became clearer. Some individuals had attempted to open a structure found floating at sea, which they thought contained money. It exploded, resulting in the death of multiple persons, for it was a mine from the war.

SPECIFIC EVENTS AND OCCASIONS: BONHOMIE

Carriacou has become known for certain planned and recurring activities, some of which the slaves brought with them from Africa, some of which came from the cultures of Europe, and some of which perhaps originated in these new homelands. Here, they are presented not in order of prominence or importance but only as they come to me in writing.

For these events, most of the villages may be hoping, if not singing, "You are my sunshine, my only sunshine … Please don't take my sunshine away."

Especially if feeling, "hot, hot, hot".

Carnival

I refer first to carnival, which was a two-day Caribbean event on the Monday and Tuesday preceding Ash Wednesday. This pre-Lenten celebration was brought from elsewhere and may have become an approved fun-day event for the slaves, but they adapted it to poke fun at the landlords.

Sometimes, on the preceding Saturday and Sunday, there were small, isolated activities termed *camboulays* in which boys and men engaged in a sport of playful stick-dancing fights, and at our home, small dishes, such as fried bakes, were prepared in the yard on the coal pot.

In Carriacou, on the Monday there was "Ole Mas", called Jouvay (J'Ouvert) elsewhere. For this, hideous cardboard face masks and head gear with attached cow horns were created and worn, together with dresses or other articles of clothing, so that the wearers resembled devils. The men or bigger boys, usually moving in groups of two or three, were frighteningly unrecognizable, so even when we younger ones, also in groups, participated, they would scare us off.

The cry, for money, was, "Way lay, way lay lambay, I want a cent, jab-jab, to pay de devil, jab-jab, to go to hell, jab-jab, and if you don't pay me, jab-jab, you go to hell." The leader would intonate whilst the others interjected with the jab-jab chants.

The groups would move from dwelling to dwelling and house to house, and if not paid, they would attempt to inflict some form of punishment on the occupants, such as throwing tar or paint on them that was usually removable but that sometimes necessitated a visit to the beach. Fortunately, this was rarely done, but it seemed harsh compared to the little that was being requested.

On Tuesday, there was "pretty mas" (masquerade). Prior to that, there would be guesses and gossiping in the village as to who the individual performers, invariably male, would be. The identity of participants was supposed to remain hidden up to and even on the day itself. But early in the morning, around seven o'clock, each would announce himself from a vantage point, though I don't think by name.

My brother Gilbert announced himself to Grand Bay from atop our cistern step and to Mt. Pleasant from another vantage point near to the kitchen. Lysander may also have once played, but I am uncertain of this.

On one occasion, I sponsored Wilcome, my friend, but we had difficulty finding shoes that fitted him. He needed maybe size 12, but we settled for a lower size. On his first jump, the shoes split wide open, but he had no choice but to keep them on.

Each player wore a fancy, commercially made, colour-variegated wire mask, together with a locally tailored, multicoloured, long, dressy skirt-like outfit that was adorned with silk, lace, mirrors, and bells, which jingled with every fanciful step, prance, or jump.

In each village, the participants acted out their parts as they walked towards a village square, which for us was Tan Dorah's Junction, to compete against each other. Throughout, the onlookers cheered, jeered, and encouraged them on.

The entire event eventually became known as "Shakespeare Mas" because, although each player may recite and display, the competition alternated between one mas-man and another and took the form of a challenge to recite passages or speeches from the play *Julius Caesar*.

When one so challenged answered, the other would respond with words of encouragement, like, 'Yes, me boy,' if right, but if wrong, he was told to go back and come again. If that person was deemed to have given consistently wrong responses, he would have to break for his crown—that is, protect it.

The crown was a beautifully crafted barrier that was made of cardboard reinforced and toughened with paint or animal skin and that covered the back of the head and upper back, a necessary protection against the blows from a bull pistle. If this was overdone or if the blow landed improperly, a real fight would ensue that would have to be broken up by older men or guards.

The fight would sometimes be a means to settle old grievances, as the players came to recognise each other.

Unrelated to carnival, in order to avenge a grievance, a man, having planned, would confront another man and lash him with a bull pistle. It is said that the first stroke freezes the victim, but after additional blows, he could easily win an Olympic sprint event. Some were known to impose their vengeance by using the flat of their cutlasses to planass someone.

Eventually, a king would be chosen to represent the village in a competition against other kings, although all the players were

SPECIFIC EVENTS AND OCCASIONS: BONHOMIE

allowed to compete against an opposing other. In our case, our king would compete first against Mt. Royal. The two villages would then combine to form the eastern group.

The end result for Carriacou, in my youth, was a gathering of two bands—the Heroes from the east and the Bon Roi from the south—consisting of all participants and other villagers. We would meet in the town of Hillsborough for the grand finale, which was meant to take the form of challenges and responses, though it was seemingly accepted that eventually, a melee would most probably result.

However, the air was one of festivity for all ages. As Iah's family members, we moved around separately but homed at Charles Cayenne's shop in the town. You may recall that Cousin Charles and his family were our next-door neighbours to the east.

I last saw the spectacle in 2011. The band from the east was led into town by colourfully dressed women singing, "Who in the way, clear out the way, because the Heroes coming down."

Of course, with time, in order to accommodate the increasing numbers of visitors, including the diaspora, the carnival activities have become better organised and well defined. They extend over more days, are run by government-aided committees, and include preliminary events, such as beauty contests for women to be judged to be the new carnival queen and calypso-singing contests to determine a new calypso king.

On the Tuesday afternoon, there is now a parade of competing colourfully costumed dancing bands, each supposedly portraying a theme and accompanied by appropriate music. There is fun and full action for and by all.

During the competition, the competing troupe remains intact for the judging, but later, as most get into the action, band members and all others become amalgamated. Unlike in the past, when the dancingly walking musicians were at the same street level as all the dancing and wining participants, the music is now blasted live or from tapes played atop big trucks, on which are scantily costumed young ladies, doing their bodily gyrations—in other words, temptingly wining.

Because of the large emigration of Caribbean peoples, there are now carnival events elsewhere with diasporic origins—for example, Toronto's Caribana (now called the Toronto Caribbean Carnival) on the first weekend in August, Brooklyn's festival on Labour Day, the first Monday in September (which I have attended many times), and London's Notting Hill Carnival in the last weekend of August.

Many years removed from my youth, during my pathology residency training in Ottawa, I got dreadfully sick while attending the festival in Toronto from the bad wine that we were drinking on one of the Toronto islands, which we had gone to by ferry for the events. It was "Pucks" McCauley, a doctor from Grenada, who took me in hand and led me to the toilet, where I vomited my guts out.

Perhaps partly in a bid to attract foreigners, some Caribbean islands have chosen dates other than the Monday and Tuesday before Lent for their carnival-like activity, knowing they could not compete with the dominance of Trinidad, the mecca of Caribbean carnival.

From 1953 to 1961, I enjoyed carnival in Grenada, where the events seemed perhaps better organised than they were at that time in Carriacou. They consisted of Dimanche Gras on Sunday, jab-jab on Monday morning, the competitive parade of costumed bands, the late-afternoon and evening street dancing, and the music of steel bands. Shakespeare Mas was peculiar to Carriacou.

Perhaps for the reason given above and probably sometime in the 1980s, carnival in Grenada was moved to a new date in August. No matter when it happened, what original began as a two-to-three-day event has progressed to many days of related but varied aspects of the celebration.

Barbados has a harvest-based carnival-type activity called Crop Over or Kadooment. Though also rooted in slavery, it is totally unrelated to the original pre-Lenten carnival show. Members of the Lucaya cricket team travelled to the show one year. Vivian went with me. We were then married and living in an apartment in Freeport, Bahamas.

In addition to the carnival-like activities, such as those taking place before lent in Dominica (Domnik Mas), in July in St Lucia, at the end June to July in St Vincent (Vincy Mas), and in July to August in Antigua, many Caribbean countries hold other festivals throughout the year for different reasons.

There are music festivals such as the World Creole Music Festival of Dominica in October, the Festival of lights in St Lucia, and Nine Mornings in St Vincent at Christmas time, as well as Junkanoo in the Bahamas. This last mentioned, competitively held during the Christmas season (on Boxing and New Year's Days) has vastly improved from what I first observed and participated in in 1968 and has outmatched the similar event in Jamaica.

Most countries also have festivities around their independence holidays.

Because of my travels, I have been fortunate enough to have seen and participated in either the entire carnival event or just parts of it not only in Carriacou and Grenada but also in Trinidad, Dominica, Tortola, and Brooklyn more than once and in St Lucia, St Vincent, Barbados, St Martin, and Toronto at least once.

It was indeed a joy to have once witnessed the stage performances of the steel bands in the Queen's Park Savannah, Port of Spain,

Trinidad. Steelpan music, though performed in other territories, originated in and remains closely linked to the island of Trinidad.

Obviously, it is possible to be serious at work but to let loose, Caribbean style, at times. And never the twain must mix, à la Kipling.

In a more genteel and at times jocular way, Da James, that man from my village, did just that, exuding a jubilant spirit.

Too much skylarking at work has been the cause of low productivity in some countries, particularly but not solely within the public service.

Carnival precedes the forty days of lent, which end at Easter. For us in Carriacou, Lent necessitated proper behaviour—no cursing, no lying, and no stealing. Some persons practised a rite on Good Friday. At 6 a.m., the white from an egg was placed in a glass of water, and it was observed again at noon. The egg was expected to produce one of three interpretative patterns for the person: a church for marriage, a boat for travel, and a coffin for death, hopefully someone else's.

Regatta

Another event in Carriacou and elsewhere was held on Fisherman's Day. It involved beach activities, flowers, and dressed-up rowboats. Of course, most events always seemed to involve the cooking of food, free or for sale; different activities, such as playing for the children and cards or dominoes for the elders; and the consumption of booze. In other words, fete for so!

Linton Rigg, a white man who owned the Mermaid Tavern in town, was responsible for exploding Fisherman's Day into the now well-established Carriacou Regatta, which has associated activities taking place over a few days during the Emancipation Day holiday beginning at the end of July. I never really followed the boat races but have always enjoyed seeing the plaiting of the Maypole, the donkey race, and the walking or climbing of the greasy pole.

Of the last two Fisherman's Days I attended, one took place when I was stationed in Dominica in the early 1980s and mainly involved partying at a home near to a river, and the other took place in March, 1997 and consisted of a small, outdoor open event in Petite Martinique, though it was called a regatta.

Regattas are fairly common throughout the Caribbean, and in the Bahamas, there are drawing cards on several of the islands, particularly on the Out Islands, like Exuma.

Christmas

Christmastime was always festive and momentous for us. Before the day itself, the house was spruced up with new blinds or curtains, the chairs were varnished anew, and a new roll of linoleum was laid on the floor.

Sometime before the actual day, in a tradition we always awaited, different carolling or hosanna bands would go from house to house in the early nights serenading the inhabitants with songs, not always carols, interspersed with short, oft repeated speeches that ended with "for Christmas comes but once a year, and every man must have his share". They did not know too many songs, but other than the traditional carols, I remember them singing, Dare to be a Daniel. Dare to stand alone. Dare to have a purpose firm and dare to make it known."

The master of the home may either intervene in short order so he could return to his needed rest or purposely allow the show to be prolonged so that the money to be given would have been earned. I would imagine that the monies were distributed proportionally, maybe just before the Christmas day itself.

Small bands of persons colourfully clad and holding musical instruments usually serenaded on the day itself, going from house to house and at times into adjacent villages. Particular homes, like the doctor's residence, the great house of the district officer in Belair, and the home of the legendary Mr. Frederick J. Paterson in Belvedere, would be targeted because it was known that worthwhile gifts, especially money, would be obtained.

Mr. Frederick "Fred" Paterson, who was of a lighter complexion, was well known in the arena of politics. Whenever I'm in Carriacou, I spend time in his son Bill's store in town, where folks, most from abroad, often gather on the back patio to pass time chatting, relieving the past, pappyshowing each other, and firing one—or as Curtis McIntosh would say, having a beverage.

In the cool of the late afternoon, the bigger boys would organise a band to parade the streets from upper Grand Bay to the far ends of Mt. Pleasant, almost to Tarleton Point, or as far as the home of Gerald McIntosh and back again. They would play more lively music, to which people danced, some in the front and some in the back of the band.

Children, all clad in their new and colourful clothes, enjoyed themselves blowing balloons, playing with toys, and eating anything and everything available but often just cakes and candies. When I attended school in Grenada, I would leave during Christmas season for vacation in Carriacou with a chain-operated motorbike or car or a view master as my toy, purchased by myself. The vehicles never lasted the entire vacation, often, like clocks, from been overwound.

Some aspects of the above were usually repeated on New Year's Day but downscaled. It was joyous, and we all had fun. At the end of day, one often heard, "Christmas done and gone, till next year again."

It is my understanding that particularly for greater visitor enticement and entertainment, a parang festival now precedes Christmas in Carriacou.

At our home there was a Christmas routine. A pig would have been reared to be slaughtered, providing us with meat not just for us to eat for the season but also to sell and acquire some money. Expectedly and without doubt, Iah would be in charge. She would estimate, I imagine with help, the pig's weight and would have her prepared list of committed buyers.

The pig was slaughtered by her chosen villagers, often with Bastapool in charge and he would be the one who would accurately plunge the dagger into the animal's heart to collect the blood while it still pumped. The other individuals assisted in holding it down. One such would be Uncle Darrell. This occurred at home a few days before Christmas, starting at about four o'clock in the morning.

The shades of the lighted lanterns would begin to blacken from the flames being too high; search lights would be glowing, and the kitchen and yard would be ablaze with fire for boiling water, necessary to completely shave the dead pig, in large pots and tins. After the boiling water was poured over the pig, they would cover it with crocus bags for a while to retain the heat. On their removal, the shavers would go to work.

The collected blood was then prepared as a delicious, especially sautéed dish to be eaten as a part of breakfast with added portions of the heart, liver, and kidneys. The meat was then taken to the shop to be sold, first to the already committed customers and then to some latecomers, who may obtain meat but certainly not the choice portions or the amount requested. Portions of the gastrointestinal tract, which we all called tripe, would be kept, but some of it was given to others. It was usually used in soups.

One of us boys would be given the pig's urinary bladder, which would be first rolled in ashes and then used as a balloon. It never lasted beyond that day. This was, for a child, a pre-Christmas gift.

Iah was known to prepare a mean baked pork, usually on the following day. Some portions of the meat would be salted and sun-dried for preservation. This went well with peas and rice or in pigeon pea and dumpling soup, both cooked with coconut milk. As already stated, it was not unusual to have to skim off a floating dead larva from the pot.

We always bought a salted, partly cured leg of ham which had to be boiled for hours and which was stored for many days. It would be sliced and usually served at breakfast with bread, as sandwiches, or as the meat in soups.

Our main Christmas dinner was mutton soup, with added provisions, dumplings, and barley, and it was usually served with the recently baked bread. The meat was from one of our sheep, slaughtered that same morning.

It was always a wonder to me that if in danger, a goat would bleat as loudly as possible and even fight back, but a sheep made not a sound when led to the slaughter nor offered any resistance to an attack, for example, by dogs.

It must be mentioned that when a ram goat was being slaughtered, the butcher had to know how to remove the testicles without contaminating the rest of the meat so as to avoid it being said to have rank smell and taste.

Also special were Christmas cakes, whether sponge, pound, or, best of all, fruit, and also the customary buns, maybe with an icing topping. Our fruits in fruit cake were raisins and currants. The Grenadian fruit cake is called black cake. Other baked sweets included coconut tarts and drops, and the drinks were either bottled soft or sweet drinks or homemade sorrel and ginger beer.

Island Tours

Within our village, without question, my mother was a known organiser for many an event. So, for example, when boats came from the Vincentian Grenadine Islands to Mt. Pleasant Beach with bags of sweet potatoes, she assumed the role of leader, got her group together to contribute towards payment for a bag, and then distributed the potatoes equally.

In a similar vein, she organised island tours.

I loved island tours. These were usually events with genesis in different villages. They were undertaken with the intention of visiting most of the island in a day as a group, with appropriate stops for relaxation, music, singing, dancing, eating, and drinking.

Iah was known to choose her friends well. Her invited villagers paid their fees and, though expecting to be entertained, were themselves expected to be active participants. Although being paid, the music band and the owner of the truck would contribute energetically. My mother was a step-dancer of regal grace, whilst most others demonstrated a more gyrating and wining style.

The hired truck was converted to a bus with partly opened sides but with an attached, rolled-up tarpaulin to be let down in the unlikely case of rain. Of course, we hoped for a sunny, breezy, not too hot day.

In my time, the band, usually a five-piece, was led by Cousin Bert Cyrus and later by his son, Doyle, on the violin. Other musical instruments included the locally made shak-shak (a sealed can containing seeds), a guitar, a steel triangle, and a grater. Bert Cyrus also owned a small shop.

The route for us started from the shop and then went through Mt. Pleasant and around Tarleton Point to Windward, with a stop along the way. It then continued via Dover to Bogles, with a stop along the way; to town, with a stop; to Six Roads, with a stop; back through the town and up Beausejour to Mt. Royal, with or without a stop; and then back home, either via Grand Bay or Nehgah House, ending at the shop or the nearby Tan Dorah Junction.

The truck was invariably that of Mr. Emmons, until Tobias McIntosh (Cousin Toby) of Mt. Pleasant acquired his truck. My mother had contributed a small sum towards its purchase with the understanding that her family would ride without charge.

Mr. Emmons, who also owned cars, lived in the town and, when necessary, was my mother's dedicated driver. There remained an overall dependency on Mr. Emmons, who was fully trusted as the one who knew how to drive with the care demanded by Sophia Brathwaite. She claimed to suffer from land sickness, but I never saw evidence of this. Perhaps Mr. Emmons was so good at driving her.

Whilst on the road, I would sit in the front of the truck between Iah's legs or to her side. It was during my first tour that I first saw the word *emporium* on the sign of a shop in Bogles. Also, at the next stop in the town, Iah bought cheese for the group. In the store, this was kept as a block on the countertop under a netted basket and sliced and weighed accordingly by the shopkeeper.

Iah told me I would not like it, but at my insistence, she gave me a small piece. She was right, as I promptly spat it out. With age, I grew to enjoy cheese, but back then, I wondered how anyone could eat that sour and even dreadfully smelly stuff.

I twice had similar reactions—once when Lysander, a lover of raw onions, gave me a bite of one and another time when I bit into a raw, very green tomato from the garden of my brother, Godwin, in Nehgah House.

Intravillage Relationships

Somehow, in writing about specific events, the relationships within the village sprung into my mind.

Whenever a car was needed for our family's use, an advanced telephone call would be made from the Mt. Pleasant post office to Mrs Mends, the operator in town, who would then inform Mr. Emmons. Even after his death, the Brathwaites relied on his sons for service.

The first person in the village to own a car, a Chevrolet, was Mr. Theophilus Nelson, who had recently returned from Aruba. Sometime after that, Charles Cayenne, our immediate neighbour, acquired his—a Ford, I think. Both cars, like most other motor vehicles at the time, had to be cranked up in the mornings or pushed for the engine to roll over and start. Even as more cars became available, the majority continued to provide taxi service.

Today, together with jitneys, they jumble up at the airport and seaports, including in St George's, signalling to attract attention.

Customarily, I would be dropped off at a junction and walk the hilly tracks to home. One night, quite tipsy, I slipped and brushed against a zooty plant. The itch was not that bad, however.

For some of my later visits to Carriacou, I made prearrangements with Dunstan, who owned a jitney, for the duration of my stay, but on my last few visits, Betty, my niece, arranged for an ATV to ascend the rugged hill of Kainash to receive me, for I could no longer foot it. For this, Napoleon, a son of Da James, was our main person. He provided the photograph of his father with permission for its publication within this presentation.

SPECIFIC EVENTS AND OCCASIONS: BONHOMIE

Somehow, and for different reasons, vehicles fell off the roads and rolled down the slopes, usually without deaths or serious injuries. However, one of the last that I knew of resulted in the death of Eslan, a villager of Grand Bay.

The most famous location for these mishaps was at a spot on the main road from Top Hill down to town called Sixteen Corner, so named perhaps because the first driver involved in an accident was paying more attention to the sweet 16-year-old female passenger or perhaps because the number of the car was sixteen. More likely, it was simply the sixteenth corner from an established point. It is accepted that it is a tricky corner, requiring full attention.

As negotiating some corners required full attention, it was also likely that drunk drivers may have contributed to some of these accidents. It should also be appreciated that although it was mandatory for one of age to formally take and pass a driver's test, the driving lessons, practice sessions, and instructions were not requirements and were more than likely informally passed on by a relative or friend.

It was in the bushes off Sixteen Corner that I earned a kiss from my then female friend as we were walking back from town to Mt. Pleasant. This lady and I had an on-and-off relationship, and to this day, we remain dear friends.

However, that was not my first kiss, for that had occurred long before with my then girlfriend Rhoda Roberts (mentioned regarding my 1964 vacation in Brooklyn). It happened in the southwest side of Tan Rose's house, where she lived. Although she had just eaten fish, it was a sweet and heavenly kiss. For some time, the memories of her sweet, soft lips and the smell of fish lingered in my mind.

As someone later uttered, "The gladness remains."

Near evening at another time, Rhoda and I had just returned to the village—me riding our donkey back from Dover and Rhoda walking back from Petite Carenage, just beyond Windward. On arriving in Mt. Pleasant, I left the donkey on the side of the road near the corn house of the school and walked with her up the short track to her home, and we kissed.

Tan Rose appeared from nowhere and started slapping Rhoda with both hands. That same lady also gave Rhoda a whipping one summer when many children were at the beach and Rhoda and I were just sitting together.

It was understood that many mothers and guardians trusted not their young girls with the male children of the Brathwaites. Of course, Tan Rose could not touch me, for then she would have had to deal with Iah, who was known then for her attitude of "Complain to me, but don't touch my children."

And yet, in the spirit of togetherness and respect for elders, a child could be chastised by an elder if considered disrespectful or if displaying bad manners, though these occasions were few and far between. Of course, this doctrine of Iah was waived for disciplinary measures at school, even though she was known to have questioned a teacher or two.

In those days, discipline in school usually included a strapping by the head teacher, on the hands of girls and younger boys but on the backsides or across the shoulders of older boys. It has been said that some head teachers toughened the leather straps by soaking it at nights in the pee pail.

Although I was only about ten years old, my relationship with Rhoda was not a mere crush, and it was certainly more than just puppy love. Our affair was encouraged by the involvement of two persons: my younger friend Wilcome, who acted as a messenger and go-between, and Theresa, a neighbour and friend of Rhoda.

In our early days of friendship, I recall saying to Rhoda that no matter what happened, we could never get vexed with each other. For me, this was cemented, for on the bark of the stem of a white cedar tree on Kainash hill, from where I could look down on where she lived near to the school, I had carved, even though not in stone, a heart around our initials. I gave her small bottles of perfume and called her the lily of the valley, for she was "not only my first kiss but also my first love, even though I never knew her."

Incredibly, things somehow changed after I entered GBSS in Grenada at age 11. On returning to Carriacou on the first vacation, I realised that our love was waning even though we continued to see each other. I was led to understand that she was then also seeing Winston Simon, and I, during the vacation, was being attracted to Susana Lang, a sister of Paul, a tailor, to whom I was once apprenticed.

Some few years later, while I was still at GBSS, Rhoda and Joyce, a more recent attraction, came to Grenada representing Carriacou for the interschool athletics. Joyce was a sprinter, and left-handed Rhoda ran the lime-and-spoon race. By the way, Carriacou won the competition, and the team was treated to ice cream at a shop on the Carenage by the coach or manager, my brother Nicholas Brathwaite. At the parlour, I gave a note to Rhoda that said, "You were once my queen, but now, someone else is."

Shortly after, Rhoda left for England.

I'm reminded of perhaps the first ice cream parlour that opened in St George's, Grenada, just opposite the produce market, in my early years at GBSS. At Nick's, one could purchase scoops of chocolate, strawberry, or vanilla ice cream, served in a cone or tub. After a little time, another opened almost directly across the street. They, and certainly other places, sold imported apples over the Christmas season.

The next time I saw Rhoda was in 1964 when we were both visiting Brooklyn, New York. Having learnt that she was going there, I purposely arranged to visit on a summer vacation from the university in Jamaica, hoping to re-establish a love that had gone astray. I tried but did not succeed. When she returned to England, she and Winston wedded. I have been told that they migrated to the USA, where Winston died.

It was some years later that I, travelling for some other reason, again visited her in Brooklyn, where she and her son were then residing. The perhaps nosey Rufina, a girl from Grand Bay to whom strange things happened, was at the apartment and would not leave, preventing any private conversation between Rhoda and me. There will be more said of Rufina.

When I resided in Freeport years later, Rhoda and I spoke a few times on the phone, and she once informed me that Euthaniel "Euthan" Noel, also from Mt. Pleasant and nephew of Hamilton Cyrus, who had a shop, was coming after her. It was not long after, on a visit to Freeport, that Euthan told me that Rhoda had become an alcoholic.

I last saw her in Carriacou, where she had moved permanently into her newly constructed home. This was in July 2012. Some of us, including Rhoda's sister, Pelerine, and Walter McIntosh, my good friend, visited her at her home in Beausejour. We had a brief chat in which we blamed each other for our breakup, which had occurred so many long years before. Although she had gargled with a mouth wash, the stale booze was still on her breath.

It is my understanding that she died in August 2014. Somehow, neither of us ever accepted any responsibility or said sorry for our separation, but then, as has been said, *love means never having to say you're sorry.*

I remind myself of this during most of my affairs with the gentler sex. I never aimed to hurt, but I was certainly not always blameless in this.

By the way, Joyce and I never got far in any kind of relationship.

Allow me to say here that the vast majority of the population of Carriacou were of African descent, but the people in the village of Windward were similar in colour to those of Mt. Moritz in Grenada, being descendants of white people from Scotland and largely remaining so identified for a long time through intermarriages. Most of their surnames began with *Mac* or *Mc*. It was in this village that a mine once exploded.

A very few persons were of other origins, like Portuguese, and there remained a few of Amerindian descent.

I am not aware that colour prejudice was ever of great relevance in Carriacou, but one may hear derogatory statements such as calling a dark-skinned person "black as coals" (to which the response would be "pot calling the kettle black") or calling one with yellowish-red complexion with scattered black spots or even with Amerindian features a "bakenegg".

At times, I used to wonder whether the shit of the queen of England was white.

As a side note, it remains strange to me that the wife of the king of England was called a queen, but if the ruling monarch was a queen, her husband was not called a king but was given another formal title or was called the queen's consort.

Some are more equal. The queen rules.

In looking back, I have the distinct impression that there was generally some degree of social nicety among the villagers. Without doubt, it seemed that many different kinds of events were taking place, and not just the usual recurring ones. There were others as conveniently arranged. Some may have been planned because of somebody's dream or because of the return of a native son or daughter. There are also the family reunions, becoming more and more popular, for which relatives come from all parts of the world.

Many events from small to large were associated with the wetting of the ground. This usually took the form of small amounts of liquor being poured onto the earth, followed by softer drinks or water. The attendees may be merely loosely assembled, or the event may take the form of a line dance led by a man pouring the liquor, followed by the ladies with their soft drinks, all accompanied by traditional music and song, at times with the drums in the background but clearly audible.

Traditionally, individuals also formed finance-related groups, such as benevolent or friendly societies, of long-term duration to assist its members if a need arose, for example, in the case of burials. A shorter-term group was the sou-sou (su-su or asue), which consisted of about six contributing persons. The members collected their lump sums in sequence, perhaps monthly, and usually earmarked the money for doing something special.

There were team sporting events and games, including cricket matches. The format varied. Sometimes the matches were between villages, sometimes between fathers and sons, sometimes between those over and under age 40, and sometimes between men and women, with some form of an advantage given to the women, like righthanded men batting lefthanded.

Other common activities of a competitive but friendly nature were tugs-of-war, rounders (from which the game baseball arose), all fours (a card game of two against two a bit similar to whist, the forerunner of bridge), and netball.

They were competitive, yes, but I now think of them in the same vein as the US All Star contests—friendly battles for bragging rights.

Once, perhaps prior to me leaving for Jamaica—I think I was travelling by boat back home to Carriacou after a short visit to Grenada—I met a man from a below-side village. An argument between us led me to organise an all-fours competition, with his team coming to Mt. Pleasant to compete against us.

We played a ten-table format that was set up in the school and would last for a timed period. The contest ended in a tie. My partner was Gaius Lang. He was not the best of players, but since no one else had chosen him, I was left no choice. Of course, drinks and food, prepared by Verna of Tahnee's house, followed.

There were always concerts and dances being promoted by different groups or agencies. If you could dance the waltz, merengue, calypso, and variations thereof, you were in good stead. The quadrille was danced also but was reserved more so for certain special performances.

Showtime!

In essence, there was a sufficient number, variety, and frequency of activities to prevent boredom. In most activities, there was general participation, but eventually, the games, in particular, became gender based. Men played cricket, and women played rounders and netball. Obviously, some activities had ethnographic significance—cricket came from England, maroon and big drum (Nation Dance) from Africa, and steel drum playing from Trinidad.

Recently, a group from Sierra Leone, West Africa, visited Carriacou to establish ties. It has been documented that many slaves who were brought to Carriacou were originally from Sierra Leone.

Some activities were more personal or family oriented. These included the wakes, which took place on the nights before burials, the rites on the ninth and fortieth nights post death, saraccas that were at times based on dreams, and as already mentioned, family reunions.

Especially for the events that drew crowds, one had to partake to appreciate the specially prepared foods, like the rolled coocoo and rolled rice, the well-seasoned meats that only those cooks knew how to prepare.

This included using the big thyme leaves for *cutting* the freshness of meats, the browning with sugar, and the cooking in huge iron pots that sat atop big rocks in the open air.

It is now my understanding that the annual Carriacou maroon-and-string-band music festival in early August, which follows the Grenada Carnival in July, is run by a committee and is government sponsored. I am not sure that some of these shows recognise their original significance, acknowledging the ancestors and making certain that the children are both welcome and fed—certainly not when they are moved from the villages to town squares and open parks and take place not in the day but at night.

Bomennaire and *bonhomie!*

My brother Gilbert, when in Carriacou from England, was very much involved in the organization and running of the Mt. Pleasant/Grand Bay maroon, I have been told. At one time, each of the two villages had its own maroon, but now they are apparently combined. A few other villages, like Bogles, still have separate maroons. As maroons may have come from Africa, that may be why I never heard of one being held in the village of Windward.

Cosnell "Puntick" McIntosh, a friend of Gilbert, on returning home to Carriacou from England, also involved himself in the promotion of carnival and, both in general and in particular, the restoration of carnival activities in his village, Mt. Pleasant, with a focus on the school children, including the girls.

The last time I saw him was in Mt. Royal in 2011. I was there on the Tuesday of carnival, in which he participated, but I did not recognise him because of his covering face mask until he came to me after his performance. Pelerine, Rhoda's elder sister, was also visiting from Atlanta. She was there, I think, to see Curtis McIntosh but was disappointed, because so too was a lady from Grenada.

Puntick died some years after Gilbert.

I now return to specific events in my village.

Events Related to Death

The announcement that a death had occurred was in itself something special. For a period of time, this was made by men aboard a truck going from one village to another, but earlier than that, in my youth, it was made by men riding on donkeys to most of the villages, loudly proclaiming, "Sake tan pale lot, who hear tell the other." This then continued with them telling everyone that *so-and-so* of such-and-such a place died the day before and that the funeral would be on such a time and day. "Come one, come all," was the final phrase of certain announcements. It seemed that it was most often at nights when we heard these announcements in Grand Bay and Mt. Pleasant.

A more formal type of communication, via the community pages, the radio, and the print media, is now the norm.

On the night preceding the burial, people gathered at the home of the dead for the wake, a solemn rite in itself. The first one that I remember attending was that of Agnes for cousin Becka, who lived near to the shop. Agnes had been pregnant for Hale Lang of Grand Bay. Her prolonged delivery proved difficult and led to her being admitted to the hospital. She died in childbirth, but her son, Little John, survived. He emigrated to England, but I saw him recently in Carriacou with his wife. He had returned, perhaps for good.

There were quite a few children who lived with Becka. In addition to Little John, there was Becka's son Godfrey, as well as Big John, Andrew, and Monica, all children of Cousin Roselia, Becka's sister, who herself resided in Grenada. Another son of Becka's, Nichol, had already left for England.

Tan Faith Charles, another sister of Becka, had two female children, Joyce and Gloria, who were always at that home. With it harbouring such beautiful young girls, I spent many hours there on vacation from high school, having an eye for both Monica and Joyce but at different times.

It was at the wake, or one of the indicated nights, for Agnes that I first experienced the big drum ceremony. I was not impressed then, not understanding or appreciating its intrigues.

Without understanding the significance, I grew up appreciating the holiness of the rituals associated with the wake and the third, ninth, and fortieth nights after death. Also, when the coffin is taken out from the home, it must be by the feet first to prevent the dead from walking back in.

All Saints' Night, which occurred on 1 November, was another annual activity that was held to remember and honour the dead. The villagers gathered at about dusk at the grave sites of their relatives. The actual rite involved lighting candles, uttering words of holy praises, and placing the candles on the tombstones.

Depending on relationships, people may have aggregated at one spot where it mattered, but largely, there was movement about to the other relevant tombstones. So, this act was not limited to the immediate family; other relatives, as well as other persons, may add a candle out of respect. This continued to between nine and ten o'clock at night.

Prior to the actual event but obviously integral to it was the parching of the dry corn seeds (parched corn, or popcorn, elsewhere), which were then pounded in the mortar with a pestle until fine and mixed with sugar to produce asham, a form of snack. Besides sharing the asham, mischievous young persons would throw it—or worse yet, flick the hot wax (sperm) from the lit candle—at other individuals.

The sperm from the melted candles was scraped off and later used to wax the convex surfaces of barrel staves, which were used by young ones for skating on grassy slopes. One time, either George or I had left a stave at the top of the northern sloped track of Kainash Hill, which led up to our home and onwards.

Cousin Flora (Fowah), our neighbour, coming home from the garden at dusk with a bucket of water obtained from the village cistern on her head, stepped on it. She ended up sliding one way lower down the track, while the bucket went another way from her. Neither of us had ever gotten so many licks before as we did that night from Iah. It's likely that she replaced the water with water from our cistern, which perhaps contributed to the extra licks.

On a day one or two years after someone's death, another serious activity was the putting-up of the tombstone. Some families would pay homage to the dead at the anniversary of death, but setting up the tombstone was meant to bring some form of finality to this until the annual All Saints' Day.

The already chosen headstone with the relevant information etched and painted had to be set into a concrete foundation built by workers under the direction of a local mason. During the day, they were supplied with food and drinks.

Other than the necessary preliminary preparations, on the day itself, the activities began at the home in the early morning with the rite of blessing given by a holy or elder respected person. This was followed by the wetting of the ground and the sacrifice and slaughter of the animals that were to be cooked.

The fowls were either held on the ground for the defeathered necks to be cut through or held by the neck and swung until the body separated from the neck. The headless body would hop around on the earth for a few minutes before finally settling for good. The cooks would go to work after the butchers had completed their jobs on all the animals.

People came from the afternoon onwards and gathered at the house, waiting to be fed. Some arrived with containers for takeaways. In the Bahamas, aluminium foil is used for takeaways at functions. However, in Carriacou, the guests travelled with special food containers.

Whether entirely true or not, it was not unknown for tales to be told about women who packed food in their bosoms, inside bras that were hiding more than the pendulous breasts. When they arrived home, with the hungry children eagerly waiting and looking, they would pull out rice, meat, provisions, bread, cakes, and finally, gravy, all from within the bosom.

This was at least preferable to the food being placed in their bloomers, which guarded the female temple.

For such events, Iah would let it be known that she would be accompanied by me, and this could not be denied her. If it were, she would not attend, and most wished that this lady of wisdom would be there.

The ceremony continued into the night, taking the form of a big drum performance, a wake, or both. Wakes were accompanied by the singing of hymns. The parents' plates of choice food were secured in a locked room, which was opened up at daybreak to be again blessed before distribution. That morning, the family would visit the cemetery to observe the handiwork, and blessings may again be offered.

Godwin wrote the words on our father's tombstone, and when last I saw him, I reminded him of them and recited them to him: *"Sleep on ye dead take thou thy rest. Thy life was one of noble deeds. Nor one of your acquaintance could deny, you proved a husband, father, and a friend."*

The last tombstone feast that I attended was that for my brother Gilbert. It took place in Grand Bay in April 1997, two years after his death. As I stood in the presence of his wife and children in the downstairs room, looking at his picture prominently displayed on the headstone and listening to the flowing words from the priest, I attempted not to cry, but my tears overcame my efforts at restraint.

Charles Gilbert

When George, the brother between Gilbert and me, went to GBSS in 1951, Gilbert and I grew closer. He would guard his little brother, of course. I don't remember when he took up fishing, but I know he did, either before or after working at the W. E. Julien store in town, which was then managed by either Mr. Toppin or Mr. Bullen. In the sea of Mt. Pleasant, Gilbert set fish pots as well as nets, and he also spearfished.

He, like all of my brothers, followed world boxing, getting the news from our box radio with the long wire antenna and also from Ring Magazine. At nights, we listened to the US Armed Forces network and other US stations, like VOA, that usually played western music.

So, we knew of Sugar Ray Robinson and Emile Griffith and the heavyweights—Joe Louis, Ezzard Charles, and Jersey Joe Walcott. One night, we heard the short-wave broadcast that

Rocky Marciano had won the heavyweight crown by defeating Jersey Joe Walcott.

The daytime stations originated out of Trinidad and Barbados. Especially in Grenada, listening to the BBC news at 7 a.m. was a must, but one had to tinkle with the tuning knob, because, as voiced by the Mighty Sparrow, the Spanish radio stations were always cutting in.

Cousin Basta (Bastapool) was known to spread the news that it was going to rain in Carriacou despite having no idea from which country the radio report originated or to where it was making reference. If it did so much as sprinkle, though, he would offer, "Ha, ha, I told you all so."

Not everyone had a radio, and especially when the transistor radios entered the scene, persons would gather around the person who possessed one, usually to listen to the broadcast of a cricket or football game.

Gilbert was so enamoured of the current heavyweight champion, Patterson, that he named his first son, with Verna Quashie, Floyd. But he requested my help in naming his second son, and I contributed the name Kempster. I never knew from where that arose, but I later used it conveniently when there was more than one lady to woo.

Even when he suffered with a scaly ichthyotic rash on his legs, Gilbert had a wooing, easy-going, casually inviting saga boy appeal to his steps, as compared with George, who had a more upright, confident, in-charge, almost demanding swagger and was well dressed. Short men swagger and dance with exceptional style.

Why this rash arose, no one knew, but it eventually disappeared. He may have been the one who had received a special meal because of this condition.

To share a secret, I believe that Gilbert once had what, to me, seemed to be bodily contact with Winnifred, one of the twin daughters of Cousin Marlain, on a crocus bag that was spread under the counter in the shop.

Gilbert moved to London in the early 1950s and sent for and married Verna in 1961. Floyd DaCosta and Clifford Charles

Kempster followed. I believe the boys moved to our home to live before they travelled.

My Family

My family, Vivian, Nika, and Dax, accompanied me when I visited him in Brockley, London in 1981, the same time as my brother George. George was then working at the UN and spent a day or two on his way to Africa. I was attending a symposium on the prevention and treatment of cancer. Whilst there, Gilbert invited me to play for his team in a game of cricket, but I declined.

Other than those already known to me, I met the children who were born in England—Ann, Mona, and Brian.

I saw Gilbert again once in Jamaica and many times after in Mt. Pleasant, where he built his home and helped in the organisation of the village maroons. Some years later in London, he was diagnosed with cancer. I reflect on that rash of his youth.

On one occasion, we met at Grenada's airport and sat for breakfast before departing, he for England and I for the Bahamas. I ordered salt fish souse, and he had the lambie (conch) water, which was so peppery that it sent him coughing after the first sip. He was not able to take another. One could see that he was a less energetic person than previously known to be. The bounce to his step had departed him.

He eventually retired for good in Carriacou, knowing that death was imminent and perhaps of eminence to him. This son born of Iah and Poopa on 19 January 1936 passed away on 5 July 1995. I was in Freeport, Bahamas, and I sent the following via W's fax machine to be read by my brother Nicholas at the rites, which would be held at the gravesite on our land that abutted the Grand Bay Cemetery:

> *I don't know that you were ever called teacher, but many are the lessons you gave me.*
>
> *You taught me bravery as we grew up in Carriacou and as we spent good times together in Jamaica and London. But, in all honesty, I am not sure that I learnt too well. For why am I sad and why do I cry—for you—as though it was the end. You saw death and asked the noble questions—Oh death! Where is thy sting, Oh grave! Where is thy victory?*
>
> *You taught me how to lose and yet benefit from losing. Mt. Pleasant versus Dover at cricket. You do remember, don't you? Dover beat us badly but we better prepared ourselves for the next time. And yet, and yet I have not prepared myself for losing you. Losing you from this earthly life but we'll meet again, I'm sure.*
>
> *We classed together in Mt. Pleasant Elementary School. You introduced me to scouting. You taught me how to*

cook, but I never learnt, for I could never prepare turtle meat as well as you could.

You taught me what it meant to be family—a family of love, a family of devotion, a family forever. I have learnt well from you.

You taught me, dear brother, how to face the fact of dying, how to accept that the Almighty grants eternal life to all of us. They will cover your body with dust and I will not be there to see this. So let me remember you for being a teacher, you will always be a brother, and to others, husband, father and friend. Let me remember you for being a man, Charles Gilbert, one who helped me to fulfill my dreams. Go for now with this message— That you were always loved and will always be loved as you are loved right now. Farewell.

Ned, Ned.

Once, when I visited Carriacou after his death, Verna invited me to have what I wished of his belongings. I took a shoe and a jersey shirt. The shoe eventually fell apart, but now and then, I wear the shirt, which I still keep in his memory.

On the way back from Chongqing, China, where I delivered a paper on forensic pathology in October 2011, Vivian and I spent four days in Beijing and another seven in London visiting his family. We stayed at Clifford's home. One evening, Floyd took us to dinner at Bella Vista Cucina Italiana in Blackheath Village, an area that reminded me of Mandeville in Jamaica.

I usually remind Vivian with a smile that, after eating various Chinese foods in Chongqing, our first meal in Beijing, the capital city, was at a KFC restaurant. But after that, it was all Chinese meals again, including, of course, roasted Peking duck, the game fowl that we only saw live in the Bahamas.

Cassava Milling

Another work activity existed because a few persons in the village grew cassava (manioc), some sweet and edible but most bitter and used to produce starch, farine, and tapioca, which we used to make a flat bread, porridge, and pudding. Other than the digging up and peeling of the tubers on the site where they were grown, all the other processes were completed elsewhere, some on the grounds of our shop.

The peeled tubers were milled in a special device that included a foot-operated, grater-covered spinning wheel. The tubers were ground by being fed to the wheel, an act that required some degree of dexterity to prevent injuries to the fingers. The mulch, collected in the boxed-in bottom of the mill's housing, was gathered into crocus bags, which were then compressed by huge slabs of rocks.

Crocus bags again, another use for.

The expressed liquid was sun-dried to make starch, whilst the shredded matter was, later that day, baked in a copper pan to produce farine. Children gathered dried corn stalks from the fields, which was used as the fuel for the fire.

A charge was levied for the use of the entire facility.

Emancipation Day

A small event took place on August Monday in celebration of the emancipation from slavery. It took the form of a morning procession, during which songs of liberation were sung and praises offered to Queen Victoria. Cousin Lillian, who lived with Cousin Shepherd, a blind fisherman, always seemed to play a role in this small ceremony, which an older Tan Cot had led for some time.

The participants initially gathered near our shop and proceeded towards Mt. Pleasant, ending at the post office. The small group of participants were well dressed. The women wore coloured dresses and adorned their heads with floral head ties and flowers. Some held bouquets in their hands. These were gathered from the blossoms of the corn plant—the yellowish white blanza (male tassel) and the orange red pupot (female ear).

Massa day done!

A Wedding

In Carriacou, there were traditional rites performed at weddings. When Godwin, my eldest brother, got married to Bonace Joseph, the ceremony was performed in the Catholic church in town, and the reception was at the home of the bride's parents in Lauriston, not that far from the town.

As an aside, in recent times, Catholic priests have featured in the news. In my youth, we knew of some of the things they did, but they did them more so to young girls. In fact, there was a story about one who used a Bible to elevate the pelvis of the girl.

He was said to have recited, "The holy book is behind you, the man of God is above you, and the rod of correction is inside you."

Whether or not Godwin had written Bonace's father to declare his intention and seek permission, I don't know. But it was common and perhaps expected for such to have occurred. If granted, the engagement and courtship would follow, and a wedding date would be set. Prior to a wedding, a flag with a suitably chosen word would usually be flown from the homes of the intending couple and their relatives for a few weeks.

Iah hired a truck to transport her invited guests, including the cooks, from our district areas, and although sharing was customary at the celebration site, she was responsible for entertaining her guests.

SPECIFIC EVENTS AND OCCASIONS: BONHOMIE

She chose her eldest brother, Darrell, to dance the groom's flag; however, he seemed inadequate when responding to his brother, and my uncle, Deeclo, who, in honour of the occasion, danced his flag from his home as the truck was passing by. Another man then took over from Darrell.

I recall that the party returned from the church with a band providing music. And as the dancing of the flags was taking place and the wedding party was walking the short distance from the road to the house, Iah danced her way to the group and placed an envelope in Godwin's jacket pocket. It was my understanding that it contained 100 dollars, then the currency of the British Islands.

I know I did not pay too much attention, but there followed the usual dancing of the cakes, the speeches, and of course, the eating, drinking, and merriment. Godwin's cake, made by Adeline in Grenada, had come by boat and was reparably damaged because of the rough seas. There must have been continuous music, but I really don't remember. On the late-day return to Grand Bay, the truck carried the weary but hopefully fully satisfied villagers, *all belly full!*

I wish to share another myth that I became aware of prior to the marriage. I had visited the Josephs and had lunch with them. The food was tasty, and I was hungry. I cleaned the plate of everything, including the last grain of rice. I was told by Howard, a younger brother of Bonace, that that was not the right thing to do. He opined that one should always leave a bit of food on the plate for the Devil, to ensure that he would not cause harm to the house.

Howard, as far as I understand, ended up in Sweden and has performed there as the lead singer in a music band. I once heard one of his songs, "Is It Fantasy or Is It Reality?" I once met a most beautiful daughter of his long after, when we were both visiting Grenada and staying at Nicho's. I'm told that her father has died.

As an expression of thanks to the bride's family, the "return thanks" rite was, as customary, held at the home of the parents of the bridegroom, now husband. So, with the wedded couple spending a day or two at our house, there was a small ceremony of praise, food, and drinks with a few invited guests.

I remember that following a bath in the small outhouse, Bonace, perhaps disturbingly, expressed that she had seen a snake. The local interpretation? She was pregnant.

Within months of the marriage, Bonace complained about Godwin's love affair with a nurse in the Belair hospital. Iah, in her known fashion, summoned him, and I was relegated to sleeping on the floor as he took my place in the bed to be lectured by his mother.

The Josephs, Innocent and Dema, had other daughters, and after this wedding, people had already lined them up for us Brathwaite boys, including the youngest one for me.

George and I made many a visit to that home, though whether before or after the wedding, I cannot remember. A swampy area was in the coastal flat land near to their home, and in it were plenty waterfowl. On one occasion, I was given two dry coconuts, which Gilbert planted in our house garden. They did fairly well for a time but did not last too long.

I also recall spending a night on the floor of their home whilst Iah was in the bedroom with Dema, who was repeating the prayer of the rosary throughout the night. We were visiting because, after weeks of waiting, there was still no word from the Joseph brothers, asea on their schooner. They eventually returned safely, after having been lost.

It so happened that Pansy, the one previously identified as the girl for George, got married to Nicholas, and I don't think they had previously known each other. I'm sure that this was all arranged, but most likely, he would have first sought permission from her parents, whether or not her opinion was sought. He was perhaps in Curaçao at that time. I don't think he was in Carriacou for Godwin's wedding either.

I do not remember when or where Nicholas got married, probably in Carriacou in the late 1950s or early 1960s. However, I do remember that in my early days as a student in GBSS, Pansy was attending the St Joseph's Convent, also in Grenada, and was singled out as one of the neatest dressed girls. Her white blouse was always tucked within the skirt with the very few creases, if there were any, equally on both sides but not at the front and back.

As Children

In our villages, we played well-known games as children. Some games could be played alone, some with one or more others. Sometimes we paired off and played competitively, one side against another. Most competitions took place just for fun, but rarely, they would lead to some type of serious disagreement.

One of the games we played, one person against another, was the matching of heads and tails, in which common pins were placed in the palm with the ends covered by the fingers of the other hand. If the second person correctly matched, that person earned the first person's pin and vice versa. The pins were usually stored in a flip-top pill container or an empty perfume vial, in which was put a small amount of talcum powder to prevent the pins from rusting. Some of us pulled magnets on the ground, hoping to find pins or coins. Some passed the time by making intricate designs with loops of string around both hands.

The games of pitching marbles, flying kites, and dancing tops were performed either individually, one on one, or in small groups. When in small groups, we could either pair up or play each man for himself. More for fun, we engaged in hop-scotch, hide-and-seek, skipping ropes, jumping jacks using pebbles, ring dancing, swinging and see-sawing on makeshift structures, asking each other riddles, and telling Nancy (Anansi) stories (crick crack, the wire bend and the story end). Magnets were also pulled to hopefully find the rare coin—Say Farm's penny. A few skated on waxed boards, some of which had wheels, and a few also rolled the metallic wheels of tyres wherever they were going. We skipped rope by ourselves or rocked to and fro, ready to jump in, when the rope was rotated by two persons. You could also graduate from one rope to two. And there were many other activities.

For example, the boys dug for crazy crabs (sand crabs) on the beach and toolooloo (doodle bugs) in their dirt burrows under houses. They also sought directions from what may have been the larva of a corn or pea beetle, requesting of it, "Bookooroombay, bookooroombay, show me Grenada." The bug would then turn its head and point. Where to did not matter, as only the truly knowledgeable knew where Grenada was located anyhow.

As noted, we boys also rummaged in the wooded areas for fruits, eating at once the ripe, esculent ones but also picking some not yet ripe but full, to be hidden at home to await the ripening. Elders would accompany us at times to pick guavas for making jams and jellies. Some fruits, like tamarind, on tall trees may be climbed for or pelted with stones.

We played wind (tennis) ball cricket anywhere and everywhere that was possible, including the street in the front of the shop, where we would close the west door to prevent the ball from breaking the drink bottles. We only rarely had to remove the stumps for the infrequently passing vehicle.

In what was left of the lunch break, we played hard-ball cricket with compost, plastic, or rarely, leather in the school yard, now and then breaking the window of the staff room but never being reprimanded.

The game of kite flying, usually during Easter, was something beyond admiring the appearance and singing sound of the kites. It extended to the sport of cutting, aided by the attachment of sharp objects, such as pieces of broken bottles or razor blades, to the kite's cloth tail.

The game involved each flyer manoeuvring so as to cut the string of the opponent's kite. A most disturbing, disheartening, and even devilish deed was doing this surreptitiously when someone's kite was flying at home and there was no competition.

Once, Soonkie, a girl of my age who was an innocent bystander, had her cheek sliced by the razor blade on a kite's tail.

Soonkie, my dear friend, where art thou? She was the daughter of Cousin Mettah, who lived with Tan Dorah. We played so joyfully together, but I have not seen her since about age 13. She currently resides in England, I was recently told.

We children knew of boyfriends and girlfriends and what would be described at first as puppy love and later as crushes. Lorna, my neighbour, was my first friend, after whom came, in no particular order, Evelyn, who lived in Trinidad but often visited her relatives, Patricia, Soonkie, Monica, Norma, Lena, Frances, and others.

Mischievously, some boys carried small mirrors around to place between the legs of unaware girls.

We all grew up knowing what sexual intercourse was, although I don't think we ever called it that. This was not strange, bearing in mind that we lived in farming villages surrounded by both domesticated and other animals plainly engaging in it. We all also knew what the outcome would be. But we children referred to the act as "doing rudeness", and even if we tried it, it was nothing more than mere crudeness.

Without doubt, this provided the real education. No birds and the bees stories for us.

Money was made by those who owned male animals and provided them for mating. Some of us would have seen how the adults facilitated the act by guiding the penis of the male correctly to its intended path, especially for donkeys and cattle.

I also remember how the men would rub zooty (nettle), an irritant plant, on the penis of the animal, which forced it to seek solace. We knew of the castration of male animals, the barren pigs intended for slaughter, and the dogs that became extra faithful and better hunters.

I was told of the wicked deed perpetrated by my half-brother, who sliced off the penis of a dog with his cutlass after the act, when the animals were stuck together. If he had done that to our dog, Iah would have deballed him.

All girls were respected and none wanted to be called a jamette, which was a derogatory word. For whatever reason, some girls stood out a bit more and maybe were treated with greater respect. Among these were Grace, who got married to Euthan Noel and in whose home I once had baked pork at lunch that was so very good that I still consider it the best I have ever eaten; Lorna Cayenne, my neighbour; the daughters of Cousin Theophilus Baptiste; Frances Francis; Myra McIntosh; Norma John; Rufina Blaize; Alcina; the Noels' two daughters, Rita and Monica, who lived close to us with their grandparents, Cousin Sheddy and Cousin Aga, because their mother, Cousin Luna, was abroad; and many others.

Cousin Theo Baptiste, married to Cousin Matay, was one kinda strict man. He would not allow anyone, and certainly not the Brathwaite boys, to fool around with his daughters, Dorothy, Atay (Princess), and Toolah (Elise). Elise, who became an author, is married to one of my best friends, Curtis Cox. Princess died in 2021.

Mr. Baptiste's home was on the southern slope of the Grand Bay main street near to one of our tracts of land. I may have been sent there for something but only once that I can recall. He also fathered male children.

Another fine-looking village gal, who I last saw in Brooklyn at Rhoda's and who was said to be something else. Her mother was in Aruba, so she lived with other relatives in the same home as her uncle, Lawrence. Over a period of time, growing up in Grand Bay, strange things happened to her. Pieces of wood flew from her bosom, her panties would just drop down, and she behaved in weird ways.

Eventually, a younger brother was blamed and considered to be bewitched and responsible for perpetuating these acts. His punishment included being locked in the kitchen loft with all doors and windows closed while it filled with smoke from a lit fire. He was also expelled from the home for a spell, but the strange happenings continued.

Her guardians engaged a shango group from Grenada to exorcise the problem. This group was probably paid and provided with free transportation and accommodation. They performed their rites mainly at nights. Some of the men were said to pursue and forcefully engage ladies of the village, some of whom were said to enjoy this.

On the final night, a ceremony was performed at the bay of Grand Bay, and food was thrown into the sea as a sacrifice to the gods. Some young boys stationed themselves in the water and happily caught and accepted the sacrifices.

It was later said that Rufina may have done those things to herself, having been guided by a black book that she had been reading. It was believed that the shango group was successful in exorcising the Dracula from within her.

Some of the bigger boys mischievously encouraged the children to do rudeness. I must have been about 6 years old when my brother Gilbert and other boys placed me and a girl of my age into the catchment tub of the cassava mill and told us to do rudeness. We knew what they meant, but I'm not sure that we accomplished or even attempted anything. At an older age, about twelve years old, the same girl and I tried again in aunt Loonie's abandoned house, without coercion and in secrecy, with better results. Even as a young boy, I knew the four-letter word, which then had an *o* instead of *u*.

I was never schooled or advised by elders about love or sex, and I think Iah knew more than she pretended, for she issued stern warnings about what she would do to me if she ever heard that I interfered with Lorna, my neighbour's child.

In my early sex noneducation, I learnt the words *cucush* (penis) and *penny* (vulva and vagina). Otherwise, boys and girls, though of course physically different, were treated alike, as those differences were of little importance to us. We all behaved in a similar fashion and did like things. For example, it was not unusual for us to sea-bathe together, with some of us naked.

The boys peed wherever they were, respectfully turning to the side away from others, whether it was along the side of the road, in nearby bushes, or behind a building.

No big thing!

When I was about 8 years old, a music band, led by Doogan McIntosh on the clarinet, practised on the veranda of the Cayenne's house, and Lorna and I would leave from there, hide behind Iah's house, and dance to the music. She allowed me to play with her breasts, but we advanced no further.

I liked Lorna. Once, as a teenager, I did try to coerce her into the sexual act, but she strongly resisted. This was that same Lorna who, without being aware of the fact, had an affair as well as a child with her half-brother and was set to marry him, causing her father, Charles, to rush to New York to abort the proceedings. So I have been told.

Between ages thirteen and sixteen, I came close to having sex twice. On one occasion, it was in a vacant house in the area called Nehgah House. We were interrupted by a bigger guy who came to macco on us, climbing over the bedroom door to peep. A macco is a person who contrives to obtain information for gossiping.

The girl demanded to see my penis, and after I showed her, she asked me to don a condom, which I had in my pocket. Nothing happened, partly because of the peeping Tom and partly because she had feelings for another, whose name was Boyfriend McIntosh.

Another time was with a girl who wanted us to try it, but now the macco was Antoo, who played cricket as a vooper—swinging wildly at bat. A few of us boys were liming at Tan Dorah's Junction one early night. The girl came to me and agreed to my request, but no matter where the girl and I went, Antoo followed. Again, nothing happened.

I always believed that women were women and men were men, both just human beings of a different body morphology, neither one superior to the other. The same was applicable to girls and boys. In this respect, just as for men, there were some women who I respected for some reason and who reinforced my beliefs, thus directly or indirectly influencing me.

Clearly and without doubt in first place was my mother. I say no more on this at this time.

Although I was not directly influenced by Mamie Eva Sylvester, it seemed no big issue when in a by-election circa 1952, she replaced her dead husband as the political representative for Carriacou, defeating men in the process. I respected what she did.

Teacher Sylvie (Ms Sylvia Charles) taught me and, as acting head teacher in Mt. Pleasant, always showed me kindness.

Nurse Alexandra Radix, of whom more will be said, graciously acted as a second mother to me.

I therefore present my appeal:

Dear ladies,

In a past, unknown time, a decision was made in which I had no choice nor have now any regrets, but I respectfully request that you continue to treat well that rib of mine—and in that regard, also me.

Thou, the first clone from my X chromosome, wert created to blindly be in life my partner, then, with opened eyes, a companion, and now also, a sister.

The story goes that a politician in his campaign visited a home where there was a pregnant dog. Even after delivery, the owner promised that she would name the pups after him and his family. Just prior to the election, he returned, only to find that the pups were named after his opponent. When questioned, the owner said, "Well, you see, their eyes open now."

It's amazing how many people, once they have opened their minds to a cause, remain closed to other possibilities, like puppies that die before seeing the light of day or horses with blinders.

* * *

Iah never wanted her children to associate with some others she considered unruly, and if we displayed an unacceptable behaviour, she would caution us to take it back where we found it. Eggs and rocks don't play together. I think we all loved, feared, and totally respected her. I don't know how far she reached in primary school, but within limits, she could read and write. At nights, she took up my lessons with me, particularly those at the back of the exercise book.

One day, my friend George, a child of Cousin Becka, who everyone called Chairman, was playing with me under the shop, which was close to his home. One of us found a shilling, which I took to my mother, an act which I later thought of as rather foolish, because I could have found a better use for it. She accused me of stealing it from the shop, having been encouraged to do so by the bad company that I was keeping. I denied it strongly.

At an older age, I did steal, especially grapes from an open bag in the supermarket or a pepper berry to plant the seeds in my garden.

Anyhow, she proceeded from the shop and went around the corner, allegedly to the post office to call my brother John, who was then working in town, to ask him to collect some holy water from the church.

That night at home, she gave me a glass of the "holy" water and said, "Alfred, you stole the shilling. Yes or no?" Well, I said yes, I did, because I wasn't drinking no holy water. It was said to cause death if one lied, and in my mind, I wondered what would happen if God had forgotten what had actually transpired. Of course, I realised, but too late, that it was just ordinary water she was holding. But how could God forget when—"(A)nd the truth shall set you free" (John 8:32).

She sent me to sleep in the fowl house. It was for maybe just a few minutes, but it seemed like frightening hours, for even when someone in a group had a flashlight, a glimpse of its glint on the shivering branches of a tree evoked the uncanny thought and accompanying fear of jombies. Imagine, therefore, the scary thoughts which were sailing within my head in the dark.

Nicho with Iah

6

MT. PLEASANT ELEMENTARY SCHOOL: TO LEARN OR NOT TO LEARN

Despite the British twist and the progression from slate and a pencil through exercise book and a lead pencil, to ink well and a feather or a nibbed dip or a fountain pen, like Platignum and Parker, it is my strong opinion that at Mt. Pleasant Elementary School, we definitely were exposed to and profited from a good, solid, strong, educational grounding in the basics—reading, writing, and arithmetic—as well as hygiene, general knowledge, some music, and handicrafts. That is perhaps questionable and open to debate, but I strongly believe it to be true.

At that time, I don't think we were using ballpoint pens in the school. In the lower classes, we used the slate and pencil. If available, we applied water with a wet rag or sponge to erase the writing, but more usually, we used either spittle or the watery stalk of the flower of a common lily plant for that purpose.

I had crayons at home, but I can't recall using them at school.

In addition to the above subjects, children also got marks or prizes for regularity and punctuality in attendance, though it was unclear to me how these were judged, especially the latter, since most children got to school before the teachers.

We were made responsible for cleaning the floor and the school grounds, as we sang, *bits of paper...pick them up,* and we received a good foundation in practising good agriculture in our school gardens. I became quite proficient in weaving the blades of cane grass and making mats from them. These plants and the lilies had been planted across the slope of our house garden as a protective barrier against soil erosion.

Particularly in the lower classes, which were referred to as standards, there were regular recitation competitions. At times, they were referred to as elocution contests. On one occasion, maybe in standard four, a competition was held over the recitation of Tennyson's "The Lady of Shallot," composed of some twenty stanzas. I feared only Curtis McIntosh then, but he was unable to finish the poem, and I easily placed first. Although my brother Nicholas was one of the judges, there was no need for nepotism.

The champion, Lord Alfred, had spoken. I have been told that at a Parents' day function, I recited Kipling's If. I am hazy about a poem I may have recited—*For the people will talk, you know.*

There once was a competition between the schools in Carriacou based on stage performances. I was a participant for my school in the category of recitations by age or class, and because I was playing outside, it was only at the end of the show that I learnt that I had won and that my sister Alethea had accepted my prize, which was a glass butter dish with its cover.

I later complained that, without my knowledge, Alethea had given my prize as a gift at a wedding. Iah was just as displeased as I was.

Let me however quickly add that this champion in Carriacou became an also-ran at the 1960 GBSS elocution contest because he could not complete, without the aid of prompting, the Gettysburg Address of President Abraham Lincoln.

One of the judges was a teacher, Osbert Benjamin, whose family and mine developed a close relationship in the 1970s when I returned to Grenada to take up an appointment. It was at his home that I was introduced to the game of bridge and also whisky with coconut water. A specialty of his wife, Verda, was roti, which we enjoyed after the games. The bridge games rotated from house to house. Benji has since passed on. Via LinkedIn, his son, Dave, and I have recently exchanged greetings.

At the above-mentioned Carriacou interschool competition, what proved outstanding were the singing performances of teachers, which I listened to. Valan Roberts, from the school in Dover, sang "Brighten the Corner" with a nasal twang, though sounding extremely well. He was competing against a stellar duet rendition of "Whispering Hope" by the Mt. Pleasant teachers Naomi John (alto) and Adelaide Blaize (soprano). I don't know who won, but in my then youthful opinion, the only fair result would have been a tie for first place.

I don't remember all of the persons who taught me in the middle and junior classes. I know they included my sister Alethea, Adelaide Blaize, Naomi John, Cuthbert Simon, and maybe Teacher Gracelyn and her sister, Louise. But the one I remember best was Teacher Ruby Cyrus, who, perhaps in standard three or four, gave me the prize for placing first in the end of year examination.

The prize was an exercise book, on the back of which were, inter alia, the multiplication tables and weights and measures. On the front outer cover, she had written, "First prize to Alfred Brathwaite, he works exceedingly well."

That was the same type of workbook that Iah questioned me on at nights, rewarding me with a knock to my knuckles from a wooden ruler if I gave a wrong answer.

In that same examination, the first test was in arithmetic, and a child from the home of Mambee scored 46 per cent, while the rest of us, all perhaps under ten, including me with 8 per cent. But I caught up in the other subjects, forged ahead, and won going away.

In this class, the other children who were bright included Norma John, a daughter of Cousin Louisa, and Horatio "Horay" Scott, who inexplicably fell backwards shortly after, and I think even left the school. I cannot explain why Curtis McIntosh does not come to mind in that class.

Curtis McIntosh at GBSS.

I know that Nicholas taught a subject or two to us in one of the middle standards and once used the strap on me. He had turned his back to the class to write on the blackboard, and one of the two bigger girls, who sat together, threw something at him. No one responded when we were asked who had done it. He proceeded to beat the entire class.

I believe that one of those girls, not too long after leaving school, carried his baby, which she lost early in the pregnancy. Whether or not she was the one who had thrown the object, I don't know. I know that he was also the head teacher at Mt. Pleasant school, though I don't remember whether that was later or at the time of the above incident.

As the head teacher, he instituted the morning assembly. We would line up by class on the school grounds, and he would personally examine each student's fingernails for cleanliness before making his morning address.

He also advised us to clean our teeth using a twig crushed to form a toothbrush, together with a paste of baking soda. Prior to that, I had never known about the brushing of teeth, except maybe rubbing them with a finger.

Nicholas may have been promoted from head teacher to the position of a supervisor of teachers or inspector of schools, and around that time, he was engaged to Joyce Cox, who was also pregnant by him. A date had been set for marriage. He was probably also either stationed in or summoned to Grenada.

I believe that he was being pressured by the head office, perhaps because of his involvement with the deputy head teacher at Mt. Pleasant school, who was also said to be pregnant by him. His proposal to postpone the wedding was met with anger, and he was chased out of the home by Mr. Cox, Joyce's father, a former head teacher himself. The deputy head teacher apparently lost the child, but Joyce gave birth to his son.

I can well imagine what our brother Godwin would have said "Nicholas Brathwaite, what a man!'

Three ladies, one plus one plus one, but one birth.

He offered his resignation to the government and escaped to Curaçao, I would imagine, in the late 1940s or early 1950s to work in the oil refinery, where he spent seven years in an administrative position. Whilst there, he captained the cricket team. He may also have done courses in navigation and begun learning handicraft, which he provided evidence of in our home in the form of a wooden plaque.

I don't remember him ever living at home with us, but on the rare visit to the home, he would clamp my flat nasal bridge with a clothes pin.

So, there it was for me—one brother to polish his shoes, one brother to smell his bottom, one brother to pin my nose, one sister to whip me, and a sister to beckon a struggling me to the deep sea—but I survived.

After my success in standard four, I moved to standard five-A in the corn house, where there were two classes—five-A and five-B, as I uncertainly recall. The five-A class was for the brighter students. It must have been in this standard that I was the lead singer at the opening morning and afternoon closing sessions in the corn house, with the rest of the class chiming in appropriately. Three of the songs we sang that come to mind were "The Lord's My Shepherd", "In the Valley, and I Couldn't Hear Nobody Pray", and "Swing Low, Sweet Chariot."

I believe that Cuthbert Simon, the music teacher, may have taught class five-B. Each teacher, besides other duties, was responsible for a class and taught most of the subjects for that class. I don't think that we had separate textbooks for each subject, although I do recall the Royal Readers series (Thomas Nelson) and the comical writings of J. O. Cutteridge. There may also have been primers.

I seem to recollect being taught the strings of the guitar—E, A, D, G, B, and E—and the backronym for space notes F, A, C, and E. It was "Papa rabbit eat Fish Augustus Cannot Eat." That for the chords is forgotten.

Teacher Cuthbert was also the scout master, and my dear brother Gilbert was an outstanding scout who mastered the art of marching, as proud as ever in his uniform. In my last year at school, I joined the movement, and under the guidance of Gilbert, I learned Morse code, tied different knots, experienced the different signs used in tracking, and passed the tests to achieve the tenderfoot rank. When I entered high school in Grenada, I considered continuing, but I could not afford the fees and had no strong inclination to do so anyway.

It was in the final 5A examination to advance to standard six, located on the stage of the main building, that I embarrassed myself. The last paper was the spelling test—an early version of a spelling bee—of twenty words, with each correct word receiving five marks. Teacher Adelaide merely called the words without any further explanation. Before this final test, I had been leading Curtis McIntosh by ten points and had boasted that he could never catch me. He scored all the words correctly, however, and I missed three of them.

Never ever brag too soon. Crow only if cocksure. And Curtis never gloated.

At age 10, it was recommended that I sit the scholarship/ entrance examination for those under age 12. The top six places would receive government funding to attend the Grenada Boys Secondary School (GBSS), the government high school for boys, located in Tanteen, St George's. Also located in the same general area and in close proximity was the Anglican High School for girls. I suspect that the girls competed separately in the examination.

I journeyed to Grenada, stayed at Adeline's, and sat the one-day exam in one of the GBSS buildings. I was not successful in obtaining a scholarship, but whether or not I had achieved the entrance pass mark was of no consequence, as George, my older brother, was already at GBSS and funds were not available for another child. Well, that issue never really arose.

I must admit that the above account, related to my time in school, has taxed the memory. I was not able to resurrect the details as clearly as I would have wished, but I stand by the generalities.

Before his marriage to Bonace, Godwin was assigned to Dover Model School as the head teacher. Iah, in her wisdom, advised that I, now nearing eleven, should go and live with him to be his messenger boy and companion and to learn from him.

In the head teacher's residence, there were two large adjacent bedrooms, Godwin slept in one and I in the other. It was the first time I had slept alone in a big bed in my own room. Not unexpectedly, the only window was closed, yet I was cold.

I don't think there were biting pests, but the house creaked all night, and I was afraid. I slept poorly from the Sunday I arrived in

Dover to the Thursday night of the same week. I left after school on Friday to return to Mt. Pleasant.

I was in the class of those expected to sit that year's scholarship examination. The star student in the class was Chester Prime. Ruby Compton was the class teacher. Many years later, when I was a resident in Freeport, Bahamas, a Mr. Gibbs from Barbados, who was then teaching in Freeport, persistently asked me about her, because many long years before, the two of them had attended the same teacher's training college and he was smitten with her.

I feel certain that years later, I, accompanied by Wilcome, attended the farewell function held for her prior to her departure for the training college. My brother Nicholas, the then head teacher at the Dover school, having succeeded Godwin, impressed me with what may have been the ending words of his address: "Vaya con Dios, or as they say in the South Sea islands, Sayonara."

During the class sessions, Godwin would sometimes walk around with the students' backs to him, looking over one child's shoulder after another. Not unusually, he would drop an anticipatory but unexpected strap on a student for the nonsense that was written.

It was customary for head teachers to walk around the compound and the classrooms, as well as to attend and even teach classes at times.

This was his specialty class, for most of the students were of the age at which they were prepared for the government's annual scholarship examination for entry into GBSS or the Anglican High school in Grenada.

Godwin beat too much and, too often, I was a recipient. Perhaps because of that or perhaps because I was somewhat lonely, after school on the Friday of the first week, I returned to Mt. Pleasant, as was expected, and spoke seriously to Iah. I indicated to this mother of mine, who somehow concurred, that I would continue schooling in Dover but preferred to walk the two to three miles there in the morning and back in the afternoon.

From home, it was along the road of Mt. Pleasant, past Works to Cousin Gerald McIntosh's house, left on Belair Hill, over into Limlair, and to the school. This Iah also had a heart.

But Godwin continued to beat that second week, and on Thursday of that week, I informed Iah that on the morrow, I would let Godwin know that that would be my last day with him, for I preferred to return to Mt. Pleasant School.

I was just too scared of receiving the licks to pay attention to learning.

So, on Friday morning, I merely strolled to Dover and paid no attention to the blowing of his whistle. At school, either a whistle or a bell or both was used to draw attention. His first whistle was for the students to stand still wherever they were, and the second required moving quickly to assemble for prayers, singing, and announcements before dispersing to the individual classrooms.

Unhurriedly, I strolled towards the school as Godwin approached me, wondering if perhaps I had gone crazy. He may have asked what was wrong with me. I looked up and unhesitatingly informed him, "Iah say I ain't coming back." He took off my cap and gave me two licks on my head with it. I turned around and headed back to Mt. Pleasant. So, I enjoyed my day off, small but feeling tall and looking forward to being a proud teenager someday.

That was my next step.

Later in life, I was visiting Grenada, and at a small celebration of Godwin's birthday at his home in Old Fort, St George's, I reminded him of the one thing that I always remembered l had learnt from him as a student in Dover: "Oh, and was she in good health yesterday?"

In those days, there were eight parts of speech, expanded to nine as the word *the,* previously an adjective, now an article—a new addition to the group. I understand that the number is now twelve.

After his marriage, I would occasionally see Godwin in Dover, especially on Sundays, when Alethea would drag me with her to visit them. On one occasion, when I was playing in the school yard,

I was suddenly thrown upward and found myself spread-eagled on the ground.

My auntie Polina's cow was in the schoolyard, and as I had run up and then backwards down a sloped concrete column, the cow had picked me up with its horn and tossed me. Fortunately, the horn entered between the leg of my short khaki pants and the back of my upper thigh.

I was OK, and my torn pants were repaired by Bonace. But to this day, I wonder what would have been my outcome in Carriacou if my flesh had been penetrated in that part of my body. Fortune was on my side. *Somebody up there!*

Both Godwin and Iah were extremely mad at Polina for letting her animal loose in a schoolyard, even though it was not a school day. However, in his waning years, Godwin doubted my story, claiming that that could never have happened in "his school". No animal would have been let loose around *his* school. He then asked me where he was at the time. He got boiling mad when I responded that he may have been with the men in a rum shop.

Likewise, he also cast doubt when I told him that our father was never birth-registered as Charles but only as DaCosta Alexander, although years before, when younger, Godwin had agreed that it was perhaps the woman in Grenada who had adopted him whomay have called him Charlie. When he had these later doubts of his, he would tell me that I was chatting nonsense.

Oh, that aging brain of his.

After I returned to Mt. Pleasant School and was in standard six, my brother Lysander, home after his spell at GBSS, was the class teacher, and Nathaniel Bascombe, the head teacher. In the final examination in standard six, I knew that I had placed first based on the scores per subject that had already been released.

The other bright sparks in the class were Myra McIntosh, daughter of Cousin Moore and brother of Lincoln, and Veda Henry from Mt. Royal. I imagine that Curtis, who had edged me out in the standard five exam, had already left school.

On the last day of classes, while at home for lunch, Lysander placed the score sheet on the house safe. I looked at it and realised that he had me as placing third or even lower. Well, on returning to school, we always passed by the shop. I left home first and related the position to Iah. When Lysander arrived, she took him aside and asked him to recheck my total. He did, and I received my true position, first place.

Even a teacher, with no calculator then, could falter in mathematical additions, resulting in changing a champion to an also-ran.

As head teacher, Mr. Bascombe, while teaching one of the lessons, once beat an entire class, save for his son, Cyril Bascombe, and me. He asked for the number that the word *couple* represented and went to each child for the answer. Cyril and I were sitting together and were the last to be asked, and Cyril had whispered the answer to me.

That's what friends were for—one plus one equal two, one and one make two.

Another situation involved my brother Gilbert, who happened to be a student in the same class and was thought not to be as bright as I was. Perhaps Iah kept him in school to avoid mischievous behaviours. There was a test of general knowledge for all class-six students of Grenada. Gilbert placed about sixteenth, and I, in the thirties. In reading the results, Mr. Bascombe remarked that it was the first time in the class that Gilbert had taken his rightful position over me.

General knowledge was never one of my better subjects, and it never was an issue for me. In that category, I accepted being an also-ran and, at times, a no-show.

I reiterate that Gilbert was always kind to me, and we always got along well. Indeed, that was true of my relationship with all my siblings, except for a troublesome period that developed with Adeline.

Gilbert emigrated to London in the 1950s, because then, England, as was said, "open up". Many young men took advantage of this and went seeking jobs, which they got. They were quite enterprising, each usually encouraged by one who was already there. As they would say in the village, "He send for him." Each newly arrived young man, after settling, would then send for his intended wife and children, if any, and would sponsor other relatives or friends.

When I was in Jamaica, Gilbert visited me at the university, and a group of us went drinking in the adjacent village of Papine. Later that day, he invited me to the Geest banana boat, a mode of transportation in those days, and from under his bed in the dormitory, he pulled out his suitcase and showed me his shiny handgun.

The schools in Carriacou were visited now and then by education officers, and on one occasion in Mt. Pleasant, it was visited by Mr. M. Z. Mark, who was probably then the chief education officer. I will always remember these words of his in the assembly: "If I could rise to speak in the Elks auditorium in New York, so too, children, you can rise."

I have always compared the influence of this on me to that of an address by T. A. Marryshow to an assembly of the students at GBSS, when I had felt as if he were speaking personally and directly to me. I don't remember his words, but years later in my reflections, he seemed to have portrayed the image of Uncle Sam—**"I want you"**—as he willed us to succeed.

Theophilus Albert was a giant of a man, both in stature and as a politician of note in Grenada and the wider Caribbean. He was a proud proponent of the idea that "the West Indies must be West Indian". He was the owner of the local newspaper *the West Indian*, the motto of which was *"Savoir c'est pouvoir"*. He did not contest the Grenadian elections for representatives to the parliament of the West Indies Federation, a union which was generally listed as one of the three unifying entities in the English Caribbean. The others were the university college and the cricket team. This was the era of

Caribbean political powerhouses—Adams, Compton, Liburd, Bird, Gairy, Bradshaw, and Joshua.

At some point in time, a West Indies football (soccer) team was also formed, but unlike the cricket team, which is still in existence, it didn't last.

Although there is a West Indies cricket team, each island or country struts its own team, as is done in football, and there are also subregional groupings. For example, there is a Windward Islands cricket team as well as one from the Leeward Islands.

Nevertheless, there seems to be greater resolve at the regional level to maintain togetherness in cricket, so there is some degree of West Indies unity. Initially, there were difficult problems within cricket, but despite disagreements and bickering, especially when the team faltered, our cricket team still exists.

There was a time when the cricketers were selected from only four territories—Jamaica, British Guiana, Barbados, and Trinidad. That has changed, and so too has the old philosophical approach that indicated that the captain had to be a white man.

As a black captain, the long-departed great Sir Frank Worrell, one of the famous three *W*s of the West Indies team, would have attested to that.

Returning to my schooling, of importance was the scholarship examination, based on which ten places were to be awarded that year of 1952 for free attendance to the secondary schools in Grenada. For the first time, we Carriacouans were allowed to sit the exam in Carriacou.

Most people seemed to think that if anyone was to be successful, it was a competition between Chester, who was taught by Godwin, and me, who was taught by Nathaniel Bascombe.

I remember two of the questions from the English test. One was, "Use an English word derived from the Latin word *luna*," and the other was, "Use the word *indeed* in a sentence. My response to the first was "lunatic" and to the second, "A friend in need is a friend indeed."

On a Saturday late afternoon, a teacher rode from town on his motorbike to announce that I had placed fourth in the examination. At that time, no word was heard about Chester, but eventually, word did come. Up to his last year of life, Godwin stated that Bascombe never let him forget that I had placed fourth in the scholarship exam and Chester, Godwin's student, had earned the final place of tenth.

I remain doubtful, but some have stated that Chester was awarded the final spot because the government wished for Carriacou to have at least two persons in the group of ten. This, most likely, was just gossip, for to me, it seemed Chester was extremely bright and earned his spot.

Throughout his life, he maintained a respectful relationship with Godwin, always visiting him whenever in Grenada and carrying *Time* magazines for him.

I earned neither first place nor 100 per cent, but nevertheless, I was regarded as a champion.

I, at this point, must indicate that secondary schools have been in existence in Carriacou for many, many years since my time. The first to be opened was Bishop's College, established in 1964.

OTHER PERSONAL INCIDENTS IN MY YOUTH: MISCHIEVOUS?

Brawn or Brain

I was never a street or brawling type of fighter, not at school or ever. Perhaps it was because no one taught me, or maybe it never appealed to me. But oh, I was quick to react if someone upset me.

The art of boxing was more interesting, and quite often, George and I, as pre-teenagers, boxed barehanded but avoided hits to the face. Invariably, we ended up fighting because he had hit me too hard.

In spite of their obvious love, my siblings took advantage of me.

Cyril, the son of my last primary school head teacher, Nathaniel Bascombe, always wanted to wrestle with me, his friend. Whenever I accepted, it never lasted, as he always easily won.

After Mt. Pleasant, Cyril and I caught up at GBSS, and on weeknights or Saturdays, I would visit the place where he boarded on Green Street. Also boarding there was a fine-looking Indian girl, a Lalsingh from the parish of St Patrick, I think. As my sister Adeline jealously guarded the use of her electricity, I would study in the guys' room at Cyril's place and then continue late into the night under a street lamp that was nearby.

Cyril's nickname then was Meracombe; I'm not sure why. The group included two other students, Neckles and Sam, who visited the boarding house just as often as I did. Sam always received help from me with zoology. We guys also limed together.

Cyril was then a heavy cigarette smoker, and after he completed schooling, he returned to a job in Carriacou, where he died. I was led to believe he died from alcoholism not too long after. Our friendship was pleasant and wholesome.

Together, we were a decent couple of guys!

I now make mention of an incident that occurred when I was about 9 years old. Somewhere on Kainash Hill, near to a tamarind tree and a plum tree, Gilbert and Cousin Mambee's boy, Cosnell, encouraged Godwin "Perro" McIntosh and me to fight.

The wiry Perro, who was nicknamed not after the Spanish dog but after the term we used for the skinny sparrow bird, took the upper part of the slope and pinned me to the ground in no time. Gilbert must have felt ashamed of me at that moment.

In those days, a fight was started by one boy placing a twig atop his shoulder and daring the other to knock it off; if done, the fight started.

Although I was usually quite passive, however, I had a readily displayed honest face, and it was not generally known that I was rather mischievous. I also did have a temper.

For example, Anstice, son of Cousin Roselia and Mr. Fred Paterson, was visiting from Grenada. Mr. Paterson lived in Carriacou but Cousin Roselia, of Carriacou origin, lived in Grenada. Anstice was probably staying at the home of Cousin Edna. As noted, Bro and Edna had three children, Celestine, Josephine, and Venus.

Anyhow, we were picking the tamarinds by throwing stones at the pods in the nearby tree. One fell, and I felt certain it was mine. But Anstice, who was about Gilbert's age, took it. I reacted by jamming his thigh with a rusting dinner fork that just happened to be nearby.

I don't think I received a flogging, but I was scolded by Adeline, who was also on that mentioned visit from Grenada, as she treated the wound. Without doubt, the usual treatment of washing the wound clean and applying iodine or Canadian healing oil, which were always present in our house, would have been done.

In this regard, there was always something of medicinal value at home, and indeed, there was recognition of the value of some of the local bushes. For example, the leaves of the soursop tree, when kept in water overnight, provided a drink that was used for cooling and cleaning the bellies of children who were on about returning to school after a vacation, and the wound-healing effects of aloes were well known.

Other than that, we could buy Epsom salt from the store. It was also sometimes given to children a few days prior to returning to school for its laxative properties. The worst tasting and most disliked by children was castor oil, a more potent laxative. It seemed important that children should cleanse the bowels before returning to school after a vacation.

On a more regular basis, perhaps weekly, Iah drank a glass of the fizzy Eno's Fruit Salts in water, and sometimes she gave me a drink of it.

It was not unusual for some of us, after a minor injury, to break out in foot sores, and we were all treated by the local nurse, Iah. There was a day that I saw her break into action as Betty fell into a trance after a passing woman commented as to how pretty Betty was. Iah immediately recognised mal jo, rushed into and through the shop garden, gathered what bushes she needed, and sponge-bathed Betty, who readily recovered.

My next fight of sorts occurred at about age 14 in the St George's bookstore in Grenada, where George and I were browsing. We were both attending GBSS at the time, he ahead of me. What happened was based on just a minor incident that involved me replacing a displaced book to its proper place on the shelf.

A nearby boy, who lived on Tyrell Street close to where I was staying and was a bit younger than I, thinking differently about my action, was displeased, causing me to throw a masterful left hook to his jaw. With the presence of George, the hurt and angry boy withdrew.

At dusk that same night, he was walking nearby with others, unbeknownst to me, and threw a rock at my face and ran. Luckily, it missed me. On the following night, I was on the wharf when I unexpectedly received a closed-hand blow to my face—we called that a cuff—from the same boy. Again, he and his companions ran away, as did I, much faster, in the other direction. From then on, I avoided him as best I could.

Another incident, not about fighting, involved Susana Lang, a girl in my class or one lower in Mt. Pleasant School who had lent me her book of Grimm's fairy tales. A week or two later, she asked for its return. I told her, without a doubt in my mind, that I had already returned it, but she said no.

Crying, she reported me to Iah. Again, with no doubt, I repeated that I had returned the book, and in this I was supported by a boy from another village who was attending our school and who ate lunch with us at the shop. He claimed that he saw when I had returned the book. Iah knew that I could not lie to her, being afraid of her holy water. The uncertainty of truth on earth, except for—"I am the way, the truth…" (John 14:16).

So, that was that.

It was not long after, without it on my mind, when to my great dismay, I found the book on the shelf in the boys' bedroom at home. I was totally surprised and too ashamed, so I threw it in the latrine pit.

Yes, now, that was that.

What had seemed to have been the truth was now revealed to be a lie.

Strangely, some years later, Susana and I developed an interest in each other, which Iah blamed for my low placement in a subsequent exam, as if eighth in a class of some twenty or so was that bad. But then, placing third or fourth was the usual. More will be said about this.

The Lang family lived off the main street of Grand Bay near to the gospel hall. During my last year in Mt. Pleasant School and into the summer holidays, I apprenticed at the shop of the eldest son, Paul, a well-known tailor of the village. This was discontinued after I moved to Grenada to attend GBSS.

The next time I recall seeing him was at his home, near to the area we called Works, after his return from the UK. He was then of advanced age, and his wife indicated that he was not completely with it. He did not recognise me. Of course, his house was large and of a block-concrete construction.

The story of another incident is preceded by the following introduction: Most families in Carriacou reared fowl. Although we once reared a few Rhode Island Red hens, which I believe we got from Godwin's in-laws, most were of a common variety. So common was raising fowl that one insult we used was to call someone a yard fowl, which meant that the target of the insult lacked mettle and gathered like fowl around the person with the corn. A politician from Grenada once referred to another in the Caribbean as a yard fowl.

When we cooked the fowl, we referred to it as fowl meat. When we spoke of chickens, we were usually referring to the baby chicks.

On the inside of our fowl house, tree branches or wooden perches stretched from one side to the other as cross bars, on which the fowl could roost. In the mornings, we piled the fireside ashes into a pan and scattered them over the fowl's doodoo on the earth floor of the coup. Occasionally, we did a general cleaning of the coup and used the matter as fertilizer.

Our meats were just chopped-up portions—no steaks. Usually, in the absence of other meats, a pullet or an older cock was sacrificed to provide meat for the main meal on Sundays. We never had fish for lunch on Sundays. It was at times necessary to parboil the tough meat of the cock on the previous day.

I am not sure why, but I indicated that I loved the head of the fowl, so that was the only portion that I was served. Eventually, I complained that it was insufficient—after all, it was mainly bone—and Iah agreed that I should get an additional piece of meat.

I don't remember who got the prized gizzard. The sternum was sometimes split apart, but at times, what looked like the clavicles, though they were not anatomically so, remained intact when served. As is still customary, we would use them in making wishes.

Rarely, some hens laid their eggs in the fowl house, but most wandered into the surrounding bushes. If we were unable to readily locate the nest, we would attach a string to the hen's leg in the mornings and then follow her to discover the eggs. Not all the eggs were to be hatched, as some were for consumption, either fried for breakfast or used as an ingredient in cakes and eggnogs.

On Sundays, when brother John was manning the shop, I had to carry his lunch from the house to him. One Sunday, William H. Mills was in the shop, and despite John's warnings, he encouraged me to eat a piece of John's fowl meat. There was obvious reluctance on my part, but with his persistence, I foolishly did.

Perhaps anticipating what was in store for me, the same W. H. was present in the house that night. After I received a good flogging from Iah, he, sitting in the rocking chair, took me onto his lap and consoled me by singing, "I'm going to take you on a slow boat to China." I believe strongly that that was the last set of licks I received from the iron lady, after the one for leaving the staves on the tract.

W. H. was another accomplished tailor in Grand Bay. He was born with incompletely formed upper limbs, and his deformed, tapered forearms looked like stakes ending without hands. And yet, he expertly manoeuvred the cloth on the sewing machine. When I later taught at GBSS for two terms in 1961, he outfitted me on an IOU agreement—gabardine pants, of course, with two pleats in the front.

As a boy, I also remember his bouts of binge drinking, which we called spells. Even Iah could not stop him for that week or two, when he drank from our shop.

The incident that I really wish to refer to relates indirectly to our neighbour Dama Cayenne. She also reared fowl, and one of her hens proudly strutted at the back of our house with some eight good-looking chicks behind her. With no one in sight, and with obvious jealously and envy, I unconsciously disjointed the legs of one of them.

I have no idea what became of it.

I must have been about 8 years old when, on an early Saturday morning before the sun was yet unkind, I found a set of roasted nuts in the yard at the front of the kitchen. Whether I called or they just happened to be there, Henry, of Fowah's upper house, and Gordon, of Dama's lower house, both a bit younger than me, joined in eating these fairly good tasting nuts.

Within the hour, all three of us were violently puking and rolling with bellyaches. Iah was in the shop and could not help us. But within the next hour, we were back in fairly decent shape. Iah, when told, was very mad with the maid who had thrown out the nuts, and in what Iah considered the wrong place.

Why they were picked, roasted, and then discarded, I don't know, but perhaps it was to obtain their oil. The nuts were from the highly poisonous physic plant, which was often planted as a hedge against soil erosion.

I have had encounters with paedophiles and obviously homosexual men. Someone from Grand Bay once pulled down his pants and asked me to do likewise, but he never touched me. We were in a garden, and I was only about seven years old.

A man called Rat befriended some of the students at GBSS and allowed us into the balcony of the Empire Theatre for free. He would then sit near to us. I think he particularly liked Snobies, who carried a razor blade in case Rat tried anything.

OTHER PERSONAL INCIDENTS IN MY YOUTH: MISCHIEVOUS?

In New York, on vacation in 1962 or 1964, Terrence invited me to spend a night at his place. All night, I was forced to fend him off. On another night, walking back to the subway from a visit to Manhattan, a white dude approached me but was repulsed. He said that if I ever changed my mind that he was listed as the last name in the telephone directory under P, Pusey.

At university, the lecturer in organic chemistry, a subject in which I excelled, once invited me to his flat in Irvine Hall. We chatted, but he made no indecent approaches. I did not even walk with a razor blade. Some years later, he was murdered in Jamaica.

Children in particular, for whatever reason, were fearful of some persons who were considered to be wicked or evil. Such was how we considered Sydney Cayenne. The image of him was of a tall black man with red eyes. He operated a shop on the main street of Grand Bay and would usually sit at the back door keeping surveillance on his fertile land near to ours in the valley below. As far as I know, he was the first in the village to own a rifle, which would be leaning next to him, as he surveyed.

I think he was also the man who gave young Godwin, my eldest brother, an old army pistol. He played with it, not realising that there was still a bullet in it. The bullet was discharged and could have ended the life of Nicholas, my next oldest brother, except it just grazed his leg. Years later, Godwin said to me, "Guess what your mother said? 'Oh, God. Godwin wanted to kill me son Nicholas.'"

Anyhow, one year, our land did not produce a good harvest, so Iah sent me to purchase dry corn seeds from Mr. Cayenne, whose production was bountiful. On returning with the bowl on my head, I was just about approaching the shop, where Iah sat on her bench looking out, when I stumped my foot and the bowl fell. The fowl rushed in with their chicks from nowhere but from everywhere. I chased them away whilst Iah retrieved the corn. Her prophetic words to me, were, "That's why you will never come first, making that bad mistake, getting ninety-nine but never a hundred per cent."

She bequeathed that I would always be an also-ran.

Somewhat later, when I was a teenager, I was back in Carriacou from Grenada on school vacation, and Iah sent me to the sea with this same man, Cousin Sydney. That first day, the water was extremely rough. I was in the front of the boat welding one oar, and he was in the back with the other. We ought to have been in synchrony, but with his strength overpowering mine, the boat turned almost completely around on every pull. He also fretted, for in order to raise the fish pot, I would have to handle both oars to keep the boat fairly stationary. That proved impossible in the bad weather conditions.

That first day was the only day, unlike quite a few days with Bastapool.

Around that time, Sydney Cayenne, as a widower, had invited my sister Alethea to be his wife. She sought my advice once when I was on vacation from Grenada, and I was against it. She married him anyhow.

I was told that he often beat her until one day when Iah cautioned him with an ultimatum, promising to kill him if he ever again laid his hands on her daughter. They never divorced, but Alethea returned to our home not long after to live out the rest of her life. All this time, I was mainly in Grenada attending GBSS.

The next one in the village to purchase a rifle was Charles Cayenne—yes, the same one who was the second person to buy a car. His dog was known to kill and eat fowl and sheep, and one day, while it was just lying in the yard, Charles, less than five feet away, aimed and fired to kill it.

After the loud sound, all that happened was that rocks were dislodged from the ground and were blown onto Say Doone and Say Beebee's house. The dog just turned its head and looked at Charles.

We children could have been hurt, as we were all standing nearby, so we did not stick around any longer. The dog may have later died from natural causes or from being attached to a brick and thrown into the sea, a not unusual act.

Say Doone and her daughter lived on the southern slope just below our house. They were often visited, perhaps daily and for long periods, by Say Doon's son, Amos, who lived about a hundred yards eastward. Whether true or not, it was believed that mental illness ran in that family, but as far as I recall, they disturbed no one. To me, they were just different and private in their dealings. A son of his, Semmie, was the one who died on the grounds of the shop, causing a rift between John and Verna.

Say Beebee was known for guarding her plum and sugar apple trees, by chasing the children away and also by tying a corked bottle filled with a coloured fluid to the plum tree. It was believed that if one stole and ate the plums, one would become corked, or constipated. The only relief would come when the bottle was uncorked. And guess what? The children believed, for a time anyhow. I don't even think that that family ate any or many of the plums. Nonetheless, I always got away with stealing the fruits, and even when I was seen doing so, Say Beebee did nothing other than talk.

I suspect that they always had a scarecrow in their house garden, as a few others also did, including us, but only rarely.

In Carriacou, like in Grenada, there were two types of plum trees. They were named after which of our two seasons in Carriacou they fruited during—one, whose fruit was purple and bumpy when ripe, was called a season plum (scarlet plum, in Bahamas), and the other, whose fruit was yellow with smooth but leathery skin, was called a dry weather plum (hog plum, in Bahamas).

Perhaps in or about 1947, about a month prior to the school's end-of-year vacation, I accompanied Iah to the village of Grand Roy in St John's parish in Grenada and stayed at the home of the Louisons, who were relatives or friends. Mr. Louison was the head teacher of Grand Roy School, and he and his family were accommodated in the provided residence.

Of course, this village became somewhat notable, as it was the birthplace of Mr. Francisco Slinger, better known far and wide as the Mighty Sparrow of calypso fame out of Trinidad.

Mrs Louison had previously visited us in Carriacou and slept in the same bed with Iah. I was then sleeping on the floor of the living room.

It was at the house of the Louisons that I participated for the first time in the gathering of the family at table to eat. Every morning, green tea was poured through a strainer from the teapot into each person's teacup. Also, only then did I realise that people ate with knives and forks.

There were other children around, and we played in the yard, on the grounds, and in the classrooms of the school. I remember that near to the residence, there was a huge cinnamon tree and other smaller trees, including a borden or bay leaf tree. Both the cinnamon bark and bay leaves were also used to make tea.

I suspect that Iah went elsewhere or back home, but for reasons I don't know, it was perhaps on this occasion that she sent me to spend time in Mt. Moritz, where my eldest brother, Godwin, was the headmaster of the village school. Adeline, the eldest of the three girls, lived with him at the head teacher's residence, as did my brother Lysander, who was then attending GBSS. Visiting us quite often from within the village was Collins, a son of Godwin who was a few years younger than me.

Later in life, I also met two of Godwin's other children from Mt. Moritz, Florence and Cecil. All three were born before his marriage, perhaps to different mothers.

Prior to that visit and in Carriacou, I had developed the habit of eating gravel stones from the track roads, especially after it had rained and the earth emanated that distinct scent, petrichor. This continued in Grenada, though I ate not the small rocks but the concrete matter of which the house was constructed. I dug it out with a nail or a knife.

On leaving, a villager gave me a puppy dog, and I took it with me when Lysander and I sailed back to Carriacou. Except for a red forehead dot, its coat was all white. We named him Spot.

OTHER PERSONAL INCIDENTS IN MY YOUTH: MISCHIEVOUS?

On the boat, I had a bellyache, and I didn't know what to do. Eventually, I shat on myself. In Carriacou, on Mr. Emmons's truck from town to Mt. Pleasant, I sat between Lysander's legs in the front passenger seat. The stench that emanated from me carried throughout the truck, and Lysander, pretending that it came from him, accepted the blame. On arrival at the shop, Iah, who was back home, immediately stripped me completely naked and bathed me.

I continued eating gravel and suffered from the obvious results of being unwell, leading Iah to take me to the hospital. The doctor, Lincoln Radix, left the interview room for an adjoining room and returned with what looked like a very shiny, long knife. He then promised to cut open my belly if I ever ate gravel again. He totally succeeded, as, being so scared, I never again purposely placed another bit of gravel in my mouth.

Was it perhaps then that I first entertained becoming a doctor, or was it already seeded in my mind? The answer is, I don't know.

In the pint that we had brought, the druggist dispensed worm medicine. Another common medication given to children was asafoetida. This was sometimes put against a child's stomach and held in place by a cloth band to treat a condition referred to as a dropped bosom, whatever that meant.

Spot was later called Pots, for no matter where in Carriacou big pots of food were being cooked for an event, Spot found his way there. One day, he disappeared as usual but never returned. We never knew what became of him. He strayed, yes, but all dogs in the village had a home, unlike in the Bahamas, where there are many stray dogs without homes, except when taken care of by the Humane Society.

At that time, we had two other dogs at home, Bingo and Romeo, both neutered, and they, together with Spot when he was around, were always fighting with Da Joe Simon's dogs, whenever they passed by our home.

One day, Bingo was lying down under the house when there occurred a good shower of rain that resulted in a rivulet being formed above but coasting downwards towards the dog. Still some few feet away, the dog arose, moved to the head of the water, dug a bypass, and went back to lie down in his spot.

Long years after, I visited the homestead to attend the funeral of my brother Lysander, who we sometimes called Lee. A service at church was now the usual. As the line of cars entered Mt. Pleasant after the church service in town, the two dogs that were then at home lay down flat with the heads on the ground and lowly moaned.

Dogs do sense things.

And now, a final bit at mischief: At a concert one night at university, I was not inside the hall but rather stood at the wide-open doors within a group of other students. A student took the stage, and as he started singing Matt Munro's "Born Free", I began loudly singing, "Walk away. Please go," from another Matt Munro song. I then immediately turned around to look at others.

Lysander

If ever there was a gentle soul—one born on 25 June 1932—it was Joseph Lysander "Lee" Brathwaite, my brother. I only vaguely remember him in Carriacou prior to my visit to Mt. Moritz in Grenada. But when he returned home on vacations, he would give me rides on his back, and after he had acquired the Cambridge Junior School certificate, he returned to live at home and teach at the village school.

I know he slept in Iah's bed, often with me between the two of them, once I was no longer peeing the bed.

He was never into working the land but was more at home, helping in the shop, or teaching. The following comes courtesy of Godwin: Once, on a visit, Godwin, John, and Lysander went to the land. He handed Lysander a cutlass to go get some wood to take home for fuel. John asked him if he was crazy, saying that Lysander would only cut himself. So said, so proven correct; Lee returned bleeding from his leg.

I know he went to Brooklyn, New York, to marry Norma Charles, a twin sister of Darnley, who had died suddenly in her sleep as a preteenager when they both were still in Carriacou.

I remember the cries and shouts from their home one Friday morning and then, throughout the day, the wailing of her guardian, Cousin Tayma, who *bind her belly* and kept repeating that the arithmetic was wrong.

"Add up that sum again."

Lysander did not stay for more than a week or two in New York and as far as I know was never again with his wife. However, the union had produced a daughter, Yvonne, who resided with her mother in New York.

After teaching, Lysander worked in the post office building in town in the revenue office. He became the revenue officer and also had tenures in this position in Grenville and Gouyave in Grenada.

When Iah was sick in 1974, I spent a night with him in Grenville on my way to Carriacou from Trinidad, where I was doing a short medical course, and when he was stationed in Gouyave, he spent the 1975 Christmas holidays with Vivian and me in St George's. It was during this period that I was employed as a pathologist in Grenada.

I became aware that his daughter, Yvonne, once visited him from New York. He accommodated her in his one-bedroom flat in Grenville, where both slept in the same bed—a situation by which, I was made to understand, she was totally appalled.

His manner was always rather casual, and he seemed not to be always thoughtful. After he returned from Gouyave to be the revenue officer in Carriacou, he displayed a posture and demeanour perhaps less than that expected for his position, although he was very respectful and seriously knowledgeable about his work.

I understand that he was promoted to the position of district officer of Carriacou, the most senior administrative post on the island, and caused a bit of back gossip when he appeared in a T-shirt for a formal function.

But he had the neatest handwriting, like Chester Prime did, and loved reciting poems. So, it does not surprise me that he may have played in carnival during the Shakespeare Mas.

When we were together at home, we always got on extremely well. He loved playing with children, running with them cradled in his arms or riding on his back. He eventually got into some trouble for this, having been accused of sexually assaulting a young girl, which he repeatedly denied doing, including to me personally when I visited.

Despite his denials, some in the village believed that he was of that disposition, but he said to me that if that were so, how was it that he never earned that reputation during his spells in Grenada.

He seemed very happy that I was in court with him when, after being advised to accept a plea bargain, he was charged EC$3,000, a third of which was for the treasury and the rest for the child's mother. This occurred in 2010.

He went often to the beach in Mt. Pleasant, and whenever I visited home, it was usual for us to go together. In his years of retirement, after the death of John, he took over running the shop. He remained at the home and had his own room when the house was remodelled.

His day started with him feeding the fowl and then going to the shop early in the morning. He would close the shop and climb the hill back home for breakfast, and then go back to the shop. He walked to the beach every day for a swim and, after sea bathing with a group of his friends that included Henry Shade and Lenny John, walked back home for lunch. He then returned to the shop until the end of the day.

I have been told that for some time, he stopped going to the beach and complained to his friends that he was no longer able to climb the hill to home without having to stop and catch his wind.

He died suddenly at home after breakfast on 7 February 2011 and was certified as having died from a myocardial infarction on the basis of severe sclerosis of the coronary arteries. I must admit that I had spoken to him before about his weight and expanded waistline.

Both Lysander and Alethea were controlled by Iah, particularly in terms of providing the finances for the home. In this regard, I owe a lot to them, for they would have supplied whatever extra monies were necessary for me to attend GBSS and the university in Jamaica. I eventually made financial contributions, but except with my love, I fell short of fully compensating them, or better yet, of offering full restitution.

I went from Freeport, Bahamas, to attend to matters concerning his funeral, and on arrival the day or two before, I spent a lonely moment with his body at the funeral home in town. I had no intention of attending the funeral, for by then, I no longer attended funeral services.

However, on the day itself, after the moaning of the dogs, I went to the cemetery, arriving just as his coffin was about to be lowered into the grave. I shouted for them to halt, placed a flower that I had picked from the yard at home on the coffin, and without a word to anyone, tearfully left.

Years before he died, he had given me his hairbrush, as he then kept his head shaved. I still have it and use it daily, though like a portion of a partly toothless prehistoric mandible, there are gaps as the bristles continue to be detached. On the last day of February, 2024, the month in which he had died, I discarded the brush.

I believe that Godwin and I, though grey and balding, were the only male siblings who kept visible hairs on our heads.

It's highly unusual for me to attend funerals because of my mournful experiences with a few of them. The first was that of a toddler who I had diagnosed with leukaemia during my stint in Grenada in the 1970s. Adequate therapy was neither available nor affordable if sought elsewhere. We had kept her alive by blood transfusions from her parents.

One day, the mother came to my office in the laboratory and said that they were no longer able to donate blood and accepted that the child's death was inevitable. I attended the funeral service at the Roman Catholic church. Not too long into the service, I was overwhelmed and ran out with my flowing tears.

The other was of the wife of my physics teacher at GBSS in Grenada. She had been the matron of the general hospital when I returned as the pathologist. I again hurriedly left the church. More will be said about my physics teacher. I, as a student, used to take flowers to her home on Church Street in St George's.

8

THE GRENADA BOYS SECONDARY SCHOOL: ANOTHER SMALL STEP

Well! Hello, GBSS. Hello, St George's. And hello, Grenada. It's January 1953, and here come two kayaks aboard the *Principal S*, ready to do battle, with brains groomed, ready and willing to absorb knowledge.

The scholarship results had placed George Griffith in first place, followed by, I think, Joslyn Winsborough in third place, and Jack Radix in fifth.

Two were from Carriacou and all others from Grenada.

In the capital, St George's, the scholarship examinations were said to be very competitive between the primary schools, with each school being identified in local lingo by both students and adults by the names of the head teachers—Fletcher, Hindsy (Hinds), Morris, for example.

Before departing Carriacou, as was customary in Mt. Pleasant, my dear mother had selectively identified homes and had made certain that I visited them to respectfully say farewell—and perhaps to receive a small financial contribution. Except for three, I don't remember all of the visits I made, but there were between ten and twenty.

I visited Uncle Deeclo and Mr. Fortune Simon, with each giving me a shilling. On the third visit, I went on a late afternoon to Mt.

Royal to see a dear older lady, who had liked me in a motherly way. I did not expect any money from her and was not offered any. We chatted for a while as she fried two fowl eggs with too much added coarse salt for my liking. From my visits, I ended up with a total of nine shillings.

It was expected, and the arrangements would have been made, that I would live at the home of my sister Adeline and her husband, Martin "Cheese" Lashley, on Bain Alley near to the Carenage (the wharf).

The Carenage was an incomplete circular promenade around the inner harbour, an extension of the Caribbean Sea. The street above it was Tyrell Street, and the next, further up the hill, was Green Street. Both ran almost horizontally above the harbour but were not as arched. Bain Alley was rather short, less than a hundred yards, and linked the above two streets.

An elderly lady, who we called Muddah (Mother), would occasionally be seen walking up from Tyrell Street, aided by a stick that she held in trembling hands, to her house at about midway up the alley. The well-known Caribbean comedian, Paul Keens-Douglas, aka Tim Tim, a son of the architect who had built the new Mt. Pleasant School, lived on Green Street above the alley and referred to Muddah in one of his comic routines.

In later years, Green Street would become very popular because of its football team's introduction of a successful, stylish, midfield draughts-board approach, with Linky loitering near the goal, ready to shoot—indeed, a winning brand of football. However, on my arrival in Grenada, children raced on the street in the evenings and into early nights, using the lamp poles, said to be spaced fifty yards apart from each other, for distance measures. I, the kayak boy, readily and easily defeated the then fastest Green Street boy, the same Paul Kings-Douglas, in our first race and every race thereafter.

Chester Merrill Prime, the other scholarship winner from Carriacou, was also going to stay at Adeline's. His father, Josiah, on saying goodbye to him at Adeline's home in my presence, gave him nine dollars and warned him to stay close to me and to follow and take my advice. I knew that this was not so much to do with me but with the respect associated with the Brathwaite name.

Two beds were in our room. One was for George, my older brother who was already attending GBSS, and the slightly larger other one was to be shared by Chester and me.

I don't remember if I took showers at the Louisons' or at Mt. Moritz when I first visited Grenada, but at Adeline's, we definitely took showers before breakfast as we got ready to go to school. My first government-supplied, piped-water showers were therefore in Grenada. The adjacent toilet was supplied with water from an overhead tank on the wall with an attached chain for pulling.

At the school, I was introduced to a new word for the toilets: *ablutions*.

The school's uniform included short khaki pants, shoes, socks, a white short-sleeved shirt, and the school tie with its pattern of blue, green, and yellow stripes on a red background. Those were the colours of the four houses—School, Archer, Hughes, and Heape. On formal occasions, our blazers with the school badge on the left pockets were also worn. The bigger boys were clad in long, grey pants.

In St George's, many homes were established as boarding houses to accommodate the out-of-town students. Proper decorum was expected in these homes. Persons who were not accustomed to using the knives and forks had a broomstick placed between both arms and the back to prevent their arms from extending to another person at table.

The charges were about equal, and the meals would have been similar, with breakfast consisting of a hot beverage, such as tea (perhaps Lipton) or an instant beverage like Ovaltine, Milo, chocolate, Fry's cocoa, or the more elaborately prepared native cocoa; a portion of canned meat, sausages, blood pudding, fish, cheese, or eggs; two small loaves of tight or leavened bread with butter or jam; and maybe a small glass of juice.

Adeline, however, only gave a loaf and a half of bread, and she tended to deceive by serving them as slices. One morning, Chester got up from the table crying, and even though Adeline added more bread to his plate, he did not return and did not respond to her questions arising from her consternation and concern. I don't think there was a problem with the other meals.

I do not remember how long Chester remained, whether for that term or the year, but he left Adeline's for the boarding house of Ma Lottie on Scott Street, where a couple of the existing boarders were Carriacouan students. Both of us and others were deeply saddened by the sudden, unexpected death of Hugh O'Neal, a fellow student, at one of these homes.

Chester and I never discussed the incident or the circumstances, and it never interfered with our friendship, which lasted beyond GBSS, through university, to our time in New York, and long after, until his death. We were born in the same year, I in April and he in July.

At school, we played lawn tennis together at the Tanteen Tennis Club, where "Redman" Kyron Charles, the coach and groundskeeper, took us under his tutelage and gave me a second-hand racquet, which was my first.

During summer vacations, we organised cricket games in Carriacou of Mt. Pleasant vs Dover, alternating the sites.

Our school tennis captain, Ronald "Doom Doom" McLean, who was staying at Ma Lottie's, once organised a Saturday morning match between a group of GBSS boys and another team of Grenadian white guys, who attended Presentation Brothers College.

The tennis court was at the home of one of them, either in the district of St Paul's or close by. I defeated a younger player, who years later became Grenada's male singles champion. Chester lost his match against one of the Alleyne boys, either Hugo or Kenny, a younger brother of Brian. The latter would be a legal mind of prominence in the Caribbean in later years.

A couple of years after Chester had left us, another Carriacouan, Winston Simon, who was entering GBSS, joined us at Adeline's, but he did not last too long at school. Years later in England, he became Rhoda's husband. I gather that he is no longer alive.

Chester and I were both in New York in medical residencies in the early 1970s, and after acquiring specialist credentials, he established a home with his wife and daughter and an obstetrics-and-gynaecology practice in Brooklyn, New York.

Whenever I happened to visit New York, he always entertained me. On one of these visits, he offered to take me to dinner and asked what food I would like to have. I responded that my preference was for Chinese. He more or less ridiculed me and instead said that he would take me to have a real New York steak. He did, and it was good.

He once took me to the US Open Tennis Grand Slam competition in Queens. As we were about to leave, he saw and hailed the Williams sisters, who were walking towards a practice court, and we had a little chat with them. They were somewhat excited to meet someone who lived in the Bahamas, where I had established my new home.

My dear friend died in New York on 29 March 2012, and I said my final farewell to him at his gravesite in Jean Pierre Cemetery in Carriacou on 14 July 2012.

In the home of the Protains along Green Street, Joy, a young daughter, would look out of the window and teasingly refer to Chester and me as "kayaks", expressed then as a derogatory term. She also called us, and some others, country bookies, a term that was broadly applied to anyone who was not from St George's, the capital. It appeared that it was customary for students from Dominica to attend GBSS; I wonder what she would have called them.

Her brother, Gary, was in my form at GBSS and befriended me, and I believe that he may have had homosexual leanings. I never knew what became of him.

In my first GBSS athletic meet, I placed third in the 80-yard dash after Bob Morris and Gregory Williams and received a belt as my prize. Weeks after, in the intercollegiate meet between Presentation Brothers College and GBSS, Robert Morris and I placed second in the wheelbarrow race, with Robert on hands and I holding the legs.

Paul Keens-Douglas never featured in any of the events.

It was not unusual for my school to defeat Presentation Brothers in athletics, but in those days, they always won at football and delighted in scoring six goals.

The next time I competed in the GBSS meet was in 1960, when I placed fourth in the javelin throw. However, throughout my stay, I always gained points for my house, Hughes, in the pre-sports-day qualifying heats, including the actual cross-country race. At that time, the other houses were School, which was changed to McGuire in honour of a previous master, Baggies; Heape, which I understand was later changed to Baptiste, in honour of a previous headmaster; and Archer, which was Chester's house.

Adeline

Adeline and author

I am aware that people can change but the transformation that I saw in my sister Adeline between about 1956 and 1960 was downright dramatic, considering that for some two years, things were going very well.

George and I were her messenger boys, which entailed getting ice from her in-laws or from the factory on the wharf, getting meat from the abattoir, getting other farm produce at the Saturday market, getting blood pudding from Mrs Nedd's shop, and responding in the early evenings to the conch shell from the wharf signalling the arrival of the fish boats with jacks.

She insisted that I attend the Anglican church, where I soon became confirmed. Later, on Sunday mornings, with her in her bed, the three of us completed the weekly newspaper crossword puzzles together.

George and I spent our vacations in Carriacou, and on returning, one of us would bring red sweeties (candy) from our shop for her, which she expected and reminded us to do.

Our relationship soured not overnight but slowly before finally erupting. Of course, I might have engineered or been partly responsible for it, but I saw a gentle, caring lady become unreasonable, taking away the usual favours that I had once enjoyed. My opinion of her then was that she had a calculating, mean, changeable personality.

In the house, I eventually had to buy a lantern or candles to study at nights after 10 p.m., so at times, I would go to study under the streetlamps where my friend Cyril Bascombe was staying. Sometimes, I also walked to GBSS to study at nights. Thinking back, I had no thought of fear on returning home that late at night. I doubt if any teenager would do that now.

Instead of including my clothes as usual in the weekly laundering, she now refused to do mine. She allowed me, for a short time, to use the newly bought washing machine, but soon, she denied me its use. So, on a weekly basis, I had to send my laundry home to Carriacou in a grip on Saturday by the mail boat, to be returned on the following

Tuesday. In the pocket of a pair of pants, Iah would have placed some money.

Adeline's three boys, Junior (Charles), Jimmy (James), and Ramon, were mischievously troublesome, especially when she went out to the YWCA meetings at nights. Once, when they spent a summer vacation in Mt. Pleasant, Iah, their grandma, was not too happy with their behaviour.

Many years later, in chatting with Godwin, I spoke of what had evolved, but Godwin indicated that our sister had always shown a tendency to behave that way, particularly by being rather mean to Lysander. When they had lived in Mt. Moritz, she would call Lysander derogatory names, like moo-moo.

In St George's, Adeline was well accepted as an accomplished seamstress. I once bought cloth from Granby's store for her to sew a shirt for me. She first made one for her son, Junior, and then made mine, which turned out to be too small.

Whatever was left of the love between us vanished when, for the first time in my life, I knew what it meant to see stars. I had received, like an explosion, the loudest, strongest slap to my face because I had bought something with the money that I'd gotten from selling one of my schoolbooks without telling her first.

The selling of second-hand books to advancing students was usual at school.

When I was finished with school and received a post as a teacher, I promptly moved to the boarding house of Nurse Alexandra Radix on the Carenage, a stone's throw from Adeline's. Miss De La Roache, a friend of Adeline, scolded me for making this move. Another friend of hers, Vicky, was also not happy.

During my stay with Nurse Radix, I was treated as a son by her; indeed, she behaved as a mother to all of her boarders, relatives or not. This continued after I returned to Grenada in 1974 as a pathologist. She, working then for the Planned Parenthood Association, loaned me their microscope and also employed me to do weekly clinics at two centres, Gouyave and Perdmontemps, during which I performed general examinations, administered Pap smears, and installed intrauterine loops. She could have found others, but she was looking out for me.

I paid Nurse Radix forty dollars per month for board and lodging, and paid another lady ten to fifteen dollars to do my laundry. That lady was also a servant in the house and was the nightly companion of a shop owner, whose shop was on the first floor of the two-storey boarding house. She enjoyed telling us boarders some tales of their love affair. She jokingly related that though her man, of an elderly age, may take long to get his sails up, once that had been achieved, he would sail her slowly into the harbour, where they would successfully land. One morning, she looked quite happy, and we asked her for the reason. Her response: *"The gladness remains."*

It was at Nurse Radix's house that I had crushes on two of the residents, Marcia Jacques and Chester's sister, Gloria, who later joined the nursing programme at the university in Jamaica and was dating a big guy from Dominica. At that time, I never seriously thought of pursuing her because of the friendship between Chester and me.

Decency prevailed, as it always should.

After I had left GBSS as a student in 1960 and lived a short distance away from Adeline's home, we became again the loving brother and sister we were meant to be and also friends. Her then youngest child, Deanna, was a true moppet, loving her uncle and wanting to leave with him whenever his visit was over.

When I left Nurse Radix's for university, Adeline presented me with gifts of linen. There were times in visiting from abroad that I and Vivian, my wife, stayed with her in Grenada, and at her home was a bottle of whisky, the consumption of which, together with our loving chats, brought us very close.

I was once on vacation in Grenada when Martin "Sticks" McLaren and his wife visited on their honeymoon. I arranged with Adeline to entertain them and a group of my friends, including George "Snobies" Griffith, a classmate from GBSS, at her home one night.

On subsequent nights, we were likewise entertained at the homes of Chasley David and Dr Lloyd Alexis, a Grenadian doctor who was employed at the university hospital in Jamaica when I was a student there.

The McLaren's honeymoon continued in Carriacou, where I arranged for a boat to take us to spend a day on Petit St Vincent. Other than enjoying the beach and the restaurant, we were also invited to the home of the owner or manager, where we were offered peanut punch, a truly delightful drink.

We, including my friend and neighbour, Gordon Cayenne, continued partying that night at the home of Sticks's mother just beyond the town.

I twice visited Adeline at her new abode in Toronto, Canada. On the first occasion, we had lunch together with her son Jimmy, who was also visiting from the USA. The second time, in August 2006, Theresa, née Moore, a Grenadian, drove me to Adeline's apartment, where we chatted for a short while.

Theresa, a most fetching young lady in the 1950s, lived in Tanteen, and on her way to the St Joseph's Convent secondary school, she would cross paths with the boys travelling in the opposite direction to GBSS. She, like Pansy, was always neatly dressed. We were in Jamaica together, she in nursing, and enjoyed a wonderfully open platonic friendship.

She has achieved the seemingly impossible, growing even more attractive with age.

I have also seen my sister when she visited her son Junior's residence in Nassau, Bahamas. Whenever I had reason to be in Nassau, I would visit with him and always received royal treatment. I saw her in November 2008 for matters related to the death of her granddaughter Lia. The last time I saw Adeline at Junior's was 13 October 2012, when he would have celebrated his sixtieth birthday.

Adeline, who lived in Canada, and I, who live in Freeport, Bahamas, continued having short telephone conversations until she passed on 10 September 2020 at the age of 95, having been born 23 December 1925. She was sadly followed by her first son, Junior, in December of that same year in Nassau.

People talk of all of my siblings and I as having the Brathwaite's features, but there were look-alikes among us—Godwin and Gilbert, George and John. Nicholas and I resembled each other in stature, but facially, I looked like Adeline. Come, Ned. Come, little Ned.

Martin, Adeline's husband, who predeceased her, never interfered in the relationship between Adeline and me. He and I got on quite well, and when I lived in Suriname, he once visited with us.

The home of F. J. Archibald was next to Adeline's on Bain Alley. The neighbourhood boys would play windball cricket in his yard, usually on Saturday afternoons before going to a matinee. Many a time, the ball ended up in the Jordan, and we would have to chase it down before it disappeared. The Jordan was a constructed, walled open drainage system running from the higher residential areas to the sea at the Carenage.

Living in that residence was Chico Archibald, who was always very friendly. He was years older than me and was a basketball player and boxer. I met his daughter, the most charming Arlene, who worked at the hospital laboratory. F. J. Archibald ran for a seat in the Grenada parliament, losing to T. A. Marryshow, more than once. I believe he may have been elected as the mayor of St George's sometime later.

Other homes in the area included that of the Boodhoos, who operated a small grocery store; the Mitchells, who owned a schooner; the Wilsons, known for working in the government's finance department; the Pattersons; the Nesfields; the Fletchers; and the Halls and Caesars, who lived at different times in the same house.

In the lower forms at GBSS, tests were held every two weeks. The first three places were announced at the morning assembly on the following Monday, and the winners would be pinned with stars to be worn until the next results.

The results for my class in forms two (the entry form) and three-A were predictable. John "Biggles" George and Nestor "Popees" Ogilvie were alternately first and second, and in third place would be either Chester "Tartar" Prime, George "Snobies"

Griffith, Alfred "Little Rice" Brathwaite, Winston "Papalee" Phillips (also called Bobby), or rarely, others.

It has been said that after he had left GBSS some years later, hundreds from John George's village in Grenada came to the town to see their black boy enter the Royal Bank of Canada as an employee. As far as I know, he ended up at Howard University, where he specialized in ob-gyn, and became well known in the Caribbean.

At school, there were the headmaster and the assistant masters, who formally addressed the students by their surnames. Most students, however, acquired nicknames, which their fellow students usually used. Some of these were aptronymic, some were something opposite from the character or appearance of the person, some were given for reasons that were not obvious, and some were given for reasons unknown to most. Many years later in Grenada, I played tennis with "B 5", his winning shout at bingo.

Nestor Ogilvie was a roly-poly, cry-baby kind of boy, earning him the nickname Popees, and John George was called Biggles because he read many of the Biggles books. Let me add here that the students were all encouraged and expected to use the facilities of the public library.

The Biggles and Gimlet series and the novels of Zane Grey were quite popular within the early forms. Of course, we also thoroughly enjoyed comic strips and books. Mutt and Jeff, Dagwood and Blondie, and Tarzan were some of my favourites.

In the higher forms, I started on the mystery books and enjoyed Agatha Christie and Erle Stanley Gardner and as my interest in science developed, I read the Popular Mechanics magazine.

As boys, we engaged in the usual youth activities, like sports, going to the movies, having girlfriends, and liming. We graduated from Chicklets to Wrigley's and on to bubble gum. Additionally, we collected and exchanged cards featuring female movie stars, on which were their vital statistics, we danced the hula hoop, and we pulled sugarcanes from the laden trucks on their way from the estates to the sugar or rum factory. Sometimes, the canes were tossed to us.

Particularly on Sunday afternoons, both young and adults took walks around St. George's, to the Botanic Gardens, and to Fort George where the police musical band occasionally performed. As older students, we, boys and girls, journeyed together to and from the Queen's Park, if our school was competing in a game.

With the popularity of sword fighting in the movies in those times—Errol Flynn in Captain Blood, Gene Kelly as d'Artagnan—we would sword fight using sticks. So wonderful! As the actor Stewart Granger said in the film *Scaramouche*, "You may turn your back on Scaramouche, my Lord, but surely you will not run away from Andre Moreau." We also made bows and arrows from twigs.

At that age, fights sometimes erupted between students, but the most well-known, reoccurring fight was between Ellis, a Grenadian, of GBSS and "Bubbles" Bullen, a Carriacouan, of Presentation Brothers College.

I seem to think that Chester Prime got his nickname Tartar from the time his head fell in a pile of cow dung whilst fighting on the playing field of the school.

To think of what Popees later became—a huge man, head of the cadets at school, who went to military school abroad (Sandhurst, England, I think), was in the military of Jamaica, and became police commissioner in Grenada. All of that would have been unthinkable in form two at GBSS.

He and his wife, Monica, who, as a nurse at the university hospital in Jamaica, always thought highly of me as a medical student, became highly religious. It was not unusual for me, when in Grenada, to visit their home when they were stationed there. One of the trees in my yard in Freeport, Bahamas, I grew from the seed of a fruit he had gathered on one of my visits. He called it condition or maybe *cornichon*. This may be the same as *bilimbi* in Guyana.

Let me add that some other nurses have expressed disappointment that I specialised in pathology, considering that during training, they thought highly of my skills at the bedside, citing, for example, how I once dealt with a deaf patient.

A man was admitted as a patient to the medical ward, and because he was deaf, there were difficulties in communicating. On my turn to examine him, I reversed my stethoscope, placing the earpieces to his ears as I spoke in the bell at the other end. His eyes brightened, and he smiled broadly.

Now I have to put up with the sad jokes of some of my friends when I am being introduced, such as, "If you are sick and on opening your eyes you see this doctor, you know you are dead. He is a pathologist."

The Ogilvie family, who hailed from Grenville (La Bay) in the parish of St Andrew, was well known. Popees had two older brothers of some prominence in the school, and all three were in Hughes house, as I was. The eldest brother who was then in GBSS was Roland. Sometime much later in life, in Grenada, I met another older brother, an orthopod or chiropractor.

Roland "Mercer" Ogilvie was an all-rounder and was picked to represent the Windward Islands in cricket against the visiting Australians. At bat, he was clean-bowled the first ball by the Australian captain, Ian Johnson, who, with another teammate, had addressed us at school the day before. Roland made a good come back to open the bowling and claimed two early wickets.

The other brother, Robert "Pye" Ogilvie, was also a cricketer as a leg break bowler at school. A few years later, being ahead of me, he passed on or sold me some of his anatomy class skeletal bones when we were studying medicine in Mona, Jamaica, at the University of the

West Indies (UWI), then called the University College of the West Indies. He did exceptionally well at university and distinguished himself by earning the award and title of Rhodes Scholar.

He finally settled in Ontario, Canada, as an ENT specialist. After university, we saw each other quite often, as we both usually attend the scientific meetings of the University of the West Indies Medical Alumni Association (UWIMAA).

Once, on a visit to Toronto in August 2006, he picked me up following my attendance at a session of the International AIDS Society Conference. He and his wife entertained me at his home, buying take-out jerk meat.

That night, they took me to a Grenadian get-together held on my behalf at George "Snobies" Griffith's home. Hensley "Beans" Miller, who had been two years ahead of me at GBSS, drove me back to the Holiday Inn Express, where I was staying in Toronto. He and his wife also regularly attend the UWIMAA conferences. These are held about every two or three years in different Caribbean territories, though they are now suspended, perhaps because of Covid. The last was in St Lucia in 2018. One is scheduled for July, 2023, in Jamaica.

At GBSS, two other prominent names of multiple siblings were the St Johns and the Steeles, and at Presentation Brothers College, there were the Fletchers. All demonstrated decent academic qualities and were keen sportsmen.

Some students, from a word of the school song, may have been considered slackers. One boy brought a goat tied to a rope with him to school. He was sent by his class master to the office of the headmaster, Sackies. On being summoned, he left the goat outside and walked in. As he entered, Sackies said, in his Barbadian accent, "Young man, bring in the other goat" From that day, the student became known as "la cabra".

During my first term at GBSS, Teacher Meemee of the gospel hall in Grand Bay, where I religiously attended Sunday school, sent me the welcome address that I was to deliver at the church's annual

Easter Tuesday entertainment ceremony of the church during my vacation after the Hilary term. It began, "Welcome, welcome, all are welcome here."

Here we go again. Recitations.

On a subsequent fun day of games at Mt. Pleasant beach, I easily defeated Antoo (Godwin Noel) in the boys' sprint event because of the practice sessions I had gotten in Grenada. At the time, Antoo was accepted as the fastest boy in Mt. Pleasant. My prize was a bag of new marbles.

Antoo was a weird individual. He rarely moved together with the other boys, particularly when we travelled to another village to engage in a cricket game. We never knew what route he took, but he would be there on time. I have already mentioned that on one occasion, at a small gathering of boys, a younger girl agreed for us to do rudeness. We tried to escape to the bushes, but Antoo kept following as a macco, so we eventually decided against it.

I believe that it was during the GBSS vacations after the Trinity term that first year that I became friendly with Susana Lang—yes, of the Grimm's Fairy Tales fiasco already mentioned. In those days, the report cards of students were mailed from the school to the home address, and in the end-of-year final examination after the Michaelmas term, I had placed eighth.

Iah was very unhappy and expressed the thought that I was being distracted because I was now studying woman, and so she blamed my relationship with Susana for my low placement.

I tried to explain that I was given a zero mark in the geography paper. The test paper had provided for the answers to be written on the question sheet itself. Unfortunately, I foolishly had not entered my name on the sheet. I had immediately explained that to the teacher after he had collected the papers, but he had refused to allow me to add my name. I had appealed no further, though thinking that it was an unjust and harsh decision on his part.

According to my recollection, the vacations were two, four, and three weeks after Hilary, Trinity, and Michaelmas terms respectively. Sometime afterwards, the "summer" vacation became much longer, and the sun in Carriacou was at its burning glory.

I think it was in the first year that a few of us received some form of training which enabled us to meet the tourists as they disembarked on the wharf. Each student, neatly attired in the school's uniform, would introduce himself and offer to accompany the visitor or group around St George's. If accepted, we usually received a small offering.

It must have been the onset of a new industry in Grenada, other than agriculture. Some boys and men dove for coins thrown by the tourists from the liners into the sea, hoping to get to them before they reached the bottom.

In addition to the above, we were exposed for a week or two to a mechanical workshop building located near to the school. I don't think we acquired any useful knowledge.

The trend of the biweekly tests and the placement order continued until form four, when it seemed that I was doing persistently better but still never surpassed George and Ogilvie. Scoring 100 per cent in that year-end exam in arithmetic earned me first place in that subject for the first time.

Where are you now, Iah? Talk that.

On entering form five-A in 1956, because I was bent on going to medical school, I included the required science subjects of biology, chemistry, and physics, in addition to English literature, mathematics, Latin, and the compulsory English language, as my choices for the Cambridge School Certificate examination. Once taken, students were advanced to form six-B, in preparation for the two years required to sit the Higher School Certificate (HSC) examination.

In form six-B, most of my day was not spent in the classroom but in the physics laboratory. From about that time or shortly after, female students from the Anglican high school attended some classes at our school. Among them and often in the lab was Cecile Lloyd, the daughter of the administrator of Grenada. His sons also attended GBSS. Miss Lloyd and I were also at UWI over the same period of time. I believe she got married to a fellow student, Carrington.

This B form was the only one that applied to all the students who had advanced from the fifth forms. In the others, the A forms were for the brighter students and the B for those not as bright, but they were otherwise equal in subjects and examinations.

One day, I realised that the results of the certificate exam must have arrived, because I saw guys carrying their desks from form six-B, which was located in another building across the quad, back to forms five-A and five-B. Based on those who I saw, I was certain that I had failed, although that would have been surprising. Chester Prime was one of those toting his desk.

The overall results were astounding, said to be perhaps the worst in the school's history. I passed but with the lowest grade, a third-division certificate, with credits in mathematics, English literature, and Latin, a pass in English language, low passes in biology and chemistry, and a failing grade in physics.

As far as I know, George and Ogilvie got higher grades. They would have left school at the end of their year in six-A, but I stayed on.

I believe that my best result in the exam was in literature, in which I earned a grade-three credit. Distinctions were reserved for grades one and two. Two books of study were Heyerdahl's *The Kon-Tiki Expedition* and Shakespeare's *Julius Caesar*. I knew the latter verbatim, end to end. I would have done well in the Carriacou Shakespeare Mas during carnival.

As I had done better in the arts subjects, the headmaster advised that I should adopt them and drop the sciences. I did not heed that advice. I was preparing to become a doctor, and my mind was set.

I must state that with time, I grew to believe that the teacher of chemistry and physics, Otto George, was certainly not the best of teachers that I have encountered, and later, I considered that the new chemistry teacher, M. O. St John, could be placed in a similar tier—neither were the best at imparting their knowledge. Otto was a loud, gruffy, short man who seemed to take delight in embarrassing the students. M. O. was big but more genteel in manner.

After advancing to form six-A, I eventually dropped physics for history, which I passed in the HSC exam in 1960. I earned a distinction in zoology in the same exam.

In my view, a few teachers—assistant masters or masters, as they were called at GBSS—at times behaved foolishly. In the form six-B final-year exam, Louis Masanto, my friend and later an accomplished pianist, was placed in a higher position than I was. The number of papers in the subjects differed, depending on the categories within each subject. So, for example, literature may have had three papers and zoology only two. This master, instead of using the average, merely added the marks of all the papers. Thus, nine results were totalled for Masanto against my seven, giving him third place, which should have been my position. I'm sure first and second would have been taken by George and Ogilvie.

I appealed to the form master, but he dismissed me. As with the zero mark that I had received in form two-A, I made no further issue of it.

Between 1959 and 1960, I reigned supreme in the sciences, earning the monikers "the walking lab" and "the lab on legs". I had an approach to study wherein if four aspects of a topic were given in the textbook, I sought a fifth. But at the end of the day, Martin "Sticks" McLaren won the biennial Grenada Island Scholar award for the year 1960, and I was an also-ran. The title I earned, proxime accessit, has been inscribed on the school's honours board. Sticks has called me by this title ever since.

The award was (and still is) granted based on the results of the HSC examination or its equivalent, and it entitled the winner to university attendance paid for by the government. Until my time and for years after, a student from GBSS was always the winner.

In 1959, I won many prizes, enough to attract a young lady, a student from the Anglican high school, to walk with me after the speech-night ceremony. We saw each other for a short time, but after seeing me with the athletes who were representing Carriacou, as already mentioned, she never spoke to me again.

My prize collection was repeated in 1960, but I lost out on the prize for botany, which was given to Winston "Dinkie" Mitchell, because he had chosen botany for his scholarship paper, and I had chosen zoology. The prize should have been based on the papers that we both sat, and in the general botany papers, I had earned better grades. This was another example of a silly decision by a master.

Despite the fact that we students competed against each other academically, we nevertheless got on very well. Certainly, as boys, we played pranks on each other, some of which I initiated but avoided being blamed for, what with that innocent face of mine.

For example, there was the time that Dinkie Mitchell left the school before the morning assembly to ride to his home in Mt. Moritz and back in less than what we considered to be the impossible time of ten minutes. He went to retrieve a memento he had taken from the agricultural fair that had been held on the preceding weekend on the school's playing field, after being told that the police had been informed of the theft.

Strangely, though Dinkie and I were together when he took the item, he never thought that it was I who had disclosed what had occurred to the rest of the class.

At another time, the rumour was spread that Tartar Prime was interfering with the daughter of the headmaster, K. I. "Sackies" Smith, and the rumour caused the headmaster's son, Maurice, a student in our class, to cry.

Rumour? Again, not from Alfred "Rice" Brathwaite.

The Windward Island's interisland secondary schools' tournament was held in Grenada in the summer of 1960. It was expected that I would be on the team, but my place was given instead to Wilfred

Charles. It was thought that one of the masters, Brim St Louis, was responsible for that, and he confirmed it years later. He was adamant, saying then that I must not make the team.

Whether he had something against me or was only fulfilling a promise to the other student, I don't know, but my general attitude was perhaps such that it generated in others a delight in putting me in my place.

I was asked to stay and help with the arrangements for the tournament, but Adeline had told me I could not stay back, at least not in her house. So, I vacationed in Carriacou. In the tournament, Sticks McLaren and Bobby Phillip had outstanding performances in cricket, with Sticks taking nine wickets in one game and being jestingly called the cricket victor ludorum.

My last year in GBSS as a student was in 1960. Many of us considered Mr. H. D. Baptiste (aka Bakes Mouth and Baksies), the master for the Hughes house, to be prejudiced. He held a ceremony in which Leon Wells, who was leaving at the end of 1959, handed over the captaincy, or head boy position, of the house to me. I was continuing on at school so as to have a stab at winning the island scholarship of 1960. However, George Briggs, a known favourite of Mr. Baptiste, who had left school but returned for the same reason, was subsequently made captain of the house by Bakes Mouth. I became the deputy.

H. D. Baptiste was the English language master in form six. It was difficult or impossible to score over ten out of twenty in the English essays, unless you were a Renwick, of nonblack looks, or a Briggs, a special boy to him. However, when A. N. Forde took over as the teacher, some of us soared to marks fourteen to sixteen.

And to think that when Choate came to GBSS from the USA for a debate, maybe in 1959, and set an exam in essay writing, the first three positions were held by nonwhite students. Neckles placed first, and I, third. Pictures of the first three of us made the front page of the local West Indian newspaper—my first photographic appearance in the media.

Anyhow, it was the same H. D. Baptiste, then the acting headmaster, who offered Dennis Toppin and me teaching positions at GBSS in 1961. The basic monthly salary was EC$145, but I earned about EC$195, the extra being for teaching botany in the higher classes. I also earned a bit more from students to whom I gave private botany lessons after hours.

I taught the form-two classes in scripture and English literature. I particularly enjoyed Tennyson's "The Charge of the Light Brigade" and Longfellow's "Paul Revere's Ride". I was not even discomforted by the student called "Big Dog"—called so for good reason. Well, maybe I was a little.

The students liked me because I never reported them for sneaking behind the physics lab, where I usually spent time during the breaks, and going through the fence to pick tamarinds. The agreement was that if they brought me some fruits, all would be well.

As a student, I spent most of the last three years in the physics lab rather than in the sixth-form classrooms. Otto George, the teacher in charge, whose office was in that lab, took advantage of my presence. I had to mix his powdered milk for him and his friends at the morning break, but I took advantage of the situation and always mixed enough to have my share.

Almost every week, he requested that I should go after school to the botanic gardens to get flowers to take to his home. And he expected us, whenever I returned home on vacation for the Christmas after the Michaelmas term, to purchase a turkey for him without an advance in cash and send it to him by the mail boat. Iah never liked this.

Nevertheless, we always did it, and we were paid on my return to school. Usually, we purchased the turkey from a below-side village in Carriacou, as they were rare in my two villages.

There was a level of friendliness between Otto and me, and I gave him the respect that he truly deserved. Over time, that changed into a true respectful friendship, which extended to his daughter and his wife, the matron at the hospital in St George's, to which I was attached on my return as a doctor.

After the death of his wife, he remarried and took up residence next door to my brother Nicholas in the area called the Villa. I therefore visited him whenever I did Nicholas. In his final years, his mind was no longer focused.

I was not at all a goody-goody boy at GBSS, and though I was a regular monitor in the lower forms and a prefect in the sixth, I must have served detention about three times. A master, during a teaching session, may punish a student by asking him to write a certain number of lines, to stand on the desk, or to stand on the steps outside the classroom. One feared that the headmaster may make his rounds at that time.

Each form was assigned a master in charge, but different masters taught the different subjects. Some masters who were admired at the time for one reason or another or who later achieved a level of significance were Mr. Naimool, the Spanish teacher from Trinidad, known for his stylish walk and dress and for always having a neatly squared-folded handkerchief barely visible from the right back pants pocket; Desmond Hoyte, who taught history, was from what was then British Guiana, and later became his country's president; Sir Paul Scoon, who was later appointed the governor general of Grenada; and Devere Pitt, who started an open university in Grenada, his homeland.

One day, I was given a three-stroke caning (strapping) by the headmaster at about 5 p.m., long after school hours, for going into his garage.

After vacations, the new terms began on a Monday, but I usually returned by boat from Carriacou on the Tuesday, thereby missing two days. Otherwise, it would have meant travelling on the preceding Thursday. That made no sense to me, for although Carriacou was hot, staying four extra days there was not only bearable but preferable to spending them in Grenada.

On the Monday in question, the headmaster had announced at assembly that students must not go into his garage via the partly unhinged door. He paid me no mind after I said I was not at the assembly. The naughty students, with whom I was playing the game of cricket, all knew why they had sent me to retrieve the ball that had gone into the garage, and it so happened that the headmaster was making his after-school rounds at the same time.

At the school's annual speech night, I think in my first year, I had a role as an animal in the play *A Midsummer Night's Dream*. And maybe in the fourth form, A. N. Forde introduced a dramatic monologue with Jack Radix at one end of the stage and I at the other. We alternately recited lines of verse of Forde's composition, which I think extoled the beauty of Grenada.

I digress here to state that in the summer of 1960, the deadline for filing applications for scholarships to enter UCWI was approaching, but I was having so much fun with my gang in Mt. Pleasant that I could not be bothered. Becoming a doctor was now remote in my mind.

But Iah demanded I do it or forced me, so I went by boat to Grenada, slept in Cheese's car that night, got some coffee the next morning from the booth of a "sissie-man" (homosexual) on the wharf, and then went to Baksies's home to fill out the necessary forms. I hung around St George's, never going by Adeline's, and departed that evening for Carriacou by sailboat, which tripled the hours it would have taken if I had gone by the motorized boats.

Also travelling on the boat was Charles Cayenne, my Carriacou neighbour, who was occupying the top bunk of a cabin. At Kick-'em-Jenny, the sea was very rough, and I therefore moved from above to below deck near to his bunk. Cousin Charles was sitting on it when the boat rolled suddenly, and his boot caught me painfully in the left eye. I don't remember how I reached Mt. Pleasant from town—most likely with Cousin Charles. It took me weeks of applying hot compresses to the eye to get rid of the clot.

Anyhow, Dinkie, Toppin, and I received three-year federal exhibition scholarships to attend the medical faculty at UWI, so we had to bargain and plead with the then minister of education R. O. Williams in Grenada to get a loan from the government to accommodate the six-year requirement for medicine. In this, we were successful, and we signed the legal documents in a lawyer's office after we had gotten to Jamaica.

In the meantime, Iah was prepared to sell a bull and the piece of land in Newland to assist, but I advised against it. However, I learned that she did sell the land. I would guess that she also sold the bull, adding the monies to the contributions that she would have demanded from Alethea and Lysander to enable her to send me some help as needed in Jamaica.

In terms of games, GBSS followed the English traditions of cricket, football, and athletics as the main sports. For about two years in the mid to late 1950s, an American coach was assigned to the school. He lived in the games master's apartment, a part of the hostel buildings. His wife strutted around the grounds, usually in shorts.

The hostel was a place where I also went to study and, especially Saturday afternoons, observe the cricket games on the Tanteen field. I usually rested in the room of Mario Bullen, from Carriacou. Some persons even thought that I lived in the hostel. This was during the period of difficulties with my sister.

Anyhow, Mr. Talaska introduced two new games—badminton and softball. In the first GBSS badminton tournament, I emerged as the singles champion and also the doubles, having paired with Bernard Coard. My main competitor was the headmaster's son, Maurice, who I defeated in singles either in the semifinal or in the final itself.

Student Gibbs was quite good at bat in softball, contributing to Hughes house winning the first tournament.

I also remember that the runners in Hughes house included "Mingie" Passee, who had an unchanging pace, and Roy Rattan.

Both were long distance runners. There was also Greene, a middle-distance runner. There was an incident during an intercollegiate meet in which it was judged that the Presentation Brothers College boys were boxing out Greene in the 400-yard race. It was called off and rerun. The Presentation boys protested by running without their shoes.

In my later years, Pope, Lloyd, Sampath, and Jeffries, not in my Hughes house, were among many others featured as sportsmen.

By the end of 1960, after eight years at GBSS, I had served as president of the Junior Science Society, the 4-H Club, the Christian Fellowship Group, and the Form-Six Literary Society, with the attractive Joan Palmer, from the high school for girls, at my side as secretary at meetings.

In addition, I was the secretary of the Lawn Tennis Club and a member of the Historical Society, the Geographical Society, the Drama Society, and the Savings Union, as well as being the subeditor of the school gazette, for which I wrote with another under the byline of FabNags. *FabNags* represented the initials of the two subeditors, mine with a reversal of the Christian initials. The other subeditor was Neville A Glean. Since then, George "Snobies" Griffith has called and written to me as FabNags, instead of Rice.

I represented my house, Hughes, in football (soccer) and cricket and represented the school in intercollegiate athletics and in the first division cricket league of Grenada. On many occasions, in the lower forms, I was named as monitor, and I was a prefect of the school for a few years in form six-A. In my final year, I was deputy head prefect of the school and deputy head boy of Hughes house.

I placed second to Papalee Phillips in the election determining the most influential GBSS student for 1960. Hip Wells, my friend and fellow classmate, of whom more will be said, managed my campaign, and in an assembly of the students, a junior student rendered his composed calypso on me, which I gather was well received. The candidates were not allowed to be at the campaign events.

These two students lived in the hostel where, as already stated, I spent a lot of time in my last few years at school on Saturday afternoons. Sometimes I studied, and other times, I used the vantage point to look at the games being played on the field.

I was also a member of the Carriacou Students Association. Through this association, I had a brief relationship with Monica Noel, who lived with Cousin Sheddy and Aga, who were upper neighbours of ours in Mt. Pleasant. During the roll call at the association's meetings, which were held at the school, everyone had to make or quote an adage, preferably profound.

For men may come and men may go, but Alfred goes on forever.

Although there was no graduation ceremony where students received graduation certificates, there was an end-of-year speech night where students received different prizes. The certificates were those earned from the Cambridge University exams. However, on leaving, one may request and receive a testimonial from the headmaster.

I want to believe that my best friend at GBSS was Desmond Deriggs, but the friendship started in the latter years. He would usually visit me at Adeline's, and I once spent a weekend at his home, somewhere in the parish of St Andrew. We walked to bushes, and for the first time, I bathed in a small pond fed by a sulphur-spring, which had the expected odour and left the whitish coating of the skin said to be beneficial health-wise.

He was an athletic sprinter and was also in Hughes house.

We often stood in the vicinity of the Empire Theatre on the wharf, and he, with his boldness, would approach passersby, asking for money for us to see a matinee show. This occurred especially in the month of October or possibly November, a month of reruns at the movies.

This was termed the anniversary month. A different picture would be shown each day. The movies were selected by the public. For all my years at school in Grenada, *Shane* always made the list, and each year, I, like most boys, saw it. There were always shouts, especially from the pit section, at Alan Ladd of "Look behind you," "Look back," or "Look out." (Brandon deWilde did.)

I suspect that the movie *Magnificent Obsession* may also have been on the list.

The lines at the entrance to the theatre for these movies were long, extending into the street, and there was pushing and jostling until one got in, sometimes during or after the trailer or short. It must have been around that time that words like Cinemascope and Panavision in movies were introduced in Grenada.

I end this phase of my life with the following: There must have been some form of consensus for nicknaming four of the masters with *-ies* endings. So, Mr. McGuire was Baggies, Mr. Baptiste was Baksies, Mr. Martineau, the French teacher, was Preppies, and Mr. Smith, the headmaster, was Sackies.

I heard those names when I entered GBSS. We all sang Lord behold (dismiss) us with thy blessing at the beginning or ending of the term; and during the term, we always listened to 1 Corinthians 13.

The Kainash/Trafalgar Boys

As already indicated, I was not a fighter, but between about 1958 and 1961, during my vacations in Carriacou, I became the leader of a gang that was composed primarily of mischievous boys, including Say Farm's boy, Alwin, who was a son of one of the Langs and was nicknamed Puff, and another Alwyn, who was the son of Cousin Lillian and was nicknamed Laca, as he was as short as the lacatan banana (not the tall gros michel). Laca lived with us, and although it was not so, he was said to have been my nephew. Also in the gang were Gordon and Dunstan, children of my immediate neighbour, Charles Cayenne, whose wife we called Dama or Cousin Mamie but whose real name was Alexandrina. Then there was Bongo, another son of Lillian, and lastly, my best friend in life, Wilcome John, who was a son of Cousin Eda and who now resides in England.

On my vacations, Wilcome and I did everything together, sharing chores and meals. We would gather wood for both our homes and make coals by slow-burning the still somewhat green logs in a dirt-covered pit. He also acted as my messenger to and from Rhoda. We got rashes from the manchineel trees and very rarely got the milk into our eyes, which resulted in pure misery.

What he carried between his thighs could be described as a weapon. It was really huge. He once told me that he had held down a young girl, and I could not believe he had entered her. Holding down a girl as a boy or a woman as a man was not uncommon; now we would call it assault. Understandably, I heard that when Wilcome moved to England, he likewise used it well, and it has also been said that, being well over six feet tall and armed with a linked chain, he beat off the white men who dared to challenge him about their women or anything else.

A story that has originated out of England was that if a black man was in a fight with more than one white man, jumping in, no questions asked, would be a Jamaican man, even though Jamaicans bore the brunt of many a joke.

The story goes that three men entered a contest which required them to supply a word to finish a sentence and then spell that word. The prompt was, **"Old McDonald had a ..."** The French man answered, "Chateau." The English man answered, "Castle." The Jamaican man answered correctly, "Farm." When asked to spell farm, he laughed and said, "Is lang time dey a teach me dat in school." Then he sang, "Old McDonald had a farm." After a pause, he gave his spelling, "Farm: E I E I O."

Another story goes that on a visit to Jamaica, the emperor of Ethiopia was said to have introduced himself to a Jamaican delegate by saying, "I'm Haile Selassie." The Jamaican responded, "I'm highly delighted."

The gang, by and large, did not engage in evil. The closest we came to a fight was when we were on Kainash Hill, which Gilbert had renamed Trafalgar, and threw rocks at a group from Nehgah House that were situated at a lower level in the valley. The group included a cousin of mine, Clifton. Our purpose was to establish turf rights but never with the intention to hurt. Clifton ended up in New York and was a guitar player in a band. For immigration reasons, he once spent some hours in my apartment.

As a pathologist, I did an autopsy on a Carriacou man who had died in the general hospital in Grenada days after receiving a beating to his head. I presented my expert opinion in court, and the accused, a close relative of Clifton, was judged to be not guilty. He approached me later with his thanks. That should have been for the jury.

We in the gang were all friends, each one very dependable. I took on the role of teaching them to box though not to fight, for indeed, I was no fighter. Almost every night, we played the card game called all fours at a vacant OPL house on the land of Jimmy McIntosh whilst drinking sweet red wine, sold from a barrel in Cousin Sydney Cayenne's shop.

We hunted crabs and, made crab soup in the yard. Iah loved the soup, so she sometimes supplied the flour from her shop to make the dumplings. During the day, we roasted green corn, not always coming from our gardens, and made and drank lime squash.

I have spoken of that tradition in Carriacou where on specific nights after death or other suitable occasion, special food was prepared for the dead. This was secured overnight and partaken of early the next day, after the dead person had supposedly eaten. Such was the case for my uncle Powell, youngest brother of Iah/ Gritillia. You may recall that the Trafalgar boys raided the house and ate some of the food.

We also went on the rocks at low tide searching for whelks and lambacks (chitons) to boil as food, and when the waters were calm, as they may be between June and September, we went diving for sea eggs (the white and not the black) and conch. I never asked and still do not know why we collected the rough-shelled whelk and not the smooth ones.

There have been times, as would have happened to others, that one of us accidentally stepped on a black sea egg/urchin only for the spine to break off and become lodged in the sole of his foot, resulting in pain and redness. Our remedy was to pee on the spot to loosen and float the spine.

We once took Jonathan Dick's boat, knowing full well at what time we should return it. I think the tide was against us on returning. When we finally managed to get around the fort rock, struggling with chafed hands on the oars, there, not too far away, was Mr. Dick, prancing up a storm and waving his cutlass threateningly. He was on time; we were not.

We abandoned the boat with the conch, jumped into the water, headed for shore, and scattered into the bushes. We never found out what happened to the conch. Maybe he didn't even bother to go to the sea again.

During my last summer vacation in Carriacou in 1961, prior to leaving for university, I visited Cousin Eda, Wilcome's mother, who no longer lived on Kainash Hill but then resided in Newland. As on Kainash, I was, as expected, a welcomed person to her home.

She took me into her garden and showed me her crops, especially the watermelons, all partly concealed and not easily seen. On my final night, the gang members played all fours in the abandoned OPL house and drank sweet red wine.

At about 2 a.m., with the moon brightly shining, we walked to the beach. What did I do then? I led the group to Cousin Eda's garden, where we feasted on melons. Not being aware of this, she, when I visited later that day to say goodbye, gave me eggs to carry with me in customary style. Of course, I don't remember what I would have done with them, but they certainly did not travel with me.

Years later, after university, she laughingly reminded me of my wickedness. "Oh! Alfred and Wilcome, they so wicked. They ate all my watermelons." She exaggerated as to how many we had eaten; it was certainly not more than two.

I last saw Wilcome when I spent a week in London in 2011. He lived out of London and joined me at a meeting of the Grenada Benevolent Society, an association of Carriacouans, in their club house. He let them know that he had come for no other reason than to see me. He had to leave before the group broke up to catch his train back home.

When this over-six-foot man embraced me, it produced a most wonderfully exhilarating yet emotionally sentimental moment and elicited a desire in me to travel back with him to his home or to Kainash.

* * *

But there was more than just spending time with the Kainash boys in my vacations in Carriacou. Particularly in the long vacation after the Trinity term at GBSS, Chester Prime and I would arrange cricket matches between Mt. Pleasant and Dover, having gotten worn-out gear from the school. In Mt. Pleasant, the game was held at the field in Works, and in Dover, it was held in the school yard.

Even at that relatively young age, we were able to involve many villagers, getting them to participate, to provide cooked food to feed everyone, and to cheer us to a well-fought conclusion. Thus, without any taught skills or knowledge of community support and youth programs, we arranged these games and fostered good competitive relationships and youth building.

It was a joy knitting together different young personalities, though some, like Godwin "Antoo" Noel, remained strange.

On the door of our shop, I chalked the announcements and the names of the playing team, each with a qualifying word. For Randolph McIntosh, who may have been the twelfth man, it was Mr. Self-Centred.

When I was in Brookdale Hospital, Brooklyn, in pathology residency in 1970, Randolph and I lived close to each other, and he once invited me to his well-prepared steak dinner.

We grew up together in Mt. Pleasant, and in 1961, we both boarded at Nurse Radix's house in Grenada. As we were growing up in Mt. Pleasant, he suffered from asthma, and I understood that he was given boiled lizard water to drink as therapy.

Winston McIntosh, later often called Socrates, was the son of my godfather, Fred, who was an older brother of Randolph. Winston lived in the same home as Randolph and had to refer to this younger person as uncle. That seemed strange at the time, for uncles were supposed to be older persons.

We of the gang and other boys often gathered in the evenings to early night at Tan Dorah's Junction to lime, chat, play music, and sing. I found out that Antoo, the macco, on a rare appearance, was one of the best movers to music. His dance always projected rhythmical legerity.

Years later, at a wedding reception held in town, I saw another young man, Faiyeh, the son of Big Sam, dance to the song "The Coocoo Soup" with the same agile swaying of the upper body and lightness of feet movements.

The mentioned song related to a well-known saying that a woman could always get her man by feeding him that specially prepared soup.

For one of the cricket games of the older adults, Gilbert, the captain, picked Antoo and me to be on his team to travel to Dover. The game was played at the school grounds, where there was a pitch. During the game, we were chased away with stones by the crowd because our umpire, Carlton Cyrus, gave out Roy Quashie, the opposing captain, wrongfully, doing so because we were losing the game.

We batted first, and I had the top score with nineteen, being foolishly run out but hitting Roy, the then fast bowler for GBSS, quite well for a couple of sixes. I then opened the bowling for my team, and in my early over, Antoo dropped a dolly of a catch.

During vacations, we boys, in the afternoons, also played both hard and windball cricket, as well as football, in the Mt. Pleasant school yard. Donald "Dan" Jackson, one of the boys, once later remarked that I had an advantage over the others, as I was one of the few or the only one wearing Keds whilst the others were playing barefooted.

Dan was the boy who had received a cut from a flying object in Hurricane Janet in 1955.

A few days before I left Carriacou, there was a sports meet in Hillsborough. I remember running on the inside track, urging Laca to a win on our jenny donkey, which he did. The political representative for Carriacou and then premier of Grenada gave the final address, and in it, he praised Bernard Bullen for his masterful show in the HSC exams that had been recently held and for being awarded a scholarship to attend UWI.

Afterwards, Mr. Bascombe, my old head teacher, walked up to me and asked if Blaize knew what he was saying. I told him to forget it. Blaize obviously confused Brathwaite from Mt. Pleasant with Bullen from Hillsborough, where Blaize lived. Was it a genuine mistake or a political ploy?

9

UWI, MONA, JAMAICA, (OCTOBER 1961—NOVEMBER 1967)

With the last words of my mother—"Don't come back until you are a doctor"—resounding in my ears, I departed Carriacou. Sometime before I left, she gave me one of her two gold rings, the other being her wedding band, which she kept on. Heretofore, she had been in control, though of diminishing influence, so I believed that by presenting that other ring, she approved and granted my complete freedom. It is worthy of mention again, that on reflection, I never missed not having a father. My upbringing was not in a single-parent home. Iah proved a manifestation of mother and father combined.

In Grenada, I spent a few days at Nurse Radix's house, visited and got a gift of towels from Adeline to take with me, and enjoyed the true love of my young niece, Deanna.

Deanna

Incoming students had received communication from the university on the expectations of campus life in Jamaica. From this, I was introduced to the cardigan, needed for the cooler climes of Jamaica.

When travelling from Grenada to Mona, Kingston, Jamaica, everything was obviously prearranged and at no expense to us, so we merely followed orders. The team leader was Barker, a Grenadian and a senior student at the university, and the rest of us were new enrolees.

The first leg of the journey, my very first flight, was from Pearls Airport on BWIA to Barbados, where we would overnight. Before departure, Dinkie Mitchell's father let him know that he must stick with me for guidance, and he certainly did so for our first years in Jamaica.

Obviously, some fathers thought that I would set good examples. I imagine that we were joined for the nonstop flight to Jamaica by others from Barbados and nearby islands who were also university bound.

In Jamaica, Dinkie and I spent the first week boarding with Ms Reid, being accommodated in her outhouse in Mona Heights at a cost of five pounds weekly, breakfast and dinner included. I want to believe that Mona Heights was purposely developed in proximity to the university, with each home having a detached apartment (outhouse), obviously to accommodate off-campus students.

The first breakfast that she served included ackee and salt fish. Dinkie took a forkful, thinking it to be scrambled eggs, gagged somewhat, and ate no more of it. I, respectfully, ate all of mine, and indeed, it tasted quite good. That would have been our first experience with ackee. At the end of the week, Dinkie, having gotten a room on campus in Taylor Hall, left.

The dollars that I had received from Iah, when exchanged in Grenada, came to twenty-nine pounds, then the currency of Jamaica. There was no way that I could have continued boarding with only that amount of money. So, I beseeched and pleaded, and with the assistance of Professor Doctor Francis "Bobo" Bowen, the warden, I was assigned a room that was next to the toilets on the second floor of block B in Chancellor Hall.

Being off campus for two weeks, I missed out on the raggings of the freshmen orientation week. From then, however, and with no bravado, I started to sprout wings.

After one year next to the toilets, I graduated to a room on the third floor that shared a balcony with an adjacent room, in which was Bill Riviere, who became a close friend. In the third year, I moved to an end room on the same floor that was previously occupied by medical students Jeff Woo Ming and, after him, Habibola Niematali. In a winning block B skit, it was said of food, "And he nyam it all ee."

Once, during a vacation, a few American students resided in the halls on campus. I don't know if it was during what is called "spring break". Anyhow, one night, one who was on block B, could not make it to the bathroom from his room before his rectum emptied explosively in the passageway.

One of our Caribbean students wrote on the door of the American's room, "We talk shit here (S T); we don't shit shit here."

Jeff was our skit writer for the interblock competition when I arrived that first year, and block B won. I played the part of the Carriacou ambassador to the United Nations and got a laugh for the words, "Carriacou is not with the east or with the west. Carriacou is with the rest."

We also won the next year with a most masterful performance by Gun Lucas and me. Habibola was the scriptwriter. It portrayed Gun not being well, lying on his back with one of his legs cramped in a lifted position, so I asked for Jack (the senior medic). Someone brought in the jack for a vehicle, and Gun was forced to maintain his leg upward until the laughter subsided.

The following year, 1964, however, after a most brilliant opening scene, we faltered and lost. Hubby Husbands was the scriptwriter. I was then the block B representative in Chancellor Hall.

The arrangements for living on campus during the terms were handled through the financial office. My expenses were covered by the contributions from the federal exhibition scholarship programme and the loan that was obtained from the Grenadian government. After the required fees were deducted, the remaining monies were passed on to me, as it was for others in similar positions. The amount proved to be quite ample if spent wisely.

However, problems arose during the vacation periods, when students were expected to make their individual arrangements. Most Jamaicans went home, and some from the Eastern Caribbean returned to their islands, usually by the *Federal Maple* or the *Federal Palm*. These two boats had been donated by Canada to the West Indies federal government.

For those who remained on campus, financial matters were dealt with by the office of the bursar on the ground floor of a building called the Nunnery. For a minimum of one week, prearrangements and payments were expected to have been made for room and at least one daily meal. But by the time vacation had come, most of the advanced sums of money we had received had dwindled, and some students experienced difficulties, especially for the long summer vacations.

Especially with the help of Dennis, the porter for block B, I was able to spend a free time in the room now and then. After my university days, whenever I visited Jamaica, I would seek out Dennis at his home in August Town to give him something, but that ended some years later after being informed that he had died.

I resided on block B for four academic years and enjoyed a most wonderful relationship with Dennis, a friend and humble gentleman. The servers in the dining room were also very overgenerous, giving those they favoured, among whom I was fortunately included, double and even triple portions. They were well aware that the food was going to be shared with others, some of whom may not even have been students.

Our single rooms sometimes accommodated an extra person or two during the days or even overnight.

Many a student became adept at using and abusing the system, and creating schemes and opportunities to get by. Some lived on campus for the entire vacation after paying for only one week, even squatting at times in the rooms of those who themselves were also squatters. Bobo, the warden, would occasionally make his rounds to check, but he hardly bothered. Anyway, the squatters, being alerted, would scatter.

The British Empire and Commonwealth Games were held in Jamaica in the summer of 1966, and Chancellor Hall served as the games village. However, some students were still around, and I was in the Nunnery. One student, Andy, dressed appropriately in shorts with water splashed on his face to make it seem he was sweating, ran past the guards and into the dining room. He may have gotten away with it once or twice.

I became friendly with a coach of the British team and with Wendell Motley, the Trinidadian quarter-miler and later politician, and I benefited from a rare meal brought by them from the athletes' cafeteria.

A goodly gentleman, a friend of mine who once lived in Carriacou but was of Trinidadian birth, portrayed his adeptness by designing with exactitude a copy of the food ticket issued during one of the summers. I made good use of it.

The kitchen staff at the supervisory levels were often at a loss to explain why though fifty meals had been paid for, they were dispensing more than that. Rarely, when near closing, a truly paid-up student would approach to find there was no more food.

Some students, especially those studying medicine, were known to conveniently visit the doctors' quarters in the university hospital compound to pilfer the food left for the doctors who were on night duty or were on call. This was made fun of in a skit about a student with the name of Sticks who, when on day duty, could not readily identify the route to the hospital, since he knew it better at nights on his way to acquiring a meal.

I, like others, would at times receive food from Jamaican friends and families. Miss Chambers, a maid at the hospital, would often bring me homemade cakes on Mondays. The Blythes, whose daughter, Grace, was my gentle and religious friend, seemed to delight in sending me roasted chicken.

Nevertheless, it was not always possible to survive by cheating, and so, deciding that it would be much less expensive than staying on campus, Magnus "Danny" Daniel and I decided to share an outhouse in Mona Heights for the summer vacation of 1963.

On some of the early mornings, we both listened to the cricket broadcasts, as it was the year that the West Indies beat England in England three games to one. In the final test, Conrad Hunt and Willie Rodriguez opened the batting and were followed by the batting stylist Rohan Kanhai and then Basil Butcher, who, with Hunt, carried us to victory.

Bobo's residence in the compound had an attached efficiency room which was occupied by medical student, Lee Lord, from Antigua. Lord went back home for the summer vacation in 1965, and Bobo kindly allowed me to occupy the room at no cost. After that, he moved me from block B to the Nunnery, which had residential rooms on the upper floor.

Within a ten-minute walk from the Nunnery was and still is the village of Papine, which was thriving, partly because of its proximity to the campus that included the university and its hospital. Other than the university students, student nurses were in residence on the hospital compound. This, together with the facts that many persons were employed there and that it was a hub for buses, meant that the area was abuzz with activity.

In Papine, there were the usual service places, like grocery stores, bars, restaurants, and, in the nearby gully, night clubs. The grocery stores did well during vacations, because the students loaded up with groceries to take to the dorms to cook for communal sharing. Some of us had hot plates and pots in our rooms. Of our especially hot drinks, Horlicks became a favourite.

At times, we scouted the campus seeking fruits like mangoes and berries, and Lloyd "Mack" McKenzie of block B served as the cook. He was good at using the ackee that we sometimes brought back as a base for soups.

Christmas dinner for me was at the home of A. C. Williams, a student on block B, and his family. Our relationship was somewhat renewed probably in the late 1970s when we were in the Bahamas. He moved to the USA, where he later died. His wife and I correspond via Facebook.

After I had moved to the Nunnery, my breakfast during vacation consisted, at times, of an avocado picked from a tree that was located behind the building. I would add milk to it and spoon-puree the two.

I remember that one Sunday night, the only money I had was ten cents. I went to the hospital to study in the lecture hall at about eight o'clock and put the coin in the slot of a coffee dispensing machine, but nothing happened, no matter how many times I punched and kicked. The machine did not return the money either. Maybe it was that experience which motivated me to change my studying pattern.

When studying at nights on block B, I would sit in my armchair with a shade-covered lamp next to me, beating the books. The shade cast a shadow on the inner wall of the room. Everyone would know that I should not be disturbed because the arc was on the wall.

After the coffee incident, I began going to bed early at nights. I would then wake up at 1 a.m. and study onward to daybreak.

In my first few months at UWI, I represented the freshmen in some of the sporting events against the seniors. I lost to Jimmy Emmanuel, a Grenadian, in badminton, but I won throwing the javelin and broke the record previously held by the same Jimmy Emmanuel. I also played football and cricket for the freshmen. No wonder Charles Thesiger, who would eventually become a well-known Caribbean psychiatrist and who always had his close mate, Lennox Pike from Belize, at his side, called me "The Champ".

Lennox Pike attended most of the UWIMAA conferences and always seemed to have a drink in hand. He was known for joking, "I don't drink any more … but I don't drink any less.

During my first year, I represented Chancellor in cricket in the interhall competitions and received the bronze medal in the javelin event. In subsequent years, I also represented my hall in badminton, one game of football (soccer), and cricket, and I was the captain of the all-fours and darts teams.

I played one game each in rugby and football for the university, and for the first two years, I was a member of the athletic team.

Chancellor athletic team

Winning Chancellor Darts Team. Author,
Gifto, James, Ramprasad, Riviere (Block B).

A few years later, after advancing from the pre-med programme to the hospital, Chester Prime and I played a game of lawn tennis against Doctors Rolf Richards and Don Christian, lecturers in medicine. We got a good thrashing, but the free drinks afterwards in the faculty club made up for it.

Without doubt, for the above and other reasons, I became a natural leader in Chancellor Hall. In this, I received support from Earl Duke, a student on block B, who showed great respect for me as a friend. He was given the nickname Finnie by David Lloyd George Calendar, another student on block D whose nickname was Priapus. The real Finnigan was a former student who Earl Duke resembled.

Finnie was chosen as one of the campus personalities one year, and on being asked whom he admired, this is what he said of me: "He can do just about anything—there isn't a game he can't play. Yet at the same time, he is brilliant, and I understand he wins his share of medals."

Long after our campus days, I saw Finnie when he visited Grenada and on one of my visits to Trinidad, where he was from. During that trip, we, including Kenneth "Kenty" Noel, who was also at the university and who lived nearby and taped Baron's calypsos for me, spent an afternoon at his home, catching up on old times. His wife, Violet, was a gem.

Strangely, without us being in contact then, Finnie named his first daughter Anika just as I was naming mine Nanika.

Dear friend, RIP! I have heard that Violet joined you in 2018.

In terms of off-campus escapades, I was still testing my wings, and that first took me to the all-girls Shortwood College. Lorraine was the first lady that I engaged. When I asked her for her impression of me, she calmly replied, "I'm not impressed."

In a general sense, I made very good, decent, and invariably lasting friendships with many persons.

I sang at the carnival calypso competitions under a moniker, Lord Riccio, that soon replaced my real name. So pervasive was that name that once, when I was sitting near the telephone on block B, where I reigned supreme for a time, and someone called asking for Alfred Brathwaite, the young man who answered the phone came to me and asked if there was such a person on block B.

First Calypso, 1963.

Singing Calypso

Singing Calypso

Riccio, derived from my nickname, Rice, started singing calypso at the university carnival in 1963 as part of the competition held at the students' union. I placed second to the president of the guild of students, Selwyn Walter, who was from Antigua. He had sung, "Run, Finnie, run. Gocking coming down." Gocking was in charge of the university library and once chased Finnie—the original Finnie—who was friendly with a staff member of the library. In my travels, long after I had left campus, I met Selwyn at his bakery in Antigua. He loaded me up with baked goodies to take back home.

My song was about the West Indies Federation, and it went like this:

First Verse

Federation dun dead and gone,
It dead and gun before it had begun
Four years of strain and pressure
As we tried to please one another,
Each man thinking of himself alone,
Wanting this and that to be his own.
And so began the decline of our nation.

Chorus

So, now I don't have no nation; I don't have no dignity.
I shame to say I'm a West Indian; I hope you'll agree with me.
I don't have no class, no creed; I don't have no race.
I only wish America would send me up in space.

Last Verse

Alexander Bustamante,
He bound to go down in history
As the man responsible
For putting us in all this trouble.
He wanted to regain lost prestige,
And so with privilege,
He told the illiterate
That they must not federate.

One Rasta man near the fence at the back of the students' union, when I finished the chorus, shouted, "Yes, sen im ras clat to space, send im up."

The next year, with the competition now held at the chapel gardens, I again placed second—I think to Edwards from Trinidad, with his song "No, you?" which was based on a then popular phrase on campus. My brother Nicholas was in the audience. My tune was the more popular one, however, as it was played at the next day's steel band jump-up on the campus ring road. The chorus went,

> It's a building here and a building there,
> buildings everywhere.
> It's a new one here and a new one there,
> about ten going down every year.
> I want to change me course and do carpentry or even masonry,
> for as far as I can see, it means the same thing to me;

I'll still be here at the university.
But it was the second verse that brought the house down:
They put down a brand-new assembly building.
You have to gather deh every morning.
And when the man say "Priapus Callendar,"
You have to answer, "Present, sir."
And the day you not feeling top,
You can go and relax in the coffee shop.
Ten empty sub-warden flat,
Dey making more room for Sammy to squat.

In the third year, 1965, I had no intention of singing. But on that night, Dr Bowen, still the warden, took a small group of us to a restaurant up in the Blue Mountains, and when I returned to block B, as drunk as ever, I could hear, every few minutes, the repeated loudspeaker announcement, "We are awaiting the Lord Riccio to compete." And so, I eventually went to the gardens.

On stage, I first explained that I was not competing, but I sang a verse of a calypso I was working on about taking the 727 jet plane to Trinidad's carnival.

As "Hip Parade" Wells would usually say, "The mighty Lord Riccio, he come here to sing caiso." The words from my last appearance included the following:

And just in case you are a bit sad,
Don't feel too bad.
You just take the sunjet 727,
And leh we go down to Trinidad.

In my first year on campus, I also played J'Ouvert Mas with a Grenadian group lead by Barker, the Grenadian already referred to as leading our first journey to Jamaica, and portrayed Adam and Eve with Lloyd McKenzie. That afternoon, I was a member of Dinkie Mitchell's band as one of the "Watusi Warriors". Dinkie also organised and put out another band, in which I also played, for the celebrations of Jamaica's 1962 independence.

Dinkie and I remained close for about two years on campus and then drifted apart, though we have remained respectfully in contact throughout our lives.

Indeed, I have always loved calypso, even though I sang other songs. On block B, I even made some small change from the student onlookers from so doing. The favourites included "Behold" by the Blues Busters, "Any Day Now" by Chuck Jackson, "Don't Play That Song" by Ben E. King, "Under the Boardwalk" by the Drifters, and "Come to Me Softly" by Jimmy James.

I also did a duet rendition of "Behold" with Trevor Castle, a good friend, and it was always well received. He was truly hurt because I did not attend his wedding, but I had no decent clothes to wear and was low on cash.

My love for calypso started in Mt. Pleasant, Carriacou, after I took a liking to the Mighty Sparrow's "Jean and Dinah", the sheet lyrics of which were given to me by Cyril from Trinidad, who was visiting his relative and our neighbour, Tahnee.

I have always believed that I, mainly because of my travels, must have seen Sparrow perform in more countries than any other person except the members of his musical troupe, though at times my seeing him was merely coincidental.

On campus, I was also a barber to my close friends, including Knolson "Gifto" Gift from Trinidad, who I once saw many years later during one of my visits. He was then a permanent secretary in one of the government ministries.

* * *

My pipe and my medical class (Author 3rd row 5th from left)

The medical course at UWI, which led to the degree of Bachelor of Medicine, Bachelor of Surgery (MB, BS), was divided into a prehospital programme of three years and then a further three clinical years in the hospital.

In first MB, year one, the subjects were physical and inorganic chemistry, general biology, and physics. One could be exempted from any of these if one had already acquired them at a prerequisite level. The only subject I had to do in my first year was physics, which I had been previously exposed to at GBSS, and I only had to attend two afternoon practical labs a week in physiology. Consequently, I was having fun, not like Da James with his donkey but with wings that started to flap stronger.

In second MB, the subjects were physiology, anatomy and histology, biochemistry, and organic chemistry, and after having passed these, one moved on to pharmacology.

I placed first in every biweekly paper for biochemistry. My fiercest competitor was Henry Fraser of Barbados. When it came time for the last paper before the big final exam of 1964, his paper was distributed before mine, and it had received an A. Jack Radix, sitting next to me, said words to the effect of "Riccio, he got you this time."

Then came mine. I received an A+.

It was perhaps at that time, in response to the apparent animosity of others, that I lost the zeal for the rivalry that seems to be born from competition.

Or is there a difference between the two? I always thought that there was, and that rivalry had a greater tendency to lead to greater conflict.

David "Jack" Radix

Jack Radix

Jack Radix and I developed a stronger and more lasting friendship from that year, and it continued to his death. In that second year, he once needed some money. I handed him my Barclay's bank book and gave him permission to take whatever he required.

Then, a few years later, while we were still students, he asked me to write his mom, Nurse Alexandra Radix, with whom I had once lived in Grenada, about his intention to get married to Pauline. I did, writing, "You will not be losing a son; you will be gaining a daughter."

I did not attend the wedding, because I did not believe he knew what he was taking on. I gathered that he was very hurt, and yet, he asked me to be the godfather for his daughter Nikoyan, who now resides in Grenada with her family, and I agreed. Long after, I, then living in Freeport, was invited to attend her wedding to Kennedy Roberts in Grenada and to toast the deceased Nurse Radix. This I also did. Nicki, like her grandma did, calls me Uncle Alfred. I visit that family anytime I'm in Grenada. His other daughter, Lisa, is an ob-gyn in the USA. We are in touch also.

I always got on well with Jack Radix, who had placed fifth in the Grenada scholarship exam for primary schools in 1952, and eventually, at the university, we began referring to ourselves as half-brothers, he being the handsome half. As already mentioned, we once performed on stage at the GBSS speech night, reciting and sharing a monologue.

He grew up with his mom and was closely attached to his uncle, Tommy Wells, a trainer of horses, and to a relative, Bruce. Up until the 1950s, horse racing was a popular sport at Queen's Park in Grenada, and it was featured especially on holiday weekends.

Jack, the dashing young daredevil, learned to ride horses, to water ski, and to love girls. Whereas I was tuned in to the likes of Pat Boone and Engelbert Humperdinck, Jack was into Elvis Presley and Tom Jones, somewhat like Sticks McLaren. And remember, he was the one who, at the university, encouraged us to purchase a Cadillac, which he kept, since he lived off-campus and was the only one with a driver's license.

He entered UWI in 1960, a year ahead of his other classmates, who had stayed back to have a chance at winning the Island Scholarship later that year. It was his room that became mine when I moved to his home in 1961.

I should state that, partly because of his escapades, he graduated in medicine after my group of Chester "Tartar" Prime, Winston "Dinkie" Mitchell, and Dennis Toppin. I don't believe that Toppin ever had a nickname, though we may have called him D. I.

To digress, the story has been told of a Grenadian, not Jack, who took such a long time to graduate in medicine that when he eventually did and wanted to return home, BWIA refused to board him on the flight. His British-Grenadian passport had expired.

One Christmas eve, Jack took a few of us, including Gun Lucas, to a roast-pork party at a gas station in Kingston, Jamaica. For some reason, we apparently annoyed a guy, who, we were told, took out his gun. The owner of the gas station came to Jack and asked him to escort us out. Jack made certain that we were OK as he led us out, never turning his back to the guy.

Let me add here that Gun Lucas, already mentioned in one of the Chancellor Hall skit competitions, was once one of the masters at GBSS. He was a student at UWI who lived on block B with me, and he became a very dear and intimate friend of mine. He was a resident of Tampa, Florida, when I last saw him. He had brought his family to visit mine on 30 December 2010 as we were holidaying in Orlando, Florida, at the Westgate Resort. He brought a bottle of sorrel drink, a favourite of Grenadians for the Christmas season. He has since died.

In my last year on campus, Jack and Pauline had already been divorced, and his new lover was Peta, who likewise adored me. As said, Jack graduated in medicine years after we did.

Once, when the Mighty Sparrow visited Jamaica, he and Jack became very close. Jack arranged for both of them to be entertained by two women, Jack aligning with his girlfriend. It was alleged that during the session, Sparrow said, "Let's switch," but Jack completely refused.

He and Peta got married, maybe after his graduation.

While I was in Grenada as the pathologist, between 1974 and 1976, I got a phone call from him at about 2 a.m. He was crying, and he informed me that he and Peta had divorced that previous day. He spoke and cried for maybe an hour on the phone.

As said, he grew up loving horses and horse racing, and he once owned one in Jamaica. "Hip Parade" Wells, the jokester, once said that the horse had placed last in every race in which it had been entered, until, after many races, it placed second to last. According to Hip, the authorities then proceeded to test the horse for drugs.

Hip Wells was himself a character known for inventing jokey situations that were often based on other persons and had enough stretching of the truth for them to be believed. One of Hip's joke on me related to my medical practice in Grenada.

I had attended to the father of Mathew Williams, a schoolmate at GBSS, at his home in Grand Bras. That part was true. According to Hip, some short time after, I met Mathew, who was visiting from the Bahamas, his then place of residence. I supposedly said to him that I was attending to his father and that he was improving by leaps and bounds under my treatment. This, of course, was not true. But according to Hip, Mathew was visiting to bury his father—true.

After graduating, Jack moved to St Croix to practise medicine, and when this ended, he moved back to Jamaica and practised in Spanish Town, where he was said to be very popular. He acquired another horse and was well known in the racing arena. On a race day in January 1980 at Caymanas, his horse placed first.

Apparently, the celebrations went on and on at the track club. On the way home, his car crashed into a tree, and the driver and maybe others died.

The driver was Jack Radix, my compatriot and dear friend. It is my understanding that a memorial cup has been established at the racetrack in his honour.

**

I think of myself as being always a bit impatient and hasty, more concerned with generalities than with small details. The virtue of patience is lost on me. However, one must appreciate that in medicine, these small details are important. That's true of life in general, but you should know them especially if questioned in academic examinations.

Thus, I was so happy and benefitted greatly when I befriended Earling Harry from St. Vincent, who suggested that we should study anatomy and histology together during the two years of second MB and microscopic pathology in third MB.

Harry made every word in the textbooks count. This was to my benefit, and he benefited from my quicker intake and astuteness. We studied together with Steve Claxton of St Kitts. Both died within less than two months of each other near the end of 2015, Harry in Illinois and Steve in his homeland.

The only other persons that I had the opportunity to study with were Jack Radix and Carmen Bowen. With Jack, I was coaching him for an oral exam in the final MB, internal medicine, as to how to guide the questions to what you were good at. We dealt with tuberculosis (TB). His first question was on pleural effusion, and he wisely guided to TB. He then went blank and failed when the first question on TB was asked.

With Carmen Bowen, I adopted the stance of Earling Harry, making every word count as I read and interpreted from the textbook of microbiology, a discipline in the third and final MB.

Long after we left university, at a UWIMAA meeting in Jamaica, we saw each other again. She seemed drawn more towards Chester Prime than to me, but she gave both of us gifts. Mine was a bottle of Sangster's Old Jamaica Blue Mountain Coffee Liqueur.

In the anatomy oral exam of the pre-med course, I was asked a question related to the location of the femoral artery, which I knew only too well. But the examiner kept asking how I would know that it was the artery. I had no clue as to the significance of his persistence until he said that it will pulsate on palpation. But at that time, and I think this may have since changed, we had no contact with live patients in pre-med, only with dead bodies.

Speaking of dead bodies, I could have been kicked out of medical school because of what transpired during an anatomy dissection session. Two students had a bet as to whether or not one would eat a piece of the formalinised dead body. Foolishly, I agreed to hold the money. Jack Radix was the student who challenged the other, who did eat it. The ladies of the class spouted it all over, and it got back to the senior lecturer, Dr Levine, who, obviously most upset, indicated that if he knew the names of the three persons involved, he would seek their immediate expulsion.

I heard nothing further. The ladies knew when to be mute. One lady in particular, Barbara, née Beckford, who called me

Kempster, has been a dear friend from then to now. Ours was a friendship of the hearts, as, I think, was that between Sidney Veitch and Chester Prime. Barbara married David "Douggie" Noel, who was a Trinidadian student at the university, and I have vacationed at their home in Jamaica on occasion. Her husband has since died.

The final second MB results were announced on my birthday, and having been awarded the 1964 Henderson Prize in Experimental Physiological Sciences, I threw a success-cum-birthday party in a room on block B.

Birthday cum success party (Author, 3rd row, middle)

I now turn to October 1964, when I was due to begin the Third and final MB in the University of the West Indies Hospital after spending the summer vacation in Brooklyn, New York, at my sister Sarah's, having gone there primarily to see Rhoda.

In travelling back, I was together with Earling Harry, who had been somewhere else in the USA but had come to Brooklyn for us to go to the World's Fair in Queens. Having spent the previous night in Brooklyn, he and I left New York by bus for Miami, but on our arrival there, our suitcases could not be located. We nevertheless continued on the scheduled flight to Jamaica.

For some three weeks in Jamaica, I awaited my suitcase and did not report to my first three-month surgical clerkship. When it eventually did arrive and I reported to the surgical ward, Mister Brooks, the surgeon, asked me to draw the anatomy of the anal canal based on the patient on whom he was teaching. I really could not fully remember it, so he ejected me from the rounds, advising that I was not to return until I had learnt it.

I never went back.

I heard that when it was time to grade the clerkship, he asked who Brathwaite was. He passed me anyhow because he was not able to link a name to each of the eight to twelve students in his team. This was my understanding.

During the third and final MB, a summer elective was mandatory. I'm not sure how seriously that was undertaken by the students, but I never completed mine under Dr George Alleyne in the Tropical Research Unit at the hospital. The topic was related to the urinary response of babies whose diet contained a certain factor.

I have no idea what his report on my elective indicated. This doctor became well known as the director of the Pan American Health Organization and for other distinguished accomplishments.

The next time my name arose meaningfully was a year or so before the big finals. Three of us, after a written exam, were named to take an oral test to decide the award of the Stockhausen Prize in obstetrics and gynaecology. At that time, I had no desire to compete, but I attended the orals anyhow. Placing first no longer mattered to me. Haig Didier of Dominica won the prize.

As we gathered on the day to await the results of the final exam, a professor of microbiology called me aside and said that my exam results were such that I should have received honours in pathology and microbiology, except that the results of my clerkship and term tests were terrible. But what was more important to me was that I had passed the final examination, which qualified me to practise as a doctor after completing an internship.

And to think that one day at medical rounds, Professor Rolf Richards asked me for the medical word given to a localised collection of fluid associated with an infection, and I couldn't come up with an answer, even after he said that it was composed of three letters, starting with p and ending with s. I thought of piss, but that was four letters.

It is my belief that it was either Professor Rolf or the dean, Prof Eric Cruickshank, who left me with "Think positive. Don't just hear; listen. Don't just see; look. And don't just feel; palpate."

For the last few days in Jamaica, my wings flapped faster, stronger, and farther afield.

During my tenure at UWI, two of my brothers also attended at different times. I was, for once, senior to them, and as their money was slow in coming out of Grenada, they were sometimes beholden to me. It felt good.

Nicholas was there, resident in Taylor Hall, pursuing a one-year certificate course in education; and later, George came for a six-week summer course in statistics, I believe. He shared an off-campus apartment with an older gentleman, maybe a head teacher from Antigua, who was probably taking the same course. It was said that one night, the Antiguan used a pint bottle on a woman and left it inside of her.

George, My Immediate Older Brother

It is my view, that of all the siblings, my brother George, like Nicholas, was one of the better logical thinkers with fertile minds. They both seemed able to arrive at a different slant to situations when most others had arrived at an obviously quick and probably myopic opinion. This came naturally to them and did not involve great effort.

We grew up together, slept on the same floor, and put out our beddings in the mornings to dry in the sun. He was three years older, having been born 12 May 1938. We often play-boxed and invariably ended up fighting because I got angry after he had hit me too hard. He was ahead of me in Mt. Pleasant School. He also attended GBSS two years ahead of me but would return home on vacations.

He had a confident swagger and was the greatest defender of our name but also the quickest to respond to his friends in need, name or no name.

At GBSS, he assumed the nickname Rice, which had originated with our older brother Lysander. Apparently, when his form was asked what food would be needed for an upcoming event, Lysander shouted, "Rice, rice." When I joined George in the high school, he became Big Rice, and I, Little Rice.

George was quite bright, and it was he who taught me that the way to master geometry was to view the image with the eyes widely opened—most illuminating, even if not scientifically ingenious. But it must have been a commendable approach, because henceforth, I seemed to be on top of that subject, so much so that I even once solved a problem that the students in form five-B and the master, Bert Callendar, had struggled with for two weeks. I was then in the adjacent form five-A, but there was an accessible door between them.

I am of the opinion that George once experienced a bit of difficulty at the school. That led my brother Godwin to later opine to me that it was a Brathwaite's trait to desperately desire and pursue women and that in this, it seemed that George took great delight to the point that he was unaccounted for over a short period of time. Nevertheless, on his return, he had the last say, earning a first-grade Cambridge School Certificate, not the easiest of accomplishments.

On leaving GBSS, he moved from Adeline's to a rental apartment and worked in the registry section of the department of health. On Saturdays, I would usually visit him. On one occasion, I sought his help, and he responded by purchasing my clothes and boots for when I was selected to represent the school as an opening bowler in Grenada's first division cricket.

In my first game, I took three wickets, the first from a slip catch by Ted Walker, a gifted school sportsman not in Hughes house. The most wickets that I took in a game was six, against St John's club, I think.

When I returned to Grenada after graduation from the UWI, he, then married, threw a party for me at his home in Tempe. His friends came from high and low, and it was obvious how they all respected and loved him, especially the one called "Green Face". But George had his peculiarities and, if necessary, would express them openly.

For example, when a few years later, Vivian and I visited Grenada for her to be introduced to my relatives, we held hands as we strolled on Grandby's Street, and George, seeing us, said that there was no reason to publicly display our attachment or affections. Love runs deeper than the show of it.

I must admit that we were not a hugging family. Our affections were expressed with a special look, a smile, or a responsive action to please. I first observed the more open physical show of affections within the Joseph family, who were introduced to us through Godwin. And this display by them was repeated throughout the day.

As an aside, Vivian and I sailed to Carriacou and got engaged in Mt. Pleasant, where Iah, feeding the fowl one morning, was the first person to be shown the ring.

George, then on campus in Jamaica, once invited me to a Chinese dinner in Papine, together with his friend, a lady I had once dated.

The lady and I exchanged friendly arguments. He interjected, "Stop splitting hairs in my presence."

He also held the view that if at home, he would not respond to the tooting horn of a vehicle that seemed to have stopped in front of his home. His dwelling had a front door which anyone could knock on, and that was his preferred choice if his attention was desired.

There was an occasion in 1974 when my friends, the Holms, from Hawaii, were visiting with me in Grenada, where I was then working. I asked George to get some lambie (conch) for a house party I had planned to have. Near to the date, I reminded him, and his response was, "Did I promise to get you lambie or not?" His word was his bond, never to be questioned or defended.

After the party, I asked how much I owed him, and he offhandedly replied that as long as I lived, I would owe him. **Show off.**

I was always welcomed at his home, wherever he lived. I would be entertained by him, his wife, Wilma, and their children. I particularly always enjoyed their salt fish souse in the evenings.

He was at the UWI for a three-year programme, I believe in economics, in the early 1970s. As the chairman of Irvine Hall, he entertained Vivian and I at the hall's end-of-year party in 1973, when we were on our way to Grenada from Canada. Within a few days, we travelled on the same flight to Grenada, I to begin working and he for vacation.

Over time, we crossed paths on many occasions. Once, we met at Grantley Adams Airport in Barbados. He was going home on vacation, and I was on my way to a meeting somewhere else.

It was there, as we sat together in a restaurant, that I gave him the worrying news that Elizabeth, his daughter, though not obviously hurt, had had an accident. She was hit when running across the road by a car that Martin, Adeline's husband, was driving. His concern was obvious, despite my reassurances. Family meant a lot to him.

As previously mentioned, we once met in 1981 at Gilbert's in London, when he was then attached to the United Nations.

On some of my travels, I stayed at his home in Grenada and also, years later, at his home in Brooklyn, where he eventually settled with his family. He has helped me on more occasions than I could ever remember, and as he has said, I cannot ever repay him, for there was never a charge.

His voice is strong on land, but back in the school days, when sailing from Grenada to Carriacou, he settled in a side corner of the boat until we docked.

We correspond with each other regularly, but the last time we saw each other was on a day when I visited both Sarah and him, having travelled to New York from Freeport for the wedding of my grandniece Dawn Odine Brathwaite, Betty's daughter, in July 2014.

Hail the man! We are brothers, and respectfully, we are bonded. At the time of writing, we are the only children of Poopa and Iah still alive.

Let me add here that in 1965, I was encouraged, nay, coerced to run and was indeed nominated for the chairmanship of Chancellor Hall. Three of us competed, and after the votes were counted, there was a two-way tie for the position. The third candidate withdrew, and in the follow-up election, I, as expected and predicted and without any true interest, lost.

It was after that that Bobo, the warden of Chancellor Hall, moved me from block B, where I had just been re-elected for a second term as block representative, to the Nunnery after the summer vacation. It was perhaps the first time that someone had been re-elected to that post, but alas, it was not to be honoured. It was in that summer of 1965 that I stayed in Bobo's apartment.

From what he may have seen, he probably had just cause to justify his opinion that I was, in his words, wasting my father's seed.

Particularly during vacations and long weekends, Bobo took students with him on his visits to other parts of Jamaica. In this, I was usually included. Steve Claxton was the usual driver of the car. The last time that I saw Bobo was at a party he threw at his newly built home in Kingston, where he had moved after he had retired as warden. I was still a student.

Be reminded that the Nunnery was a two-storey wooden building with offices, including that of the bursar, at the ground level and with students' rooms on the second.

In the Nunnery, I was still affiliated with block B and the Busy Bees sports team. Others in the Nunnery, where I spent two academic years, included the likes of Ralph Nimchan, Clive Mohess, Steve Claxton, Earling Harry, Chester Prime, Trevor Lindsay, and Headley Rose.

Nimchan was known for sharing his bananas only after they had begun to rot and also for putting pin holes in his tin of condensed milk so that those who borrowed never had the time to take too much of it. For another good reason, someone referred to him as "Pound for Pound".

Chester had his Sprite car, and Steve had another model.

Every morning, Headley Rose, a Jamaican, reminded me of the three esses—shave, shit, shower. The last time I saw him was some years post-graduation when I, on a visit to Jamaica and staying at the Pegasus, was invited to a doubles game of tennis at the Liguanea Club.

At one point, I was at the nets as he was serving, and as I moved laterally to take a return, Headley, going for the same ball, hit me at the back of my head with his racquet. At the Nunnery, I think he was dating Betty, who later married Dr James Ling, who was once a lecturer at the university hospital.

Another Great Thinker, One with a Knighthood

Having mentioned Nicholas (called Nick by his wife, Pansy) in my caricature of George, I now present my association with him. He, my second eldest brother, had a genteel, rather casual demeanour but was very deep minded in his approach to life. Whereas the eldest, Godwin, was emotional and heart-driven, Nicholas was brain-controlled.

He preferred a simple life and was known to enjoy a meal of corned beef and sardines directly from the containers, served with white rice.

When I was a small boy, on any occasion when he visited the home in Carriacou, he would pin my nasal bridge with a clothes pin because my nose was too flat. Later, in my first year in Grenada at GBSS, he was visiting from Curaçao, and on my asking, he gave me his wristwatch.

When I first invited Vivian to Grenada, we stayed at his home in Mt. Moritz, and after that in his home in The Villa in the town of St George's. When I was stationed in Suriname, I also visited him in Guyana. He had moved there from Grenada, where he was the permanent secretary in the ministry of education, to take up the post of regional director of the Commonwealth Secretariat Youth Programme in 1974.

In his travels related to this position, he visited me in Nassau, Bahamas, in the late 1970s. His daughter Charmaine, his sons, Earle, Sammy, and Ben, and his wife, Pansy, were all very gracious people.

After his ten-year spell in Guyana, he moved back to Grenada, and whenever I visited, whether or not I stayed with him, I had full use of his car. It was not unusual for persons to hail me, thinking it was him. This happened especially during his four-year spell as the prime minister of Grenada, because they knew his car and perhaps because he and I looked alike.

Once when I stayed with him, I was accompanied by my son, Dax, who subsequently changed his major at FAMU in Tallahassee, Florida, to politics, I guess having been so impressed by the experience.

My dear brother held total respect and appreciation for the downtrodden and the hard worker. He once told me that he haggled not the price of the farmer's produce. If he wanted something, he bought it. Whether or not he was following the advice offered in 1

Thessalonians 5:12–13, I have no idea, but it seemed to be just in his nature. If I were to be asked to name the siblings I considered to be or to have been very religious, I would say Godwin, Adeline, Alethea, and Balvina.

As far as I know, Nicholas's life in Grenada was mainly spent in the field of education, as the head person in primary schools and in college and as an administrator in the ministry of education, from entry levels to higher positions.

He also held positions within unions, was the head of the interim government after the US invasion, was the parliamentary representative for the constituency of Carriacou and Petite Martinique, and finally, was prime minister of Grenada.

He enjoyed the respect of many, in large measure just for being the person he was, for his contributions to the region, and for his respect for others. He wished no fuss to ever be made over him.

He was a wise man. He held strong views, not believing in local government, as he believed that it divided people at the grass-roots level where togetherness was so important.

In his conversations, he liked to use certain phrases like *that kind of thing* and *and so on*.

His handwriting, in script, cursive, and print, was very neat. One day, Nicho, as we at home called him, telephoned me in Freeport to request that I visit so as to accompany him to Trinidad, where he was to have surgery for colon cancer, which I gladly did in October 2013.

A friend of his family, Angela Pierre, took time off from her job to manage his stay and chauffeured us around Port of Spain for his different appointments. On his last night at the hotel before his admission to the hospital, we had a small argument on a relatively unimportant issue in the room we shared. He had spoken to the maid concerning his belongings during his stay at the hospital. I thought he should have spoken to the manager. "Let's go to sleep and not argue" was what he may have said to me.

The hotel was the Kapok, where I had stayed umpteen times, the first being in 1974. This time would be the last. On the day he was admitted, we were joined by Earle, one of his sons. Following his operation, I returned to the Bahamas, first spending a couple of days in Puerto Rico to seek parts for my car.

I saw him at least twice after that on my usual visits to Grenada, but the news was relayed to me that Sir Nicholas Alexander Brathwaite, OBE, who entered this life on 8 July 1925, departed it on 28 October 2016. He received a state funeral and was laid to rest beneath the oceanic waters.

Other Friends and Episodes

I now present a hodgepodge of some aspects of my life.

I was always involved not just in sports but also in personally keeping relatively fit, except for the times of my medical internship in the Bahamas in 1968 and my residencies in New York and Canada. After university, when I felt that I had arrived, I anticipated strutting around displaying the sprout of a paunch. The wings needed rest.

Back then, when I attended GBSS, every form had a weekly games afternoon, usually of cricket, football, or athletics. On vacations in Carriacou, we younger ones ran the length of the beach and back and then swam, especially on Saturdays, near noon and into the afternoons.

In Grenada, after hurricane Janet, I cycled every morning to Grand Anse Beach to run and swim. The bicycle was an OPL army type, easily disassembled and reassembled, that I borrowed from Gordon Lashley, a brother of Cheese, Adeline's husband.

When Betty, as a child, was admitted to the hospital in Grenada, I visited her every morning after my ride, leaving the bike at the bottom of the steps that led from the esplanade at one end of the Kendall Tunnel upward to the hospital. I basked in the experience of sincere love that I received from a 2-year-old child, so similar to that I later received from Deanna, Adeline's first daughter.

Keeping fit and playing games continued in Jamaica. I ran around the ring road every morning, and in an intra-university relay race, when I was residing at the Nunnery, I was picked for the relay team of four persons from Chancellor. I ran the third leg, each leg being once around the ring road, and Derek Hanlan was on the home leg. We won, and the prize was a case of Cremo chocolate milk.

There were two ring roads, one around most of the university buildings and the other around the adjacent hospital complex.

Sebastian "Sambas" Peter and Curtis "King Solomon" Cox, who's in-dwelling antenna identified every location of a possible party, resided on block B for a summer vacation. One morning, I woke them up at 6 a.m. to go running. Sambas afterwards remarked that I took off like Kipchoge Keino, leaving them way behind.

My dear friend Sanbas, an endocrinologist, was at one time attached to the UWI medical programme in the Bahamas as a senior lecturer.

He transitioned on 11 November 2022 to a place unknown whilst he was living in his homeland, Grenada. RIP, dear friend.

I have had multiple interpersonal affairs of different depths with women, and I hold the view that the love of many does not diminish the love for each and that love may exist at different forms and levels. But as I often say, like flowers, women should not be plucked—whatever that means. And of course, love comes sometimes in its purest form and is at other times accompanied by opposite feelings. The question therefore remains: can anyone truly define that word, *love*?

As someone once said, one may think that someone dislikes or even hates, when the truth is that that person just does not know how to show a liking or love.

I did have a special girlfriend who was very precious to me. I once referred to her as my destiny, and I enjoyed a loving relationship with her from about 1964, when I was a medical student, to 1970. Now, though very much apart, we are still together in friendship. Once, travelling there by train, I spent a weekend with her in Portsmouth. She stayed at her home, and I, at her aunt's.

My friendships with many ladies in my university days have continued to this day, and how fondly I remember the Jamaicans—Elaine "Ditty" Gweneth Martin, Maxine Brown, Yvonne Gardner, Deena, Pat "Spartacus" Beek (who danced to "Let It Be Me" by Jerry Butler and Betty Everett), Yvonne Samuels, Beverly Domville, and many others, including Audrey, a field hockey player. All were very friendly ladies who demonstrated a gentle liking for me. I did not collect women, as some thought—my friendship was with selected ladies—but I did and still do collect souvenirs, like paintings and especially trinket bells, from places I have visited.

One night, a group of us went barhopping and ending at a place where I ordered whisky from the lady. Spartacus had taken us to her home. The lady was her mom.

On campus, I had the unwavering and undying friendship of Ermina Davis, from Antigua; her twin sister, Evie; a brother, Gregson; and maybe another, Edgar. That friendship has continued since their return to Antigua, where I have visited them more than once, and to this day, we keep in touch. I can't think of going to Antigua and not contacting them—gems all. It is my understanding that on 27 July 2022, Edgar died. At lunch at her home, Evie introduced me to Malbec wine from Argentina.

To friendship, Ermina

Lady Grace

Grace Blythe, who resided in the Bastille (the name given to the nurses' hostel) and who has referred to me as her kissing friend, encouraged her mom from Savana-la-Mar to send cooked food to me on campus and encouraged the entire family to befriend me.

Once, Vivian and I, on a visit to Montego Bay, were picked up by one of her brothers and were well entertained by Grace, her brothers, and her mom and dad. She drove us to a picnic at the beach, and people mistook me for P. J. Paterson, the prime minister.

That night, one of the brothers had a party at his home, and we were invited. When we returned to Montego Bay, the small hotel was closed, our room door was locked, and the guard had no keys. Vivian climbed through another room to get to ours.

The very religious Grace once invited me to a revival/crusade service in Kingston. Near the end, when the song "Oh Lamb of God, I Come" was being played and an invitation to approach was issued, I got up. Grace was pleased, but I walked straight outside.

As mentioned, I have been mistaken throughout my life for other persons. Once, in Durban, South Africa, where I was attending the IAS conference, I was wearing a dashiki and walking with a long rod.

A white couple, in seeming admiration, thought I was Mandela. My attire was not that of Moses, for then they may have knelt.

Especially because of my slightly bent back and the swaying or rocking style to my walk, I have been mistaken for Sobers of cricket fame, who may be related to the Brathwaites in Barbados. Someone thought that I looked like Kirk Douglas in *Spartacus*. They need spectacles.

On my landing from a boat in Phnom Penh, capital of Cambodia, I was approached and surrounded by many who were shouting, "Kofi Annan!" and someone stole something small from my open shoulder bag. Vivian and I were travelling from Siem Reap, the province of ruined temples, after attending the IAS conference on AIDS in Bangkok in July 2004. Of course, a part of our visit included going to Golgotha, the place of skulls.

On the way back to the USA from Phnom Penh, we stopped in Tokyo for almost a full day. Yasutake collected us from the airport, gave us a tour of Asakusa Temple, and then took us to a tempura lunch.

Most have likened me to the actor Morgan Freeman. I'm OK with that.

I was never highly religious; but, at Iah's insistence, I went to Sunday school at the gospel hall in Grand Bay in my youth, though I always hoped it would rain heavily so that it would be cancelled—never in Carriacou. Adeline made certain that I attended church when I moved to Grenada in my early teenage years. Either Archdeacon Piggott or the bishop of the Anglican church promised that we would feel the entry of the Holy Spirit at confirmation. I felt nothing.

In my last years at GBSS, I became serious about becoming religious because of an address given by a priest at the usual Friday service at the school. The subject chosen by Father Huggins was the scriptural command to "be of good cheer". I welcomed my renewed interest in the Lord and, after a lapse, again went back to the Sunday morning service, willingly putting my copper coin into the collection or offertory plate.

From then, it was in and out again. On occasions, there were persons coercing me to kneel and accept the Lord, which did not result in any change in me. At the university, I once asked the Lord for a sign and was certain that I had found it, for in walking back from the Bastille to the Nunnery one late night, I was certain that a star had followed me all the way and was convinced it was from the Lord. Having later learnt that was a natural phenomenon, I reverted.

For a long period during and after university, I did not go to church, except for my wedding. That changed when I took up residence in Freeport, Bahamas, in 1985 and became a member of the Pro-Cathedral of Christ the King (Anglican). Since then, no matter where I am, be it Carriacou, Bermuda, or Tortola,

I have usually worshiped on Sundays, though now, because of the Covid-19 pandemic, there has been some hesitancy and delinquency.

I particularly enjoyed the Sunday morning services in Tortola at St Paul's Episcopal Church in Sea Cows Bay for the church's unpretentious approach, as well as the Wednesday noon services at St George's Episcopal in Road Town. The latter took an informal approach to a formal service, usually led by Father Branch of Trinidadian origin. On more than one occasion, I enjoyed the rendition of Psalm 126 in the versions that refer to the watercourse of the Negev, for it somehow reminded me of the rainy seasons in Carriacou.

Other than fooling around with the corn cob and its blossom, the first cigarette I smoked was one offered to me in 1961 by Mr. Coomansingh, a fellow teacher in GBSS. Thereafter, I smoked regularly at the university, an average of two to four per day after meals and prior to studying. I followed this pattern, with the amount increasing in spells at stressful times, until about 2017, when I quit completely. My upper respiratory allergies to dust and cold wind worsened on smoking, as did the wheezing in my chest.

My skin itches more than now and again. It is sensitive to polyester material and it erupts with large bumps and severe itching from bites and stings. My blood eosinophil count tends to be higher than normal. No matter how many are in a room, the mosquito chooses me.

In the wintry months on Grand Bahama, there are occasional fronts of skeleto-cerebral, bone-invading, shiver-inducing atmospheric chills that worsened all my health problems.

My drinking of alcohol followed the pattern of smoking. I usually drank socially but occasionally in binges, perhaps too often. It was in those latter periods when I discovered that, in the words of a teacher at university, "alcohol enhances desire but diminishes performance".

I must have developed hypertension in the 1990s, but I only accepted that diagnosis in Tortola in 2007 when I started to experience constant dizziness. I had grown up on salted foods, and as an adult, it was not uncommon for me to sprinkle a bit more onto my food. Likewise, in that same land, it became obvious that my knees were arthritic—not surprising, with those games I had played and continued to play even after my return to Freeport in 2008. I tried but never took to golf, quite popular in Freeport. Sometimes, now, I use a cane for support. I have already been told that I need bilateral replacements.

It was in 1996 that I ruptured a tendon in my left ankle, which was repaired under general anaesthesia by my friend and colleague Dr Janakiram. Some years after, he died suddenly at Rand Memorial Hospital, where he worked.

That I am not too far from death has occupied my mind more than once in my life. The first must have been in 1998, when I experienced a most debilitating form of vertigo in the Pegasus Hotel in Jamaica on my way to breakfast. The experience was mildly recurrent, but the not-too-rare heightened episodes were such that I had doubts that I would see the new millennium.

I was diagnosed with glaucoma on 11 November 1996. On 4 February 1999, I had right lens replacement for cataract, and I had the same procedure performed on the left eye on 16 August 2016. At this second time, my haemoglobin was under eleven grams per cent. Though I did not have symptoms, I learnt that it had fallen below eight grams in 2019, and when I subsequently developed symptoms, primarily dizziness, I learned that it was under six grams. Investigations did not uncover an obvious cause for the anaemia, but my haemoglobin levels have rebounded to normal on iron therapy. Obviously, I had been bleeding slowly. Again, death was foremost in my mind.

I experienced right ulnar nerve entrapment and on 19 October 2017 had transposition plastic surgery in Nassau, with a regional anaesthetic block at the neck. The surgeon was Dr Neil. I had begun to drop things from my right hand, but when that happened with money, I promptly sought the doctor. Before, I had never realised the importance of the pinkie.

My inconsistently taken medications now include a multivitamin, an occasional pain killer, and antihypertensives, and Vivian feeds me a daily concoction made from seaweed. I was recently placed on prostate-shrinking capsules. On an uneven terrain, a cane offers support.

One disappointment that I experienced was as block B representative in 1965. I was all prepared to receive the first ever presentation of the Warden's Plate, donated by Bobo himself, on behalf of my block. We had been assessed based on the points we'd accrued in various categories during the year.

At the end of the committee meeting, all representatives from the five blocks agreed to abide by the decision reached. However, Clive Mohess of block A was unhappy with the result and complained to the warden, who decided to withdraw the offer for that initial year. I lost a bit of my respect for my esteemed friend and warden, as I felt he should have consulted with all others before withdrawing his award.

Another disappointment occurred when I visited Chancellor Hall years later. I did not see my name on the Wall of Lions in Chancellor's meeting and dining room. I believed and still do that I was a worthy Chancellorite. And another disappointment was that my classmate and subsequent professor of pathology at UWI never invited me to be an external examiner.

Although he was ahead of me, Priapus and I were inseparable during my first three years on campus, except when we attended classes during the week. I was on block B, and he, on block D. He was ahead of me at GBSS and went, like Jack Radix, to university before I did, but we developed a very close friendship. And if I may say so, we were both of us brilliantly clownish.

We were loud and confident, moved about together, and repeated phrases like "What the men say, now," "Hi, hi, hi," and "The men gat to move, yes, move as one." We mixed and drank different combinations of beverages, and if asked about any of them, we referred to each concoction as a "man-you-must".

As a group that included Magnus "Danny" Daniel, who we also called Dano, we often went nightclubbing on weekends in well-known whorehouses. We would sometimes drink and dance until it was time to catch the 5 a.m. or 6 a.m. bus, the first of the morning, back to campus. We always went out with the understanding that we would stay at the club until every man was ready to leave and would never speak of what had transpired during the night. On Sundays, we merely fooled around, if possible, after a good sleep.

Once, Priapus invited about five of us out, despite knowing that the rest of us had no money, for he would be the one spending. At the bus stop, he ushered us in. When we arrived at the next stop, the conductor came to collect the fare, so we pointed to the back; to our dismay, there was no Priapus, and we therefore had to make our exit.

On one occasion, we took Bill Riviere, my friend from block B, with us to the Hole in the gully not far from Papine to dance the hully gully. On returning, we took a shortcut track up the hill. Well, Danny fell. The next day, Bill was, with a wagging tongue, spouting all over Chancellor about how Danny not only fell but rolled like a dumpling back down the hill.

What happen in da gully, stay in da gully!

He never was invited again on our outings, though he and I remained friends, usually rolling the *r*'s in our names when calling to each other. I also rolled the *r* when calling to Roberts (aka Roberto), an older student on campus from Trinidad who was a strong proponent of my candidacy for hall chairman and who lived not too far from Danny in Trinidad.

Bill and I both had girlfriends, and we often went out as a foursome, I with Beverly and he with Loretta.

Beverly

Beverly was an extraordinary lady who treated me with great kindness. I believe she introduced me to the stage shows in Jamaica, to the pantomimes, to Ranny and Lou, and maybe, though I'm not sure, to the concerts of Bob Marley and the Wailers, the Blues Busters, Toots and the Maytals, Desmond Dekker and the Aces, and others. She once gave me a stereo set for my room at the Nunnery.

I met other members of her family, including her dear sister, Sharon, who resides in Florida. Bev later lived in Barbados with her husband, Hal Parris, who is now deceased, but now she is back in New York living with her son, Darren.

What wonderful people.

For the vacations, as mentioned, it was necessary to make financial arrangements with the bursar's office for room and board if one stayed on campus. It was surprising how many persons squatted successfully. One person may possess a single dinner card, but he would collect more than one serving for sharing, and admittedly, the servers assisted us.

For one summer vacation, Chancellor's kitchen was closed, and we ate at Taylor's. As usual, one person would collect enough food for three or four. Well, one night, we were all eating when the kitchen supervisor came out. She chose Danny to approach and asked to see his card. Danny jumped on top of the table and proceeded to lambaste the lady. "You think the government of Trinidad and Tobago sent me all these miles to be asked by you for a card?"

Even though the lady supervisor seemed completely taken aback at what Danny had said, we, the others, gulped as fast as possible, in a hurry to leave. But one had to admit that Danny's impressive speech would have awed anyone.

Long after my days on campus, I was quite often in Trinidad and visited Danny many times, witnessing the deterioration of his sight from glaucoma to the point of total blindness. I also saw his general health decline from pulmonary fibrosis. He was taken care of by his wife, Ida, and their adopted daughter, Bernadine.

Whilst he was still able, he fulfilled his desire to visit Carriacou and Petite Martinique. He travelled to Grenada in maybe 1975 and stayed with me, and we also went to Carriacou by boat. When we arrived, it was too dark for him to deboard, and even the next morning, when he descended by ladder from the main boat to the rowing boat, he almost fell into the sea. But that day, he swam in the town's bay, and afterwards, he met my mother and all others at home. On the return trip, he was allowed to step ashore on the sister isle of Petite Martinique.

All these moments were cherished by him.

One night in Grenada, he, Priapus, and I went to a nightclub and bar in Belmont, and at about 2 a.m., Danny declared that he wished to have a woman. So, this was arranged, and we drove to the Grand Anse area, where he fulfilled his wish on the back seat of my Humber.

To digress slightly, that car was, according to my daughter Nika, "Daddy's pretty car". If in driving, another car was ahead of mine, Nika would say, "Move, ugly car. Move, ugly car. Let Daddy's pretty car pass."

Anyhow, from Grand Anse, we dropped the woman off at the wharf, and when we got to my home in Morne Jaloux, Danny realised that all his money was gone. So, that was that.

I last saw him in 1993, and he died on 11 October of that year, though it was not until the following year that I learnt that.

A true and everlasting friendship bound us together.

At the university in Jamaica, most thought of Priapus as an intelligent student, but he was always thought to take second place in history, his field of study, to Walter Rodney from Guyana.

Walter obtained first-class honours, and Priapus, after graduating with second-class honours, moved off campus and began postgraduate studies. After that, we did not see each other as often, but it became obvious that he was not the same person. When we heard that he was not well, a few of us Grenadians visited him, and some of us who were medical students were fooled by his acting into believing that he suffered from a foot drop.

It was not long after that he was admitted to the psychiatric ward of the university hospital with a diagnosis of schizophrenia. He refused to eat the food that was served on the ward, and whenever I visited, he predicted that I would win the Nobel Prize in medicine for proving that man could live without eating.

I, as a teenager, once opined that we were all born normal but that at birth, a germ entered the body of some and contributed to their bad outcomes. This germ theory of mine was a seeming combination of hereditary and acquired diseases (nature/nurture).

For this, I had hoped to receive recognition. Now, having become better educated, I'm no longer waiting.

Some have expressed the view that Priapus had experienced difficulties with his sponsor, Professor Roy Augier, in defending his thesis, which was not accepted, and that after that, things went wrong and he was never again the same. But, maybe in jest, there were those who believed that he was never normal to begin with. Hip Parade Wells always claimed that I was partly responsible, because it was I who had encouraged Priapus to talk nonsense on campus—"Let the men move; we must move as one."

There was a rumour that his marriage to a Trinidadian lady in 1966 in Jamaica had precipitated his illness. I didn't even know that he was married and have never met his wife or the daughter of the union. I have nothing more to say on this.

My next encounter with him was when I returned to Grenada at the end of 1973 to take up my employment. He was then teaching at GBSS. Dr Evelyn Mahy, the resident psychiatrist, was treating him for his mental problem, and he was doing very well. We renewed our friendship and spent most Fridays or Saturdays playing 500-rummy for almost the entire night at my home in Morne Jaloux.

Sometimes, I played this game with my brother Godwin at his home, and he passed on some basic techniques for winning, but only when I was due to leave Grenada.

During the uprisings in 1974 in Grenada, Mahy left for Barbados, so George Clarke, a psychologist, continued Mahy's regimen. George either got sick or died, and so I continued to manage Priapus's treatment. Then I left in 1976 for Suriname, and when I visited Grenada in 1977, I found Priapus in a bad way.

He had left or had been terminated from teaching and lived alone in the old homestead that was partly without a roof in Mt. Fendue in the parish of St Patrick. When I went to the homestead, there was a pot containing his food of boiled sprat fish that was obviously days old. Eventually, his relatives repaired the house and arranged for his care.

Though at times he spoke gibberish, he was still functional, and his memory remained good; some nine years after we had left Grenada, I returned with my wife and children, and he called them all by their names.

Most times when I happen to be in Grenada, I would visit him. I saw him when I attended a Caribbean Public Health Conference in 2004 and was accompanied by others, including my daughter Nanika, who had coauthored my poster presentation, and Brian Weiz, well known for his air ambulance service from Florida, USA. (Let me say that Nanika and I have coauthored a few scientific papers.)

I next saw Priapus on 12 November 2005 together with King Solomon Cox, Big Stiff Francis, Sambas Peter, and his friend Errol. All of us were attending a UWIMAA meeting. Our last chat was on 25 June 2008 when my wife and I visited him. At that time, we met his sister, Ruby.

I sometimes find myself humming his song, a rallying cry for the football finals at UWI in 1964. At first, I did not expect the song to succeed, but it did.

> We want a goal, Chancellor if you please.
> Bear down on Irvine; bring them to their knees.
> We don't want no other place,
> And so just in case,
> Down here in Mona Bowl,
> Chancellor, we want a goal.

My friend died in March 2009, I've been told.

What de men say now, Priapus? No gibberish, bro. Talk sense!

In my first year at the university, the finals in football was between Chancellor and Taylor. The refrain was—When Chancellor goes a marching on, hurrah, hurrah. (repeat), no man, no beast no other place could front the mighty lion's face. Today we add to Taylor Hall disgrace. Chancellor won the game.

I thoroughly enjoyed my life as a university student and Jamaica. When I arrived, Jamaicans treated the students with reverence. At times, we would turn up at a party uninvited and declare that we were doing research, and we would get away with it. But the situation started changing in my final years, and as far as I heard, it only worsened.

Herbie Husbands delighted in playing pranks on the unsuspecting. Having learnt the location of a party, he would invite a group to show up at a certain time. Sometimes he even invited people to show up at a place where there was no party. Many have been embarrassed on knocking at a door unannounced, especially if there was no party. He is present in the photo—Chancellor scores a goal.

Perhaps not that often, but on or about midday on some Saturdays, a small group of us would catch the number six bus to downtown Kingston to shop at Woolworths. We would then have a look around and a drink at the crafts market before heading back to campus. Although there was a supply of good watches—including Bulovas and Omegas, the latter of which Chester Prime bought—most went for the reliable and cheap Timex. Many hustlers paraded the streets. Once, "Stinky Joe" Bullen, who had been praised by the member of parliament for Carriacou, bought a watch from one of them. Even before he returned to the campus, it was turning greenish. It was not a Bulova but a Bolova.

I bathed at Dunn's River Falls, Negril Beach, and elsewhere. I drove through Fern Gully. I ate jerk pork and drank mannish water. I enjoyed being "the Riccio". I have used most presented opportunities to return.

On my last night on campus, there was a dance at the students' union, and it was one of bad behaviour on my part. Everyone wanted a piece of the Riccio, so as to say their farewells. Drinks poured freely, and I kept adding black and hot pepper to mine, foolishly boasting that I had an iron stomach. Things were such that I had no idea that my precious lady had left, and hence, we did not spend that last night together.

On leaving the lights of the students' union, I walked gently into the night back to the Nunnery.

I was nearing departure from a country where I had been introduced to the hully gully, to ska, to rocky steady, and to reggae. My walk back to the Nunnery was filled with sadness.

My lady felt ignored, she said, and she refused to come to the Nunnery after I had gotten her on the phone at the Bastille. I spent the rest of the night, my last as a medical student, alone at the Nunnery.

However, she kept her promise and had her friend take me to the airport the next morning.

I almost missed my flight, for neither Ramdhat nor I nor my lady nor any of the others who were seeing me off had heard the announcements. But my watch indicated that something was wrong.

After double-checking at the counter, I had to run to the BWIA plane. I climbed the steps only to be told that that plane was leaving for New York and had to backtrack to the other one for Barbados.

As the plane took off and smoothly soared, Jamaica drifted away, and in silence, I, in quiet sombre, cried.

In Barbados, I think I spent the night in a student's room arranged by Herbie Husbands, who was previously at Mona but was then finishing his studies at Queen Elizabeth Hospital.

That night, he took me to a house party and introduced me to Charlie Griffith of West Indies cricket fame. I have since sat twice at the same table with Mr. Griffith at UWIMAA meetings, both in Barbados.

For his internship, Herbie, then married, also went to Nassau as I had done and was lodged in a special apartment near to the intern's mess. I'm not sure that I ever saw him again, though I think I did. He died in 1999, years after becoming a radiologist.

Although my group was not the first from UWI to intern in the Bahamas, it seemed as if we provided an impetus for others to follow. At that time, the year of internship that followed graduation, was, for us, generally spent in hospitals in Jamaica, Trinidad, and Barbados.

As I liked none of those choices, I went to see the dean, who indicated that the hospital in the Bahamas had been recently approved for the internship programme. I knew that my decision was made.

Another country, here I come!

In a similar manner, I have reflected, and perhaps with good reason, that after Chester Prime and I went to GBSS, there was an influx of bright boys and girls following in our footsteps. Winston "Socrates" McIntosh from Mt. Pleasant, the young man who had to refer to Randolph as uncle, and my nephew James "Jimmie" Lashley, Adeline's son, were both winners of the Grenada Island Scholarship award as students of GBSS.

No wonder so many of us extol the virtues of our alma mater, the song of which says, "The feats of fathers and brothers are beacons marking the way. The torch handed down by others we must keep alive today." Its motto is *"Non palma sine labore."*

Having departed Jamaica in November, I went to Grenada and Carriacou for the rest of the year, before leaving in 1968 to begin my internship in Nassau, Bahamas.

I missed my precious lady. I yearned for her and just wanted to get married to her and for us to get lost together. Being together in mind but physically apart was not my cup of tea, and I was very disappointed when she did not come to me, as I had requested from Carriacou, even though her decision was the logical one.

Using logic was the better approach, but love, in the Mt. Pleasant tide, suffered me just a wee bit.

On my way to Nassau, I stopped off in Jamaica and was put up by King Solomon and Sambas at the Nunnery. The lady was still mine, but I said farewell to Maxine, Yvonne, and another attractive nurse who had just been jilted by her Guyanese boyfriend.

From room to room, the Riccio went.

In Nassau, there would be four others from UWI—Toppin, Trotman, Duncombe (a Bahamian from Bimini), and Hyacinth Chin Sang. The men stayed in the interns' quarters, where two British female interns were ending their terms, and Hyacinth was roomed further uphill on the compound in the nursing sisters' residence. Of the two women from the UK in our quarters, one, Jenny, was entertained by Dr Cecil Bethel, and the other was entertained by a male Bahamian nurse.

The intern's salary was B$250, on par with the US, and lodging with meals and laundry were provided at no cost to us.

PART 2

EXTENDED MEDICAL TRAINING—WITH A SALARY

10

PRINCESS MARGARET HOSPITAL, NASSAU, BAHAMAS

At that time in Nassau, there were many men from the Caribbean islands who had been recruited and employed as, inter alia, prison and police officers, including a group from Grenada who behaved as if they were the masters of the land. They gladly welcomed Toppin and I, showing concern for our welfare. However, it soon became noticeable that they were also bent on abusing the sick-day privilege, seeking sick slips from us, which, after a time, neither Toppin nor I was too happy about.

On the day of my arrival, I was whisked from the plane by a few of them, bypassing immigration and customs. That seemed a wonderful way to travel, but it backfired later on returning from Jamaica, where I had gone to sit and pass the ECFMG examination, which was a requirement for pursuing medical residency programmes in the USA. I must add here that I got some revenge on Sticks McLaren, as I received a higher mark than him in that exam. Also, it was good to spend time with my dear lady friend.

Anyhow, on returning from Jamaica, the entry stop to the Bahamas was in Freeport, Grand Bahama Island. I was taken to a room to be questioned as to why I should be allowed entry or allowed to go to Nassau when there was no previous entry in my passport. Eventually, after much explanation, the immigration officers became convinced that I was legit and allowed me to board the already delayed flight.

My three-month programmes at Princess Margaret Hospital were in chest diseases, with Dr Mark Bown, an American consultant; internal medicine, with Dr John Lunn, a Bahamian consultant; surgery, with Dr Earl Farrington, a Bahamian, consultant; and obstetrics and gynaecology, with Dr Cecil Alexander, a British consultant.

My initial impression of Nassau was of a clean and colourfully pretty city with buildings of pastel colours—one where it seemed to rain a lot and the streets were easily flooded. It appeared to be a crime-free city in which one could walk about without fear any time of day or night, as I often did in the Bay Street area near downtown.

Especially after my university spell in Jamaica, I was lonely in the first six months, not so much in the day but at nights. The Grenadian prison officers did provide some companionship, as they knew the ropes and invited us out. Of them, I remember Dave Noel, Boca Julien, "Stumpy" Bruno, Wavell Munroe, "Bondo" Edison Roberts, "Shark" Robinson, and Tony "Beaver" Barker. I eventually also met some non-Grenadians, especially from Barbados and Trinidad.

In addition, there were some other men working elsewhere with whom I developed close friendships. Coming to my mind are Stephen "Mossy" Redhead from Grenada, a bookkeeper at ABC Motors; Leon "Hip Parade" Wells from Grenada, a teacher; and Joseph "Joey" Alfred from Trinidad, a magistrate and, later, a judge.

Hip Wells, the comedian, was already known to me from my GBSS and university days. I knew Mossy's brother, Fabian, who was at the university during my time. Fabian entertained me years later on a trip I made to Caracas, Venezuela, when working with the Pan American Health Organization (PAHO). He was Grenada's ambassador there.

Trotman, one of the interns, was thought to be gay and showed an interest in Mossy Redhead, but Mossy, not of that leaning, had his eyes on a student nurse who was, however, then seeing someone else.

Joey Alfred gave me my last driving instructions and practice towards getting my license. When I took the test, I made certain that my stethoscope and white coat were in the car. My first driving lessons were with Godwin in Grenada. Those were followed by a short spell with Jack Radix in our car in Jamaica, and after that, I received lessons from a delightful friend, Joy Bogle, a medical student at the university. Joy and I message each other at times. I think she specialised in radiology.

I introduced Joey to Evelyn Boyd, a student nurse who also was my friend in Nassau. They got married, and, years later, we developed a very close family relationship.

In February 2014, Joseph Bernard Emmanuel Alfred, my long-lasting friend, died at age 78 in his homeland, Trinidad.

After a few months in Nassau, I was introduced to Vivian Isaacs, a student nurse. I believe it was Daisy Johnson, another nursing student, who introduced us. At that time, I was friendly with Zelia Thompson, another student nurse who occasionally, invited me to her parents' home for a Sunday dinner. When I, at year's end, left Nassau for Newfoundland, I did not say goodbye to her parents, who were not very pleased, according to Zelia, who had already left for England to finish the nursing programme. I gather that after that year, the Bahamas school of nursing was granted the necessary accreditation and recognition by the British Council to award the title of registered nurse (RN) to its graduates.

My lady friend from Jamaica visited Nassau, where she had relatives. Once, when she came to see me at the interns' mess, I introduced her to Vivian, who was then my usual date but who I had already asked to rest herself and lay low for a while. Before leaving, the Jamaican said to me, "Riccio, that girl is in love with you."

My primary reason for being in the Bahamas was for my internship. Overall, it was pleasant, but the schedule of alternate nights and weekends on-call was a bit too much. Nevertheless, we accepted it as the norm and did not complain.

Yet, primarily for other reasons, our group withheld our services starting on a Monday in November, the penultimate month of the internship. The issues included poor physical accommodation, poor meal planning, and being conveniently on-call at nights for the consultants' private patients, whom we did not know beforehand.

The Bahamian media was fair in their reports of what was transpiring, and the seemingly sympathetic public responded by bringing us food. Someone was assigned to plan our meals, and the accommodation was repaired. The then minister of health, Dr McMillan, said we ought not to strike because we were not yet even doctors, but Dr Lunn defended us on this.

Dennis Toppin was asked by the group to speak to Professor Annamunthoodo, the dean of the faculty of medicine at UWI, who expressed concern about the programme at PMH but also annoyance with us because, as he rightly said, we should have sought his advice before taking our action.

I think we met with the ministry of health authorities at 4 p.m. on the Friday of the same week and returned to work.

Incidentally, the University College of the West Indies was part of the University of London until it became an established university in 1962, at which point it became UWI. Thus, at games, our chants went from "U-cee!" to "U-wee!"

One good thing about the internship was that there was always a party in the doctors' mess.

11

RESIDENCY PROGRAMMES

The programmes of residency, as they are called in the USA and Canada, represent hospital-based training towards specialisation in a branch of medicine. Surgery, paediatrics, internal medicine, pathology, and obstetrics and gynaecology are but a few examples of an ever-expanding field, to which are added subspecialities.

I always thought that ob-gyn was the easiest of the specialties, requiring no great depth of knowledge, and I was therefore seriously considering doing it. However, with my love for children in general and the enjoyment and fulfilment I got from taking care of them at the university hospital in Jamaica, paediatrics was my first choice.

At First, an Educational Interlude

After internship, I left for Grenada and Carriacou for a short period. On my departure from there, I stopped over in Jamaica to obtain Canadian entry visa and then stopped in Nassau, where I stayed at the nurses' residence for free. Finally, after overnighting in Montreal, I journeyed to St John's, Newfoundland, to begin a residency in paediatrics in January 1969.

There, over a three-week period, I saw only one other black person in downtown, St John's. Upon seeing me, some children stared at me in amazement. The overall atmosphere was bleak, and the ground, like the people, was white, being covered with snow. I lacked the required enthusiasm. It did not take long for me to resolve that neither paediatrics nor Newfoundland were for me.

My love perhaps was for the well, playful children and not the sick ones. It was certainly not for those with strange neurological conditions, as I was exposed to in Newfoundland.

I headed back to Nassau unannounced, where I believe I again stayed at the senior nurses' residence.

Whilst in Nassau, I received an appointment to see Dr Jeffery Wilson, the chief medical officer, who promised me a job in pathology to start in March. With a month to spare, and with an offer of a place to stay from an Indian teacher, we left for Trinidad, his homeland, for the carnival festivities on the Sunday preceding Ash Wednesday.

On the Monday, we went to downtown Port of Spain for J'Ouvert. We spent that Monday night sleeping on a mattress placed on the floor at the family home of Gloria Roach, who I had met in Nassau. We spent most of Tuesday on the balcony looking at the parade of bands on Henry Street. On Tuesday night, we went back to the Indian's home.

Early Wednesday morning, I boarded a flight to Grenada, but I spent most of that time in Carriacou, often visiting Miss Kanie's granddaughter, Nella, for whom I felt an attraction.

I returned again to Nassau by 1 March 1969, on which day I began my job as a house officer in the Rand pathology department, with Dr Joan Read, from England, in charge.

I was placed under a more junior doctor, G. Curd, who taught me to do autopsies and to read histology slides. Later on, I became friendly with the British lady who was the histology technologist in the department.

I think that I may have spent the first week after my return to Nassau at the Parliament Hotel at the government's expense, and after that, I believe that I may have spent a week or two at Mossy Redhead's apartment.

Then, a lady friend from Grenada named Barbara, who was leaving on vacation, allowed me to use her apartment on Bay Street.

I had met her through her uncle, Duncan Rapier, the manager of the Nassau Beach Hotel. On her return, I spent a month in Mr. Darling's apartment building on Deveaux Street, close to the hospital, and then another week in a room of a house on West Street that was within walking distance of the hospital. Finally, I stayed in a one-bedroom apartment in a new complex owned by a Jamaican man on Constitution Drive in Boyd's Subdivision.

It was during this time that Vivian and I cemented our relationship, becoming extra close.

Also, this was when I again started to play cricket, not having played since leaving Jamaica in 1967, and even there, I had not played in my last years, spending more time studying for the final exams.

My first game of the league, representing Paradise Club under the captaincy of Mr. Colin Dean, was against St Agnes Club. Earl Alleyne, under the byline "First Slip", reported in one of the local newspapers that "Dr Brathwaite made a most inglorious (or inauspicious) entry into the league by being bowled first ball by Woods." However, in that game, I did claim three wickets and took a well-judged running catch on the long leg boundary. I believe we won the game. I continued to represent my club until I left for residency in Brooklyn, NY.

Once in Nassau, being a novice, I poured water into the engine of my car, which I had bought for $800. It was a second-hand Morris Minor, which I gave to Vivian when I again departed Nassau.

This short time in Nassau was also a time for parties. From the carnival in Trinidad, I had brought back Sparrow's latest LP albums, with songs like "Mr. Walker", "The Lizard", and "Sa Sa Ye". They proved to be the raison d'être for many an invitation for me and my close friends, Joey Alfred, Leon Wells, and Stephen Redhead to attend, provided we travelled with the albums.

Sometimes, after partying, we went swimming in the wee moonlit hours of the morning at different beaches.

It was on this leg of my journeys that I met Norris Gordon, his wife, Leila, and their children. He was a nurse psychologist attached to the Sandilands Rehabilitation Centre on the same general compound as the prisons. A close friendship ensued.

Another Grenadian then in Nassau who I saw fairly often with his Bahamian lady friend, Norma, was Raymond Briggs.

My mind tells me that it was at that time in Nassau that I met "Bigman" Laffleur, and his living-in lady, Miss Lily. She had burnt her hand, and after she was discharged from the hospital, I continued to visit to clean and dress the unhealed areas.

They lived in an enclosed beach locale in a hut adjacent to the second home of an executive of CBS in the USA. Bigman provided managerial oversight for the property. My friends and I visited for the above reason but continued afterwards so as to swim and party and to catch land crabs. On one occasion, we met the man himself, Mr. William S. Paley, owner of the property. He granted us permission to continue with our exploits there.

This was a time that Hip Wells related another story—certainly his version of it. A Jamaican doctor, Dr Fergus, worked as a haematologist in the laboratory at PMH during my internship. After I left, he departed for the USA. Being allowed to travel only with less than $10,000 without declaration, he put the rest of his money in the spare tyre of his car, which he shipped. On arrival in Miami, his car was sans the spare. So far, this was apparently true, but Hip claimed that the good doctor then sat at a street junction for weeks, looking at cars and hoping to spot his spare tyre.

The Second Act

During this stint in Nassau, I applied for residency jobs in both Pathology and obstetrics and gynaecology, deciding to accept whichever was the first positive response but hoping that it would be the one in pathology. In my view, pathology was the most demanding

RESIDENCY PROGRAMMES

knowledge-wise of all the medical disciplines. Not only that, but pregnant women always seem to begin labour contractions that lead to deliveries at nights—a disturbance of good sleep.

Somehow, this reminds me of what someone once said about menstruation—that it was a bloody waste of good fucking time.

My first positive response came from the residency in pathology.

I left Nassau in early July 1969 to begin the residency in pathology at the Lutheran Medical Center (LMC) in South Brooklyn. Loneliness again crept into my life. However, I managed, and it was then that I became acquainted with, learnt, and mastered the public transportation system. I could then easily and readily find my way to wherever it was necessary to go in New York.

This was also a time when I often went to the movies, especially to see those that had won or had been nominated for Academy Awards. Other than Charlton Heston, who I was first exposed to in Grenada when I saw *The Ten Commandments* and *Ben-Hur*, among others he acted in, at the new Deluxe Cinema, I thought very highly of Dustin Hoffman. I went to see *Midnight Cowboy* and was so engrossed in the action that it was only on the way home that I realised that he had played the role of Ratso, also known as Enrico "Rico" Rizzo—well, that was somewhat close to *Riccio*!

Always a place of excitement, New York was abuzz with an extra sparkle in its atmosphere. The euphoria accompanying Broadway Joe's guaranteed victory in the super bowl rolled over to the amazing Miracle Mets, with the likes of Cleon Jones, Tommy Agee, Jerry Koosman, and Tom Seaver. They were well on their way to winning the World Series of baseball, and the Knicks, with Willis Reed, Walt Frazier, Dick Barnette, and others, were shooting baskets in their pretty shorts towards capturing the NBA championship over the LA Lakers in 1970.

The director of pathology was Dr Ted Ehrenreich, an expert in kidney pathology. There were two other pathologists on staff, Dr Stoll and Dr Libman. The latter knew the fine and theoretical details of all pathologic conditions but apparently had difficulties in arriving at a diagnosis. He was soon replaced by, I think, Dr Campbell.

After weighing the odds and assessing the pros and cons, one must come to a decision.

Dr Libman left one in limbo. I promised myself to be more decisive.

My associate resident was Mario Wernicke, who stayed with his wife, Susana, in the same apartment complex as I. He owned a Volkswagen, and at times, I rode with him to and from work, though it was but a short walking distance. Part of our association was for me to guide him in the use of the English language.

One Saturday, we drove to Glen Falls in upper New York to see the Dr Libman at his new position. We had always enjoyed listening to him. After he had taken us for a bite in the hospital cafeteria, we took our leave, and on the way back, I drove without a license until we approached the city.

Mario and I both left LMC after that year. I remained in Brooklyn, and he went to Manhattan. In the following year, though separate, we kept in touch, and at his invitation, we saw the rock musical *Hair* together on Broadway.

I next saw Mario in his homeland, Argentina, while I was stationed in the Republic of Suriname. We were both attending a pathology conference in Buenos Aires. One day, we had lunch together.

Within a month or two of being at LMC, I tendered my letter of resignation because the chief of surgery, a white man, referred to me as a liar and made racially-tinged remarks in the mortuary, where I was performing an autopsy. My words in the letter included, "Though black I am, I am no less a man." My letter and resignation were not accepted.

It was not always things of a pathologic nature that occupied my time at the Lutheran Medical Center. The institution had occasional outings for the staff, the departments organised get-togethers, people were generally friendly, and I was even a regular member of one of its bowling teams.

My precious Jamaican lady was either making a visit or was moving permanently to New York, and I awaited her arrival at the apartment where she was expected to stay. On her exit from the elevator, I was standing in the hallway, and it was as if we both realised that the spark was no longer aglow.

From then, we drifted apart; however, we have since remained friends and now and then exchange greetings through the internet.

Vivian also visited, and one night, with a well-placed contribution, we saw Dionne Warwick's show at the Copacabana from stage-side.

Whilst still at LMC, I developed close friendships with two of the three Grenadian ladies who had vacationed in Nassau when I was working there for four months in 1969 and who were now living in New York. Years later, I became acquainted with the third, who was then living in Barbados. If there was anything involving Grenadians, Pauline made certain that I was invited if I happened to be in Barbados.

Toppin's old girlfriend from Carriacou, also in New York as a nurse, invited me to a night party that went till six or seven the next morning. At the party, I met a nurse from South Africa who expressed that I was a most dynamic and charming individual, and I agreed. On my return to Grenada years later, another lady said, whilst we were dancing, "You are the most charming of the Brathwaites". I did not disagree.

We left the party together in over a foot of fresh snow that had fallen during the night, and we frolicked in it as we wended our way to the subway station. We saw each other again. One time we ran into each other when going to the Brooklyn Museum, on the grounds of which we observed an eclipse of the sun. On another occasion, she invited me to the Village for a concert featuring Miriam Makeba—"Pata, pata, pata."

I became friendly with a lady who also lived in Brooklyn but who was from Jamaica. She paid a visit to her homeland, and on her return, she informed me that she was pregnant and that she intended to have an abortion, which she did. Sadly, she developed serious complications afterwards. The parents, thinking that I was involved, suggested that to the Brooklyn Police, and they interviewed me at the hospital, which proved a bit embarrassing for me.

It was also then that I began to date a dear lady named Bernadette from Petite Martinique. She was staying with Carriacouans Martin Roberts, his wife, and his sister, Daphne. Daphne was a young lady that I was very fond of from the days that I was schooling in Grenada, but it was not our turn.

In July the next year, 1970, I moved from LMC to Brookdale Hospital Center and lived in its adjacent apartment building for staff. In charge of pathology was Dr David Spain, an expert in pulmonary pathology. He was assisted by two others, one being Dr. Kauffman. I befriended the secretary of the department, who introduced me around within the hospital. Not remembering names, I would greet people afterwards with just "Hello!"

This hospital was much closer to where many West Indians lived. I therefore visited my sister Sarah much more often and strengthened my friendship with Norris Gordon and his family, who lived near to the hospital. That was a friendship that had begun in Nassau.

On Saturday nights, it was the custom to dance in the basement of Wisco Manor on Eastern Parkway, which was owned by the Caesars, who were said to be related to my maternal grandmother. That was where Mobile Olliviere's music band played. Both names had roots in Petite Martinique.

In winter, when one exited the basement onto the street at two or three o'clock at night, it was wonderfully exhilarating to inhale that cold air after the smoky atmosphere on the inside.

In thinking back, it was during my time at Brookdale that I received a call from Jacklyn Creft asking about my interest in politics.

Perhaps because of my response that I preferred to be behind the scenes, I was never called again. To appreciate this diversion, one is forced back to the political circumstances in Grenada from the 1970s through 1983—protests, strikes, a coup d'état, executions, interim administration. I had already left Grenada when the coup d'état took place.

A significant milestone occurred on 9 January 1971 in Nassau, to which I had journeyed from New York. On the morning of that day, Father Cooper, in St George's Anglican Church, joined Vivian and I and proclaimed us husband and wife after we each had declared, "I do."

So far, we still do, but not without misunderstandings. Praise the Lord!

Mossy Redhead was the best man, and Hip Parade Wells, a groomsman. My sister Sarah was there from Brooklyn. We spent our honeymoon first in Mexico City and then in Freeport, Grand Bahama, at the home of Vivian's "aunt" Brenda and her husband, Wilber Major. We ended in Nassau.

Vivian moved back with me to Brooklyn. The pathology department held a small reception for us. She managed to get a job in a nursing home, and most nights, I went to Manhattan to accompany her home on the train. My residency at Brookdale Hospital ended in June of that year.

One of the things we enjoyed in downtown Manhattan on a late Saturday morning was breakfast cooked on an open grill just behind the counter where we sat—hashbrown potatoes, sunny-side-up fried eggs, New York steak, and a tall, ice-filled glass of Coca-Cola. No wonder my arteries are calcific.

My wedding

The Gods Dwell here

My travels continued, as I was accepted to continue my residency in pathology and laboratory medicine at the Queen's Medical Center in Honolulu.

Vivian and I left for Hawaii at the end of June, taking an organised tour. We travelled first by bus to Washington, D.C., where we spent a night or two with Reverend Jeremiah, who had extended the invitation to me, and his wife, Maude, and children.

The invitation had been offered when he had visited Brooklyn to attend the wedding of his relative and we had gotten into an argument about politics in Grenada. Maude was my first cousin, a daughter of Uncle Deeclo.

On the Sunday morning of our stay, the goodly reverend woke us up to go with him to church. We declined, and he, a bit upset, questioned how we could stay at the home of a preacher and not accompany him to his church. This did not lessen the spirit of hospitality that we received.

From there, it was on to Richmond, West Virginia. On the first night, we went to a bar, where I thought I was looking at women but, alas, realised that they were all homosexual men, differently dressed and adorned. We left after one drink because of the strange and questioning looks we were receiving from some of them.

Next we flew to Boulder, Colorado, where we stopped for a few days. Then we travelled again by bus via Reno, Nevada, with a stop to view a part of the Grand Canyon, to San Francisco, California. We spent a few day there doing the usual—visiting a national park, riding the trams, and eating at Fisherman's Wharf.

The flight from San Francisco to Oahu was fantastic. On the large jet plane, there was an upper deck with a bar and easy chairs for just relaxing away from one's assigned seat where backpacks cannot damage your face. On arrival, the people who promised to meet us at the airport never materialised due, as we later learnt, to an unfortunate mix up regarding our time of arrival. So, we took a taxi to Honolulu and checked into a cheap apartment hotel.

We rented a car for the first few days, but pretty soon, we bought a second-hand one. Fortunately, we were lucky in finding an apartment for rent on the top floor (fourth or fifth) of the building within walking distance of the Queen's Medical Center. I was a third-year resident in laboratory medicine (general pathology), and Vivian got a job as a nursing assistant in the hospital.

I had good times in Hawaii, but Vivian, apparently, not so much. Other than working, we did what most tourists would do after work, at nights, and on weekends in Oahu. We swam a lot, attended at least one luau, and visited the USS *Arizona* Memorial. We not only saw Diamond Head at a distance every day but took tours to it. We went to different shows and saw a game by the Harlem Globetrotters. And it was there in Honolulu that we saw performances by Bill Cosby and Sarah Vaughn. To me, Hawaii was not dull.

Curtis Cox was also there, having come from Grenada, as I had put in a good word for him for a residency position in surgery, which he got. Our friendship, which started in our teenage years and was strengthened at UWI in Jamaica, has grown and indeed has blossomed into a very warm, friendly relationship. He was supposed to have been the best man in my wedding, but unfortunately, he had to return to Grenada from Nassau.

My first, most impressive Old Year's Night in Hawaii was in a Honolulu establishment in 1972 with Vivian and Curtis. We were feted to the utmost, at a cost of course. As the changeover was welcomed, one of us atop a table loudly proclaimed, "Happy New Year."

Curtis has given one of his sons my name—no, no, no, not Riccio, but Fitzgerald.

We left for home after 6 a.m. on New Year's Day in a dense haze of smoke, for everyone had launched fireworks and firecrackers.

My friendship with the Holms, Roger and Colleen, was tremendous. She and Ms Jerry Cravalho, a lab technician in bacteriology, together with Dr Will and Curtis Cox were the godparents of our first child, Nanika Veanna (born May 12, 1972). The post-baptism party was held at the home of the Cravalhos. Mr. Cravalho was an easy-going, friendly person who took a liking to Mama, Vivian's mother, but his wife was not very friendly and hardly took part in the celebrations.

In the hospital, I also had good relations with the chief histotechnologist, Laura, and with ladies in haematology and chemistry. All were decent and genuine individuals. However, the strongest of the friendships was with Colleen and Roger, who in 1974 visited us in Morne Jaloux in Grenada. They arrived perhaps the day after Dax, our second child, was born, on 20 July. Colleen gave a monetary donation to the hospital through me, and she always presents gifts to her goddaughter. On retirement, they returned to Stanley, North Dakota. In the latter part of 2021, Roger departed this life.

I rotated through the disciplines of microbiology, haematology, and chemistry but had on-call duties for the autopsy service.

It was nearing the end of my period in Hawaii when Mama came from Nassau to visit us, accompanied by her first daughter, Bobbi, and Bobbi's infant son, Scotty.

We developed good friendships, with the chief of the laboratory, Dr Drake Will, who also headed the microbiology unit within the lab and proved to be a great supporter of the family throughout our stay.

The knowledge that I gained was tremendous. Dr Namiki was the most knowledgeable anatomic pathologist I have ever met—someone who always bowed and said, *"Arigato."* Near to the end of my stay, we had a falling out, but that was readily patched up by the chief. Dr Ann Catts was most reliable, and Dr Ben Hom, though sound in haematology, proved a difficult person to fathom. However, without doubt, my strength in Hawaii was always derived from Dr Drake Will, so much so that he encouraged me to remain at the laboratory, promising me the post of chief resident for the ensuing year and an all-expense paid trip to a conference in Vienna.

But my mind had been made up long before. I was moving to Ottawa, as part of my desire to see as much of the world as I could during my years of education to become a qualified pathologist before returning to serve in my country. Of course, because of my love to travel, I planned to see more of the world after that during my vacations from work.

We received invitations to his home, and whilst Vivian enjoyed the pool, he and I sat back, chatted, watched her, and drank. He marvelled at her powerful thighs. When he once travelled abroad, he gave us his home to take care of. We had a party one night, drank him out, had a bash, and left the place for him to clean and restock.

Vivian and I visited Kauai for a few days during her pregnancy. We also went to the big island, Hawaii, with Nika, Bobbi, Scott, and Mama, to be guided through the steam and flames within Volcanoes National Park.

From somewhere there, I walked a short distance towards a cliff overlooking the sea and beheld the most breathtaking scene that I have ever seen—a sharp drop off the mountain to a black, sandy cove that appeared as if unchanged from its inception. The hazy grey of the pacific extended beyond, as if endlessly and forever. The photo I took has faded.

The other volcano that I similarly twice ventured into with the prominent pitons in the area was the Soufriere in St Lucia, but Hawaii projected a mystic majesty.

All in all, I don't think Vivian was happy in Hawaii, and I was peeved during the visit of her relatives. But all things considered, I thoroughly enjoyed my stay in the lands of such outstanding and dramatic topography, so much so that I have always felt that Hawaii, where once there was royalty, **'tis but where the gods reside.**

Near the end of my residency, Vivian returned to Nassau with her relatives, and I took a Pacific Affordables tour for about two weeks. The first country I went to was Japan. I arrived in Kyoto and rode the bullet train to Tokyo. Then followed Taiwan and Hong Kong.

On the night before beginning the tour, after attending a small party thrown by Curtis at a girlfriend's house, I was on my way to see another friend who worked at the lab but got involved in a road traffic accident. I was thought by the police to be in the wrong but, thankfully, was not considered to be inebriated.

I never knew what the outcome was, although I received some form of communication from the insurance company telling me to return to Hawaii to present evidence. By then, I was back in Grenada.

In Tokyo, I learned not to drink in so-called clubs but instead to drink in bars, because there was a big difference in price. Also, the ladies at the clubs offered table companionship but drank more than the customer and had much more exquisite tastes.

After the tour, I returned to Hawaii in the early morning and left for Ottawa at 11 p.m. that same night. The send-off at the airport by my friends, which included Colleen, Jerry, and Curtis, was indeed truly, memorably grand.

Ottawa, Canada

I was accepted as a fourth-year resident in clinical pathology at Ottawa General Hospital for the period from July 1972 to June 1973. Because the Royal College's certificate examination in general pathology was to be held in November, arrangements were kindly made for a five-month extension at Ottawa Civic Hospital, where I would work in anatomic pathology, to occupy me until then.

In the practice of general pathology, there are two divisions: clinical and anatomic. The basic subdivisions in clinical pathology are microbiology, haematology, and chemistry. Anatomic pathology includes autopsy and histopathology, which is the examination of biopsies, resections, and organs, generally requiring microscopy. At Ottawa General, my programmes were in all three disciplines.

Microbiology and chemistry were each run by a nonmedical scientist employed on a part-time basis. I particularly enjoyed haematology (including blood banking) under Bill McLeish, who delivered and published our paper, "Anti-N Antibodies in Patients on Renal Dialysis".

It was in haematology that I met Lorraine, the supervisor, who, with her boyfriend, once took me to an American football game involving the Ottawa Rough Riders. Clothing-wise, I was unprepared, so instead of freezing to death in the open air, I spent more time near to or in the warm bathrooms, thereby missing most of the game.

It was during my stay in haematology that I examined the blood film from a seemingly clinically undiagnosable patient and recognised the microscopic forms of the malarial parasite. Another resident, a female from Egypt, having heard of my discovery, hurried to the ward to inform the clinicians, thereby giving the impression that she had made the discovery.

In addition to the formal programmes listed above, each resident was on-call to perform autopsies on the weekends. We also had journal clubs, for which the meetings were held monthly at the home of a senior staff member, who always provided good fare.

The chief of the pathology department was Professor Desmond Magner. Once, when asked a question, I told him that I had not delved deeper into the clinical aspects of a lymphoma topic, and at the elevator, as he was leaving, he remarked that in pathology, the more knowledge one acquires, the better a doctor one will be. That has remained with me, even though I have not consistently followed the advice.

Within the department, Dr Donald Hill was head of anatomic pathology, and he took a special interest in my performances. Near the end of my tenure, he suggested that I should remain in Canada, for my expertise would be lost in a small island like Grenada. He told me that he would go no further but that he would place me within the top four residents he had ever had the honour to teach.

In Ottawa, I spent the first weekend, or a few days, in the interns' residence. The games-and-recreation room was located in the basement of the building, available to all the hospital doctors.

During breaks, throughout my stay at Ottawa General, I played table tennis and pool there.

I was fortunate to quickly find an apartment on Andrews Avenue that was within walking distance of the hospital. In my first week there, on returning home from the hospital, I found my apartment in shambles and my camera and other treasured items that I had procured in Hong Kong all gone. I was so unhappy and angry that for the first and only time in my life, I felt I could have committed murder. The police appeared, but to this day, I have heard nothing from them.

Within a month, Vivian came with Nanika from Nassau, to where she had returned on leaving Hawaii with the baby and her relatives. She had no problem finding a nursing job, the British system, in the same hospital.

The winter in Ottawa was cold though on many a day enjoyable. One day, I really felt that freeze as I walked from the bus stop to an affiliate laboratory. It was minus ten degrees, and with the wind chill, it felt like minus twenty-five. The warmth of the laboratory was a welcome and precious relief.

On mornings, we had to bundle and bungle Nika to the babysitter and collect her in the evenings after work. Of course, I minded her on the nights when Vivian worked.

One night, I went along with a group from the lab to a TGIF get-together at a club, and it snowed heavily. On leaving, we had difficulty freeing the cars. By the time I got home, Vivian was fuming, as there was not much time remaining for her to get to work and she had been wondering what she would do with Nika, but as it turned out, she did have sufficient time.

Nika was a child of fun, somewhat wildly active, but she vomited very often, and we never knew why. But oh, how much I loved her. The Rideau Canal within Ottawa is converted into a skating rink in the winter, and it was there that she joyfully learnt to ice skate, doing so as her proud parents admired their Hawaiian princess!

Other than work, the family engaged in other activities. Vivian and I enjoyed many television shows together, with one of our favourites being *The Sonny and Cher Show*. We loved their song "I Got You Babe". We made fondue and drank Canadian beers, like Labatt and Molson. I also drank Seagram's whiskey. Every so often, we bought freshly baked bread at the bakery of the nearby supermarket and unashamedly splashed it with butter and ate it right there.

We once drove with Frederick Albert, a university classmate from Trinidad, and his wife to Montreal to a Byron Lee concert. Albert was nicknamed Federgel because he lived on that medication at university. At the concert, Junior, a member of the band who I had first met in Jamaica through Pat Beek, introduced us to the great Mr. Lee himself.

Dr Federgel once had a group of us over to his home for dinner. The snowy weather that night was terrible, and the delivery of the catered food took so long that his wife quickly put something together for us to nibble on. Her small preparation was so good that we did not do justice to the late-arriving meal. I have been told that my classmate has died.

Over a long weekend, we went to Kingston, Ontario, for a conference in pathology, and on the way back to Ottawa, we spent a night with Ralph Nimchan and his wife, Theresa, in Toronto.

EXTENDED MEDICAL TRAINING—WITH A SALARY

I knew him from the Nunnery at UWI in Jamaica. Remember? Mr. Pound-for-Pound!

Just before leaving Ottawa for Grenada, we took a bus tour within Ontario, passing a night in Wilno, said to be Canada's first Polish village. We then went on to Niagara Falls, where I recall walking with Nika huddled against me to gain protection from the spray.

We were visited for a few days by Daisy Johnson, Vivian's friend from Nassau, and one night, we went to a stage show (?Show Boat) at a theatre. She and Vivian talked so much during the show that I left.

I headed directly to a party at the hospital, where Chester Pitter, a medical graduate of UWI, was the DJ. I was edging closer and closer to a young white lady who was one of a group of students studying medical records. Their restroom was in the same building that was used as an office for the pathology residents. As we danced and she was becoming quite responsive, out of nowhere arrived Vivian, with Daisy in tow, cutting in on the dance floor. I was maddened. I left at once and walked home alone to Andrews Avenue.

I think it was in Ottawa that we saw performances by Tom Jones and possibly the Mighty Sparrow.

We partied a lot in Ottawa. Sambas and his wife, Missouri, were there. Stumpy Bruno was there. Ben, from Africa, and his wife were there. And Luc Charlot (who I nicknamed Mr. Solo) and his wife were there. Luc's first child, Ruthy, became my second godchild. Sadly, she has since died. I thought that Luc resembled Napoleon of the show—*The Man from U.N.C.L.E.*

My first godchild was the daughter of my adopted half-brother, Jack Radix. As already noted, she resides in Grenada with her husband, Kennedy Roberts, and their children. I, at her invitation, travelled to Grenada for their wedding and toasted her dead grandmother, Nurse Alexandra Radix, my second mother, at the reception.

I would want to believe that it was because I never stayed in any location long enough, and especially not in my homeland, that I only acquired two godchildren. Even the friendships I acquired faded as time elapsed. The very first time I was entitled to vote in a land where I resided was in the Bahamas on 27 February 2002 at age 60.

Perhaps another one of my biggest disappointments in my journeys was taking the Canadian pathology certificate/fellowship exam in November. I had done very well in the written section and passed all the orals, save for that in chemistry, but the word came out that I was purposely failed so as to put me in my place. To this day, I think I answered the questions as best as possible, but the examiner, Dr Hill, an elderly man, not Donald at Ottawa General, kept asking me the same question over and over and over. I kept searching and searching and searching for what else he wanted from me. It was thought that the head of chemistry at Ottawa Civic had something to do with failing me, because he thought I was too pompous and needed to be taught a lesson. I recall being asked about seven times the same question related to an elevated alkaline phosphatase in a teenager.

I remain convinced that I did not fail that exam, but I guess that is what everyone who has failed says. But I *did not fail* that examination.

Nevertheless, the family left for Grenada, where I soon learnt that I had passed the American Board of Pathology's examination that I had sat in San Diego prior to my departure from Ottawa. I was so happy that I still don't know how or where I lost the letter that had conveyed the good news. I was expected to return to Canada in six months to repeat that oral examination, but I never did.

On the way to Grenada, we passed through Jamaica, first staying at Montego Bay, courtesy of Miss John and Aunt Jerry, Vivian's relatives. In their yard, Nika fell and hit her head. I sometimes think that this has had lasting effects. Ha ha ha!

Having rented a car, we toured the area, and after a couple of days in Montego Bay, we drove to Kingston and stayed with George Hamlet, a GBSS classmate, and his wife. It is my understanding that they subsequently relocated to Canada and that George has since died.

We attended the Christmas party of Irvine Hall courtesy of the chairman, George Brathwaite. One day, we drove to the Blue Mountains, and Nika vomited in the car. On the way back, I was speeding so as to keep a luncheon appointment with Ramdhat Chadeesingh at the crown dining room of the Pegasus Hotel. At a junctional stop in Papine, a man said to me that I could kill myself if I wanted but not the child.

I had become very good friends with Ramdhat, a student at UWI in my time who had also lived on block B, but since then, we have been out of touch. His father was known for owning a clothing outlet that had a brand of shirt that I liked and usually bought and wore in Jamaica. I am uncertain of the name of that shirt (perhaps Tropical), but I haven't forgotten the brand of the short-sleeved dress shirts that I bought in the Baker & Sons store on Bay Street and wore in Nassau, Bahamas: Van Heusen.

On departing Jamaica, we were told at the airport check-in that we had not reconfirmed our flight and that there were no available seats. I argued and defended us strongly, claiming that I had reconfirmed in Montego Bay, although that was doubtful. It was a mess at the airport, with many university students travelling back to their homes on vacation. In the end, we were accommodated in first class, and I kept bringing drinks from there back to my brother George in the economy section, although I don't think he was a user of alcohol.

The episode at the airport again reminded me of that medical student from Grenada who had taken so long to graduate that he was denied passage back home at the airport because his passport had expired.

PART 3

AN INDEPENDENT WORKING MAN

12

GRENADA: WHAT? NO FATTED CALF?

I had made it generally known that it was my intention and that I felt committed to return and serve in my country, Grenada. Long before I departed Canada, Dr Leonard Comissiong, the chief medical officer (CMO) of Grenada, and I were in communication, and it was obvious that he was prepared to fully assist me in returning and to make certain that I would enjoy and be contented with working in my homeland and be professionally happy.

At that time, there was no established post of pathologist, and rather than waiting for its creation, he offered the available post of medical specialist. He also made certain that I was duly registered and licensed to practice.

New Year's Day being a holiday, I suppose that I reported for duty on 2 January 1974, but before that, housing would have been arranged. Mr. Franklyn St Paul, an employee of the government, was most helpful not only in this but continually, in other matters.

I was first assigned living quarters in one of the Carifta Cottages in Morne Rouge near Grand Anse beach, which had been constructed for the Caribbean junior athletic games when they were hosted by Grenada. It was a two-bedroom, well-accommodated residence, but it was meant to be only a temporary one for us. In the interim, I was shown other government-owned houses.

After about a month, we were moved to the vacant Mt. Wheldale property, the official home of the chief justice of the Windward

Islands. When that judge was later stationed in Grenada, we were moved to a vacant home in Morne Jaloux that normally housed a stipendiary judge. When one was appointed, we again moved to another government property in Parade called Carlton House. It was near Richmond Hill on the way to St Paul's. Whilst there, I planted a young breadfruit tree in the back garden, and I moved my private practice office from Tyrell Street into what may have been the maid's quarters downstairs.

It was from Mt. Wheldale that Prime Minister Maurice Bishop was freed from house arrest on 19 October 1983. He was shot the same day. I have learnt that Carlton House has since become a rehab centre.

Not only was Grenada a country in political turmoil when I arrived, but it was also, at that time, completely shut down by the *Committee of 22*. Being a government worker, it was possible to manage, but it certainly was not the best of times to introduce my Bahamian wife to a country where we expected to stay permanently.

And for me, I did not anticipate or imagine that the first autopsy I would perform in Grenada would be on the father of Maurice Bishop, Mr. Rupert Bishop, who died from a rifle shot on Bloody Monday. Sometime later, I gave evidence at a hearing of the Duffus Commission, which had been appointed to investigate the breakdown of law and order in the country.

Because of the protests and other happenings, the police were on extra alert. My car was once stopped by the police, and I was asked if I had any arms. Of course, I said no. Afterwards, I wondered what would have happened if I had given a smartass answer of, "Yes, two."

Quite early in my appointment, Dr Comissiong arranged for me to be granted a one-week fellowship, offered by PAHO, to attend the Trinidad Research Virus Laboratory (TRVL) to gain an exposure to and an understanding of the principles of epidemiology.

Before the week was up, I had to leave, having received a telephone call that my mother was very sick. On the way to Carriacou, I overnighted in Grenville at the rental room of my brother Lysander, where he and I slept on the same bed. I left the next morning by plane to see and attend to my mother.

My mother was in bed but obviously not in agony. As I attended her, I laughed and even teased her that she got scared because of a simple bellyache. She was not amused with my manner and made another one of her prophetic pronouncements: "The next time I get sick, I will die, and you wouldn't even know."

This was etched in my mind—kismet.

Continuing to make all efforts to accommodate me, the CMO requested that I accompany him as one of the two delegates from Grenada for the conference being held in Jamaica in 1974 to establish the Caribbean Epidemiology Centre (CAREC) in Trinidad, which would incorporate and succeed the TRVL. He asked for my views and advice on his intended address to the conference, which, in essence, was about how the Middle Passage was not just for the transportation of slaves but also of cholera to the Caribbean.

It was the first of multiple conferences that I would attend at the Pegasus Hotel in Jamaica. At the conference, I met a doctor in public health from Suriname who informed me that his country needed a pathologist. My initial response was, "Where is Suriname?"

At another time, maybe that same year, I was Grenada's representative at the first Caribbean Sexually Transmitted Diseases Workshop, which may have been held at CAREC, though I resided, I think, at the (upside-down) Trinidad Hilton Hotel. Again, I was informed by a dermatologist, Dr Paul Niemel, from Suriname about the country's urgent need for a pathologist, and he offered me a dinner invitation to talk about it.

Gloria Roach, a friend who I had met in Nassau, was then back at home in Trinidad, and she arranged with another lady to accompany us to dinner. It was at her mother's home that I had observed carnival in 1969. During the dinner at a fancy restaurant, the Surinamer realised that he had forgotten to bring his wallet with his money and had to return to the hotel for it.

The ladies were not particularly attracted to him and asked me to find another man to go dancing the following night. I invited Dr Gerald Grell, who hailed from Dominica and was a class colleague at Mona. We went dancing at the Trinidad Holiday Inn in downtown Port of Spain.

At this time, I will say something hopefully not too distracting about my impressions of Trinidad, a land I have visited multiple times. Culturally, it has its carnival, its calypso, and its steel band, but for me, culture in Trinidad is actively alive every day on every street and street corner, around the supposedly largest roundabout in the world (Queen's Park Savannah), and in the upside-down hotel. It is also alive when a native attempt to mamaguy or bamboozle you—a very interesting place.

On the streets, I have eaten cups of their small oysters in a peppery tomato sauce, and at a concert, I ate the best boiled corn in a milky liquid served from a kerosene tin on an outside fire. Around the Savannah, I have drunk jelly coconut water and eaten doubles and roast corn after jogging from where I have usually stayed, the Kapok Hotel.

In December 2005, I was the British Virgin Islands representative to a Cariforum/European Union course entitled Training Laboratory Assessors. During my stay, I took a taxi tour to the pitch lake, said to be the largest natural deposit of asphalt in the world. At its periphery are houses atilt as they sink overtime into the soft earth. Included in this tour were visits to Chaguanas, Claxton Bay (known for its bajohns and the Grenadian Uriah Butler), San Fernando, the wild fowl sanctuary, Point Lisas, and Temple in the Sea.

On an offer by Joan Belle-Eversley, introduced by a mutual friend, we toured the west coast of Trinidad through Chaguaramas, Carenage, Point Cumana, and the Falls at Westmall shopping centre. It was at that same time that we stopped to pay a visit to see my campus friend, Knolson Gift, the permanent secretary in the Ministry of Foreign Affairs.

GRENADA: WHAT? NO FATTED CALF?

One night, at Club 51, I saw a show by Paul Keens-Douglas, who I knew from my GBSS days. I also saw performances by calypsonian, Scrunter, and ate wild meat of boar and deer. On another night, I attended performances at Silver Stars pan yard and saw a performance by Los Dynamicos, a parang group.

On the last night, I and others attending the same seminar attended a party at the home of Valerie Wilson, known to me from CAREC. There was entertainment from the calypsonian Black Sage and Los Numeros, another parang group.

During my stay, I spoke with Dr Mervyn Henry, then retired from the CPC/PAHO office in Barbados, who informed that a fellow Trinidadian pathologist we both knew, Val Massiah, had died. Dr Henry has also since passed.

At the STD workshop referred to above, Dr Alfred R. Brathwaite, another born Grenadian who was the lecturer on STDs and taught my class at the university in Jamaica, also attended as the Caribbean expert specialist on STDs. After that, we met again and again and were establishing a strong, friendly relationship. The next time that we met was in Grenada, when he came to lecture the nursing class. I was happy to occasionally drive him around.

We again met in Puerto Rico in 1981 at the first STD World Congress. It was at this conference that Dr Jim Curran, at a special session, presented a paper on a disease that was affecting gay men in the USA. This was later identified as STLV-3 and was eventually labelled HIV/AIDS.

Because of the similarity of our names, Freddy and I often caused confusion among the delegates and administrators, and I happily and readily offered no denials—and even, at times, readily and happily accepted it—when anyone referred to me as the specialist.

On one of the lighter days at the conference, I went over to St Thomas for a day's visit and was asked by Freddie to bring back a special bottle for him to take back to Jamaica for an upcoming party.

At the airport in St Thomas, I must admit that I was slightly taken aback on seeing the dark-skinned, flat-nosed middle-aged women manning some of the stalls at the airport, having being just ushered by the fairer-skinned, straight-nosed younger women at the conference in Puerto Rico.

As said, Freddy and I crossed paths on quite a few other occasions, and it began to embarrassingly dawn on me, once in Grenada and again in Dominica, that he fully enjoyed his drinks.

Now, back to Grenada. The CMO also requested my assistance in holding clinics at the Grand Bras district in Grenville, St Andrews. This was convenient for him, because the assigned doctor had left on vacation and there was no obvious generalist physician available, but he proposed that it would provide me with an opportunity to be exposed to and appreciate the health system of the country. Regardless, it was likewise convenient for me, as I did not yet have much to do in the lab, and it was also a means of earning some extra money, as the doctor was allowed to charge persons who were registered as private patients.

It later provided an occasion for Hip Wells to make fun at my expense, as I had attended to Mathew Williams's father.

Later, when there was a case of typhoid in Gouyave, the town of St Johns, the CMO appointed me to lead the investigation. It seemed to me that my welfare was always on his mind, and I seized every opportunity he tossed my way.

At the end of my first year, I titled my annual report "The Year That Never Was". His advice was that this would not go well politically, so I should change it. I respected him too much not to accept his advice.

In March of my second year in the job, he nominated me to be Grenada's representative at a medical conference on cerebrovascular accidents under the auspices of the Foundation of Higher Medical Education Nederland Antilles in Curaçao. I gladly accepted.

However, in overnighting in Antigua, I suffered from an asthmatic attack and used up all my inhaler. When it again occurred on the next night in Curaçao, I only gained some comfort by lying next to the air conditioning unit.

After that, I was better for the rest of my stay, and one night in the casino, I won $350, with which I bought a slide projector and brought it back, customs-duty free, to Grenada.

On the departure from Curaçao, I overnighted in St Martin, sharing a room with Dr Freddie Ballantyne of St Vincent. I believe that I again met Freddie in Trinidad later that year at the Windward Islands Medical Association meeting, where I presented a paper on sexually transmitted diseases, and again in St Vincent in the early 1980s when he was then the CMO of his country and I was project-managing a workshop on hepatitis B laboratory testing.

One night, the participants at the workshop were entertained on his tourist isle, a ferry ride away from the mainland, as arranged by Mr. Owen Jackson, the director of the laboratory.

Despite the disturbances arising from politics, we had some good times in Grenada. Vivian received employment as a registered nurse and was also accepted into the midwifery course, which she successfully completed. Sometime after that, she quit the government job and joined Oxfam, together with Nurse Mildred Cruickshank, under the direction of Pearl de la Mothe, who I understand was later murdered.

Pearl was the lady from whom I had bought a parcel of land in Grenada that Godwin was afterwards able to sell. This was done after I had decided that I was no longer going to make my home in Grenada.

I was able to spend some close moments with three of my brothers, Godwin in Old Fort, Nicholas in the Villa, and George in Tempe. Later in 1974, Nicho left for Guyana, where I once visited him from Suriname. Adeline was a most genteel lady, and we got on marvellously well—a far cry from our previously troubled days.

I was also able to sail to Carriacou to stay in my home of old; to see and feel the love of my sister, Alethea; to chat with another two brothers, Lysander and John; to become better acquainted with my niece, Betty, and other relatives; to meet with many other persons, including Da James; and to still be able to anger my dear mother. The home is astir as morning breaks, there is movement in and out, and the radio plays softly the soothing songs of gospel.

My brother Gilbert was then in England.

In Grenada, we had a special party group of families and individuals that included, inter alia, "Satan" Dowden and his wife, Felix Alexander and Mildred, Eric Pierre (of the Seamen and Waterfront Workers Union) and his lady friend, and few others. Felix would bring crayfish to my home, and Satan, the coconuts. Many were the get-togethers that we organised as I was being introduced to different beaches and hideaways in Grenada.

There was a group of professionals and their families who met regularly at the residence of the manager of the Bank of Nova Scotia that included him; Dr Alistair Budhlall, an internist at the general hospital; Justice Lyle St Paul; me; and others.

Dr Barry Rapier at the hospital provided profound counselling on intrahospital relations, and Dr Desmond Noel threw great parties.

Throughout my tenure in Grenada, many persons, not counting my relatives from Carriacou, visited from abroad at different times. I have already mentioned the Holms, but others included Vivian's mother; Vivian's sister Les; another sister, Pam, and her male friend, McNair Brown; Hip Wells and his lady friend; and Raymond, the son of mine with Bernadette.

I would like to think that Dennis Toppin, who graduated with me, also had intentions of returning to Grenada with his Bahamian wife, Leila. I suspect, though I am not certain, that my return may have influenced him so to do, but soon after they had arrived, they learned that I was leaving.

My understanding is that they did not stay for too long. Since then, I have been entertained by them at their home in Vancouver, Canada. To me, Dennis was the strong but quiet one in our medical group from Grenada, the no-nickname one.

When we left Grenada, we gave our dog, Fluffy, to Mr. Dowden.

After I later took up residence in Freeport, Bahamas, Eric Pierre visited on union matters, and we spent a day together.

Sadly, Eric, Satan, and Felix have departed this life, the last in Canada and the other two in Grenada.

During my period in Grenada and on a trip to Carriacou, I left the home in Mt. Pleasant at about seven o'clock in the morning. One thing led to another, and I did not get back until after one o'clock the next morning. Iah was waiting, and she laid into me. My special breakfast (salt fish and bakes) was on the table, as was lunch (peas and dumpling soup) and, just for me, an evening fish broth. She went on and on and on. As usual, she threw the remark "You is doctor now and have no regard," at me. I sat at the table and ate everything, despite having feted all hours before.

She had once told me by letter that I was very ungrateful. This happened in 1968 during my internship in Nassau. She had asked for financial assistance to repair the tombstone of her husband, my father, and I had written back that money must not be spent on the dead. Her response filled me with remorse.

Who was I to have hurt this lady, who had somehow guided me from undesirable tendencies?

Love does not in sorry dwell but is rather sweeter and better in acknowledging thanks.

Without doubt, there were good times, but Grenada was not as welcoming—and more so, not as rewarding—as we had hoped, especially for a wife who hailed from the Bahamas. Yes, we made friends, wonderful friends, but in 1976, a decision was made to leave.

Workwise, Miss McBurnie, a technologist, and I started processing tissue specimens for microscopic examination, but this was not too successful. When I requested help from the pathology department of UWI in terms of preparing slides for me, this was denied.

I made an application to Jamaica, which was my second choice, and the CMO, Dr Jeffery Wilson, who I had met before in Nassau, assured me that a job would be available at the Montego Bay Hospital but said that I must await the official letter from the public service commission.

The Bahamas, our first choice, had already responded that no job was available. In addition, although Suriname needed a pathologist, as I had been told in Jamaica and Trinidad, it never featured as a choice.

However, at the conference in Curaçao, I was approached by Professor Fritz Jessurun, dean of the medical faculty at the University of Suriname. Having being told about me, he presented a case for me to join the faculty as the pathologist. Perhaps because I seemed unenthusiastic, he bulldozed me into accepting an all-expenses-paid two-week visiting professorship at the university. I thought, what the hell? So, I accepted, went, and delivered addresses to students and to the medical association.

Suriname, as I was first introduced to it at this visit, was physically unattractive, a flat land with stagnant water in ditches and canals, and was inhabited by people who spoke a language that was foreign to me. But after that visit, Professor Jessurun, not satisfied with calling almost every day about his verbal offer, came to Grenada to have dinner at my home and again appealed to me. I, then feeling adventurous, gave him my word that if I did not hear from Jamaica by the end of January, I would accept the Suriname offer. He called me the first day of February, and just like that, I was going to Suriname. The acceptance letter from Jamaica arrived in the post on the following day.

After working in Grenada for two years, playing tennis with a steady group that included the prime minister, Eric "Uncle" Gairy, being invited to many parties, and gaining some degree of recognition in my homeland, I still remained not fully satisfied.

I have mentioned being committed to returning to Grenada, but I never meant committing to stay forever, though it would have been my preference. This reminds me of the difference between being involved and being committed. Bacon and eggs at breakfast requires the hen's involvement but the pig's commitment. The prime minister and I were on respectful terms, but he treated me with some degree of friendliness. He appointed me, through the proper channels, to the maternal and child welfare committee and also to the metrification board. At one of the meetings, the question of the government leasing land to the residents in need arose. I suggested that studies be done and the residents advised what crops they ought to grow in the different locales. I was accused of being communistic with that idea.

He expected persons in reasonably high positions to attend dinners at Rock Gardens Inn, which I think he owned, on Wednesdays and at another restaurant in Grand Anse, Therese, on Saturdays. Both were buffets, and there was a tussle in the former but better behaviour in the other. I once stayed at the inn or guest house on a government-sponsored visit from Suriname. I did not attend too many of these unaffordable dinners.

He once, after first calling me, sent his attendant to collect medicine from me at my office, having indicated that he felt a bit off and sniffly but had an important meeting to attend.

He had a close friendship with the Surinamer, Mr. R. Dobru (Robin Raveles), the minister of culture and an accomplished poet and politician. I saw him at one of Gairy's parties in Grenada. I believe that it was because of this friendship that I left for Suriname in February 1976 with the prime minister's blessings.

I was no pig.

Vivian and the children departed for Nassau to await joining me in Suriname.

Despite the turmoil that I have mentioned, it is nevertheless with some pride that I say that I was in Grenada on 7 February 1974 and witnessed the ceremony in which Grenada was declared to be an independent nation. Let the annals of history record words from our national anthem: "Hail! Grenada, land of ours ... God bless our nation.

There is no doubt that Gairy had transformed the political climate of Grenada. There were those who thought he practised voodoo, and he was criticised for his interest in UFOs and was said to be the person who had organised the ugliest man competition in Grenada. In the first contest, the runner-up complained that the judging was unfair because the winner had worn dark glasses.

I do recall, however, that it was in the 1950s that he was upsetting persons and things in Grenada as the leader of the Sky Red uprising—so much so that when he first visited Carriacou, people were most concerned. When he announced his political campaign in Mt. Pleasant, some of the men of the village were armed with bull pistles to beat him if he misbehaved. Nothing happened, but I don't think his party has ever won the seat of Carriacou and Petit Martinique. It is claimed that he often said that if your neighbour's house is on fire, start wetting yours.

All things considered, I owe my thanks and gratitude to the man who accommodated my transfer to another country that I grew to love. This was a man for whom many sang, to the tune of an old British song with similar lyrics, "We will never let the leader fall, for we love him the best of all."

As my friend, Norris Gordon, would say, Gairy transferred in August 1997. RIP.

13

ONE OF THE ORIGINAL THREE GUIANAS

The Republic of Suriname was a land of 400,000 people of different ethnicities with an abundance of young women of stunning, unsurpassed beauty, a variety of foods that I would willingly return for, and the friendliest and most disciplined people I have ever encountered—so much so that I, at times, have referred to them, complimentarily, as sheep. I have said many a time that if you should ask a Surinamer for something and the response is no, ask again, for you were perhaps not heard the first time.

Unlike in Grenada, it was beyond my imagination that a coup d'état would ever happen in Suriname, but it did in February 1980, two years after I had left. But it probably was easier to achieve there, the people being like sheep.

I was the sole pathologist attached to the Academisch Zeekenhuis (Academic Hospital), providing service to three other general hospitals. I was the head of the pathology department and the only lecturer in pathology for the two-year classes of the University of Suriname medical faculty, and I was the forensic pathologist for the department of justice.

I earned a salary from the hospital and a separate one from the university. I also billed the other private hospitals and received payment from the justice ministry for performing forensic autopsies. Unlike in Grenada, where it was survival on a month-to-month basis, I became more financially secure, and with permission, I was able to remit money regularly to Iah for her personal use and deposit some in my bank in Carriacou.

However, within the first two months, I encountered a problem. The students complained, and with good reason, that I had not yet begun my lectures. On my arrival, I had indicated that it would take me about three months to be ready, what with having to prepare the lectures and, even more importantly, having to attack the heavy backlog of pathology cases at the hospital that were awaiting reports.

When I did start, my lectures were delivered in English and remained so throughout my stay. This seemed not to be a problem to the students, and indeed, there developed a bond of love and respect between the students and me, which was a most wonderful thing to me. One student, in particular, became a family friend. My daughter, who adored her father, was also very fond of the student, Kenneth Middelijn, but she got mad with him on two occasions.

Once, maybe on Christmas Day or near to it, Kenneth and another student, Ramon, were on their way to a luncheon engagement elsewhere and stopped at my home. We ate rabbit meat and kept drinking until about 3 a.m. Of course, Nika was not drinking, but she was not very pleased that they seemed bent on emptying the mini bar in my chest, which they eventually did, with my help.

Thesis Night, Defending a thesis

Thesis night with students

The next time was at the reception that the students had organised on the night after I had defended my thesis, 'The Pathology of the Thyroid Gland in Suriname'. On our departure from the party, as Vivian and the children were leaving that early morning for Nassau, the students, with Kenneth the leader, soaked me down with Parbo beer. Nika was very, very mad, and I seem to recall that she even cried.

Kenneth and Nika

Thesis Night, Minister of Health-Suriname

Thesis Night, Mortuary Group

As indicated, in my travels, I seem incapable of escaping being involved in problems, so I was not too surprised when, in addition to the complaints of the students, I encountered another problem in Suriname. This problem occurred when I applied for a driver's license.

After much running around at a lower level, the chief of that service denied my request, having decided that he could not authenticate my Grenada license because it did not have my photograph. I sent it to Grenada to have that corrected by my brother George.

In the interim, I refused to do the police autopsies, claiming that my certificates in pathology also had no photographs. Deputy Prime Minister Mike Brahim intervened, and from then on, he became a close and reliable friend of the family. He always invited us out. He cautioned me and advised that I should never make an issue of problematic matters that arise in Suriname, and if perchance any issue did arise, I should just come to him.

A local newspaper had already put me on the front page with an article in Dutch, with one part interpreted as, "Who is this Jamaican telling Surinamers what to do?" Indeed, I love Jamaica and had the opportunity to become a Jamaican in 1962, but I never did.

The work hours of the government and the general public followed the Spanish custom of having a siesta time on weekdays after working from 7 a.m. to 2 p.m. The business sector extended the workday after 4 p.m. I think that on Saturdays, the work hours ended at noon or 1 p.m.

Heer Mijnals was head of the hospital mortuary, and he and his three assistants made sure that I was well taken care of in a most respectful manner. In the attached sitting room, they often held get-togethers, which they made me a part of, and they regularly invited me out to different functions. One of the assistants belonged to a group, and I once saw them as pallbearers dancing with the coffin and its dead on their shoulders.

I also made money from the embalming and preparation of bodies for shipment, usually to Holland. The mortuary staff embalmed and prepared. I signed the documents, and the funeral home paid me a decent sum, which I gladly shared.

Every so often, we did autopsies in the district of Nickerie, with Mijnals and I travelling from Paramaribo on a small Suriname Airways plane, probably a sixteen-seater, at 7 a.m. It was about an hour's flight. Usually, we would finish the autopsy by 10 a.m., and afterwards we feted with Indian friends, drinking Parbo beer and eating roti with curried chicken using our fingers.

Sometimes we patronised a local food joint to have a fish broth made from the fish that climbed the mangrove roots. We did all of this before leaving for the plane, with me not having spent a cent and with each of us laden with agricultural goodies. Woe betide me if I took that 4 p.m. flight back to Paramaribo without first having emptied my bladder.

My family and I once journeyed there by car to spend a weekend at the home of one of the Indians to attend the ceremony of marriage of his daughter.

I played tennis with a group on two afternoons of the week, and I belonged to a Keep Fit club that met from four o'clock in the afternoon on Saturdays. At Keep Fit, the drill master, Paul Leflang, managed the routines. We ran and played basketball, volleyball, and football, both within the group and in friendly games with other groups.

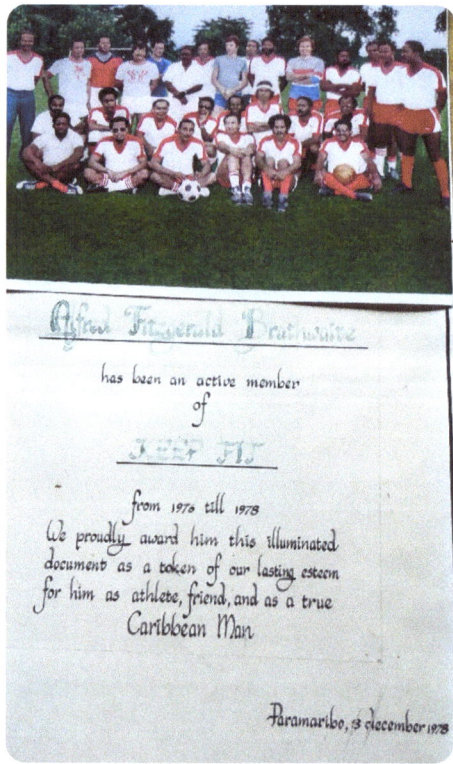

Keep Fit

At the end of most sessions, we celebrated with food and drinks as necessary, especially on members' birthdays. Some spouses jokingly referred to us as the keep fat club.

Once, the group was invited to tour the Parbo brewery, and did we have a ball. There was beer and a bountiful display of exceptional hors d'oeuvres. Another time, we visited a Bush Negro village via canoes and also had a good time. The group held a final farewell party for me and presented me with a photograph of the group. Included in the testament were the words *a true Caribbean man*.

I have kept this with pride.

Suriname was a fun place, a party place, and as I usually say, it was the first place I saw that the Chinese knew how to dance. Suriname was the first place I visited where, instead of being served beer in a pint, as is customary, a litre bottle of Parbo beer would be placed on a table to be shared. It was also the first place I encountered people who drank whisky and cola, instead of whisky with water, ginger, or in some islands, coconut water. And for me, it was the first place where rotisserie-roasted suckling pigs were not unusual at parties.

Thesis Night, Suriname President and Vivian

Outside of the workplace, I had many friendships, but the one that springs to a failing memory is that with Robert and Martha Power and their relatives. Robert was a plant pathologist.

The family also enjoyed picnicking at Cola Creek and travelling throughout the country by car (the Humber that I had shipped from Grenada). We would cross the rivers by ferry. Some rivers were quite big, but some were small and required a mere barge holding no more than three cars per crossing.

On one occasion in Nickerie, we crossed over by ferry to New Amsterdam in Guyana. From Paramaribo, we also travelled to the district of Albina and across the river by the bridge to the adjacent French Guiana. On one of these trips, we took a tour of the prison where Papillon had been incarcerated.

Two of my favourite actors were in the movie of the same name—Dustin Hoffmann and Steve McQueen of *The Sand Pebbles*, *The Magnificent Seven*, and *The Great Escape*.

At the hospital, Dr Dinesh De, a radiologist from Bangladesh, and his wife, a medical generalist, were very entertaining. I, in later years, arranged for them to be hired in Freeport, Bahamas. They are now retired and reside in Nassau but with the hope of returning to Suriname due to health reasons.

In the hospital pathology lab, Mevrouw Yvonne Van Leesden, the administrator, and her pathology assistants, especially Ms Ong a Quie, were extremely friendly and exceptionally helpful. At the university, the histotechnician, Juffrouw Gracita Redan, who was also the locally well-known singer of "Mi Lobi Wan", fell in love with me, or so I thought.

Thesis Night, Gracita

The practice of dermatology was well established in Suriname, largely through the well-known accomplishments of Dr Paul Niemel, who in Trinidad had been the second person to invite me to his country.

During my stay, the department held regular sessions with me to discuss recent cases. My interest in and knowledge of skin diseases developed from these. Dr Niemel was also one who demonstrated concern for my welfare, for which I remain forever grateful. He is no longer alive.

The hospital, led by Director S. O. Bergen, held a farewell function for me and presented me with a wooden clock in the shape of Suriname. Vivian did not attend, claiming the invitation came too late.

The university medical school also held a function for me at which one of the students sang "To Sir with Love". Professor Oostburg remarked in his address that maybe I was leaving Suriname because I had not been fed enough of a fruit called mope (pronounced as "mopay"), which may be called a hog plum or June plum elsewhere. Supposedly, when consumed, it ensures that visitors remain in the country. Just within the Caribbean, a fruit may be known by different names in different places.

In my remarks, I countered with the rejoinder that what I wanted was *more pay*.

The students presented me with a bauxite memento on which was engraved, "*Een tastbaar aandenken van vriendship.*"

Bauxite memento

Despite realising with absolute certainty that the past three years had been the most professionally fulfilling, exciting, and rewarding of my life, I nevertheless left Suriname for Nassau prior to Christmas, spending my last week at the home of Dr Stuart Watson of PAHO, who I had first met in Grenada. We had held different views on the question of children's vaccinations.

He agreed with the government's position that these should be mandatory for entry into the schools. I preferred a different approach, for which I offered good reasons. I favoured utilising profoundly simple and widespread public education methods.

During my sojourn with him, Dr Watson remarked that never had so many beautiful women visited his home as did during my short stay. Even just after three years, as in Jamaica, where I'd spent six years, many friends wanted to bid farewell.

Ramon and Kenneth took me to the airport.

Whilst in Suriname, I took Spanish lessons at the Andres Bello Venezuelan Institute. I can manage, though only barely, to say or write what I wish, but if someone speaks Spanish to me, it sounds like mere gibberish. The director of the institute, Sylvia Ogilvie, was related to the Oglivies of Grenada, who I had first met at GBSS.

My journey through that language must go down as somewhat of a waste, for in GBSS, I had had classes in Spanish for three years, but the teachings had been highlighted to pass exams and little else.

Living in Suriname, a Dutch-speaking country, I also took lessons to learn Dutch as well as French, but I left without speaking either. Likewise, I never understood the local Sranantongo (Taki-Taki) dialect.

It therefore appears that when it comes to languages, though it has always been one of my desires to be competent in them, I seem incapable of readily grasping any but my native English.

Even today, I continue my escapades in learning Spanish at home. However, as I age, I'm becoming less fluent in English, as words steadily disappear from my vocabulary, so perhaps I'm merely spinning my tyres in the mud of Spain. I never remember when to use *ser* vs *estar* or *por* vs *para*. To begin with, I have not been to Ireland, so I've never kissed the Blarney Stone.

Nika and Dax, as children at school, had no difficulties speaking the Dutch language, although now, after so many years, I doubt they would recognise it anymore. Dax, because of his own circumstances, now speaks Spanish, but Vivian, Nika, Chandre, and I remain confined to English.

With the opportunity to travel to a new country, some relatives visited with us on separate occasions. Among these were my brother-in-law Martin, his son Junior, Vivian's sister and aunt, and others.

A young lady from Carriacou, Shirley, who worked with us in Grenada as a maid, also joined us in Suriname in the same capacity.

I, by myself, also took the opportunity to see other places whilst in Suriname. I have already referred to my visits to Argentina, where I met up with Mario Wernicke, and to Guyana to see my brother, but I also spent a few days in Belem for relaxation and Rio de Janeiro in Brazil for a pathology conference.

In Rio, there was an organised tour to see a football game in the famous Maracaná Stadium. We were seated and the game was on, but there was no excitement. At the end, the teams just exited. After a while, however, there was the greatest of roars in the stadium, heralding the game we had actually come to see, the Vasco de Gama Club, with its star player, Roberto, against another team. So impressive was the response of the stadium to every move made by the players that I was often in awe.

I have already mentioned visits to French Guiana and to Guyana to see my brother Nicho. In Guyana, I met with a former classmate, Floyd Neckles, who took me to his jungle farm and then to Mr. Ramsahoye, who had once taught at GBSS.

On two occasions, I was recalled to Grenada, with permission, to present evidence in court cases, and after I left Suriname, I was provided the opportunity to return there on two occasions. The first was a request from PAHO to report and advise on establishing small laboratories throughout the country. I stayed at the Krasnapolsky Hotel. I saw a few of my past students but not too many other persons, because of my job constraints and because many had died.

On one occasion, a gentleman approached me at a riverside park and, in a questioning manner, called me by name. I did not recognise him, but we chatted a bit. He left me with this: "It's not who you know but who knows you."

I did learn then that Kenneth had quit medical school and held a political appointment with the government, which had him stationed in French Guiana. I did not meet him then.

Thesis night, with Kenneth and his dad.

The second opportunity came when I was attending the annual research meeting of the CHRC at the Torarica Hotel. Kenneth was then back in Suriname, and at his invitations, we had dinner twice and attended a nightclub one night.

One of my past students, Dharma Ramautar, and her husband, Rudy, took me around, including on a visit to my old Keep Fit haunts.

Other than what has been presented, I encountered two stressful situations in Suriname: an eviction and a death.

Before acquiring a house for rent, I was permitted to reside in a room attached to the Centro Andres Bello run by a director,

Sylvia Ogilvie, who had Grenadian roots. One night at the centre, a reception was held to welcome a higher-up person visiting from Venezuela. I attended together with Vivian. He questioned the director about us and demanded our immediate eviction.

Vivian, Nika, Dax, and I packed all of our belongings into my Humber and went to the Krasnapolsky Hotel. The owner allowed us to stay in a suite at a very affordable price.

Within a few days, we luckily found a suitable house for rent on Jan Zweers Straat, a short walk from the compound that housed the medical faculty of the university and the hospital, where Vivian also worked as an assistant in the department of anaesthesia.

The other situation began one morning as I was peering down the microscope at work. I got a call from the telegraph office. The gentleman read it to me, but with his Dutch accent, I understood not what he had said until I turned back to the microscope. Only then did it hit me that he had said, "Iah died this morning at ten o'clock."

All of that week, my house phone had been dysfunctional, and despite daily requests from Vivian for me to report it, I had refused. During that time, my brother George had been trying to get me to alert me to her illness but without success.

I collected US money from my tennis friends, hoping to travel the following day, but I did not, for I remembered her usual words to her children to the effect of "When I die, don't travel just to attend my funeral. Bury me the same day, for I don't want the hypocrisy of people coming and gathering to drink rum and eat food." And I remembered her more prophetic words to me: "The next time I get sick, I will die, and you wouldn't even know."

Kismet, once again!

As I was told, she, who was born in Carriacou on 4 September 1899, died, after drinking a cup of tea, in the arms of Sarah, who was visiting for this likely departure, on 13 October 1977.

The cause of death: Senility.

No! Nonsense! Never applicable to Caroline Sophia Brathwaite, née McLeod. No, no. Never.

My thesis for the University of Suriname was also dedicated to my mother, "who inspired persistence." To me, she exemplified percipience, inherent wisdom, and a decency of character that will survive beyond the tombstone. But for now, rest on, dear mother.

On my trips to Carriacou, it is usual for me to pay my respects to the dead. Now lying apart beneath the earth but being together in spirit wherever else are the bodily remains of the Brathwaites—Charles, Sophia, Alethea, Lysander, and Gilbert. She would have cast doubt on this spiritual existence and my respects, for she was known for saying, "Take care of me when I'm alive, for when you dead, you done."

14

NASSAU, BAHAMAS, 1978–1981

Although I refer to my stay in Suriname as one of great joy, I had committed myself to serving only one three-year contract, and particularly to please my dear wife, I was fully prepared to return to Princess Margaret Hospital in Nassau, Bahamas, as a consultant pathologist, starting in December 1978.

In the beginning, conditions were quite favourable both socially and professionally. I rented a decently priced house that was owned by an in-law of Vivian, and a friend lent us his car pro bono. Within a few months, I purchased a car whilst awaiting the arrival of the Humber, being shipped from Suriname, and I bought a house.

The director of laboratory services (DoLS) made my introduction quite pleasurable. I was assigned to be the pathologist in charge of the sections of blood banking, serology, and microbiology and was conveniently offered the then unoccupied erstwhile office of the DoLS. The present DoLS was established in another office.

Another pathologist, a Bahamian who had graduated from UWI after me, was also a consultant on staff, and the two of us got together quite often and pleasantly discussed changes we felt were necessary to be implemented in the service.

The chief laboratory technologist, Mr. James Sands, became my fun and close friend, and I spent much time in his office. He was known for using peculiar words and phrases—for example, calling someone a *poo-shaker* or referring to them such. Another phrase of his—*the fungus among us*—perhaps reflected his expertise in microbiology.

I teased him quite a bit, telling him on more than one occasion that it was people like him who reinforced my belief that God exists, for otherwise, he, Sands, would have already self-destructed. Janet Debarros, the supervisor in microbiology, was a knowledgeable and dependable worker, and we also got along well.

However, after a few months, things at work started sliding downwards, compounded by some imagined difficulties on the home front. Unfortunately, matters worsened after the DoLS, Dr Joan Read, resigned or retired and recommended that the vacated post should be offered to me. Well, all hell broke loose, because there were those who thought that the position should be offered to the Bahamian. At that time, I was a foreigner on contract.

Socially however, things progressed quite well, especially because it was customary for consultants working in the hospital to receive invitations to virtually all government-sponsored activities, including parties. I was introduced to Muhammad Ali at a party at the home of the US ambassador. The Drama in Bahama pitted Ali against Trevor Berbick in December 1981.

Nika and Ali

Not only did I attend the Paradise Island performance of Tavares, but I also met all the brothers when they visited the home of my in-law parents.

"Heaven must be missing an angel."

I played competitive cricket and practised with a team at football. I also played tennis both with a dedicated group of guys—members of the racquet club at the Nassau Beach Hotel—and, sometimes, at the police barracks at the invitation of my friend Mathew Williams. At times, the governor general, Sir Gerald Cash, played with us, and food and Champagne would follow. Neil Headley, who later moved to Freeport, was in this group.

I jogged most mornings and felt physically fit. I also began playing hockey, having been introduced to it by Garry Brathwaite, a prison officer who was originally from Barbados. Our team, the Finco Warriors, won the league in 1980.

However, in the lab, relationships deteriorated. Swords were drawn between the two candidates for the directorship and their supporters, not just within the lab but elsewhere within the hospital and beyond.

For the first time, I recognised what I considered to be a weakness in the then minister of health, who I thought demonstrated a lack of decision-making abilities. My opinion was only reinforced in my mind as years went by for different reasons.

But he was wily enough to express to me that, although he supported me, I ought to understand and appreciate that his hands were tied. He blamed others for what was to happen. I left his office wondering what he had actually said, and to this day, his use of many lofty but meaningless words baffles me.

It was also then that I thought that I was having difficulties with the women in official positions—the permanent secretary in health, the CMO, the hospital administrator, the medical chief of staff, and the Bahamian pathologist.

The Bahamian eventually received the appointment, and despite my friendships and the support I received from some staff members in the lab and throughout the hospital, the relationships were worsening. The situations and conditions between her and me were such that I thought of quitting.

Particularly nasty was the gossip about me that emanated from two of the supervisors within the lab—an obvious attempt to derail my character. The conspiracy would have debased any lesser person, except that I was able to stand tall and to repel or disprove whatever they conspired to throw my way.

In those difficult times within the lab, I continued to receive an understanding of support from persons who I considered decent and genuine individuals. I was strengthened by the friendships of James Sands (of *the fungus among us*), Marvie Seymour-Major and Ms Stefanie Lightbourne in cytology, Ms Edna Morris in supplies, Crystal Wildgoose in serology, Danny Price in chemistry, and others in histology.

Of course, there were those to whom whatever was happening, made no difference and did not matter to them.

I was then assigned to the autopsy service and to the office which Dr Read had been using.

It seemed that Dr Read had established a relationship with the police in which she had been called to make scene-of-crime investigations. I was not prepared to accept that responsibility and appealed to the CMO, who directed me to continue the practice. It was not long after, perhaps on legal advice, that she called to say that indeed such was not my responsibility.

I welcomed the opportunities to travel, usually to attend meetings or conferences of an educational nature, and was once invited to Grand Turk, capital of the Turks and Caicos Islands (TCI), to perform a forensic autopsy and subsequently to offer evidence to the courts. I visited Providenciales, TCI, with the cricket team in 2005 and also played in Miami, Florida, more than once. I attended a medical conference in Panama, where Vivian and I ate large country steaks and took a day's tour to one or two of the San Blas Islands.

I taught microbiology to a class of nursing students and also prepared the blood banking course curriculum for the soon-to-be-introduced more formal training of nurses.

However, as the situation was fast becoming untenable, I decided to leave as soon as possible. My brother George, in Brooklyn, was ready to receive me. There appeared a glow of light in the darkened tunnel.

I received a call from the PAHO country representative, Mr. Sam Aymer, who indicated that the PAHO headquarters in Washington, D.C., wanted to know if I would still be interested in a position with them, one which had been first mentioned when I worked in Suriname. I readily expressed my interest and was offered an appointment

Let me state here that, over time, I have always looked forward to fulfilling my daydreams, like I would imagine most persons do. One dream I had was to become a professor. I, however, had accepted that that opportunity, presented after my thesis had been accepted, was lost because of my decision to leave Suriname. But indeed, some of my then students have since referred to me as Professor, and Nicholas always called me that.

To be a competent musician and to be fluent in languages were other unfulfilled wishes.

Another desire of mine was to work for an international agency, and now that the opportunity to do so had arisen, I gladly agreed with no reservations and accepted the opportunity, even though I had not been offered the opportunity to fulfil my other dream of being labelled as a director.

With the agreement in place, I served out my three-year contract with the government of the Bahamas.

When I look back at my stint in Nassau, I believe the situation could have been dealt with differently. I could have been given a position as acting director until the end of my contract, after which the position could have been offered to the Bahamian. Strangely, a few years later, when I was in Freeport, Bahamas, I was asked by the then CMO and permanent secretary to return to PMH to direct the pathology service.

I refused.

My Humber was left with Vivian in Nassau. Our house, initially rented out was eventually sold, as Vivian moved in with her parents, who themselves had relocated to a rather big government-owned property, where I stayed on some visits back home.

15

SPORTING A LAISSEZ-PASSER

I accepted the offer to be the project manager of the two-year United Nations–funded, WHO/PAHO-administered, Caribbean laboratory strengthening project to be based in Dominica.

Beginning 2 January 1982, I first spent an orientation week at the PAHO headquarters in Washington, D.C., under the guidance of one of the most pleasant men I have ever met, my boss from headquarters, Dr Ramiro Martinez Da Silva.

The following week was spent in the PAHO Caribbean Programme Coordination (CPC) office located in Barbados under Dr Mervyn Henry, who to me was another weak leader. With my forthrightness and stubbornness, we fell out after my first year—another bit of trouble.

After Barbados, on arrival in Dominica on or about 20 January 1982, I was informed by the taxi driver that the ride from the Melville Hall Airport to the capital town of Roseau would be two hours, but I never expected it to be through the worst roads and terrain that I have ever been exposed to.

After roughly two hours, I said to the driver that we should be close to Roseau now. He responded that we had just passed it. My unexpressed inner reaction was that 1979's Hurricane David should have flattened it instead of leaving what seemed a slum. The Caribbean joke that if Columbus returned to the islands today, the only one he would recognise would be Dominica seemed well referenced.

I was accommodated at the Sisserou Hotel, which was located just beyond the city. On my second night, a Sunday, things were uneventful until about 1 a.m., when I experienced a most severe case of gastroenteritis. I thought it was due to a powdered milk drink that I had consumed at supper. Of course, I was ill at ease for my meeting with the authorities later that day.

When my fourteen-day courtesy stay at the hotel had expired, I moved to a smaller hotel, Continental Inn, in the centre of town and then to the less-expensive Vena's Guest House. Vena was a tremendously dramatic lady, often taking me out on weekends to see her different properties and, in so doing, the wider country.

On one such venture, we spent a day in the country at a stopover place that she owned. It catered on request to persons travelling to and from the airport. Whilst there, Jack, a taxi driver coming from the airport, stopped in.

I needed no introduction to hail his passenger, who was none other than Lance Gibbs of West Indies cricket fame. I have since met him once in Nassau at a cricket game and once at the airport in St Kitts, when I believe he was in the shipping business.

At Vena's in the town, a lawyer named Anslem Clouden from Carriacou stayed for a while, having arrived from Canada with his son. He was there during the pre-Lenten carnival festivities, and we partied together.

From Vena's I went to another less-expensive guest house (bed, breakfast, and dinner), and then, after a few months found an apartment in Goodwill owned by Mr. Gilbert, whose son, Nicholas, I had known at UWI as a friend. Eventually, I rented a house further up the road in Goodwill owned by a Mrs Chambers, who lived abroad.

My office was in the laboratory of the Princess Margaret Hospital in Goodwill.

Although I grew to enjoy my time in Dominica, the first few months in what seemed a rather dreary land where it rained daily were rather dismal—so much so that on landing in Antigua on my first trip away from Dominica, I felt so relieved that I wanted to kiss the tarmac.

My job in Dominica took me to many of the Caribbean islands. Amusingly, I then became one of those briefcase-carrying persons that I had usually joked about who, after a week's visit to a country, became self-proclaimed experts of that country.

Something that seemed to be becoming a usual for me occurred at my first meeting with the minister of health, the Hon. Charles Maynard. We got into a civil argument that was based on a misunderstanding about autopsies. He expected me to perform them, particularly the forensic ones, when needed. I responded that that was not my responsibility. He disagreed and promised that he was willing to complain that my being stationed in Dominica was then of no consequence and that he would consider withdrawing Dominica from the agreement.

Later, his permanent secretary told me that he had to explain to the minister that my stance was correct. Nothing more came of that. As a matter of fact, when the project did put on a workshop in Dominica, the honourable minister as the featured speaker at the opening, praised my performance up to that date.

Workshops were also held in St Vincent and St Lucia. Another one initially planned for Grenada was moved to Barbados, as Grenada was then no longer available because of an upsetting political imbroglio.

As said, although stationed in Dominica, the nature of the job entailed frequent travel, and in addition to the islands of the project—Grenada, St Vincent, St Lucia, Antigua, St Kitts/Nevis, Anguilla, the British Virgin Islands, and Montserrat—I also visited other islands in both an official and unofficial capacity. My official visits included Barbados; Trinidad, which I visited at least annually to attend the CAREC's Laboratory directors meeting; Guyana; Jamaica, where I went for a blood bank conference; Chile, where I went for a laboratory conference; and Venezuela, where I went for a conference on the reorganisation of laboratory services to meet the goal of health for all. Unofficially, I visited St Thomas and St Croix, where Joseph "JT" Mark, who I had known at GBSS and as a resident of block B at UWI, worked and where I met the lovely Flavia Logie, also from Grenada, who was then a well-known reporter on Radio Antilles.

Since I first met her, she has studied at FAMU in Florida, graduating as a qualified lawyer, and she now has her own practice in St Croix. She is a lady of many parts, well known in the Caribbean—a former reporter on Radio Antilles, a multisports enthusiast, and a poet. With me as the novice, we have since exchanged our poetry, and we continue to converse through the internet. We saw each other when she was in Tortola on business and later coincidentally in St Kitts at a cricket game that I, Laca, and others were attending. I include two poems by her, with her permission:

I have also bounced up just by chance on more than one island with Curtis McIntosh, a classmate of mine from Mt. Pleasant school who also attended GBSS, some years after me. At the time, he was working for the Caribbean Food and Nutrition Institute, a job that also entailed travel. His travelling had preceded mine, and he gave me his personal contacts on different islands. Curtis was the student who mastered me in the spelling exam. Before leaving for Dominica, he advised me to make the acquaintance of Ms Alice Leytang, a senior person in Barclay's bank. She once invited me to dinner. Her husband accused me of being aloof.

The first by-chance meeting with Curtis happened in St Kitts—a land where I once looked in awe at a crown of white atop a coastal hill created by a conglomerate of birds, the guano of which makes good fertilizer—then in St Vincent, Grenada, and Nassau, Bahamas. He once said of many women of Nassau that in walking, after the top half of their bodies has disappeared around a building, the bottom half still remains visible—the Peking duck appearance.

Today, this is even more obvious with the high rate of obesity. Sitting in my car outside a grocery store in Freeport, some six out of ten women going in would appear to be overweight or obese (fat).

During those times, Curtis resided in Trinidad, and on one of my visits, I spent my last night at his home. Both of us were drinking, but he promised that he would get me to the airport on time.

It seems the usual departure time for most first flights from Trinidad is 6 a.m.

Anyhow, when I awoke at about ten minutes after five, he was still asleep. In the hurry, I forgot to pack my pyjamas, the pants of which had a big hole in the crotch. What an embarrassment. Maybe a year or so later, on another of my visits, I was presented with my pyjamas by his wife, Claudette, cleaned, pressed, and fully repaired.

Curtis is now retired and still maintains his home in Trinidad, one in Carriacou, and another in Atlanta, Georgia, where his family resides. On my visits to Carriacou, if he is there, he makes certain that we enjoy some time together over a cold "beverage", his name for a drink. We last spoke by phone sometime in 2022.

However, in most of my later visits to Carriacou, Curtis's brother, Walter, who lived in Mt. Pleasant, and I drew closer. On my last few visits, he was no longer there, having remigrated to England, where he died. *Whohpah!*

To me, all of Toby's children, as well as he and his wife, Cousin Leenie, were most pleasant and courteous individuals. Cousin Toby was the man once beaten by Charles Cayenne. He had once contested the elections for the representative from Carriacou in the country's parliament. He received the most votes in Mt. Pleasant but lost overall.

Socially, things were OK in Dominica, as they were throughout my outside travels. I played cricket in a bush league, played tennis at the Dominica Club, and got on well with the lab staff under the directorship of Mr. Roderick Fortune.

I had special friends, like Seraphine Cognet; Jacqueline Carter, whose father was a Grenadian; Zina Cuffy, whose sister rode in my Honda Accord EX for her wedding; Alex, Bill Riviere's former girlfriend, and her children; Angella Bacchus of St Vincent; Magdalene

Hippolyte and family of St Lucia; and a Grenadian, Pauline Louison, who I first met when she vacationed in Nassau and who lives in Barbados. My secretary was Angela Julien.

Cognet and her family are close friends of me and mine. She graduated as a nurse in Dominica and emigrated to New York, where she got married. She invited me to be the father giver at the wedding. Now she is divorced, has earned a doctorate, and resides in Atlanta, Georgia.

Father giver at Cognet's wedding

She has visited Freeport since my residence there, and our families met up in Savanah, Georgia, in August 2019. I had met her mother and sisters in Portsmouth in Dominica, and I once had a breakfast of salt fish and bakes at their home.

On my St Lucia visits, there was a room available to me at the Hippolytes' home with a bottle of Johnny Walker at the bedside. Magdalene's mother has died, but I'm still very welcome in Magda's new home. I have met all her siblings. I don't remember their names, but they are all wonderful people. on my last visit to St Lucia, Vincent, a brother of hers, drove me around.

Life is worth living when one has such friends.

I was especially happy to have met the Lavilles on my brother Godwin's advice; he had previously met and been befriended by Andy Laville on one of his travels. On some weekends, I danced at a club operated by Ophelia Marie, née Olevache, a singer who my nephew Junior had met at university. I sought out and met Jeff Joseph, a singer-musician, having so enjoyed his album *Hot Music (La Fiesta)*.

Of course, I renewed friendships in the countries I revisited, and whenever I visited Grenada, I would try to spend at least a day in Carriacou.

My duties required me to spend time in the PAHO office in Barbados fairly often, and I was always well entertained by a former GBSS classmate, Bob Morris, with whom I played tennis. He always now calls me Uncle Alfred. At school, he was the fastest sprinter in our age group.

Charlie Sayers, a former West Indies fast bowler from Guyana, stayed with me when visiting Dominica. He once said to me in jest, that previously when he had travelled, he had lived off a suitcase and fucked women, but now, fuck the suitcase, as he lives off women.

Dr Lawrence Charles, a recognised Caribbean expert in leprosy and PAHO consultant, lived in Antigua but was originally from Dominica. He was also a traveller and was well known for timing his visits to a Caribbean country to coincide with when an international cricket game was being played there.

This good doctor, a former CMO of the Bahamas, became my friend, and as a pathologist, I received and reported on the dermatologic specimens that he referred to me. My experience in Suriname was earning dividends. Let me reinforce here that my knowledge of leprosy and other tropical diseases was gained during my tenure in Suriname.

Besides our friendship, I mention Dr Charles because his sister, Dame Eugenia Charles, was then the prime minister of Dominica. She was living in the original homestead where Lawrence had stayed when he was visiting Dominica and where he had sometimes invited me to have some of his famous rum punch. I was once invited there by the prime minister herself for a formal luncheon for visiting PAHO delegates.

On the grounds of the house was an outside bathroom that was supplied with water directly from a flowing river; Dr Charles was proud to show me.

Their father, at that time, was alive. He was a centenarian and was still fully functional mentally. When he became ill, I made a diagnosis of multiple myeloma from his bone marrow specimen. He died shortly after.

Once, when I overnighted in Antigua, Dr Charles provided a resting place for me at his home, where I met his wife. Two of his sons were at UWI during my time there.

I have neither walked with kings nor met royalty, but I have been introduced to many high-placed persons, particularly within the Caribbean but also elsewhere. I have stayed at the home of the prime minister of Grenada, met the prime ministers of many other Caribbean countries, and met both the prime minister and the president of Suriname. I have been invited to the residence of the Governor General (GG) of Grenada, Sir Paul Scoon, who sent his driver to pick me up from Adeline's, where I was visiting. I have been introduced to the GsG of St Kitts and Jamaica, have met with more than one GG of the Bahamas, have known two of the directors of PAHO, as well as other persons of note, and once danced with the governor general of Grenada.

When appropriate, my family, having increased by another daughter, Chandre, on 20 April 1983, visited me in Dominica from Nassau on more than one occasion.

Because there was ample leisure time, especially in my first year, I pursued a course in management by postal mail with the Trans-World Tutorial College, earning a certificate in the principles and practice of management with distinction.

Management certificate

The original two-year project was extended to March 1985 but not beyond, as the funds were no longer forthcoming from the international bodies. The project territories were now being asked to provide the finances for further extension.

At the PAHO meeting of Caribbean country delegates in 1984 to decide the direction and future of the CPC/PAHO, the project was discussed, but no commitments could be given. As usual, decisions were only going to be made by governments after receiving the reports of the returning delegates.

But it was doubtful that it would have been extended any further, bearing in mind that Grenada, St Lucia, and Antigua then had pathologists on staff, that Anguilla usually depended on St Martin, and that the BVI referred their pathology specimens either to St Thomas or Puerto Rico. Administratively, each country was open to being advised on the direction of its laboratory service but was not obliged to accept any recommendations—reserved rights.

It was obvious that my future with the project would soon end and now required my attention—the creation and prediction of Drucker. An arrangement was arrived at between the government of Grenada and Project Hope, who then had an office in the country, and I was offered a position. The government would recruit me as a pathologist, and Project Hope would pay me another salary to be the public health medical coordinator of the hospital or of the island.

I was also in touch with the Bahamas, and the CMO had indicated that there was now a position for a pathologist in Freeport, Grand Bahama Island, at Rand Memorial Hospital, which could be offered to me.

I sought the advice of my brother Godwin, who thought it would be a wonderful exercise for me to return to serve in my country. I gave it due consideration and felt hopeful that if I accepted, maybe one of those dreams of mine could be achieved. That dream was to receive an honour from the British royalty, which would acknowledge Grenada's first pathologist who had returned and served his country well.

I then spoke to my brother Nicho, and with his usual "Oh, oh," he asked me if I had gone crazy in thinking of returning to work in Grenada.

One night, sitting at home in Dominica in front of the TV, courtesy of Marpin Enterprises, I prayed to God for advice with my head bent. When I looked back up at the screen, a commercial immediately came on saying, *"It's better in the Bahamas."*

I seemed destined for the Bahamas, and to there I returned.

As of this writing, unrelated to the original project, I have revisited some of the islands of the project for professional but more so for personal reasons. These include Antigua, St Lucia, the British Virgin Islands, St Kitts and Nevis, Anguilla, St Vincent, and Grenada, and of course, besides Petite Martinique, the once sun-blazed and torrid but now culturally hot show-wise isle that we call Carriacou.

A political party in the Bahamas once campaigned on the slogan "Two Straight", but for me, here I went again, a fourth time.

16

ONE MORE TIME

With time, I settled very well in Dominica, basking in its natural beauty and bathing and at times luxuriating in the rivers, the Emerald Pool, Trafalgar Falls, and a nearby sulphur pool. I enjoyed the scenery and ate wild strawberries, a souse made from the cow's skin called franchine (fasheen, vwashin), and crapauds' legs. My part-time Dominican maid, Gertrude, was a true gem of a lady in her duties of cooking, laundering, and cleaning, all of which she performed with the greatest concern. I refused to be encouraged to journey to the boiling lake; it just appeared to be too hazardous for me.

The farewell send-off from Dominica was held at the home of Augustus Fadelle, a technologist at the lab. I left without learning the French patois that is widely spoken there, although I did make an effort, trying to learn from a lady named Kerry Zamore from the Royal Bank of Canada.

Dominica—the nature isle!

I travelled from Dominica to my home in Nassau for some relaxation. Again, not unexpectedly, on our initial conversation, the CMO created hiccups concerning my appointment in Freeport. I was about to call Grenada to accept their offer when she called me back to say that all was in order.

I made an exploratory trip to Freeport, where I met with the administrator, Mrs Michaela Storr, who has remained a truly honest person and a friend, and with Mr. Jacob Cooper, chief supervisor of the lab. I was also introduced to the rest of the staff. I began my term as a consultant pathologist at Rand Memorial Hospital on 1 April 1985. There were persons living in Freeport who were already known to me and who readily assisted me to settle in. One of these was Daisy Glass, née Johnson, who I had met during my internship in Nassau in 1968 and who lent me her car. She and her family, including her husband, Donald, children, Donny and Denver, and brothers, CJ and BJ, have remained faithful friends. In addition, there was Dr Pamela Etuk, née Bethel, who I also first met during my internship, and Euthaniel Noel, a teacher from Mt. Pleasant, Carriacou, who lived alone, was a good cook, and introduced me to the Lucaya Cricket Club.

Lab Staff, Rand Hospital

Others from Grenada who were resident in Freeport included Simon Alexis and Ann Alexis (both teachers) and a gentleman called Briggs. For different reasons, only Simon and I are still here from that group.

As expected, under the courtesy of the government, I spent a week at an apartment hotel. One morning when I woke up, naked as usual at that time of year, I soon realised that the room had been broken into and that my travellers cheques had been stolen. I was able to recuperate the monies from the bank, but for the second time in a new land, I had no follow-up report from the police.

My family joined me from Nassau after I had found a three-bedroom apartment in the Tudor Gardens complex owned by Dusty Miller, with Lester Taylor as resident manager and Crystal as secretary. In 1988, with the help of Barclay's bank, we were able to buy a house on Hawaii Avenue, from which this penmanship is taking place.

My first role at work was to compose and complete intra-and inter-laboratory manuals. A histotechnologist from Nassau, Stephanie Lightbourne, visited Freeport to set up the anatomic pathology area and to compile a list of equipment and supplies to be ordered. Bear in mind that the lab was already functioning as a clinical laboratory in the disciplines of haematology and blood banking, chemistry, serology, and microbiology.

Of course, it was essential that a technologist be recruited for the histopathology section so that the tissue specimens being sent from the hospital to Nassau for reporting could henceforth be handled locally. Fortunately, a Grenadian lady named Maria McBurnie, already known to me, accepted the position. She has since moved with her son, Avery, now a married man, to Florida, and we remain in contact.

I must admit that I was already acquainted with the lab, as it had been necessary at times for me to travel to Freeport to perform post-mortem examinations in the hospital mortuary during those difficult times in Nassau after the departure of Dr Read, who previously had done them,.

In Freeport, autopsies were performed by Dr Ronald Bourne, though when he was on vacation, they were done by some other doctor from Nassau. I established a close relationship with him and his dear wife, Rosalie, when I moved to Freeport. The autopsy suite has since been renamed in his honour.

He liked to share an occasional item of witticism. As a proud member of the Rotary Club, he invited me to become a member, but I declined, not wishing then to be tied up in other meetings. Jacob Cooper at the lab wanted me to become a member of his Lions Club. As far as I remember, I was not asked to be a member of Kiwanis, but I was invited to give a talk, as I have done at the other clubs, by John Fraser, a coworker at the hospital.

Dr Bourne held that the Rotary Club was the king of clubs, Kiwanis, the prince, and Lions Club, the pauper. Once, at the introductory prayer, a Rotary member at the back of the room shouted, "Can't hear you!" The speaker replied, "I wasn't talking to you."

Freeport proved profitable to me professionally and socially but was only so-so financially. After the initial problems I had encountered, the CMO became my most prominent supporter and a dear friend.

My primary work was related to the practice of both anatomic pathology and clinical laboratory medicine. However, in August 1986, I was appointed, on her recommendation, to act as the medical staff coordinator (MSC) of the hospital, following the departure of the previous holder, Dr Sethi. This was in addition to my substantive post in the laboratory.

This position was the equivalent of what is now termed the medical chief of staff, and I was thus a member of the hospital management committee (HMC), which was later expanded to manage all Grand Bahama health services. The portfolio was thus extended beyond the hospital to the entire island and some cays. Therefore, it included the five public health clinics and also, at that time, the environmental health services.

The management of this newly created entity was in the hands of the executive management committee (EMC), composed of the administrator, who headed the committee, the principal nursing officer (PNO), the MSC, and later, the financial officer (Mr. Alexander Burrows). Mr. Burrows' wife, Valeria, a senior employee at the hospital, must be one of the few Bahamians who call me Lord Riccio, and at times, The King.

As the MSC, but also as a member of the HMC and then the EMC, I was involved in many activities throughout the island and its cays. Doctors at the district clinics during my time included, among others, Nehru, Kavala, Gutam, Ebarle, and Fernandez. My input was needed in health policy decisions related to disease outbreaks, disaster management, and the establishment of the statutory body, the Public Hospitals Authority. I also served on the education committee of the UWI Clinical Training Programme in Nassau. I have participated in the functions of some government, regional, and British Commonwealth agencies.

During my fifteen-year service as the MSC, several different persons held the positions of administrator, PNO, and minister of health, as well as that of the governor general, who made an annual visit at Christmastime to the health institutions. The administrators included, after Mrs Storr, Herbert Brown, Janet Hall, Catherine Weech, and Sharon Williams. The PNOs included Mrs Lula Knowles, Sylvia Davis, Veronica Poitier, Anna Hall, Paula Neymour, and Cheryl Bain. From the business office, Gretel Stuart was stationed in the lab. Secretaries to me and the lab included Shawn Mader followed by Hilda McDonald, and Cynthia Sealy was attached to the MSC office.

Non-Bahamian visitors to Rand that I met included Demond Wilson (Lamont on *Sanford and Son*) and Nelson Mandela—yes, the man himself, who I was once mistaken for in Durban.

Within the hospital, my added responsibilities included the oversight of the pharmacy, EKG, physiotherapy, ambulance, and the emergency departments. I was the chairman of the safety committee.

I had a close relationship with Robinson, the head of ambulance, and the driver "G. O." Cumberbatch. I have been told that a visitor to the Bahamas was constipated for many days and requested the ambulance because he was in very painful agony. G. O. drove so fast and seemingly recklessly that when the white man arrived at the hospital, as scared as ever, he had already emptied his bowels.

The opportunity for official representative participation within the country extended regionally and internationally, and I seized it, with the willing encouragement and support of the CMO of the Commonwealth of the Bahamas, Dr Vernell Allen.

I received a grant in 1992 from CAREC for a study on chlamydia in Grand Bahama, the results of which were published in the Bahamas Journal of Science. Gabriella Adderley, a lab technician and loyal friend, did most of the testing. And PAHO recruited me on a temporary basis for a laboratory strengthening project for the family islands of the Bahamas in 1993.

Outside of the country, I visited Antigua, both Trinidad and Tobago, and Ottawa, Canada, to attend conferences; Florida, USA, and Puerto Rico to establish ties with laboratory suppliers, air ambulance services, and hospitals; Alberta, Canada, to observe health services systems; and other lands. I have been recruited on short-term bases by PAHO either as adviser or consultant to report on services in Trinidad, Anguilla, Guyana, and Suriname.

Partly because of the 1981 meeting that I had attended in Puerto Rico, I developed an interest in HIV/AIDS and became a founding member and medical adviser of the Grand Bahama AIDS Awareness Committee (GBAAC). I also became the voice for this disease entity in the local health service and throughout Grand Bahama and indeed was recognised nationally for this in 2005. Locally, I have also been an honouree of the GBAAC, and in 2018, I was honoured by HASB

(HIV/AIDS Survivors Benefit). In this regard, I worked closely with administrative personnel and nurses, including Dixie Jones, Millicent Brooks, Charles Pratt, Vivian Brathwaite, Veronica Poitier, Pearlene Burrows, and others, all under the directors of the programme in Nassau, Dr Perry Gomez and Rosemay Bain. I headed the local activities around the 1 December World AIDS Day more than once, funds for which were provided by the PAHO office in Nassau.

At the meeting in Puerto Rico, I became closely acquainted with an attendee from the University of Shizuoka, Japan, Yasutake Yanagihara, and we exchanged online greetings after that. He even spent a few days with me at my home in Freeport in November 2002. He was mentioned earlier in the account of our stopover in Tokyo.

HIV-AIDS lecture to school students.

I held and still hold membership in the International Aids Society, and I attended some of its conferences—Vancouver, 1996; Geneva, 1998; Durban, 2000; Barcelona, 2002; Bangkok, 2004; Toronto, 2006; and Mexico City, 2008. After the conference, I, and others of my family, would tour the city, nearby noteworthy attractions, and other places in that country and elsewhere, usually but not always by ground transportation. From Durban, we went to Port Elizabeth and Cape Town; from Barcelona we went to Valencia and Madrid; and from Bangkok, we went to Cambodia. For two years, I served as president of the Grand Bahama Medical and Dental Association, and I was GB's representative on the Bahamas Medical Council, of which monthly meetings were held in Nassau, except during the summer. The then retired CMO Dr Allen was the registrar of the council, so we continued to see each other quite often for that two-year period.

I was also one of Grand Bahama's representatives on the National Blood Bank Strengthening Committee and the National Laboratory Strengthening Committee, so the trips to Nassau were frequent. In Grand Bahama, I was instrumental in founding the Grand Bahama Blood Bank Committee and was elected the first president. The membership included persons from the industrial firms and the general public. Grand Bahama Island was considered the industrial capital of the Bahamas.

I, as a member and medical adviser of the Grand Bahama branch of the Bahamas Cancer Society, was also a public voice for cancer. Likewise, the same appearances applied to a similar position in the GB chapter of Us Too International, which was started mainly through the efforts of Ms Dorith Collie, Mr. Rudy Sands, and myself. In this regard, I received, as did three other local members, the 2012 Edward C Kapps Award from Us TOO, which is headquartered in Chicago. Us TOO is a voice of concern for prostate cancer.

Dorith Collie and I enjoyed a close friendship, which started with our official positions in the Bahamas Cancer Society's GB branch. She has since died, but it's not unusual fo4r me to read the words "You have such good heart, and I am proud to know you," in a card addressed to me.

I must admit that I feel a sense of pride when I am acknowledged privately and publicly as having influenced others positively. In this regard, and from the lab, I have influenced the career paths of Kevin Carroll, Meritta Strachan, Tameka Bain, and Mandi Pedican. I feel very proud of the respect and praises of thanks that Marcus Garvey, an emergency medical technician, offers me as he, now in the Turks and Caicos Islands, advances further.

I have presented many papers orally, as posters, and as publications on the above medical conditions, and it was not unusual for me to be in the local daily Freeport News and on ZNS, the local Bahamas television network, because of this or because I had given expert evidence in court, generally in cases of homicide, based on the autopsies that I had performed.

Someone once said in jest that if you have a medical issue or problem in Grand Bahama, go see the mayor, Dr Brathwaite. Many, especially within the hospital, called me Doctor B or Chief. I was retired as the MSC in 2001 but was retained in the position of consultant pathologist into April 2005, when I retired from public service. However, I was asked to provide advisory input, and this I did into June.

I have continued active membership in the above organizations. It should be appreciated that I also still hold some wider memberships in the Medical Association of the Bahamas, the Ontario Association of Pathologists, the Canadian Association of Pathologists, the American Association of Clinical Chemistry, the International AIDS Society, the University of the West Indies Medical Alumni Association, and the New York Academy of Sciences.

I am a life fellow of the International Biographical Association and a fellow of the American College of Pathologists.

On a different note, I have played cricket as a member of the Lucaya Cricket Club, under President Dusty Miller, and have also had my spell as coach, co-vice chairman, and then chairman. On one occasion, I travelled with the team to Providenciales, Turks and Caicos, where Francis Scott, a team player, and I solidified our friendship. Years later, I visited Francis at the hospital in Freeport on the day he died.

I have played hockey and football (soccer) as a member of the Freeport Rugby and Football Club, and I also hold membership in the GB Tennis and Squash Club, where I have played an occasional game of squash with Vivian and with a dear friend, Oplyn Ferguson.

A dedicated group of us played tennis on a court at the home of Clint Moultrie and then on the courts of the Princess Hotels. Players included Neil Headley, who had moved from Nassau, and Eddy Granger, but my usual partner, and good friend, was Ivan "P. J." Deveaux. We were described as the winning losers, for even when losing, we blended so beautifully that onlookers swore that we were winning. I usually attended the local private Kwan Yin tennis tournament over the August Monday holiday. I was once invited to compete as a senior but lost in the finals to Churchill Tener-Knowles.

We had a group of hospital workers that would get together for evening beach parties. Sherry Jones and Norlon Rolle were the primary organisers and the preparers of the food. Like me, Norlon is retired, but Sherry has since died.

My travels to the capital, Nassau, were frequent and undertaken for different reasons. On such visits, I usually called on my friend Hip Wells and my nephew Junior. On one occasion, I was in town to catch a flight to Cuba for a trip organised by Mathew Williams for his student Spanish class at the College of the Bahamas (now a university).

I saw Hip on 14 April 2009, on my return from Cuba. He died the next month on 12 May.

At writing, I am a member of the Freeport Players Guild, the Grand Bahamas Performing Arts Society, and the Rand Nature Centre (Bahamas National Trust).

During my spell in Freeport, to aid in dispensing my responsibilities, I completed an online course/program in disaster management, reinforced by attending conferences and submitting a study guide publication—*Natural Phenomena, Hazards and Disasters for 1995*—which earned me a Disaster Management Diploma from the University of Wisconsin Madison College of Engineering in June 1999. I have also pursued studies in epidemiology, a three-week summer program at Tufts University, Boston, in 1987, and a one-week course at Michigan University the following year.

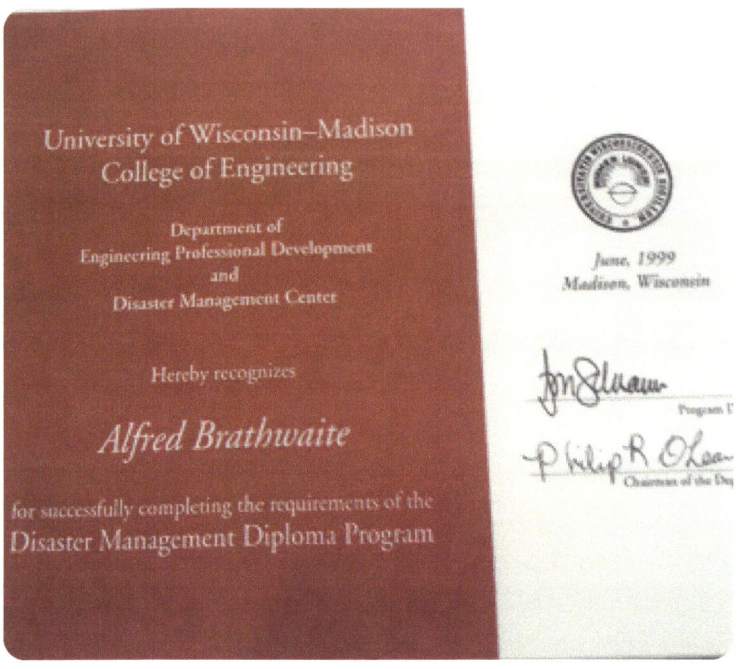

Disaster diploma

I served as locum tenens in pathology in Bermuda, at the invitation of Dr John Obafunwa, in May 2002 and again in April 2003. Unlike in the Bahamas and the BVI, the justice department in Bermuda paid the hospital pathologists for performing forensic autopsies.

I visited the usual sights and saw the Bermuda Day parade, Harbour Nights, concerts, and other events. I also met government officials, including the minister of health, Nelson Bascome, and the premier, Ms Jennifer Smith. I met a doctor/politician, I think, who knew Dr Conville Brown of the Bahamas. I also met a senator who knew Cynthia "Mother" Pratt of the Bahamas, and I reacquainted with Meredith Smith, who I knew from our times in CAREC's laboratory directors' meetings.

I had such wonderful times in Bermuda that I will list other persons I met and who extended kindness to me. Those with connections to Grenada included Ms Aileen Rattaray(?), sister of Dr Dennis Noel; Eddie Belfon, who worked for the Bank of Bermuda; James Dumont, who I later met in Grenada on his return there; and Franklyn DeAllie. Those with Bahamas connections included Don Mitchell, who later moved back to Bahamas (Freeport, Us TOO); Dr Farquharson, on an elective in surgery from studies in Canada; and Dr Barry Whalley, a former PAHO representative to the Bahamas who provided funds for some of my projects there. Those with Jamaica connections included Nurse Ann Wilson and Roger Wong, who was once on block B in Chancellor Hall, with me. Those with Barbados connections included Colin Blades, who was on campus in Jamaica with me and who presented me a gift of a Statesman stamp album; and Judge Archie Warner.

Nurse Wilson and I have maintained contact, sometimes conversing on the phone or sending text messages.

I also met Bermudans Dr Miller and his wife, who knew Justice Weekes of the Bahamas, and Trinidadian Tricia Lares, who had worked in the radiology department at RMH in Freeport. And finally, I often chatted with Nurse Michelle Siew Ling, from the Far East, and Ms Leoni Dyer, the receptionist at the nurses' residence. A most friendly laboratory staff held a farewell function for me in 2003

My close friends in Freeport included many of the doctors, of which Dr Babu, now back in India, assumed first place. I say no more except that there are now many others that I consider as friends.

My daughter Nanika makes every effort to keep her parents happy. She gifted us a trip to Las Vegas in September 2001 for our thirtieth wedding anniversary. We got stuck there for a few extra days because of the terrorist attack on the US buildings on the 11th. When we eventually left, every bearded Arab-looking man was viewed with a hint of suspicion. But we did get to visit the west rim of the Grand

Canyon in Arizona, though the Hoover Dam aspect of the tour was disallowed.

For our fortieth wedding anniversary, she gave us a cruise to Alaska with stopover days in Seattle.

A most caring daughter!

During and after my spell at Rand Hospital, it hit me that agencies and organisations compose and use slogans and themes for many of their promotions, advocacies, and championed issues. The WHO's slogan "Health for All by the Year 2000" has always stuck with me. I often wonder whether or not such slogans ever result in meaningful change. And during my spell in PAHO, I became acquainted with acronyms like AMPES, TCDC, and NCD.

The following is special to me. After moving to a house in 1988 in Freeport, a friend of my wife came to my home carrying a nodding head in a basket. I did not want a dog, but my children, enamoured by this tan, furry puppy, promised to take care of it. Despite my reservations, it was allowed to reside in my home.

I grew up accepting that animals are cared for outside of the house, and that's where Fluffy—my name for this pet—was kept. For different reasons, neither my wife nor my kids offered further great concern for the dog. Fluffy became my friend. I taught her tricks, like shaking hands, and both of us ran after balls in the backyard. But she was aware of who the boss was. A look from me and she knew what to do. She would sit in the back seat of my Toyota, staring out the window, as we went to the beach to swim. She became arthritic with age and eventually lost her sight, but she knew where she was and how to get around. I came home from work one day and could not find her. There was no dog in the yard, in the roads, in the neighbourhood, or in the bushes. The gardener had left a back gate open. Fluffy was never seen again.

We never said goodbye.

17

THE YACHTING CAPITAL

At a meeting of the UWIMAA in St Kitts in 2001, I saw Dr Orlando Smith, a former colleague from Mona, Jamaica, who had spent some time in the Bahamas but was then the chief minister of the British Virgin Islands. He and I relived some days of old, and he invited me to visit his country and to consider performing some duties there. This was a renewal of a similar request he had made in 1994.

A few years later, I first made an exploratory visit, and shortly after that, I responded positively, having by then retired from the Bahamas government service at the end of April, though I was to provide assistance till June. In July of the same year, 2005, I began work as a consultant medical officer with duties in pathology attached to Peebles Hospital in Road Town, Tortola, the capital island and seat of government.

In the past, a pathologist had established such a service from within a trailer, but a new two-storey complex had been recently built as an addition to the hospital. My first role was to set up the anatomic pathology practice within it. Two adjacent areas at the ground level had already been set aside for a mortuary and a histopathology lab, but there was, as yet, no office for a pathologist. Until arrangements could be made, I worked out of a temporary office in the administrative building, dominated by Mrs Winnifred Charles, the hospital general manager. Eventually, with the help of

Dr Heskith Vanterpool, I was given another office within the area of anatomic pathology—a most unsatisfactory situation, in my opinion. After many complaints from me, I was moved to a more suitable office on the second floor of the new complex.

I quickly recruited a histotechnologist, Devye Ann Nicholson, a Guyanese woman then working in St Lucia, but it took more than the first year of my two-year contract for the mortuary and histopathology lab to be equipped. For my professional satisfaction, therefore, I requested and received a one-year extension on my contract to make certain that these were functional.

During my stay, I performed forensic autopsies at a funeral home, but the hospital cases were done at the hospital mortuary when it had become fully equipped. My usual assistant was Mr. Andrew Cito.

My relationship with the coroner (a magistrate in the British system) also started on a good note but deteriorated inexplicably in my final year, although I have contemplated the reasons for it. Nevertheless, I was placed on the questioning block as if I were in the wrong on a professional matter and forced to defend myself. Our relationship, as I said, went south.

Here we go again with another bit of difficulty.

At the beginning, I also had a decent professional relationship with another person, the chief surgeon, but I later thought of her as demonstrating a most unethical behaviour in something she had done. At one time, this individual had also held the position of the chief of medical staff at the hospital.

My social life was very good. Vivian joined me in September of my first year and remained until September 2007, working as a senior nurse in public health. Now and then, we played lawn tennis, but because I too often had to retrieve the balls from surrounding bushes or just lost them, we more usually played squash at the sports club, where we sometimes also used the gym.

Laca, a member of my Kainash gang who had lived with us in Carriacou, lived with his wife, Elnora, and family in Tortola and still does. He made certain that I was happy. On Friday nights, he cooked and sold food to the public from under a tent. His specialty was broiled fish.

Earlier on Friday nights, a group of us, including Johana Boyd, Sauda Smith, Sanjay and Osha Amin, Stephanie Kerins, and the Farraras met at the Tortola Sports Club, usually for wine and snacks. After this, Vivian and I would go to Laca's.

Stephanie Kerins was known for throwing excellent parties. As far as I know, she and her family moved to Scotland. She regularly posts on Facebook.

On Saturday afternoons, another group of us would meet for drinks and food at different places but more so at the home of Eustace and Joanna Ferguson. Some of the other members, most of whom were from other Caribbean islands, included Robert Harewood, Herman Creque, and Tony Palmer.

The chief minister invited me to everything possible—receptions, parties, trips, and his home. In 2006, Vivian and I went with him to the Rock Café in Virgin Gorda at his insistence. He also brought along Sanjay and his family and others.

I was treated well by Mr. Armstrong, a lab technologist at the hospital who hailed from Guyana; Kimberly Parker; Takiyah Penn; Edwin "Juckotou" Sylvester and his wife, Claudette; Antonia Pena and her sister, Leuris; Lucy Lettsome; Juan Varela, a saxophonist from the Dominican Republic, and his wife, Flavia, whose wedding at a seaside locale I attended; and many others. The staff of the hospital laboratory were very friendly and accommodating. I played an occasional game of tennis with a group that included Israel "Sarge" Sergent, a police officer, and was usually organised by Mr. Carl Armstrong. I spent my lunch breaks chatting with Diana Lucy Lettsome in her shop of home-cooked products, sometimes enjoying a tasty light meal. Lucy died in either 2020 or early 2021. Two daughters of hers have been my gentle friends, with Tresha and I still sometimes exchanging hellos. I have written a poem reflecting my thoughts about her.

I exercised at home in the mornings and jogged almost daily on the fields in the afternoons. A Grenadian young man working in Tortola introduced me to a local anaesthetic, Nutmed, which instantly relieved my leg pains when I first used it but was not as effective after that. Anyhow, one day, as I was leaving the field, I said to him in our dialect that we would catch up. His response was "That's what one tomato said to the other."

Life moved along very well, and all in all, we were having a wonderful time. There was always something happening. There were plays—I saw one with Oliver Samuels—stage shows, and movies, especially at the HLSC College. There were parties aplenty, both private and open, including Bomba's Full Moon party and Guy Fawkes bonfires (gunpowder, treason, and plot). There were also festivals, food fairs, farmer's week activities, and arts and crafts displays. One year, the Caribbean artists' arts and crafts festival was held there. The people were friendly, and there was little crime. But like in Dominica, someone told me that my manner was one of aloofness; this time, it was a lady. I ask myself, am I aloof or humbly self-confident?

I seem to think that in one of the years that I spent there, there was a total of four murders, which raised concerns.

A large percentage of Tortola's population had moved there from elsewhere, many from the Caribbean, with perhaps the majority of these coming from the Dominican Republic. Obviously, employment possibilities were then very high.

The British Virgin Islands constitute a British overseas territory, the economy of which is based, inter alia, on tourism and financial services.

It is considered the yachting capital of the Caribbean. The spring regatta is an annual event that is in itself a festival. I have attended and was feted aboard an anchored boat, courtesy of friends at First Caribbean Bank.

In terms of music, the Bahamas has its rake-and-scrape; Trinidad, its steel band; Carriacou, its big drum and string band; and the US Virgin Islands, its quelbe. Likewise, the BVI has its fungi music. So often have I danced to the music of the Lashing Dogs band.

Music festivals are held not only in Road Town, the capital, but also elsewhere on the island, with the big annual event held on Memorial Day in Cane Garden Bay. I have seen performances by Byron Lee and the Dragonnaires, Roberta Flack, Bunny Wailer, Destra, Lucky Dube, Percy Sledge, David Rudder, Arrow, En Vogue, and Jerry Butler.

Mr. Butler arranged for a picture to be taken of Vivian and me together with him and his wife. I add here that in Orlando, Florida, 16 October 2001, Vivian and I met and chatted with Clifton Davis, who was an actor in the TV sitcom *Amen*.

Travelling to St Kitts for its music festival in 2007, we saw Alison Hinds, Crazy, Machel Montana, and Michael Bolton. For both islands, I have only identified the big guns.

The annual carnival-like Emancipation Festival in Tortola, held July through August, included J'Ouvert, beauty contests, cultural parades, and horseracing at the Little A track, where we witnessed the record win of Actspectation. We attended many of the activities.

We visited most of the other inhabited islands of the BVI, as well as other close islands, including Puerto Rico (a hub for American Airlines), Anguilla, St Martin, St Eustacia, and the Rock, Saba. We experienced a carnival in both St John and St Thomas of the US Virgin Islands.

During my stay, I attended a UWIMAA meeting in Grenada in 2005; CHRC meetings in St Kitts in 2006, Jamaica in 2007, and Suriname in 2008; the IAS AIDS conference in Mexico; an India vs West Indies cricket match in St Kitts in 2006; and ICC cricket in both St Kitts and Antigua in 2007. In 2008, I attended a Stanford

20/20 cricket match in Antigua, where my acquaintance with the Davis family was reinvigorated.

At the CHRC meeting, I met two very attractive student presenters. Now and again, I say hello to Anika Mitchell online, but I have had the good fortune to meet with Kathryn Warner at subsequent medical meetings. She's a most caring lady. Both have advanced in their careers.

I regularly attended local medical conferences and workshops in Tortola and became a member of the Cancer Society and of the New Day Foundation, an organization addressing HIV/AIDS issues.

The following are some activities Vivian and I attended and participated in within the BVI, as best as possibly remembered by me: We went to Jost Van Dyke, for its world-renowned New Year's party; to Anegada, a coral island not unlike islands of the Bahamas, to enjoy its beaches and lobsters at Loblolly Bay; and to Virgin Gorda for The Baths, for the Easter festival and fishing tournament in Spanish Town, and for the sea sports in Leverick Bay. On a weekend while we were in Leverick Bay, we spent half a day touring Saba Rock.

At Loblolly Bay, the lobsters were served whole, including the legs, in an open beach-front restaurant. This reminded me of Carriacou, where we roasted lobsters, and of Antigua, where I had lobsters on two separate occasions in indoor restaurants at the invitation first of Clavis Joseph and Pat and then of Ermina Davis-Osoba. All three had been on campus with me in Jamaica in the 1960s.

We once took an all-day boat tour with friends around Tortola, swimming in coves, eating at restaurants, and ending at night by boarding an anchored yacht in the open seas with spring-break students seemingly showing orgiastic behaviours.

My children—Nika, Dax, and Chandre—have visited, sometimes with their friends, and Dax got married in Tortola in 2007. The family once took a sailing trip with Captain Thomas, who was originally from Grenada, to Jost Van Dyke, where we had lunch, and to Green Cay, where we swam.

Other visitors have included Lorna and Kay, Vivian's nurse friends from Miami, and Errol Bodie, my friend from Freeport. Errol was visiting as the squash coach for the Bahamas junior team in 2007, and we accommodated him in our apartment on the last night he was there. Whilst on the island, we took him to the opening of the Emancipation August Festival and took him the following day to Jost Van Dyke, where we went swimming at White Bay. It was not the first or last time that Vivian and I have been to White Bay and to the famous Soggy Dollar Bar.

We took Elaine Toote and Gail Saunders, who were visiting on archival business, to dinner at Pirates Bight Restaurant on Norman Island on 28 August 2007.

At a reception at the chief minister's home, I met the owner of that island, Dr Henry Jarecki, and sometime later, I met his niece, Dr Lianna Jarecki, a very entertaining lady.

Les, Vivian's sister, visited from Nassau. They spent a day at Peter Island. At that time, I was attending a meeting in Jamaica.

With much spare time in the BVI, I commenced a criminal justice course online through the postal service that I completed in Freeport. I graduated summa cum laude in July 2012 and now have an associate of science degree in criminal justice from Penn Foster College. This complemented other courses and programmes I have pursued, not only to improve my knowledge in pathology and laboratory medicine but to enable me to better perform the other functions allotted to or expected of me.

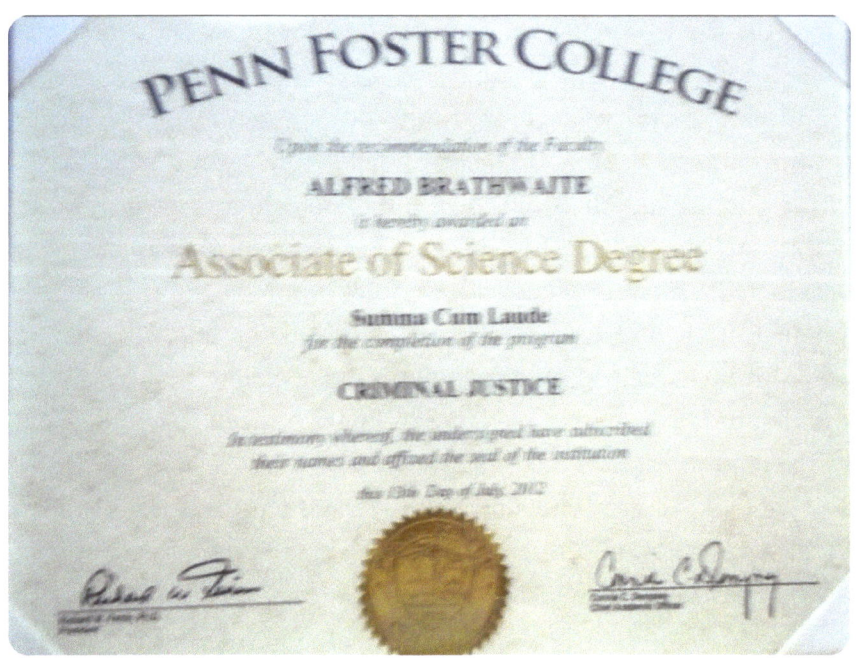

Penn Foster

Whilst in Tortola, I have also had the good fortune to return to the Bahamas to present evidence in court cases, with expenses paid by the court. On one occasion in April 2007, I returned to walk down the aisle at St Mathews Church in Nassau with Chandre, my daughter. She now carries the name Tillman and is the mother of seven children. On another occasion in March 2008, I again journeyed to the Bahamas, accompanied by Laca, to join in the sixtieth birthday celebrations of Vivian and her twin brother, Irrington (aka Minkey). On the night of 21 March, courtesy of Nika, Vivian, Laca, and I dined at the world-renowned Gray Cliff Restaurant. But afterwards, we returned to the wonderful BVI—*nature's little secret.*

I have little respect for defence lawyers who in courts attempt to belittle me or my evidence. I have held deep regards for the late Sir Cecil Wallace-Whitfield. He may ask only one or two questions. But, beware of the trap.

PART 4

THE REVOLVING DOOR: A TIME TO GO

18

WHITHER GOEST THOU?: BACK HOME

Having left Tortola after spending three years there, I retired fully from the active practice of medicine and took to backyard gardening at my home in Freeport. I found time to walk alongside my eldest, Nika, when she changed her name to Clark on 21 April 2017 in Nassau. Years later, she represented the family by going to Costa Rica for the second wedding of her brother, Dax, on 17 June 2021. I once sported a T-shirt that said "I Slept on a Virgin" in large, bold letters on the upper front and "Island" in smaller letters lower down. One guy asked me, "Is that all you can do on a virgin?" I responded,

"Since my stay there, they are no longer called Virgin Islands."

With Laca, Nassau

With Nanika, an outdoor aisle

One day, I got a call from Sir Albert Miller, one of the players of the eventually disbanded tennis group. He was a man of great prominence in Freeport and the wider Bahamas, being one of the triumvirate owners of the Grand Bahama Port Authority in addition to having his own private businesses.

One of these was Immuno-Augmentative Therapy, a part of the Immune Research Centre originally established in Freeport by Dr Lawrence Burton from the USA. Sir Albert outlined that he was prepared to offer me part-time employment to be in charge of the laboratory at the centre.

It was my opinion that the offer was extended partly because the facility was being denied a licensure by the national accrediting body, but he said meaningfully that it was to save me from the Devil, who finds work for idle hands. This reminded me of once hearing, "You are wasting your father's seed."

I accepted the offer and provided supervision two mornings per week. I was handsomely paid, as he had promised, and had one of those dreams of mine, fulfilled—I was given the title of director (of the laboratory). I therefore set out to make my second million, since the first not only never materialised but was quite short of ever being realised.

Within a short period after starting my position, the laboratory received its license.

This part-time job lasted for three years, and during that period, I enjoyed times with a wonderful group of people that included Jacob Cooper, who was the former chief supervisor of the lab at Rand Hospital and my wonderful friend. He has since died. I continue my friendship with his family, all wonderful and gracious people. One of his beautiful daughters, Gigi, and I talk often.

Not too long after the death of Sir Albert, Immuno-Augmentative Therapy, no longer viable, was closed.

Life continues, the second million forgotten, but the public still remembers me. Some suggest that it's time to get rid of my old 1983 Toyota Cressida. I remind them that my wife is even older. My neighbours are friendly. The one called Basil, who is of my age, visits me almost daily, and though he usually repeats the same things he said back when I bought the car, last year, last week, and even the day before, he makes for good companionship. He is a friend in times of need, a friend indeed. At a younger age, in an exam, I had written those words.

When there had been a spate of murders, said to be gang related, particularly in Nassau and primarily of young men, Basil caused me to smile when he said, "These young people must be don't know how long you does be dead for."

Clayton, Coralee, Charlie and his family, and Joe Darville are also immediate or close neighbours, some of whom have a propensity for saying *bye-bye* and *okay* too many times when chatting. However, we look out for each other.

Those further afield who are nevertheless like neighbours include Terecita Kemp and her sons, with whom we usually have Christmas dinner; David Long, an excellent cook, and his wife, Terry; and others from within the different membership groups. We have also had Christmas dinners with the Romers, have close friendships with E T and Procker, and the Tynes, and continue to enjoy the soups of Cynthia Cooper.

Foreign friends include Elijah Crawford and Dr. Odell McCants, the former a frequent traveller to the Bahamas.

Presently, I am living through the devastation of Grand Bahama by hurricanes, including Frances and Jeanne in 2004 and, more recently, Mathew and Dorian. On top of this, Covid came to the Bahamas, took its toll and may still be around.

Those who speak of returning Freeport, the Magic City, to its glory days need more than just words to make it happen. I have heard of ghost towns of the Old West, and without doubt, Freeport, despite the oft-mentioned resilience of its people, seems to be slowly descending into that category with a little nudge here and there along the way. Perhaps it is because there have been such limited efforts to stem the decline. But for Freeport and Grand Bahama, my present home, I hope and wish all will turn out well.

Grand children in my yard in Freeport

Backyard Garden

A Jumbled Miscellany of Thoughts—Nondoctrinal

As I weed, prepare beds, dig holes, sow seeds, and pot plants in my home garden, and as the curly-tail lizards and chirpers follow to seize the unearthed worms, my mind wanders over a multitude of things, other than what's already written. Just within me, some of these seem reasonable and are acceptable, some I question, and some merely make me smile, hum, and sing. And on many a time, incidents I've deemed worthy to be included in this story have sprung into my mind only to vanish when later I get to my desk. I'm then tempted to return to the yard to seek their reappearance. Am I losing it?

Anyhow, here are some of them:

1. There are words that we have used from way back, some still in use, and there are some of more recent usage. In Carriacou, we did not use the word *singlet* to refer to an inner vest. Instead, we

called it a merino, a name taken from that of the sheep's wool. In a similar vein, outboard motors were all called Johnsons, sports utility vehicles were Jeeps or Land Rovers, and jeans were Wranglers. Are these examples of eponyms, as *cardigan is*, which I first read of prior to my journey to university on being advised to get one because of the cooler climes there? I believe that it is perhaps well known that *sandwich* is an eponym.

Two words have been frequently used, one from the 1990s used in reference to HIV/AIDS and the other more recently used in reference to Covid-19, both diseases of pandemic proportions. I am aware that two separate words may be combined to form a new word, but these two became in vogue. I refer to the word *upscale*, used in reference to the treatment of the first disease, and *uptick*, used when referring to the number of cases of the second.

And as vaccines arrived in Freeport, I learnt of tranches. There are some words that continue to put me in a quandary,

such as *default*, as used in computer language; *predate* and *postdate*, regarding changing the date for an event; and *turn down* or *turn up* in reference to an air conditioning unit. When I face a challenge, do I put my head up or down? And why in the stores is a boned fish without bones?

Many times, I'm sure, people say or write of concepts with words and phrases that have been similarly used before without being plagiaristic. The writer does not indicate a quote, being unaware of its previous usage. In my view, it's axiomatic that the use of these words of wisdom may well seem repetitious, having been formed and expressed over time in more minds than one.

The Beatles were not the first to say "let it be", so instead, they sang it. And of a different significance, just attaching the pronoun *me* to its end, also rendered in song, gave the phrase a different meaning.

Speaking of songs, I have read them many times but cannot ever remember the words of "Auld Lang Syne" when the clock strikes or the ball drops in New York City. Sir Isaac may well wonder why it is a ball and not an apple.

2. Many a time, one Carriacouan would say to another, "After one time is two times." I was never certain of its meaning, but late in adulthood, I have used it to mean "I don't make mistakes." The first time that I'm aggrieved by someone, I say, "That's your mistake." But were it to happen a second time, then that would be my mistake, and I don't make mistakes—once bitten, twice shy, but for me, there is never a twice.

   Of course, *two times* may refer to the seventh stage as a return to the first if one lives that long in the Bard's tale. Some have never matured beyond stages two or three, and there are those who have never navigated through all seven.

   And yet, in each of us, there is a tendency to forgive but perhaps not to forget, unless it is of no consequence. If it is, when I'm the one involved, I just let the matter rest. So, most times I relegate a hurtful experience to the land of forgiveness, but indeed, some hurts can remain burdensome in my mind forever, to be *upscaled* conveniently.

   In this regard, I generally trust most people—but only once if I discover that I was deceived or obviously taken for a ride. I am always prepared to grant favours if I'm able to, but I strongly oppose the development of dependency in someone who is bent on using others when they possess the capabilities to better themselves. I despise the attitude of expecting things for free, especially when the person no longer requests but increasingly demands. Parasitism! And so good are some at spinning yarns that you are placed in a quandary trying to determine whether to judge the man or his tale.

3. Quite often, I make telephone calls to agencies. More and more often, a mechanical voice responds and advises me of my options.

I'm asked questions, and then the voice either says goodbye or requests that I hold the line to be connected to an agent, a representative, a customer service professional, an associate—an eventual live person. Whilst waiting for this, I listen to a repeat of music, advertisements, further advice, and the message "Your call is important to us. Please continue to hold."

After twenty minutes, I begin to wonder about what is important to them—my call, my time, or me. By the time one gets connected, it's possible to have forgotten why the call was made. In thinking of time, I question the wisdom of continuing to refer to 12:00 as either a.m. or p.m. *Noon* and *midnight* seem to be more telling and less burdensome.

4. Some may not seek power but most willingly accept it if it is given to or thrust upon them or merely coincidentally obtained. Some even snatch it. No matter the circumstances, when power is acquired, they thrive on and cling to it, unwilling to ever relinquish it unless it's taken away. One only has to look within the realms of politics, religion, and life itself to witness individuals' abuse of power over many, over few, or over just another entity. Let others judge the issue of hypocrisy, unplanned or deliberate. I also tend to cringe on hearing, I won because I put God first. I guess that the also-ran thanks God for just being in the race.

    With the death of Archbishop Desmond Tutu, I am reminded that there were, and hopefully are, humble giants with power who use it for the benefit of mankind.

    Some are known to cite the scripture which says that it's not the acquisition of money that's evil but the love of so doing. But how they love the titles—*el presidente*, most honourable, executive director—which they either choose themselves or direct others to enact them. However, once acquired, such titles promote gigantic egos and convey power. With power, be it of conservative, liberal, moderate, right, or left views, humility becomes humbled. It wanes and is invariably eventually extinguished.

The joke goes that someone with utmost power approached God claiming that he also can create man. Go ahead, he was told. He heaped up mud, but was stopped as God said, first go and make your own mud.

I see too many in power who grow larger waistlines, have bigger pockets, and acquire more magnificent dwellings, called homes and palaces, and they encourage more and more hangers-on and sycophants. Many who adorn themselves and their surroundings know not or care not that it is written that even Solomon in all his splendour …Matthew 6:29.

But they all attend church regularly as parishioners, patrons, or preachers.

5. I use the US Supreme Court as an example of times when significant decisions made by a majority of one may be formidable in their effects, being conceived as the law of the land. How can a 5-4 split decision be used to adversely affect so many?

That is the power of one perhaps of independent views but nevertheless politically appointed.

I admit that I do not have a solution to offer, but I have difficulties accepting that something that will affect so many lives can be determined by one vote, particularly when the decision made by five men involves an issue affecting women.

Just as they have once banished women's names at marriage, so too they banish women's rights to make personal decisions.

Dictatorship, even within the democratic system, may be reflected in more ways than one and may even be classed as being benevolent. This notwithstanding, it is well appreciated that democracy has its limitations and imperfections.

At least, for a certain level of felony, I think a unanimous verdict must be arrived at and so proclaimed by a jury. However,

Henry Fonda's character in *12 Angry Men* may be cited as a reverse of the above, in that one person may be holding up the show. But it seems to me a fairer system for certain situations. **But, what is truth?**

6. My brother Nicholas, as head teacher, advised us to brush our teeth. However, I only began regular brushing on entering secondary school in Grenada at age 11. Colgate and Listerine toothpastes were already well known, as also was Pepsodent—"You'll wonder where the yellow went." And the soaps then included Palmolive and Lifebuoy.

   There were always prizes offered of these products as a part of the advertising process. I often wondered how many tubes or bars constituted a month's supply of toothpaste or soap, the winning prize.

7. Because I have high insteps, I used to buy longer shoes to get a not-too-uncomfortable fit, but I always ended up kicking low-lying objects—until triple E width appeared in the stores. I found it strange, however, and still do, that when trying on shoes at the stores—starting with Bata in Grenada and Payless in the USA—my right foot aims towards the right, but the shoe seems to be heading to the left, and oppositely but likewise on the left foot.

   Were it not for my bowed legs, I may well have been six feet tall. Gradually, with age and arthritis, my height has decreased even further as the convexity of the bows increase. Who needs knees when, even though not as strong, the wings can still flap.

8. Although I may be briefly upset by it at times, I have never been overly critical of being disciplined at home, at school, at work, or otherwise. Responding sharply to the whistle or the bell at school was normal. There was some form of gratification in doing so, even though generally delayed, such as receiving a prize for good behaviour or even decorum at a later date. But a

no or an untoward response was met with punishment—justice, immediate and swift. Justice delayed is justice denied, so it is said, but the same should apply to praise.

To me, this punishment seemed a form of (Pavlovian?) conditioning, but despite this—nay, perhaps because of it—I believe I became a better person.

Debatable!

In the time of my youth, the concepts of good and bad, right and wrong were fairly well established as if engraved in stone. There may have been grey areas, but now, though some basics remain, there seems to be no bad or wrong anymore. Today, the same things of old are still done, but all are now considered to be right. And as my friend Hip Parade has said, if a young man has stepped on your foot, you are the one to say sorry. Your foot was in the wrong place.

For us older ones, adaptation is a necessity for survival, or else one can just withdraw from this world. It is no longer a matter of so much good in the worst of us, for worst exists no more.

9. I welcome the changes that technology has brought to mankind and this world, although like Monk on TV, I marvel at but remain bewildered on seeing these weighty vehicles called planes take to the skies and wonder how concrete boats can stay afloat. I believe in an almighty. Advances in technology are quickly followed by increases in danger. Life continues but does it become better for the majority of people? Evolution ceased with the creation of man whose nature remains unchanged.

I remember how persons once pursued courses in stenography and typewriting, but now, my grandchildren have learned these by themselves and are adept at the new form of shorthand writing. Although I continue my attempts to adopt and adapt in order to be with it, with my limited success, I often seek comfort in a nostalgic yearning for the return of the good old days, the bygone years.

Though humankind's nature has not changed, I still enjoy interactions with people. Banks appreciate my money but no longer welcome me. Visiting the post office once a week instead of daily is now the norm for me. This new interactive form of technology alienates man from man, just as religion has been guilty of doing from time immemorial.

I once entertained the idea that on retirement from medical practice, I would work as a janitor in a public place, like an airport, mainly sweeping. I would silently study individuals to determine their minds, their moods, and who they are, even striking up conversations.

At my high school, GBSS, we were encouraged to save in the banks, and in this, we were supported by the Penny Bank. Gaining interest was the norm. Today, many banks no longer grant interest, but with their protected power, they extract taxes from the accounts or impose ad-hoc penalties. The profit-to-people ratio weighs heavily on the side of the former.

I believe in an almighty or supreme being, though in a form unknown to me. I avoid judging any person, though I do sometimes judge humankind, and I admit to wondering why the Being's rest didn't occur on the sixth day. It is perhaps with a hint of cynicism that I venture that the patient Almighty need not end the world; mankind will do it. One can always lay the blame on Adam.

Sometimes a question enters my mind: when the world ends, as predicted, would the Almighty need to exist anymore, or would he still continue to judge those who have already been judged by him?

There are persons who have been most unkind to others and are now repentant; they truly, contritely accept their God and henceforth behave accordingly. But for some, their God is but a convenience, called on in times of trouble. As the Good Book says (an outstanding performance by Topol in *Fiddler on the Roof*), first make amends with your brother before appealing for mercy and absolution. It's not for me to question why persons make drastic changes in their behaviours, but admittedly, I do, at times.

In my time, I have hurt others. Sometimes I have done it while being fully aware that my action would have that result, but in most instances, I have done it unknowingly.

10. I was always of the opinion that the original approach of waiting for AIDS to progress to a disturbing state before starting treatment was wrong, for even when a pregnant woman received antiviral drugs, it was not for her health but for that of the unborn. An aggressive approach should begin at diagnosis or even be taken prophylactically, as is done now.

    And lastly, in jest, I know about being embarrassed. I once almost wet my pants—an embarrassment in itself—when the only available toilet emanated a most horrible stench. Without a choice,

    I went in, hurriedly relieved myself, and exited with that stench following me. And at the door, waiting to enter, stood a lady I had eyes for.

    Only one toilet in a rest station? But it was just my imagination.

POEMS

Two poems by Flavia Logie are acknowledged, with thanks. All others are by the author, written over the years.

Animating Pollination

The softness of the petals
           Protecting the fruiting bud
Brought out by the wetness
           Of the clear mountain dew,
Caressingly smooth, as droplets
           Form along the pink inner walls.
The petals respond by opening
           Ever so slowly,
Quivering as they do, like lips
           Not quite certain of what to do,
Partly opening, partly closing, unsure, to expose the bud
           Before the time is due.
The bird hovers.
           The nectar lies deep.
The bird also quivers,
           Brushes the petals.
Entry is nigh. It happens.
           Honey flows.

Bridled Happiness

Let our lives mirror nature
the sunrise and the dawn
the clouds
the rain
and the cleansing it brings
the twilight
the night
the moon
and yes,
another new day …

Each cycle
we experience
in Love.

—Flavia Elisa Logie

Acceptance

Each moment is precious
breaths
smiles
kisses … jewels
and your words … so many
delicious and enchanting
soothing … sweet music to the ear.
Later, your words come to me
soft, sweet whispers in my ear
they come to remind me
that you were here
and even if you are not
today … no
you were
and I accept that.
acceptance of the moments
and the bliss they provide brings solitude to the anxious heart
warmth to the cooling spirit
peace within.

—Flavia Elisa Logie

Golden Nature

I gazed at the moon

                                              last night.

It was full and golden.
came the dawn of the morn
with an early sun.

                                              It too was golden.

the day warms, and
butterflies manoeuver
from flower to flower.
their wings flitter. they hover,
portraying their colours
of yellow, orange, and brown,

                                              all golden.

I dwell on my most cherished thought
never to be forgot —
you, I hold in my hands
to roam throughout lands
to see and behold
all your treasures unfold
like the sunset horizon

                                            before and for, me

a chest laden with fruits,

                                            all golden.

Tensions

Deep down inside of you
are feelings that need to surface.
Let me search and find, removing the lace
that covers the bud that protects the space
that extends to the spine, the pleasure to encase.
But first, let me prepare you—
let me touch your face.
Close your eyes and let
my fingers play and roam along the crevasse
of your thighs, of your breasts, of your navel,
of your soul, or your mind,
soon to cry for the entry that brings
the release that must come, with peace.

Projections

Yesterday, I looked marvellous,
someone, a friend, told me
today.
The total me.

I need to feel marvellous
tomorrow and all ways,
because I want it that way
entirely.

I wish to have this friend again
repeat this wanting phrase.
But I cannot ask,
lest it betrays
this sweet evil of my ways.

The Love Call

In saying
I love you,
My words could thus end,
My friend,
And they will be true.
But such simple words
May not truly tell,
Nor do they reflect,
The true depths of my feelings
Nor my yearnings
Nor my desires
To be with you, forever,
To satisfy all my burnings and longings
To be with only you
Now and ever in love.

It Never Ends

Life's pace is so varied,
So up and down, but it never ends.
Think of the races, the horses, so strong,
So magnificently studied, streaming along,
Being plotted to win in a blaze of glory
And yet continuing on at the end of the
race and beyond.

Think of the student, day after day,
Weary so often but continuing on,
And only sad joy when it's successfully over
But only to start again.

Think of the Dawn as the darkness fades
And earth unfolds its beauty.
But what of the dusk, the darkness it heralds,
With such dull shades to brighten again in the morn?
But is there no sun?
Is there no spark?
Where is the shine?
Where is the craze?
Is this just a phase, or is it the end?

Where is the you?

Eating Ice Cream: The Wings of Love

At first it was calm,
      serene, and peaceful, undisturbingly
      calming.
Then came the gentle breeze,
      soft and whispering, delightfully
      soothing.
The wind grew stronger,
      swaying and confusing, questioning
      emotions.
From Heaven to Earth, exciting imaginations of the storm,
      wild and unyieldingly yielding
      explosions!
Fulfilment. Satisfaction. Serenity. Smilingly restful.

The Triangle of Changing Emotions

Side One

When first I saw her, just by chance
Slim and Oh! Exuding radiance
So triangularly feminine,
In nose and facial outline,
in chest and pointed breast
The slender hips in graceful walk
The hesitation to talk—with me.
Seemingly so fragile
The innocence of a child,
And so I thought in her cute pants outfit,
And so I sought, mine eyes again to be lit
on this most elegant young lady of this land.
To take her hand,
to guide across the street
on each and every day we meet.
To make and keep her safe in every way.

Side Two

And then one day,
the pants gave way
to blouse and skirt,
rather short,
fitting snuggly and holding in place,
as if encased,
twin mounts of north and south, of front and back,
straining to escape from being restrained

from this attack
upon their freedom, from this constraint
imposed on them by this most desirable lady of this land.
To hold her hand,
But not to cross the street.

Side Three

We have begun to converse,
at first somewhat nervous.
But soon, one detects
or at least suspects
a dose of double trouble.
The quietly, softly given gentle
words of the accepting and unknowing youth in truth
contrasts, though evanescent,
with the barbs of mischief and even a touch of insolence.
From those lips and from the look of slightly widening eyes,
with knowingly tempting words, not obviously lies,
from lips slightly parted with tongue curling upward,
one wonders, the mind wonders on the sweetness of those soft
and yielding petals and the taste of glorious nectar, as the triangle
uncurls forwards,
as one gently rests hands
on the most seductive female of this land.

Within the Triangle

Ever so rarely, the mind falls prey
      and thoughts betray
the captivation by this woman,
the most beautiful in this land.
Desirous to be fully discovered, designed

Hesitance
For one to seek, disrobe, and find
that ultimate triangle of her Mount

Allowance
For delicately demilking and deliciously drinking, gradually delighting in defoliating, deflowering, defruiting, but without defiling such a dainty—surrendering

Acceptance—for one to delve, descending deeply without digging.

Yielding—gradually declaring open, gently distending, not destroying, never devastating such beauty. Tentatively

Responding to one's demands to taste, sip and eat without devouring. Temporarily distorting but never dismantling nor degrading.
The synergistic rise and fall, joyfully

Participating.
Giving and taking, teasingly rendering and receiving, been held and holding in arms darlingly, as one delivers oneself, now deflated, old but not discarded.
Receivingly dedicated to being lost together, in time
For one to cherish that Triangles have curves, depth, parabolae, and definitely, more than three sides—three linear enclosing
An Inside.

Hotchpotching

           With me you will lay
Not because I ask
              But you may
So wish to do.
           You will open to me.
I demand it not,
           But you may feel you ought.
You lose if someone else takes.
Nothing I wish of you will not be pleasantly given
             Willingly
Along a road that passes by Heaven.

           If there is nothing to lose,
How could one give?
            If there is nothing to give,
How then could one love?
             When two together surrender to each other,
There is no loss.

Raindrops will not destroy
But just enough to annoy.
But oh! You will seize the moment to enjoy
That cross. Look upward
To say to the Almighty
OK, enough is enough.
Now stop it.

Heaven must have moved to another place.
I feel that way whenever I see your face.
Otherwise, as Tavares sang clearly,
"Heaven must be missing an angel."

The people of Day look for the Sun.
The rising of the Moon
is for the people of Night.

To elevate without lifting,
To chastise without beating,
To feel without touching,
To love without consuming.

I heard your voice,
So soft but clear.
Most, I heard not what was said,
But I held it oh so dear.
No name was given,
And yet I knew
That voice belonged to you.
The simple joy, the happiness.
My day, the Lord did bless.

When I was young and was afraid,
I ran to my mother.
Time passed, and at an older age,
I ran to my brother
And other times to my friend.
When will I run to me?

How wonderful and beautiful it is
To think but to dwell not on thoughts,
To wish
But to want and ask naught,
To love
But never to demand,
To walk
But to no more than hold hands,

To talk
But never of each other,
To kiss
But not devour each other,
To live
But not expect forever
In this uncertain joyful journey through life.

Those smiles that are forever present,
The dimples they enhance,
Both denoting pleasantries,
These days so hard to find.
The statuesque build,
    Of Royal Blood
From Henri and Toussaint.
Go fly, thou dearest,
For the freedom reigneth
In thine heart, now and forever.

What a High Sensation
It must be
To celebrate another Day,
A Special one at that.
Thou Taurean, so strong,
Give vent to your emotion.

Summer Blues

It is not yet summer,
But it's hot,
       hot, hot, hot
            and muggy.
But looking through my window,
      the colours aglow,
Green predominates both above
      and below.
But what variates of hue the
      flowers ensure,
Bright pink and reds,
       even blue and yellow.
Butterflies and hummingbirds
      flit to and fro.
The fronds of the palms, are
      they waving to me?
They stand so tall, so proud and
      majestic,
As if they too share in my gin
      and tonic.

To Dream

I sleep.
My dreams are of you.
I awake,
But I keep dreaming
of you with me,
Dreams I seem unable to control.
But why are my conscious
Thoughts of runaway dreams.
This lord of life,
This king of deeds,
Stays quagmire,
Both day and night in slumber,
Dreaming.

To Pass Over

I ask not whether
        you believe or not.
I know not whether
        or not you care.
But remember
        a man
who cried to his father,
one who did suffer,
one who died but word has awoke again.
No, not Lazarus.
        The one called Jesus.
Whichever
        What way.
Happy Easter

EPILOGUE

One has the power so to do, but it is not easy to write about oneself. Nevertheless, I have done so, and not just about myself but of others and also of circumstances from earlier times. Whenever the memory lagged about happenings in Carriacou, I sought and received help from my sister Sarah; my brother George; Valda, my uncle Powell's daughter; Verna, my sister-in-law; Godfrey Louis Napoleon Roberts, a son of Cousin Becka; and nieces Kisha and Deanna and nephew Jeffery of Carriacou. My heartfelt thanks go to them and to all others who have contributed and to whom I remain indebted.

My son Dax, in Costa Rica, deserves special thanks for using his skills on the computer to link me and the manuscript to the publishing house.

The staff of The Ewings Publishing LLC have, without doubt, been pleasantly helpful; I particularly mention Ethan Jones.

I must have wished to include everyone that I had encountered in my journey or to say more on any matter, but that has proven an impossibility for different reasons. My apologies. However, other than those already mentioned, I wish to acknowledge the friendship of Leroy McLeod and his wife, Venetia; the expression of concerns by Cavel Green and her daughter Leisha-Gaye; and the joy derived from knowing the wife and daughters of Jacob Cooper.

The coronavirus pandemic has cramped my style, as it has for many others. My usually yearly travels, which I enjoy and have always

EPILOGUE

planned and looked forward to, whether to new places or familiar ones, were put on hold from August 2019, when some of my family members and Cognet's met in Savannah, Georgia, USA. Whilst there, Hurricane Dorian caused catastrophic damage to the island of Grand Bahama, where I have resided since 1985.

Protocols, restrictions, curfews, and lockdowns, some of which are still in effect, became the order of the day, all together a damper of enthusiasm and initiative. Perhaps I ought not to complain, for

I spend more time gardening and landscaping in my backyard, but the surges and the steady results of more and more people getting infected and dying are of great concern and certainly most disturbing. I refer not just to the situation in the Bahamas but in so many other lands.

But that daughter of ours called on my fifty-first wedding anniversary about a gift of travel to Cancun, Mexico, in 2022. And my response was, why not? Only, when? Maybe in June. Vivian and I did make the trip in June, and especially because of the reduced restrictions, I journeyed to Jamaica for the sixty-sixth research meeting of CARPHA in September 2022, spending a few days in Miami on the return leg.

Since retiring from the active practice of pathology, I have lived a rather simple life. No more arguments about strong disagreements. I read the headlines of newspapers with not much time spent on details and others' opinions. Instead, I enjoy reading the comics and completing the easy crosswords. My interest in sporting events, once so vibrant, is now limited to just the outcomes. And yet, my life is not an unhappy one. I do, however, miss the opportunities I had to attend elaborate stage shows whenever I travelled.

I have fallen prey too often to being criticised for offering advice to someone seeking it in a controversy with another, for the seeker goes to the other and utters, "Alfred says," after which the other tells me to mind my own business. As such, I now, when two persons disagree, don't get involved unilaterally, or better yet, at all. Nevertheless, I still consider it one of my strengths to be able to deal with all persons of different levels.

I have read some of the best literary volumes, mainly British (because they were requirements at schools), American (because I've so desired), and Caribbean (because they received critical acclaim. Among the Caribbean authors are Naipaul, Braithwaite, Walcott, and others.

I have read biographies and autobiographies, the latest ones being those of Mandela, Obama, and a few Caribbean cricketers. I have read Maya Angelou, Maya Banks, Toni Morrison, and so many others with appreciative awareness, but I have not, for various reasons, felt overwhelmingly informed or educated by them. I must have been influenced, but they did not contribute to the values in my life. Hemingway's *Old Man and the Sea* reminds me of Cousin Basta, even though our quest was only to catch small fish.

Some things I have read now provide me with good questions for the Jeopardy answers or answers to crossword puzzles.

In my readings, I do appreciate striking alliterations, oxymorons, and, in Latin at high school, the ablative absolute construction—Caesar, having crossed the Rubicon, civil war followed. I have just finished reading John Buchan's *The Thirty-Nine Steps*—of literary worth, no doubt, but a seeming fanciful adventure. Not being versed in the geography of Scotland myself, it proved a bit difficult to appreciate, for my knowledge of Scotland resides only on the Loch Ness Monster and Glenfiddich single malt.

I was fascinated by the baseball skills of Roberto Clemente and have read Arnold Hano's biography of him. I have read Robert Kennedy's *To Seek a Newer World*—"to see or ask why or why not"—as well as a biography by Arthur M. Schlesinger, Jr. Though I have not met either of them, I've admired both *el jugador y el politico*—I'm still learning Spanish—for exuding a level of compassion that truly impressed me, and for this and other reasons, I consider them to be heroes. *Champions!*

EPILOGUE

Now, I read lightly the novels of many writers, one of whom is Harold Robbins from long ago. I think I have read all his books, and my son received his name from the protagonist of *The Adventurers*, blended with that of my father, DaCosta. Robbins, Nora Roberts (aka J. D. Robb), James Paterson, Lisa Jackson, John Grisham, Sidney Sheldon, Ken Follett, Sandra Brown, Danielle Steele, David Baldacci, and Dan Brown rank as favourites.

I have been known to purchase a book that I have previously read, having forgotten that I have already done so. And my novels are penmarked with page numbers that refer to what was mentioned before.

I seem to have more to do on a daily basis and have no feelings of guilt when postponing some for another day, but I tend to overdo this on the weekends. Monday arrives, and the unfinished pile has grown larger. But then, I hardly know which day of the week it is. Most seem like Saturdays.

The majority of Sundays are planned—early morning church services, computer updates, wonderful dinners prepared by Vivian, television, rest, nothing, sleep. Whatever it means, I am at peace with myself and happy with my life, though I am always questioning why hairs and nails continue to grow, and unceasingly, rapidly so. Too often, my trousers seem to have a smaller waist and have only one leg, and when I do manage to get into the two legs, they are longer.

It's no longer that easy to cut my toenails; they are more hardened in texture and more difficult to reach. And I have no desire to spend my time in salons.

I still enjoy listening to music but spend less time doing so, and I have not been to a movie house for years and years and years. On TV, I watch reruns of very old movies with stars like Kirk Douglas (Spartacus), Charlton Heston (Moses), Anthony Quinn (Zorba), Victor Mature (Demetrius), Debra Paget (Lilia), and Deborah Kerr (Anna), to name a few. I also like the old westerns (with Audie Murphy, Randolph Scott, and others), detective stories and court room scenes (Perry Mason, Matlock, and Cannon), and a bit of comedy.

EPILOGUE

And, within the inner home, I'm either in the bedroom or at my desk. I spend very little time in the living room, but I do dine at table.

I still enjoy the typical Bahamian breakfasts—souses, boils, and stews that are served with grits or johnnycake—and I may still have a Kalik or Sands cold beverage.

Dancing, for me, now revolves around movements of the upper body only; my arthritic knees—post cricket, football, hockey, tennis, and jogging—are just for walking, and I usually require the support of a cane. I have discovered that the best way to travel by air is to indicate the need for a wheelchair.

Some have said that age is nothing but a number. Whatever, but I would venture that I presently qualify for act six on the world's stage, *As You Like It*. I'm forgetful, without doubt, but if I seem oblivious, then it's purposely so for good reason. I'm unsure as to whether or not my mentation has dipped or is not as keen, but my attention span has decreased, especially at meetings and sermons. I despise the constant repetitions and unending perorations, and after words have been repeated three times; OK, OK, I've gotten the picture, or as Dusty Miller of the cricket club would say, "Get on with it."

At those times, my ears hear nothing more, as I begin to reminisce.

I'm still a product of the universe, consciously evolving and pursuing a higher standard of life, but I've taken my licks, usually for having behaved foolishly or having done wrong. Perfection seems an unending challenge. But when I'm sometimes introduced as the Caribbean pathologist, there goes an extra beat of the heart, not unlike when one gets an unexpected responding kiss, and then the pursuit of perfection matters not. And time stands still.

As said in Carriacou, this sun is a bitch, and so some say of old age. In my memoirs, memories have been revealed. Mirrors reflect what the now is, but mirthfully, whichever way the dawn unfolds, in mind, body, and spirit, I hope to age youthfully as a light continues to shine down on a certain dear lady, in whose radiance I continue to bask. And even though I cannot be what I'm not, *I've got to be me.* Quintessentially so!

Natural beauty   The 1983 Toyota Cressida

APPENDIX

CURRICULUM VITAE
of
DR. ALFRED FITZGERALD BRATHWAITE
M.B.B.S., M.D., F.C.A.P.

BORN: April 22, 1941 in Grenada

MARRIED: Vivian nee Isaacs in 1971

Children:		
	Nanika	1972
	Ricio	1974
	Chandre	1983

EDUCATION:

1. **PRIMARY:** Mt. Pleasant Government School 1946 - 1952

    Awarded a Scholarship to attend Secondary School

2. **SECONDARY:** Grenada Boys Secondary School 1953 – 1960
    Passed examinations (Certificates) of Cambridge
    University School Certificate – 1956

    Higher School Certificate – 1959 and 1960 with distinction in Zoology.

    Taught at the G.BS.S. January – August, 1961

3. **UNIVERSITY:** University College of the West Indies as external student of London University to study medicine 1961 – 1967

    Graduated M.B.B.S. November, 1967

4. **POST-GRADUATE:**
    (a) Internship (rotating at Princess Margaret Hospital, Bahamas, January – December, 1968
    E.C.F.M.G. 1968 (109-453-1)
    (b) Residency in Pathology:
    Lutheran Medical Centre, N.Y. July 1969–June 1970
    Brookdale Hospital Centre, N.Y. July 1970-June 1971
    Queens Medical Centre, Hawaii, July 1971-June 1972
    Ottawa General Hospital, Canada, July 1972- June 1973
    Ottawa Civic Hospital, Canada, July 1973- Nov. 1973

<u>American Board Certification</u> in Anatomic and Clinical Pathology – November, 1973

PROFESSIONAL EMPLOYMENT

1974 – 1976		Specialist Pathologist, Government of Grenada, Grenada.
1976 – 1978	(1)	Anatomic Pathologist, Academisch Ziekenhuis, Paramaribo, Surinam.
	(2)	Head, Department of Pathology and Lecturer, Medical Faculty, University of Surinam, Paramaribo.
		Presented M.D. Thesis: "Pathology of the Thyroid Gland in Surinam", November 1978.
1978 – 1981		Consultant Pathologist, Princess Margaret Hospital, Bahamas
1982 – 1985		Project Manager and Pathologist, PAHO/WHO-UNDP Caribbean Health Laboratory Improvement Project, based in Dominica.
1985 – present		Consultant Pathologist, Rand Memorial Hospital, Bahamas
		Acting Medical Staff Coordinator from 1986 to June 2001

Between 1974 – 2005 General duties included:

(1) Practice of Anatomic Pathology including autopsies, surgicals, and Cytology.

(2) Practice of Clinical Pathology.

(3) Practice of Forensic Pathology.

(4) Teaching of Laboratory medicine.

(5) Supervision and management of laboratories.

(6) Hospital and Health Services management (Bahamas) to June 2001.

AWARDS AND CITATIONS

1952: Government of Grenada – Primary School Scholarship.

1961: Federation of the West Indies (Federal) Scholarship.

1964:   Henderson Medal for Physiological Sciences, University of the West Indies.

1974:   PAHO – One week Fellowship.

1975:   Guest lecturer, Medical Faculty, University of Surinam.

1978:   MD. (Thesis), University of Surinam.

1980:   Marquis Who's Who in the World, 1980 – 1981.

1982:   Letter of appreciation from Caribbean Association of Medical Technologists.

1986:   PAHO STC on Laboratory services, Guyana and Surinam.

1988:   Plaque for Outstanding Service, Caribbean Association of Medical Technologists (CASMET).
Also elected Fellow (Honoris Causa).

1987:   (Mar. 11 - 18): PAHO Advisor on Laboratory services in Anguilla.

1991 (Jan. 13 – 27):   PAHO Advisor on Laboratory services in Trinidad.

1999 (June):   Diploma in Disaster Management, University of Wisconsin (Madison).

Nov. 2000:   Award for dedicated services in Medicine, Public Hospitals Authority, Bahamas.

Nov. 2001:   Award for Immeasurable Contribution to HIV Education, P.H. Authority and Grand Bahama AIDS Awareness Committee.

2003:   Distinguished Service Award (CASMET)

ASSOCIATIONS, etc.

MEMBER: N. Y. Academy of Sciences
Ontario Association of Pathologists
Canadian Association of Pathologists
International Academy of Pathology
American Association for Clinical Chemistry
Paradise Cricket Club, Bahamas (former)
Cricket Club of Lucaya
Dominica Club (former)
Bahamas Hockey Association
Past Member – Maternal and Child Welfare Committee and Metrification Board, Grenada

Associations, etc. Contd

                Former member Bahamas Medical Council
                Founding President Caribbean Association of Lab. Med.
                Bahamas National Blood Bank Committee.
                Bahamas National Laboratory Strengthening Committee.

1987 to present: Medical Advisor to Grand Bahama Cancer Society

1988: Former Member of National Committee on Trauma, Bahamas.

1995 to present: Medical Advisor to Grand Bahama Aids Awareness Committee.

                Former President G.B. Medical & Dental Association.

FELLOW: American Society of Clinical Pathologists
                College of American Pathologists
                International Biographical Association
                Caribbean Association of Medical Technologists (Hon).

PUBLICATIONS:

                Many papers including Cancer trends in Caribbean islands, Chlamydia prevalence in Grand Bahama, Anti N antibodies, HIV/AIDS in Grand Bahama and Mortality Statistics for Grand Bahama have been published. Also, presenter at regional and International meetings on diverse medical topics.

Alfred F. Brathwaite

PAPERS DELIVERED

1. "Iron Metabolism" 1975
   To Medical Association of Surinam

2. "Venereal Disease Control" 1975
   Annual Meeting, Windward and Leeward Islands Medical Association

3. "Medico-Legal autopsies" 1977
   Medical Association of Surinam

4. "Cancer Statistics Surinam" 1977
   Conference on Management of Cancer,
   University of Surinam.

5. "Cancer Statistics from Autopsies in the Bahamas" 1980
   Medical Association of the Bahamas Conference

6. "Cancer Statistics in Caribbean Islands" 1980
   Conferences on Cancer; St. Georges Medical School, Grenada

7. "A Laboratory Network in the Caribbean" 1982
   Intercaribbean Immunology Conference – Jamaica

8. "Diarrhael Diseases" 1982
   Caribbean Association of Medical Technologists,
   Annual Meeting, Bahamas.

9. "Leprosy" – The Disease Process"
   Leprosy Training Workshop – Dominica

10. "Laboratory Systems" 1983
    PAHO seminar on Laboratory services, Chile

11. "Etiology of Cancer" 1986
    Bahamas Cancer Society.

12. "What is Pathology" 1985
    Rotary Club of Lucaya

13. "Laboratory Medicine" Bahamia Women's Club 1986

PAPERS DELIVERED, Contd:

14.	"General Aspects of Cancer" Elks Lodge Convention, Bahamas	1986

Oct. 7, 1986:	"Respiratory Diseases" to seven Day Adventist Health Week, Freeport.
Oct. 20, 1987:	"AIDS" to Pilot Club, Freeport.
Oct. 29, 1987:	"AIDS" to Kiwanis Club, Eight Mile Rock, Grand Bahama
Oct. 30, 1987:	Panelist on AIDS Seminar, Rand Memorial Hospital Staff, Freeport.
Feb. 20, 1988:	"AIDS" to Seven Day Adventist Health Week, Freeport.
April, 1988:	Panelist on AIDS, Nurses Forum, Freeport.
May 14, 1988:	"Warning Signs of Cancer" to High Rock Community for Grand Bahama Cancer Society.
June 23, 1988:	"AIDS" to Life Underwriters Association of Bahamas.
Oct. 18, 1988:	"AIDS" and "Aspects of the Grand Bahama Health Services" to Rotary Club of Lucaya.
Oct. 20, 1988:	"Parasitology" to Senior class, Freeport Anglican High School.
Nov. 2, 1988:	"AIDS" to St. Pauls Church Group, Freeport.
Nov. 5, 1988:	"AIDS" to Life Underwriters Association, Bahamas.
Feb. 16, 1989:	"Let's Talk About Cancer" to Rotary Club of Freeport, Bahamas.
April 22, 1989:	Participated in Rotary Club Careers Seminar for students, Grand Bahama.
April 24, 1989:	"AIDS" as part of World Health Activities, to Catholic High school students, Grand Bahama.
May 5, 1989:	Speaker in Cancer Seminar for Rand Memorial Hospital Staff.
May 27, 1989:	Speaker at Cancer Society "Lets Talk About Cancer", Grand Bahama.

PAPERS DELIVERED Contd:

1990:	Moderator/Host "Your Health & Hygiene" Radio Show, Grand Bahama Medical & Dental Association.
Sept. 20, 1990:	"Medical Ethics" to L. U. Association, Grand Bahama.
May 19, 1991:	Cancer – A reminder. Freeport Rotary Club
May 27, 1991:	Overview of Cancer Cancer Society/Pilot Club Seminar. Freeport.
July 1, 1991:	Pap test and Mammograms. Bahamian Women's Club. Freeport.
Nov. 15, 1991:	Minisymposium on Cancer. Rand Memorial Hospital. Overview of Cancer.
Nov. 22, 1991:	AIDS. Youth Group of Grace Nazarene Church, EMR.
Mar. 13, 1992:	AIDS. Youth Group of Calvary Baptist Church. Freeport.
May 21, 1992:	Panel member on Cancer Society, Pilot Club Cancer Seminar. Freeport.
July 25, 1992:	Preventative Medicine in Bahamas. South Western Alumni Association.
Feb. 11-12, 1993:	Maternal and Child Health Workshop. The adolescent.
Mar. 3, 1993:	AIDS. Women's Group of Zion Baptist Church. Freeport.
Mar. 18, 1993:	Target the Children. Rotary Club of Lucaya.

PAPERS DELIVERED Contd

Mar. 29, 1993:	AIDS. Grade 12 Freeport Anglican High School.
Apr. 7, 1993:	AIDS. Adult group of Calvary Baptist Church.
Apr. 21, 1993:	Elected President of C A L M.
May 4, 1993:	AIDS. Bahamas Customs.
May 11, 1993:	AIDS. Blood Transfusion. Cancer. Kiwanis Club of Lucaya.
May 11, 1993:	Moderator for Cancer Society/Pilot Club Cancer Seminar. Freeport.
May 18, 1993:	Changing Patterns of Disease. Rotary Club of Lucaya.
Apr. 20-23, 1994:	Cancer in Bahamas. CALM Meeting in Jamaica.
May 3, 1994:	Moderator of Cancer Society/Pilot Club Cancer Seminar.
May 25, 1994:	Radio Show. The Autopsy.
Feb. 18, 1995:	AIDS. Seventh Day Adventist Health Forum.
Feb. 24, 1995:	Teens and Sex. Freeport Anglican High School. Grade 8.
Jan. 15, 1995:	AIDS and Your Family. Panelist. Calvary Temple Church.
July 11, 1995:	Ebola. Rotary of Lucaya.
Oct. 22-27, 1995:	Chlamydia in Grand Bahama. CASMET Symposium. Freeport.
Mar. 21, 1996:	Cancer. Grand Bahama Cancer Association Seminar at Guiding Star Society, Eight Mile Rock.
Sept. 6, 1996:	Epidemiology Surveillance in Disaster. R.M.H.

PAPERS DELIVERED Contd:

Oct. 29, 1996: Cancer of Prostate.
Rotary Club of Lucaya.

Feb. 7, 1997: Talk of AIDS-HIV
G. B. Girls Brigade at Calvary Baptist Church in E.M.R.

Feb. 18, 1998: AIDS Lecture Candlestick Outreach Church,
Grand Bahama.

Oct. 27, 1998: Speaker at Cancer Society Seminar,
Grand Bahama.

Jan. 21, 1999: Presented paper at Dept. Environmental Health Emergency
Preparedness Forum. Grand Bahama.

Apr. 21-24, 1999: Presented paper on "Antibiotic Patterns", Rand Memorial Hospital
at CHRC annual meeting in Barbados – Satellite.

Aug. 29, 1999: Spoke to the Jamaican residents of Grand Bahama
Association on Government Health Services.

Aug. 1, 2001: The Coroner's Legal System at CASMET/AMT Meeting
In Nassau.

Nov. 7, 2001: HIV in Grand Bahama 1991 – 1995 at UWI Medical Association
Meeting in St. Kitts.

Aug. 29, 2002: Presented an update on "AIDS" at G.B.H.S. – G.B.A.A.C.
Annual HIV/AIDS Seminar for Health Care Workers.

Nov. 6, 2003: "Mortality Statistics for Grand Bahama" at UWI Medical
Alumni Association Meeting in Nassau.

April, 2004: Poster Presentation "Epidemiology of Cancer in
G.B." (Co-author) at CHRC annual meeting In Grenada.

COURSES, MEETINGS ATTENDED, Etc.

1974:	Meeting for the setting up of the Caribbean Epidemiology Centre, held in Jamaica.
1975:	Windward Island Medical Association Annual Meeting, held in Trinidad.
	Post graduate course on Cerebrovascular Accidents held in Curacao. Meeting for he Control of Sexually Transmitted Diseases, held in Trinidad (PAHO sponsored).
1977:	Handling of Malignant Diseases Conference, Surinam.
1978:	X Triennial Congress of Pathology, Rio de Janeiro. X11 Int. Congress of Cancer, Buenos Aires.
1979:	Annual Meeting Medical Association of Bahamas (Theme – Cancer) and in 1980, 1981.
1980:	International Symposium on Cancer, London, England. Conference on Cancer, St. George's Medical School, Grenada.
1981:	Management Course, Bahamas. Latin American Health Care Exposition, Panama. 1st STD World Congress, Puerto Rico.
1982:	CAREC'S Annual Laboratory Directors Workshop, also in 1979. 1983.
	CASMET'S Annual Meeting, also in 1979.
1983:	ASCP – CAP Fall Meeting, Miami. National Workshop on Intersectoral Approach to Primary Health Care, Dominica.
	Intercaribbean Immunology Meeting, Jamaica.
1983:	PAHO Meeting on Reorientation of Laboratory Services, Chile.
1983:	PAHO Laboratory Management Course, St. Lucia. CANDI Annual Meeting, Session on Rastafarian Diets, Dominica.
1985:	AFIP Hematology seminar, Washington D.C.
1986:	Grand Bahama Medical Association Bahamas annual seminar.

COURSES, MEETINGS ATTENDED etc.

Oct. 13, 1986:	Commonwealth Health Ministers V111 Meeting, Nassau.
Nov. 7, 1986:	Grand Bahama Dental and Medical Association Annual meeting.
1987:	PAHO Teleconference on AIDS.
July 26 - Aug. 14, 1987:	Summer Course in Epidemiology, Tufts University.
Nov. 18 - 21, 1987:	CASMET'S Health Educators Congress and annual meeting, Barbados, (Sponsored by the Commonwealth Foundation).
July 4 - 8, 1988:	Workshop (PAHO) on Development of an Intersectoral Protocol on Health Promotion in Primary Health, Jamaica.
July 18 – 22, 1988:	Epidemiology for Developing Counties, University of Michigan.
Oct. 26 – 28, 1988:	Train the Trainer Workshop on AIDS, Nassau, (AIDSCOM).
Dec. 12 – 14, 1988:	AIDS Teleconference (PAHO) in Nassau, Bahamas.
Mar. 28 – 31, 1989:	Computer Course for Senior Management Staff, Rand Memorial Hospital, Bahamas.
May 23, 1989:	Syntex Seminar for Doctors on Industrial Health Surveillance Programs.
Aug. 14 -18, 1989:	International Conference on Emergency Medical Services, Crystal City, Virginia, U.S.A.
Aug. 21 – 25, 1989:	Course on Diagnostic Pathology 1989, I.A.P. New Hampshire, U.S.A.
Oct. 23 – 25, 1989:	Family Island Health Services Conference, Nassau.
Oct. 27 – 28, 1989:	CASMET 35th Biennial Conference, Miami.
Nov. 21 – 25, 1989:	CAREC/AIDSTECH Workshop on AIDS/STD, Jamaica.
December 8, 1989:	Grand Bahama Medical & Dental Association annual seminar "Acute Care".
Feb. 24, 1990:	Cancer Society seminar "All you wanted to know about Cancer", Nassau.

COURSES, MEETINGS ATTENDED etc.

May 28, 1990:	Cancer seminars at Rand Memorial Hospital and Princess Hotel.
Sept. 26, 1990:	"Cocaine Addiction – The Aftermath" M.A.B. and U S I S, Grand Bahama.
Sept. 27, - 28, 1990:	Workshop on "Domestic Violence", Rand Memorial Hospital.
Oct. 13 – 21, 1990:	Member of Bahamas Team to Edmonton, Canada to observe delivery of Health Care.
Oct. 22 – 25, 1990:	Family Island Health Services Workshop, Nassau.
Apr. 1996:	Disaster Management Seminar. Wisconsin.
July, 1996:	International Conference on AIDS. Vancouver.
Jan. 17, 1997:	Medical Certification of Death Seminar at Rand. CAREC/PAHO/MOH.
Apr. 16 – 19, 1997:	CCMRC Annual Meeting in St. Martin.
Sept. 3 – 6, 1997:	AIDS Perinatal Transmission Conference in Virginia, U.S.A.
Sept. 6, 1997:	Disaster Seminar at Rand. Delivered paper on Epid. Serv. of Disease after a National Disaster.
Oct. 5, 1997:	GBMDA Annual Seminar.
Mar. 5 – 6, 1998:	AIDS Vaccine Trial W/S in Nassau, Bahamas.
June 28 – July 3, 1998:	XII International AIDS conference, Geneva
July 18 – 26, 1998:	V UWI Medical Alumni Reunion Activities.
Aug. 28, 1998:	Emergency Response Course in Grand Bahama, Dept. of Environmental Health.
Dec. 2, 1998:	Symposium on Medical Response Documentation, Nassau, Bahamas.
Mar. 18 – 21, 1999:	Health Strategic Planning meeting, Nassau, Bahamas.

COURSES, MEETINGS ATTENDED etc.

Nov. 4, 1999: CASMET Annual Activities in Curacao.

Feb. 13 – 17, 2000: Central American Society of Dermatopathology Conference on Dermatology in Costa Rica, Quepos.

Feb. 24 - 25, 2000: Conference of Heightening Awareness in HIV/AIDS in Caribbean Region, Nassau, Bahamas.

Apr. 12, 2000: WINSIG Management Information System W/S, PAHO, Nassau, Bahamas.

May 22 – 26, 2000: Logical Framework W/S, Nassau. PAHO.

July 9 – 14, 2000: XIII International AIDS, Conference, Durban, S.A.

Aug. 2 – 3, 2001: CAREC/PAHO meeting for the launching of standards in Blood Banking/Transfusion for the Caribbean, in Nassau.

Nov. 7 – 11, 2001: UWI Medical Alumni Association Reunion and Scientific Meeting in St. Kitts. Delivered a paper.

Three separate Public Seminars in 2001 of G.B. Cancer Society including on April 27th, when Dr. Brathwaite presented G.B. Statistics followed by Dr. Dewitty of Howard Medical School, Washington, D.C.

July 7 – 12, 2002: XIV International conference on AIDS, Barcelona. Attended Skills Building W/S on HIV Rapid diagnostic methods on July 10th.

Oct. 4 – 5, 2002: GBMDA annual conference: Royal Oasis Hotel, G. B. Theme "Advancing Health Care in the Bahamas".

Oct. 25 – 29, 2002: AABB annual Scientific Meeting, Orlando, Florida.

Nov. 26, 2002: Opening ceremony of AIDS Week at Christ the King Church Hall, Grand Bahama.

Jan. 17, 2003: PHA forum on FTAA at Christ the King Church Hall,

COURSES, MEETINGS ATTENDED etc.

	Grand Bahama.
Jan. 23, 2003:	Emergency Preparedness Forum VII at Carraway Building, Grand Bahama.
Mar. 13 – 14, 2003:	Seminar on Productivity and Flexibility in the Work Place (GBHS, BPSU).
Mar. 20, 2003:	MSD presentation on Asthma and Allergic Rhinitis, Grand Bahama.
May 1 – 3, 2003:	CHRC Scientific Meeting, Nassau.
May 16, 2003:	Grand Bahama Cancer Society Public Seminar.
Nov. 4 – 9, 2003:	UWI MAA 7th international Medical Conference in Nassau. Theme "Research and Caribbean Health Care". Made presentation.

PUBLICATIONS

1. Part Author – Anti-N Antibodies in Hemodialysis patients.
   Transfusion 15:43, 1975.

2. Hemoglobin values in Grenada
   Caribbean Medical Journal Vol. 2. 1978.

3. Ectopic pregnancy in Surinam
   Surinam Medical Bull. 1:52, 1977.

4. Experience with medicolegal autopsies in Surinam
   Surinam Medical Bull. 1:97. 1977.

5. Surgical Pathology of the Thyroid in Surinam
   Surinam Medical Bull. 2:43. 1978.

6. Pathologic lesions of the fallopian tubes in Surinam
   Surinam Medical Bull. 2:13, 1978

7. Carcinoma of the breast in Surinam
   Journal of Trop. & Geog. Medicine 31:81, 1978.

8. Doctorate Thesis, "A Study on the Pathology of the Thyroid Gland in Surinam".
   Accepted by the University of Surinam, November 29, 1978.

9. The Accessory Spleen in a Surinam Study
   Surinam Medical Bull. 3:5, 1979.

10. Part Author – Pathology of the Appendix in Surinam
    Surinam Medical Bull. 3:17, 1979.

11. Helminth Investigation in a Grenada Population. Submitted to the Grenada Government.

12. Cancer patterns and trends in the Bahamas.
    PAHO Bulletin 18 (1), 1984.

13. Histopathological Cancers in the Commonwealth of Dominica.
    PAHO Bulletin 20 (3), 1986.

14. Part author – Wilson's Disease in the Commonwealth of Dominica, a case report.
    Trop and Geog. Medicine 38:84, 1986.

PUBLICATIONS, Contd.

15. Surgical Pathology of the Thyroid Gland in Surinam, 1971 – 1977.
    Caribbean Medical Journal 41 (1), 1980.

16. Cardiac Disease at Autopsy in the Bahamas.
    CAREC S. Report, July, 1984.

17. Aortic Aneurysms in the Bahamas – an autopsy review
    CAREC S. Report, July, 1984.

18. Liver Biopsy Diagnoses in Surinam.
    Submitted for Publication.

19. The normal value from the Laboratory.
    Bahamas Medical Newsletter 1979.

20. Accident Related Fatalities in Grand Bahama
    Bahama Medical Journal, July 1989.

21. Cancer in Grand Bahama
    Caribbean Lab. Action News (CLAN)
    Vol. 4:1 June, 1994.

22. Prevalence o Chlamydia
    Genital Infection on Grand Bahama
    Bahamas Journal of Science, Vol. 3 #3 June 1996.

23. The first six years of HIV in Grand Bahama Clan 5:2, 1996 (Nov.)

24. Pregnancy in Grand Bahama: The untold numbers.
    A. Brathwaite, R. Butler, V. Allen.
    Bahamas Journal of Science Vol. 4 #2, Feb. 1997.

25. Natural Phenomena, Hazards and Disasters: A report for 1995. Accepted June 1999 by University of Wisconsin (Madison) as Professional Study Project towards Diploma in Disaster Management.

26. Co-author "Resistencia a los antimicrobianos en el Caribe in PAHO Publication of Antimicrobial resistance in the Americas.

27. Abstracts of HIV in Grand Bahama, W.I.M.J. Supplement, 2001.

PUBLICATIONS, Contd:

28.   Overview of Forensic Pathology in the Caribbean.
        Pg Doctor, C/Bean 18 #3, 2002.

29.   Mortality Statistics for Grand Bahama (Abstract)
        WIMJ Supplement, Nov., 2002.

CV Update for Alfred Brathwaite---2008 to April, 2017

2008
 Oct 2nd-3rd –Attended Grand Bahama Medical and Dental Association (GBMDA) Medical Conference at The Westin.

 Oct 30th----General Meeting of Lucaya Cricket Club (LCC). Elected Vice Chairman (Coach).

2009
 April 22nd to 25th —Attended Caribbean Health Research Council (CHRC) Annual Scientific Meeting, Sandals Grande Hotel, St. Lucia.

 Oct 1st–3rd---Attended GBMDA Annual Medical Meeting Freeport.

 Oct 28th–31st—Attended American Society of Clinical Pathologists (ASCP) Annual Meeting in Chicago, Sheraton Towers.

2010
 Feb 10—Spoke to Men of Education Ministry on Cancer, Freeport.

 April 22nd to 24th---Attended CHRC Annual Scientific Meeting. Hyatt, Trinidad.

 Sept 8th—Made presentation on HIV/AIDS at Agape House, Freeport.

 Oct 1st. Attended GBMDA Annual Medical Meeting at Pelican Bay Hotel, Freeport.

 Oct 4th---Attended Opening Ceremony of CASMET Council Meeting at Our Lucaya Hotel. Guest speaker-Hon. Laing.

 Nov 16th to 20th University West Indies (UWI) Medical Reunion at Accra Beach Hotel, Barbados.
 Made Presentation "Update on Breast Cancer in Women on Grand Bahama Island, Bahamas" on the 19th

 Dec 4th---Elected Chairman of LCC at the AGM.

2011
July 24th – 27th American Association of Clinical Chemistry (AACC) Meeting in Atlanta, Marriott Marquis Hotel.

July 31st to Aug 4th, CASMET/AMT Meeting, Intercontinental Hotel, Miami.
Sept 13th GBMDA, Glaxo Smith Kline sponsorship meeting—Dr. Robin Roberts on Benign Prostatic Hypertrophy.

Sept 29th to 30th GBMDA Annual Meeting.

Oct---Appointed Laboratory Director at The Immune Research Centre (IRC--IAT) to May, 2015.

Oct 15th to 18th, Meeting in Chongqing, China. Made presentation on Forensic Medicine in the Caribbean.

Nov 20th, Attended 2011 Caribbean HIV Conference at Atlantis Hotel.

2012
Jan 18th to 21st University of Miami Pathology Conference at Eden Roc Hotel, Miami Beach.
Oct 5th, Attended GBMDA Annual Meeting.
Dec 7th, Received Edward C. Kaps Hope Us Too Award, O' Hare Hyatt Hotel, Chicago.

2013
Feb 19th to 21st, Attended American Academy of Forensic Sciences (AAFS) Meeting, Washington DC.

Apr 4th, Attended Cleveland Clinic Seminar on Prostate Cancer, as part of the Us Too --Alpheus 'Hawk' Finlayson Events.

May 2nd to 4th, Attended CHRC (58th)/CARPHA (Caribbean Public Health Agency) Annual Meeting, Hilton Hotel, Barbados.

Aug 25th to 26th, CCAS 10th meeting, Breezes Resort, Nassau.

Oct 4th, Attended GBMDA Annual Meeting.

Oct 25th to 26th, Attended CASMET BGM, Atlantis Hotel, Nassau.

Nov 4th to 9th Attended (Pegasus, Kingston; Ibero star Rose Hall Suites), UWIMAA

Scientific Meeting. Made presentation "Breast Cancer in Grand Bahama Women: Ten-year Survival Data."

2014

Mar 8th, Honoree at Award Ceremony, 40th Independence Anniversary, Medical Association of Bahamas, Government House, Nassau.

May 1st to 3rd, Attended CARPHA Conference in Aruba, Convention Center, stayed Renaissance Marina Hotel.

Nov 20th, Us Too Regional Southeast. Leadership Meeting, Dattoli Cancer Center, Sarasota, Florida.

2015

Jun 19th to 20th, Attended Us Too Educational Conference and Banquet, Hyatt O' Hare, Chicago.

Jun 25th to 27th, Attended CARPHA Annual Conference, St. Georges Medical School, Grenada.

Jun 30th, Attended talk by Dr. Rivet Amico at 10th International HIV Treatment and Prevention Conference, Eden Roc Hotel, Miami Beach (IAPAC).

Sept 5th, Attended Us Too Town meeting at Church of Grace for all Nations, Freeport, GB. Dr. George Charite presented.

Sept 25th, GBMDAssn. Annual Medical Conference, Pelican Bay Hotel, GB. Was one of two Honorees on the 26th.

2016

Sept 29–30, GBMDA Annual Educational Scientific Conference, Pelican Bay Hotel, GB. "Emerging Trends in Medicine."

Nov 12–17, UWIMAA 12th Int'l Medical Reunion Conference, Jewel Runaway Bay Beach and Golf Resort and The Pegasus Hotel, Jamaica. "UWI and Medicine in the 21st Century—Solving health Priorities—Past—Present—Future.

2017

APR 27–29, CARPHA 62nd Annual Health Research Conference, Marriott Hotel, George Town, Guyana. "Climate Change, The Environment and Human Health."

More CV updates to 2024

1. Retired from Bahamas Government service—April 2005.
2. Specialist Medical Officer, BVI, July, 2005—July 2008.
3. Coauthored "Epidemiological Profile of Cancer for Grand Bahama Residents: 1988–2002". Poster presentation at CHRC Scientific Meeting in Grenada, 21–24 April 2004. Published in W I Med J, 56:1, 2007.
4. Coauthored "Mortality Data for Residents of Grand Bahama: A Ten-Year Analysis (1993–2002)". Published in Bah J of Sci. 11:2, 2004. First presented at UWIMAA meeting in Nassau, Bahamas, 2003.
5. Coauthored "Benign Lesions of the Breast in Residents of Grand Bahama". Published in Bahamas Naturalist and J of Sci. 1:1, 2006.
6. Coauthored "Ten-Year Survival Rates for Women of Grand Bahama Island, The Bahamas, Diagnosed with Breast Cancer in 1988–2002". W I Med J 2018; 67 (3): 197.

Meetings

Attended and made presentation at the Laboratory Directors Meeting on HIV in Vancouver, Canada, January 1995.

Attended CHRC Scientific Meeting in Barbados, April 1999.

Attended MD International seminar Purchasing of Medical Equipment, Miami, Florida, July 1999.

Attended ASCP meeting, New Orleans, September 2003.

Attended Caribbean HIV meeting in Santo Domingo, DR, March 2004.

Attended IAS International AIDS Conference, Durban, S. Africa, July 2004. Coauthored "HIV Disease in Grand Bahama: The Third Five-Year Period, 1996–2000".

Poster presentation at CHRC Scientific Meeting in Tobago, 20– 22 April 2005. Published in W I Med J Suppl. 54:2.

Attended Sickle Cell Association of BVI in Tortola, 12–14 September 2005.

Attended CASMET meeting in Jamaica, 27–29 October 2005. Honoured for dedicated service to laboratory technology.

Attended UWIMAA meeting in Grenada, 8–11 November 2005. Presented a paper "When and Whence Cometh Death in Grand Bahama, Bahamas". Published in Bah Naturalist and J of Sci. 1:2, 2006.

Attended CARIFORUM Lab Strengthening Project Workshop— Training Laboratory Assessors, Trinidad, 2–10 December 2005.

Attended North American Plastic Surgeons meetings in Tortola, BVI, January 2006 and 2007. CME course of the College of American Pathologists, "Archives Test Your Memory", 2006.

Attended CHRC Scientific Meeting in St Kitts, 26–28 April 2006.

Attended AIDS International Conference in Toronto, Canada, 11–19 August 2006.

Attended PAHO workshop: Mass Casualty Handling of the Dead, Tortola, BVI, 6–8 December 2006.

Attended CHRC 52nd Scientific Meeting in Montego Bay, Jamaica, 3–4 May 2007. Attended CHRC Scientific Meeting in Suriname, 24–26 April 2008.

Attended UWIMAA meeting in Ocho Rios and Kingston, Jamaica, 13–18 July, and UWI 60th Anniversary celebrations, 2008. Presented "Survival Times of Breast Cancer Patients in Grand Bahama".

Attended Parrish Medical Centre seminar UWI: Caribbean Impact, Global Reach, 13–18 July 2008.

Attended AIDS International Conference in Mexico City, 4–8 August 2008 in Mexico City.

Awards

Received an award for distinguished service to GBHS, presented by the Governor General, 12 December 2003.

Received the Honouring Men Pioneers for Outstanding Service in the Fight Against HIV/AIDS award from the National Foundation of Women's Association of the Bahamas in collaboration with the ministry of health, Bahamas, March 2005.

Received the Health Hero service award in medicine from the ministry of health, Bahamas, November 2005.

Other Activities

Attended Venereal Disease Seminar—Control of Sexually Transmitted Diseases, at CAREC, May 1975.

Attended 1st World Congress on STDs, Puerto Rico, November 1981.

PAHO consultant to Suriname on improving laboratory support to primary health care, January 1986.

Successfully completed the AHA/ACLS Provider Course, Rand Memorial Hospital, April 1992.

Attended workshop Cholera for Laboratory Directors, Buenos Aires, Venezuela, June 1993.

Attended CCMRC? CALM Meeting, Barbados, April, 1995.

Attended CHRC Scientific Meeting, Barbados, April, 1999.

Attended CHRC Scientific Meeting in Guyana, April 2002.

Attended IAS International Conference on AIDS, Barcelona, Spain, July 2002.

Attended IAS International Conference on AIDS, Bangkok, Thailand, 11–16 July 2004.

Attended UWIMAA meeting in Jamaica, July 2008.

Attended satellite workshop of CBCE entitled The Pathologist Role in the Future of Personalized Medicine at ASCP meeting in Chicago, Illinois, October–November 2009.

Attended UWIMAA meeting in St Lucia, July 2018.

Attended CARPHA 66th Annual Health Research Conference (Hybrid), Kingston, Jamaica, 15–17 September 2022.

Attended CARPHA 67th Annual Health Research Conference, Paradise Island, Bahamas, April 27-29, 2023.

Attended CARPHA 68th Annual Research Conference in St. Lucia, April 25-27, 2024.

Attended 8th Annual C/bean Medicolegal and Forensic Symposium, November, 2024, Grenada.

ADDITIONAL PHOTOS

A young medical student

As a teenager

Awards for HIV work, Nassau. Hip Parade, Vivian, a friend, Alfred, Merlene, Nika, Jacob.

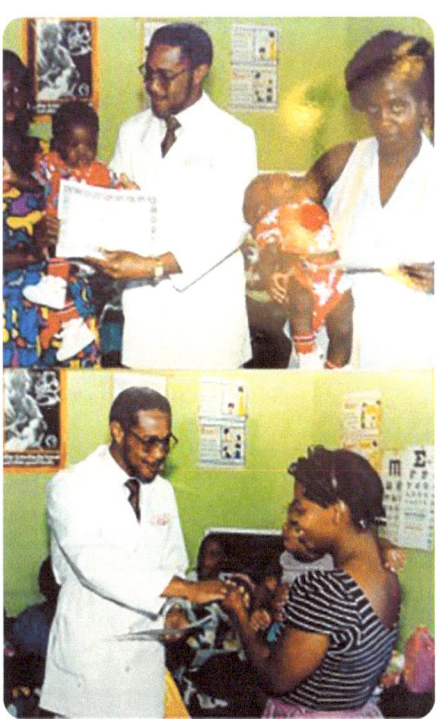

As MSC, giving out birth certificates at clinic.

Babu, Doctor of the year.

UWI, Block B. (Author 2nd row middle)

Chancelor scores a goal

Chester at UWIMAA

Dr. Harohali and author, RMH beach party

FINCO Hockey Team.

From Grenada to UCWI, 1961

Harry and Steve, colleagues at university.

UWIMAA Meeting, Author, King Solomon,
Sir Paul Scoon, "Big Stiff" Francis.

Lucaya Cricket Team, Freeport

Mijnals and Co., Suriname

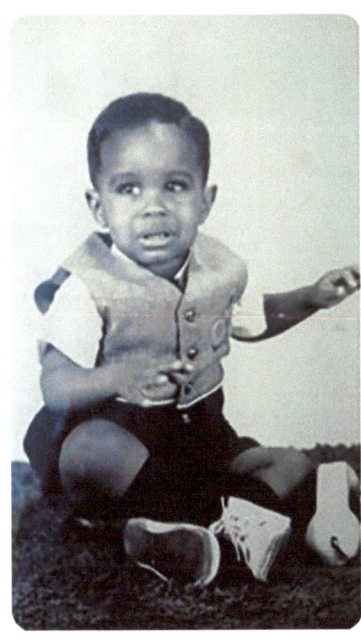

My son, Tony

Priapus, extreme left, Jab Jab, UCWI

Singing with Trevor Castle, UWI

Singing With Trevor

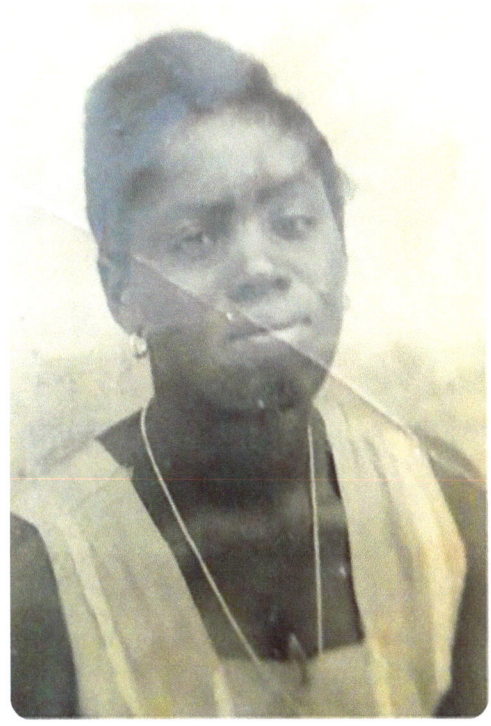

Soonkie, schoolmate

Sportsman soccer award, Freeport

The friends at UWIMAA

With Bobo, escape to Montego Bay

With Cox, Holm, Cravalho, Hawaii airport

A special person, Magda Hippolyte

Basil, my neighbour

Despite the mask of Covid, I'm in my driveway.

Flavia Logie, my poetic friend

Friend from Mt. Pleasant

Grenadians at UWIMAA

Ivan and Clint, Freeport.

Jouvert-Adam and Eve, UWI.

Kathryn at CARPHA

La Flora Pena.

My Godchild Nikoyan

Rhoda

Shirley

Surveying from Block B, UWI

The Lady I call Spartacus.

Wedding of George Baker and Olive

Remembering Pegasus-A true friend.

Being an Honouree of the GBMDA.

www.ingramcontent.com/pod-product-compliance
Lightning Source LLC
LaVergne TN
LVHW070938070526
838199LV00035B/642